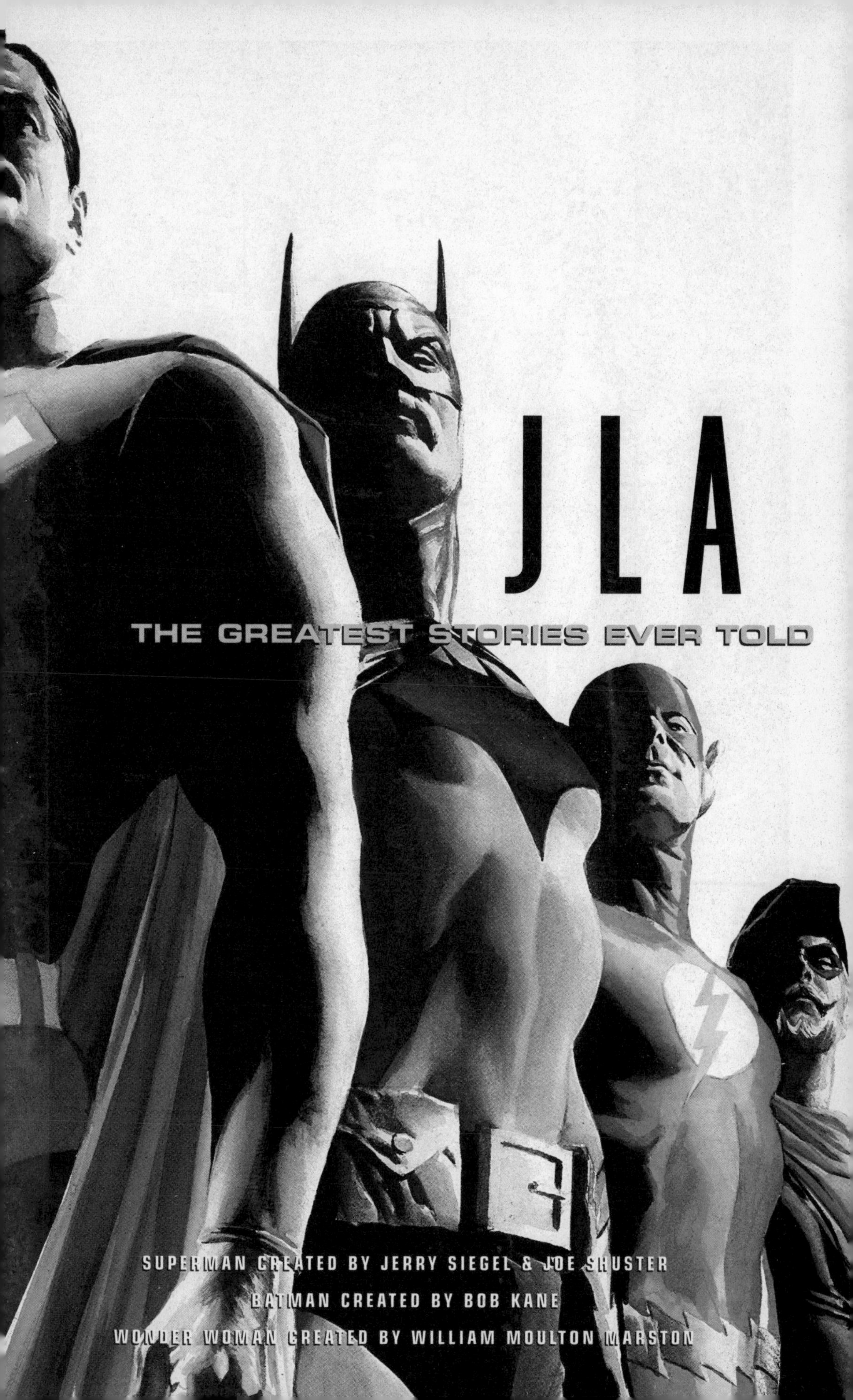

JLA

THE GREATEST STORIES EVER TOLD

SUPERMAN CREATED BY JERRY SIEGEL & JOE SHUSTER

BATMAN CREATED BY BOB KANE

WONDER WOMAN CREATED BY WILLIAM MOULTON MARSTON

Dan DiDio Senior VP-Executive Editor   Anton Kawasaki Editor-collected edition   Robbin Brosterman Senior Art Director   Paul Levitz President & Publisher
Georg Brewer VP-Design & DC Direct Creative   Richard Bruning Senior VP-Creative Director   Patrick Caldon Executive VP-Finance & Operations   Chris Caramalis VP-Finance
John Cunningham VP-Marketing   Terri Cunningham VP-Managing Editor   Stephanie Fierman Senior VP-Sales & Marketing   Alison Gill VP-Manufacturing
Rich Johnson VP-Book Trade Sales   Hank Kanalz VP-General Manager, WildStorm   Lillian Laserson Senior VP & General Counsel   Jim Lee Editorial Director-WildStorm
Paula Lowitt Senior VP-Business & Legal Affairs   David McKillips VP-Advertising & Custom Publishing   John Nee VP-Business Development
Gregory Noveck Senior VP-Creative Affairs   Cheryl Rubin Senior VP-Brand Management   Jeff Trojan VP-Business Development, DC Direct   Bob Wayne VP-Sales

JLA: THE GREATEST STORIES EVER TOLD

CONTENTS

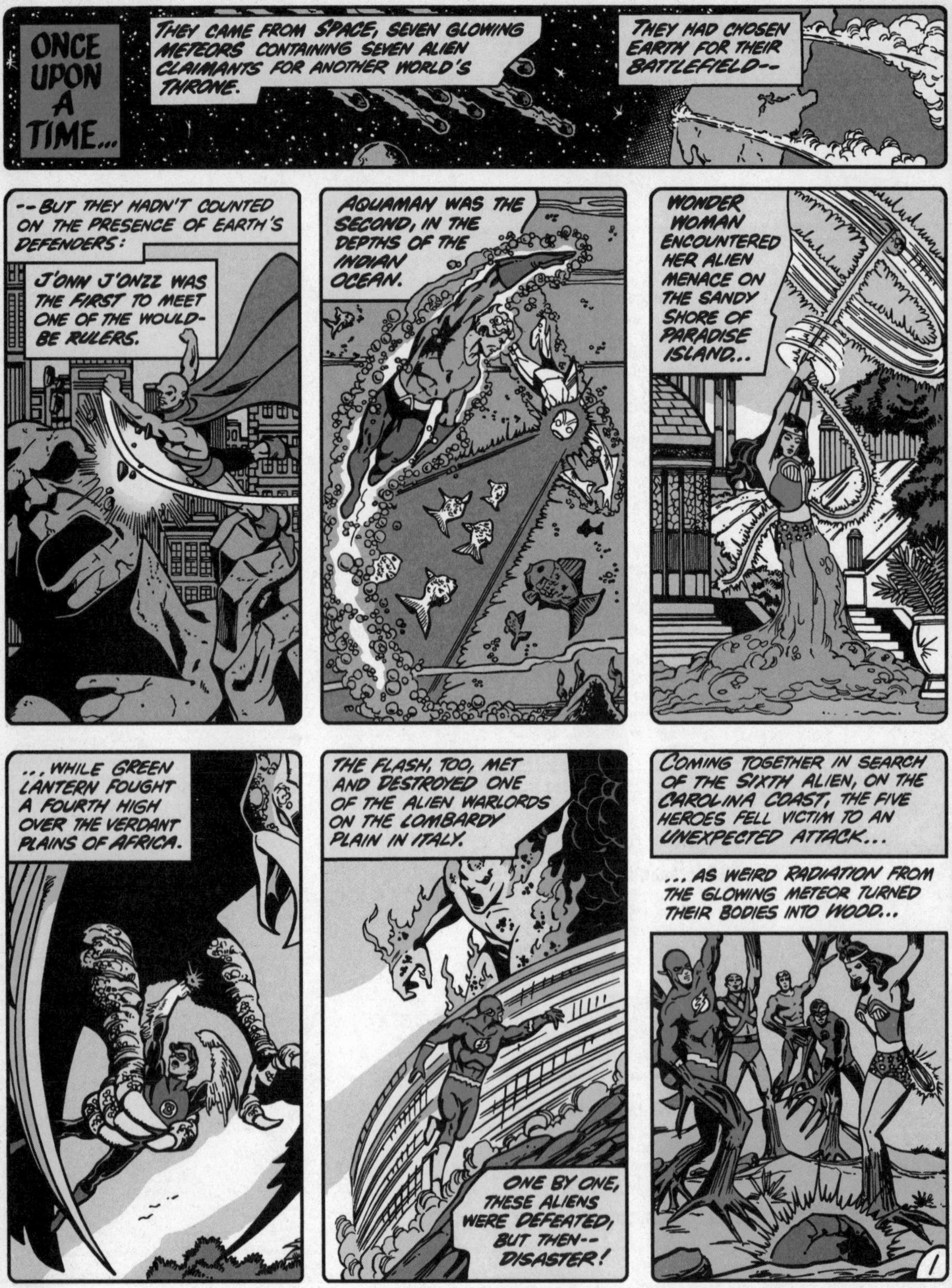
ONCE UPON A TIME...
THEY CAME FROM SPACE, SEVEN GLOWING METEORS CONTAINING SEVEN ALIEN CLAIMANTS FOR ANOTHER WORLD'S THRONE.
THEY HAD CHOSEN EARTH FOR THEIR BATTLEFIELD--
--BUT THEY HADN'T COUNTED ON THE PRESENCE OF EARTH'S DEFENDERS:
J'ONN J'ONZZ WAS THE FIRST TO MEET ONE OF THE WOULD-BE RULERS.
AQUAMAN WAS THE SECOND, IN THE DEPTHS OF THE INDIAN OCEAN.
WONDER WOMAN ENCOUNTERED HER ALIEN MENACE ON THE SANDY SHORE OF PARADISE ISLAND...
...WHILE GREEN LANTERN FOUGHT A FOURTH HIGH OVER THE VERDANT PLAINS OF AFRICA.
THE FLASH, TOO, MET AND DESTROYED ONE OF THE ALIEN WARLORDS ON THE LOMBARDY PLAIN IN ITALY.
ONE BY ONE, THESE ALIENS WERE DEFEATED, BUT THEN-- DISASTER!
COMING TOGETHER IN SEARCH OF THE SIXTH ALIEN, ON THE CAROLINA COAST, THE FIVE HEROES FELL VICTIM TO AN UNEXPECTED ATTACK...
...AS WEIRD RADIATION FROM THE GLOWING METEOR TURNED THEIR BODIES INTO WOOD...
1

Writer: Gerry Conway **Penciller:** George Pérez **Inker:** Brett Breeding
Colorist: Carl Gafford **Letterer:** John Costanza

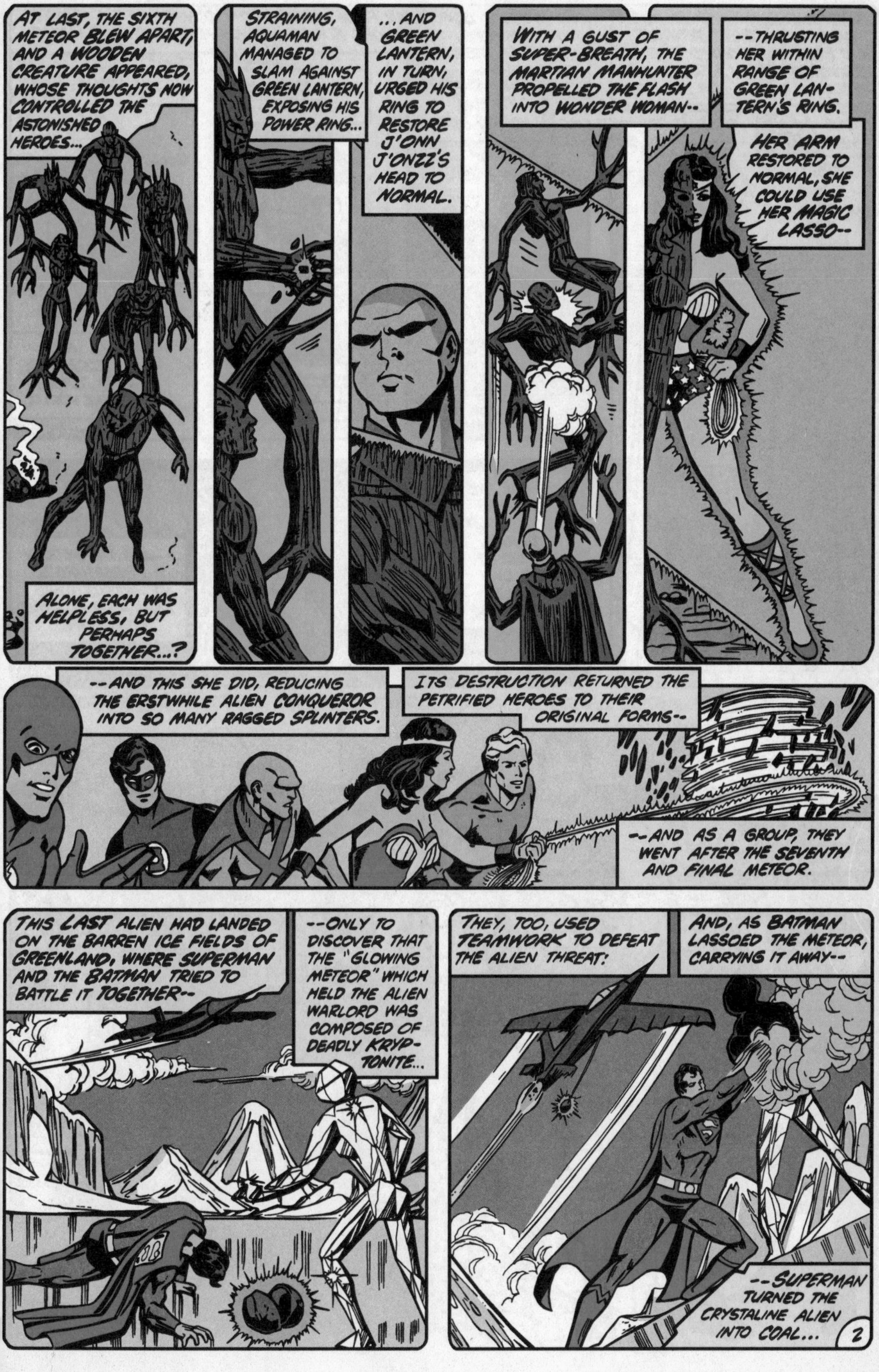
AT LAST, THE SIXTH METEOR BLEW APART, AND A WOODEN CREATURE APPEARED, WHOSE THOUGHTS NOW CONTROLLED THE ASTONISHED HEROES...
ALONE, EACH WAS HELPLESS, BUT PERHAPS TOGETHER...?
STRAINING, AQUAMAN MANAGED TO SLAM AGAINST GREEN LANTERN, EXPOSING HIS POWER RING...
...AND GREEN LANTERN, IN TURN, URGED HIS RING TO RESTORE J'ONN J'ONZZ'S HEAD TO NORMAL.
WITH A GUST OF SUPER-BREATH, THE MARTIAN MANHUNTER PROPELLED THE FLASH INTO WONDER WOMAN--
--THRUSTING HER WITHIN RANGE OF GREEN LANTERN'S RING.
HER ARM RESTORED TO NORMAL, SHE COULD USE HER MAGIC LASSO--
--AND THIS SHE DID, REDUCING THE ERSTWHILE ALIEN CONQUEROR INTO SO MANY RAGGED SPLINTERS.
ITS DESTRUCTION RETURNED THE PETRIFIED HEROES TO THEIR ORIGINAL FORMS--
--AND AS A GROUP, THEY WENT AFTER THE SEVENTH AND FINAL METEOR.
THIS LAST ALIEN HAD LANDED ON THE BARREN ICE FIELDS OF GREENLAND, WHERE SUPERMAN AND THE BATMAN TRIED TO BATTLE IT TOGETHER--
--ONLY TO DISCOVER THAT THE "GLOWING METEOR" WHICH HELD THE ALIEN WARLORD WAS COMPOSED OF DEADLY KRYPTONITE...
THEY, TOO, USED TEAMWORK TO DEFEAT THE ALIEN THREAT:
AND, AS BATMAN LASSOED THE METEOR, CARRYING IT AWAY--
--SUPERMAN TURNED THE CRYSTALINE ALIEN INTO COAL...
2

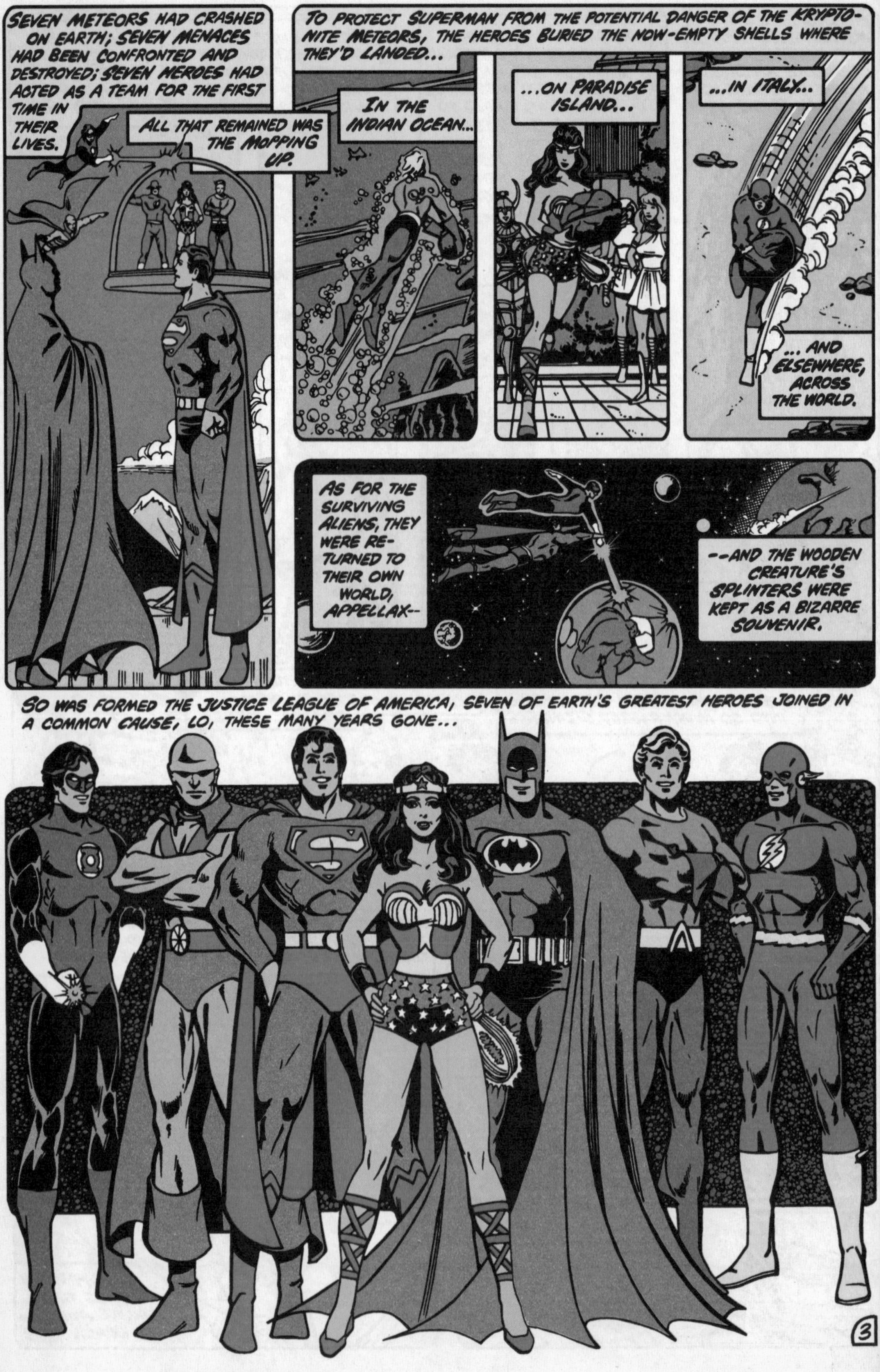
SEVEN METEORS HAD CRASHED ON EARTH; SEVEN MENACES HAD BEEN CONFRONTED AND DESTROYED; SEVEN HEROES HAD ACTED AS A TEAM FOR THE FIRST TIME IN THEIR LIVES.
ALL THAT REMAINED WAS THE MOPPING UP.
TO PROTECT SUPERMAN FROM THE POTENTIAL DANGER OF THE KRYPTO-NITE METEORS, THE HEROES BURIED THE NOW-EMPTY SHELLS WHERE THEY'D LANDED...
IN THE INDIAN OCEAN...
...ON PARADISE ISLAND...
...IN ITALY...
... AND ELSEWHERE, ACROSS THE WORLD.
AS FOR THE SURVIVING ALIENS, THEY WERE RE-TURNED TO THEIR OWN WORLD, APPELLAX--
--AND THE WOODEN CREATURE'S SPLINTERS WERE KEPT AS A BIZARRE SOUVENIR.
SO WAS FORMED THE JUSTICE LEAGUE OF AMERICA, SEVEN OF EARTH'S GREATEST HEROES JOINED IN A COMMON CAUSE, LO, THESE MANY YEARS GONE...
3

INTRODUCTION
BY MIKE TIEFENBACHER

I've loved the JLA since 1960 — even though I never actually read an issue until 1963.

My cousins bought and read hundreds of comic books in the 1950s and early '60s. When I visited them I always read as many as I could, and thus, at age seven or eight, before ever buying any comics of my own, I was aware of DC's super-heroes. (I recall reading SUPERMAN ANNUAL, in fascination at all the various Super-family members.) I especially enjoyed WORLD'S FINEST COMICS, which made it clear that Superman, Batman and Robin knew each other and lived in the same world, something which rarely happened back then. At 10 cents an issue my cousins' comic books were routinely discarded once it was clear that everyone who wanted to had read them. Seeing my interest, my aunt gave me a large stack of those much-read issues. While mere jetsam to them, to me these comics offered a banquet of tales to be devoured again and again. None of them, however, were issues of JUSTICE LEAGUE OF AMERICA. But one was ACTION COMICS #269 — which featured the house ad for JUSTICE LEAGUE OF AMERICA #1!

JLA editor Julius Schwartz had many talents, but one of his strongest was writing house-ad copy.

"Just Imagine! The mightiest heroes of our time...Superman! Batman! Flash! Green Lantern! Wonder Woman! Aquaman! J'onn J'onzz — Manhunter From Mars!...have banded together as the JUSTICE LEAGUE OF AMERICA to stamp out the forces of evil wherever and whenever they appear! The thrilling exploits of these famous champions appear in the new Superman DC National Comics Magazine on sale on August 25th!"

Julie's words, Ira Schnapp's magnificent lettering — I was hypnotized. Murphy Anderson's wonderful cover was the source of continuing questions, too, as I dreamed of actually reading the story it reflected. Who was this red-skinned guy with the reptilian halo, and why was he playing chess with the Flash? Why weren't my favorites Superman and Batman seated at the JLA's table with the others, but shown only as tiny figures on a chessboard? And where could I get my *own* set of JLA chess pieces?

What was the attraction? I believe it was the communicated feeling of *friendship*, the notion that these like-minded individuals would not only band together to fight a common cause, but become true comrades whose demeanor showed they enjoyed one another's company. The egalitarian attitude of the group, which I felt in that ad, had begun in the 1940s Justice Society of America (in ALL STAR COMICS), though I didn't know that then. JSA scripter Gardner Fox, in fact, seemed so intent on making each member equal to the others that whatever happened to one member, happened to each of them, in each super-group. The conceit was simple: no matter which member you liked, he or she got equal play in every issue.

And the Justice League heroes looked as if they belonged together. Created by many artists and writers, their disparate costumes seemed as if they could have been tailored by the same costume

shop, and their coloring was completely complementary. The fact that this was all chance — except for Green Arrow, who'd join in #4 at the fans' insistence, these seven heroes were just about the entirety of DC's then-current super-hero population — makes it all the more remarkable. They couldn't have chosen a better lineup.

In the summer of '63 I finally read a friend's copy of JLA (#22, part two of the first of the annual team-ups between the Justice League and Justice Society). It took a full year (and the release of JLA #30) for me to buy my first issue, but I was finally hooked for good. I resolved to find every solo appearance of every JLA member, and it's become a lifetime commitment.

The evolution of the JLA over the decades is quite confusing. I love the team as I first encountered it, the work of writer Gardner Fox, penciller Mike Sekowsky, and inker Bernard Sachs. Sachs was the first to depart (with #43, eventually replaced by Sid Greene), followed by Sekowsky (#63), then Fox (#65), leaving behind a tenure just short of a decade. Fox's variances in story formula were what made it entertaining for me, as in the first story found in this volume, from JLA #19. Its villain, Dr. Destiny, originally appeared in JLA #5, though his Materioptikon and focus on dreams originated in this story. By this point, the Atom had also joined the group (in #14). What endears this story to me is the charming staging of the revelation of the nine JLA members' secret identities to one another (even if Aquaman didn't have one, per se). Having it done en masse as Fox did it goes along with the camaraderie theme I mentioned, made all the more special because it was so ephemeral.

It was at the time important to maintain the idea of secret identities, though soon it became all the rage for super-heroes in groups to call each other by their first names rather than by their code names. For me, this familiarity removed the air of mystery I like super-heroes to have, besides being a horrible breach of secrecy which endangers their loved ones. The JLA's means of removing that

knowledge from one another — and the world at large — was accomplished through the use of *amnesium*, an alien mineral housed in Superman's Fortress of Solitude, which had first appeared in SUPERBOY #55 (reprinted in that aforementioned SUPERMAN ANNUAL #1 — and probably where Schwartz and Fox found it). It was par for the time, straining credulity so that amnesium managed to extract the exact identity information from the entire world (clearly not altering any memories created before the adventure shown here), but it was otherwise uncontroversial. This was an example of the JLA employing what would later be termed "mind-wiping," which had happened often in those early issues.

Over the next few years, the JLA/JSA crossovers began and Hawkman joined (#31). Batman became the focus of most covers of JLA and every other title he appeared in when the *Batman* TV series took off and became a national rage, and sales went through the roof. By 1968, though, sales were on a downward trend, threatening super-hero comics in general, and, fueled by a

changeover in publisher from Irwin Donenfeld to Carmine Infantino, what could be considered the original "Crisis on Earth-One" occurred. Virtually every character's status quo was altered, with creators removed or switched from book to book to reignite sales. The JLA was no exception.

Sekowsky left to become editor, writer and artist on WONDER WOMAN and METAL MEN, while Fox, who'd been at DC since at least 1939, would write very little for DC thereafter. Dick Dillin, who'd spent the prior 18 years drawing BLACKHAWK, became the new JLA penciller, lasting through 1980 (#183), a run that surpassed Sekowsky's by several years. Fox's replacement was Dennis O'Neil, who had written several series for Marvel, and for Charlton (as "Sergius O'Shaugnessy") under editor Dick Giordano. When Infantino brought Giordano to DC, Giordano brought O'Neil along, and he was given JLA. Soon after, the members were again aware of one another's first names, animosities began to crop up, and DC's formerly stoic heroes would never be the same. Some of it was inevitable, as the

WANNA MAKE SOMETHIN' OF IT?

preponderance of descriptive captions was reduced in favor of expository dialogue. But filling-in character blanks previously left to the readers' imaginations altered the flavor of DC's world. And to see these adult heroes, who had never before evinced overt personality traits, suddenly appear to be regressing in maturity, seemed shocking at the time.

O'Neil wrote Wonder Woman (who'd lost her powers) out of the book and imported Black Canary from Earth-Two to replace her, brought the new Red Tornado created by Fox to Earth-One, and wrote J'onn J'onzz out of the group, simultaneously altering his origin. Because Schwartz did not edit his solo adventures, Fox had always portrayed the Manhunter as an ersatz Superman, perhaps due to the diminished role the Man of Steel originally had in JLA (Mort Weisinger, Superman's editor, and Jack Schiff, who edited Batman, feared overexposure and perhaps loss of character control), utilizing only J'onn's super-strength, speed, flight, invulnerability to everything but fire, and Martian vision. In his own strip in DETECTIVE COMICS, and, later, HOUSE OF MYSTERY, he was walking through walls, turning invisible, changing his features, and employing myriad powers only seen once, making him much less a reflection of Superman than he appeared in JLA. As Superman and Batman became more prominent on the covers and in the stories (their lack of prominence overruled by the publisher), Fox probably felt no need for two Supermen, and began to use J'onn less and less. When written out, the Martian Manhunter had not been seen in the comic for over a year, rather a sad end for a charter member.

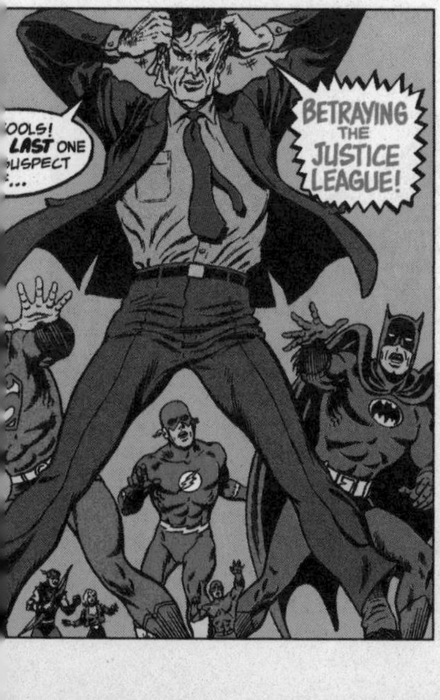
BETRAYING THE JUSTICE LEAGUE!

Our second story, #77's "Snapper Carr – Super Traitor!" is also sad. Snapper Carr had appeared in JUSTICE LEAGUE since the beginning. The unpowered Snapper (created by Fox in emulation of Edd "Kookie" Byrnes of TV's 77 *Sunset Strip*), was given honorary membership in the group for his aid in capturing Starro the Conqueror in their first appearance, along with a signal device and the "keys" to the Secret Sanctuary (a cave in an unnamed North American mountain range, which only added to the romantic image I had of the group). His unwavering support and admiration for the League was unquestioned throughout Fox's run on the strip, and even in O'Neil's first story in #66. But it seemed as if any vestige of the old days (especially a "beatnik" from 1959!) was anathema by 1969, and thus appeared the historically important story reprinted here. Just as shocking today as it was then to those of use who "knew" him, it also served as the stated reason the JLA was forced to abandon their mountain HQ for a satellite and its *Star Trek*-inspired teleporters.

Issue #122's "The Great Identity Crisis," besides perhaps inspiring the title of the recent miniseries, was a clever attempt to plug the hole created when it became clear that the members had exchanged identities for good (it has to have occurred after #74, because Green Arrow had lost his fortune and gained his new costume and his beard by #75). Written by Martin Pasko, the story not only explains the identity revelation, but also features *amnesium*'s reappearance in JLA and the participation of Dr. Light, a personage of recent importance to the DC Universe. While the identity exchange still seemed unneeded, I was thankful that the issue was finally addressed.

JUSTICE LEAGUE OF AMERICA #166 through #168's three-parter was the start of another new era as its founding editor, Julius Schwartz, was replaced by Ross Andru. Gerry Conway (the regular writer since #151) and Dick Dillin remained in their roles through the changeover. Elongated Man, Zatanna, and Hawkgirl had been added to the team by this time. The Secret Society of Super-Villains, a band of whichever villains seemed to be out of prison at the moment, appeared in their own title for fifteen issues. The story itself is all about identities and secrets, and is a fine representative of its era. And as the recent IDENTITY CRISIS miniseries pointed out, it again necessitated the memory-wiping of many of their foes to maintain their secrets. The same band of villains recently reappeared in 2005's JLA #115-119 to renew the conflict.

George Pérez was briefly the regular JLA artist, and the three-page origin from JLA #200 (which starts off this volume) shows the kind of work that got him the assignment to draw the later CRISIS ON INFINITE EARTHS series which put an end to the previous thirty years' continuity in 1985.

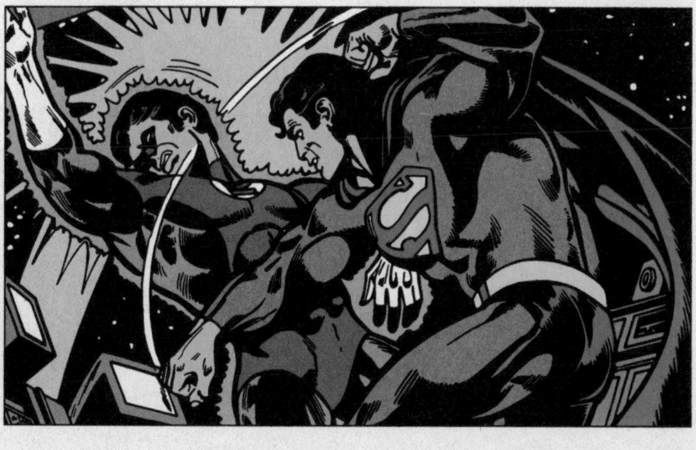

Leap forward nearly a decade for "Born Again," from 1987's JUSTICE LEAGUE #1. Things had begun falling apart a few years previous. The satellite headquarters was destroyed, the existing Justice League was disbanded by Aquaman, then replaced by one with full-time members including J'onn J'onzz (who'd since returned to Earth), Elongated Man and his wife Sue Dibny, newcomer Vixen, and a never-before-seen Steel (grandson of the original Steel, who also made appearances), Gypsy and Vibe. In a short time, Steel and Vibe were killed off. By then, of course, all the Earths of the JLA's past had been collapsed into one in 1985-86's CRISIS ON INFINITE EARTHS.

The subsequent miniseries LEGENDS relaunched JUSTICE LEAGUE, featuring an all-new line-up with roots on multiple Earths (including a new, heroic Dr. Light). Unlike the "darker, more realistic" slant of the post-CRISIS DC created by the deaths of old favorites like the JLA's Barry "Flash" Allen, JUSTICE LEAGUE, under writers Keith Giffen and J. Marc DeMatteis and artists Kevin Maguire and Terry Austin, became a smashing success by going in the other direction, emphasizing humor above all else. Their run was long and influential and retained a following which resulted in 2003's FORMERLY KNOWN AS THE JUSTICE LEAGUE and its 2005 sequel.

The most recent stories here involve the changing face of the Justice League in the ensuing years. Still bearing the same code names as their predecessors, the membership in "Star Seed" (JLA SECRET FILES #1) from 1997 (a modern retelling of the original Starro the Conqueror story) by Grant Morrison, Mark Millar, Howard Porter and John Dell, and "Two-Minute Warning" (JLA #61) by Joe Kelly, Doug Mahnke and Tom Nguyen from 2002, show heroes in a much grimmer state than shown in any of their earlier incarnations. Flash and Green Lantern are completely different people under their masks (Wally West and Kyle Rayner, respectively), while Aquaman, Batman, and Wonder Woman, most notably, are very different personalities, and recent inductee Plastic Man is seen without his goggles! Those of you who grew up with these versions are probably as amazed at the earlier characters as I am by the contemporary owners of the costumes. Dozens of other recent members have come and gone, and, I'm guessing, when the smoke clears from the newest INFINITE CRISIS, we'll be seeing something similar to the charter line-up again, or perhaps something all-new.

While we wait, ten (counting Hawkman and the Atom as two) JLA statues are staring down at me as I write this, alongside the PVC Justice League sets (though sans Superman and Batman, who must still be stuck on Despero's chessboard). And I hope we'll soon see the release of the fine cartoon series JUSTICE LEAGUE and JUSTICE LEAGUE UNLIMITED on DVD in season sets, since they frequently capture exactly what I love about the classic JLA.

So I am as in love with the Justice League as I was in 1960 and 1963, and undoubtedly, I will be till the day I die. And, very probably, four years beyond.

Mike Tiefenbacher 2005
(acknowledgments to Murray Ward and John Wells for all their feedback, and to Chuck Huber for remembering everything I forgot about amnesium!)

— Mike Tiefenbacher was once described as the Hardest Working Man In Comics Fandom, turning out nearly 500 issues as editor, writer and art director (with Jerry Sinkovec) of various comic-strip reprint magazines and fandom's leading news magazine *The Comic Reader*. In 1977 he co-founded the Amateur Press Alliance, and, has indexed many long-running DC titles — the results of which are also available online in the Grand Comics Database.

Mike's passion for comics had led to many achievements in his favorite field, including writing several stories for DC Comics (DC COMICS PRESENTS, FUNNY STUFF STOCKING STUFFER, and NEW TALENT SHOWCASE — which featured his own kid hero, Bobcat). Plus, he has had dozens of articles in nearly every major comics magazine, stints as a letterer and inker, and also compiled the ComicKeeper computer inventory index. He currently writes an online column on comics at nostalgia-zone.com, and consults with DC on various reprints and licensed products.

JUSTICE LEAGUE of AMERICA

★★★ ★★★

NEVERMORE SHALL THE *JUSTICE LEAGUE OF AMERICA* STAND LIKE A MIGHTY BULWARK BETWEEN CRIME AND HELPLESS PEOPLE! NEVERMORE SHALL ITS MEMBERS UPHOLD LAW AND ORDER AGAINST ALL WRONGDOERS! BY COURT ORDER, THESE CHAMPIONS OF RIGHT AND JUSTICE HAVE BEEN BANISHED INTO SPACE, NEVER TO RETURN TO EARTH!
SINCE THEY ARE SWORN TO UPHOLD THE LAW, THEY REFUSE TO DISOBEY THE AWESOME SENTENCE WHICH HAS TURNED THEM INTO...

the SUPER-EXILES OF EARTH!

THE ROLL CALL

ATOM
AQUAMAN
BATMAN
FLASH
GREEN ARROW
GREEN LANTERN
J'ONN J'ONZZ
SNAPPER CARR
SUPERMAN
WONDER WOMAN

THIS IS **ALL WE'LL** SEE OF **EARTH** FROM NOW ON-- SINCE WE HAVE BEEN EXILED INTO SPACE FOREVER!

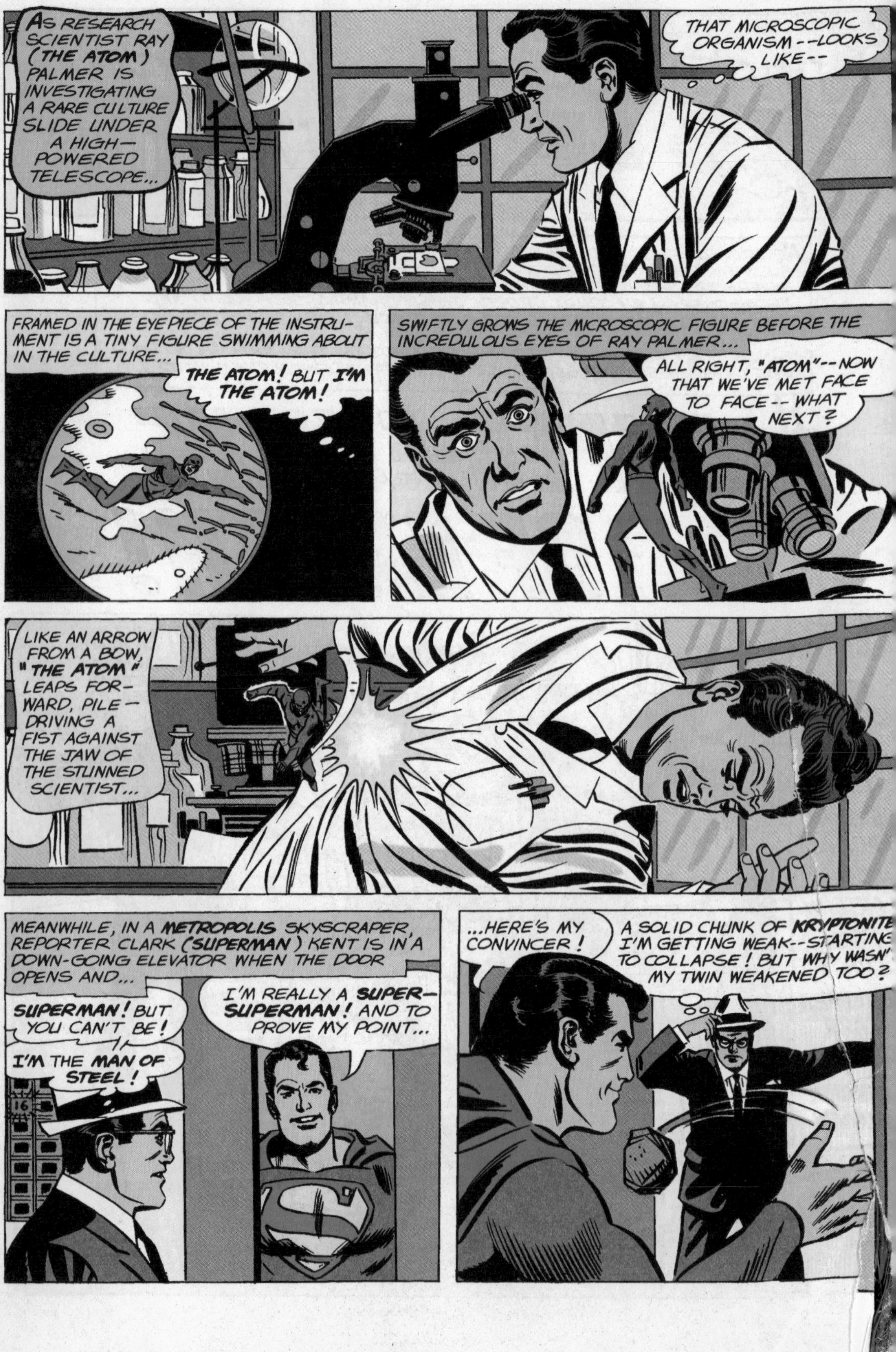
AS RESEARCH SCIENTIST RAY (THE ATOM) PALMER IS INVESTIGATING A RARE CULTURE SLIDE UNDER A HIGH-POWERED TELESCOPE...
THAT MICROSCOPIC ORGANISM--LOOKS LIKE--
FRAMED IN THE EYEPIECE OF THE INSTRUMENT IS A TINY FIGURE SWIMMING ABOUT IN THE CULTURE...
THE ATOM! BUT I'M THE ATOM!
SWIFTLY GROWS THE MICROSCOPIC FIGURE BEFORE THE INCREDULOUS EYES OF RAY PALMER...
ALL RIGHT, "ATOM"--NOW THAT WE'VE MET FACE TO FACE--WHAT NEXT?
LIKE AN ARROW FROM A BOW, "THE ATOM" LEAPS FORWARD, PILE-DRIVING A FIST AGAINST THE JAW OF THE STUNNED SCIENTIST...
MEANWHILE, IN A METROPOLIS SKYSCRAPER, REPORTER CLARK (SUPERMAN) KENT IS IN A DOWN-GOING ELEVATOR WHEN THE DOOR OPENS AND...
SUPERMAN! BUT YOU CAN'T BE!
I'M THE MAN OF STEEL!
I'M REALLY A SUPER-SUPERMAN! AND TO PROVE MY POINT...
...HERE'S MY CONVINCER!
A SOLID CHUNK OF KRYPTONITE! I'M GETTING WEAK--STARTING TO COLLAPSE! BUT WHY WASN'T MY TWIN WEAKENED TOO?

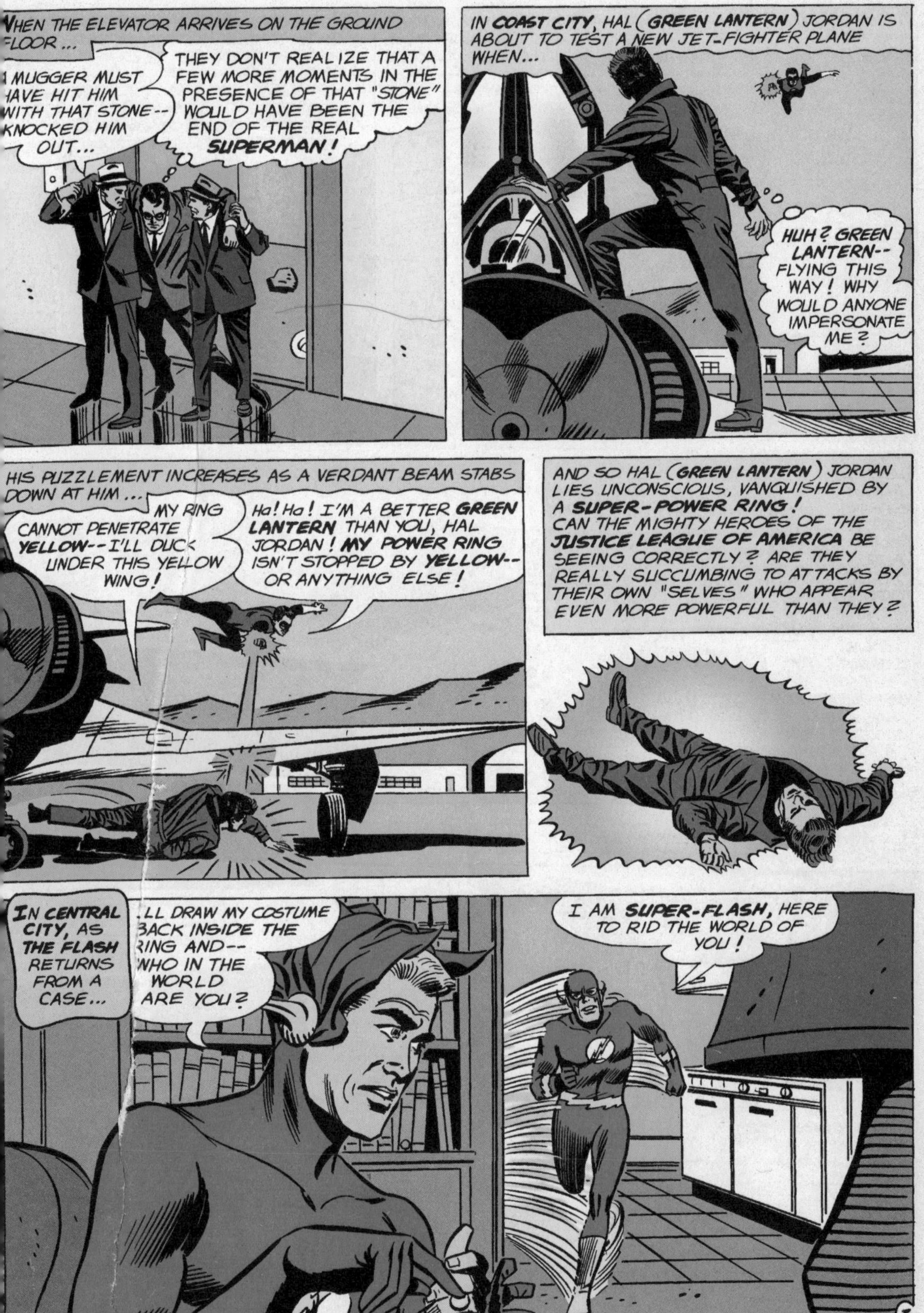
WHEN THE ELEVATOR ARRIVES ON THE GROUND FLOOR ...
A MUGGER MUST HAVE HIT HIM WITH THAT STONE-- KNOCKED HIM OUT...
THEY DON'T REALIZE THAT A FEW MORE MOMENTS IN THE PRESENCE OF THAT "STONE" WOULD HAVE BEEN THE END OF THE REAL SUPERMAN!
IN COAST CITY, HAL (GREEN LANTERN) JORDAN IS ABOUT TO TEST A NEW JET-FIGHTER PLANE WHEN...
HUH? GREEN LANTERN-- FLYING THIS WAY! WHY WOULD ANYONE IMPERSONATE ME?
HIS PUZZLEMENT INCREASES AS A VERDANT BEAM STABS DOWN AT HIM ...
MY RING CANNOT PENETRATE YELLOW--I'LL DUCK UNDER THIS YELLOW WING!
Ha! Ha! I'M A BETTER GREEN LANTERN THAN YOU, HAL JORDAN! MY POWER RING ISN'T STOPPED BY YELLOW-- OR ANYTHING ELSE!
AND SO HAL (GREEN LANTERN) JORDAN LIES UNCONSCIOUS, VANQUISHED BY A SUPER-POWER RING! CAN THE MIGHTY HEROES OF THE JUSTICE LEAGUE OF AMERICA BE SEEING CORRECTLY? ARE THEY REALLY SUCCUMBING TO ATTACKS BY THEIR OWN "SELVES" WHO APPEAR EVEN MORE POWERFUL THAN THEY?
IN CENTRAL CITY, AS THE FLASH RETURNS FROM A CASE...
I'LL DRAW MY COSTUME BACK INSIDE THE RING AND-- WHO IN THE WORLD ARE YOU?
I AM SUPER-FLASH, HERE TO RID THE WORLD OF YOU!
3

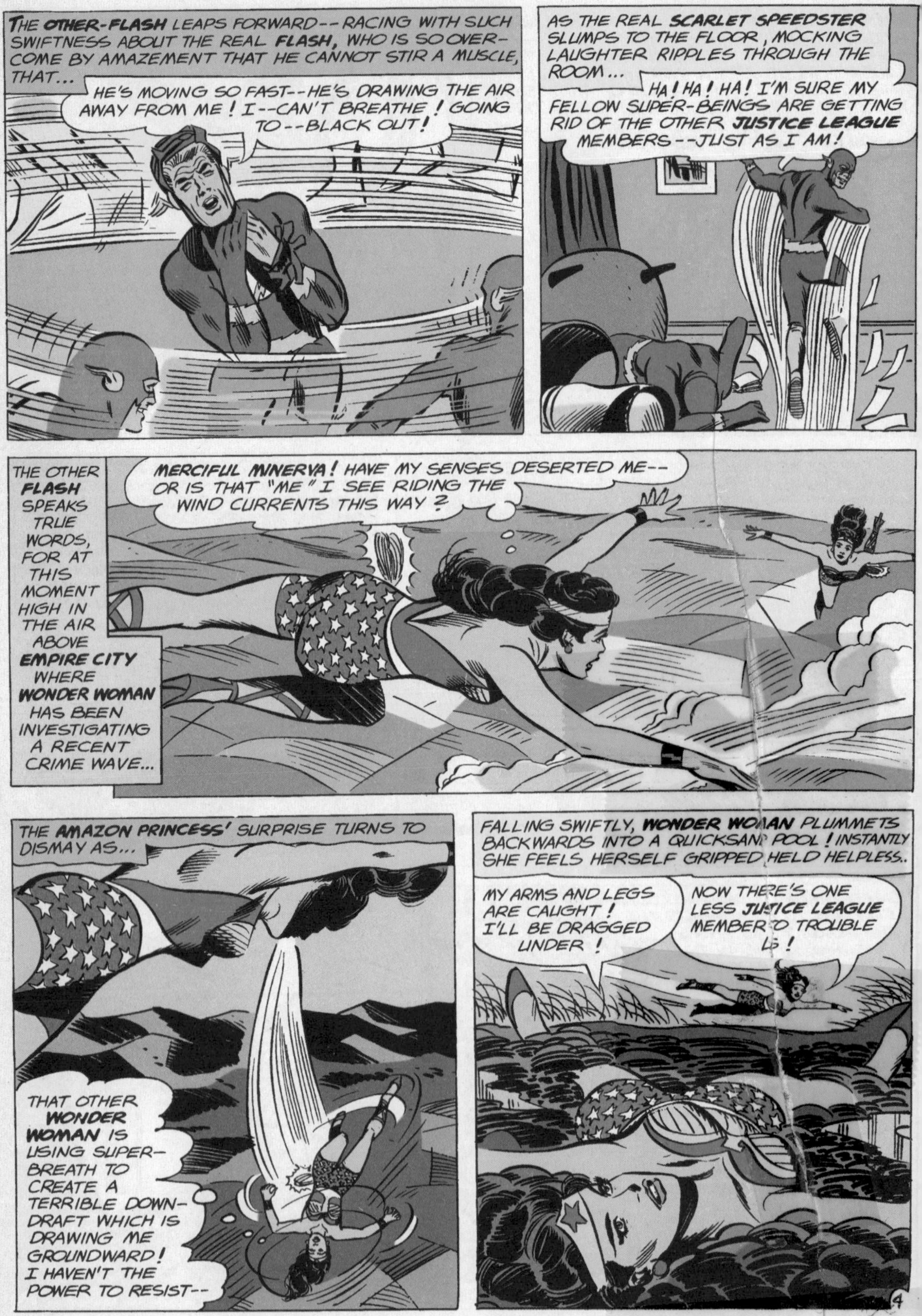
THE OTHER-FLASH LEAPS FORWARD-- RACING WITH SUCH SWIFTNESS ABOUT THE REAL FLASH, WHO IS SO OVER-COME BY AMAZEMENT THAT HE CANNOT STIR A MUSCLE, THAT...
HE'S MOVING SO FAST--HE'S DRAWING THE AIR AWAY FROM ME! I--CAN'T BREATHE! GOING TO--BLACK OUT!
AS THE REAL SCARLET SPEEDSTER SLUMPS TO THE FLOOR, MOCKING LAUGHTER RIPPLES THROUGH THE ROOM...
HA! HA! HA! I'M SURE MY FELLOW SUPER-BEINGS ARE GETTING RID OF THE OTHER JUSTICE LEAGUE MEMBERS--JUST AS I AM!
THE OTHER FLASH SPEAKS TRUE WORDS, FOR AT THIS MOMENT HIGH IN THE AIR ABOVE EMPIRE CITY WHERE WONDER WOMAN HAS BEEN INVESTIGATING A RECENT CRIME WAVE...
MERCIFUL MINERVA! HAVE MY SENSES DESERTED ME--OR IS THAT "ME" I SEE RIDING THE WIND CURRENTS THIS WAY?
THE AMAZON PRINCESS' SURPRISE TURNS TO DISMAY AS...
THAT OTHER WONDER WOMAN IS USING SUPER-BREATH TO CREATE A TERRIBLE DOWN-DRAFT WHICH IS DRAWING ME GROUNDWARD! I HAVEN'T THE POWER TO RESIST--
FALLING SWIFTLY, WONDER WOMAN PLUMMETS BACKWARDS INTO A QUICKSAND POOL! INSTANTLY SHE FEELS HERSELF GRIPPED HELD HELPLESS..
MY ARMS AND LEGS ARE CAUGHT! I'LL BE DRAGGED UNDER!
NOW THERE'S ONE LESS JUSTICE LEAGUE MEMBER TO TROUBLE US!

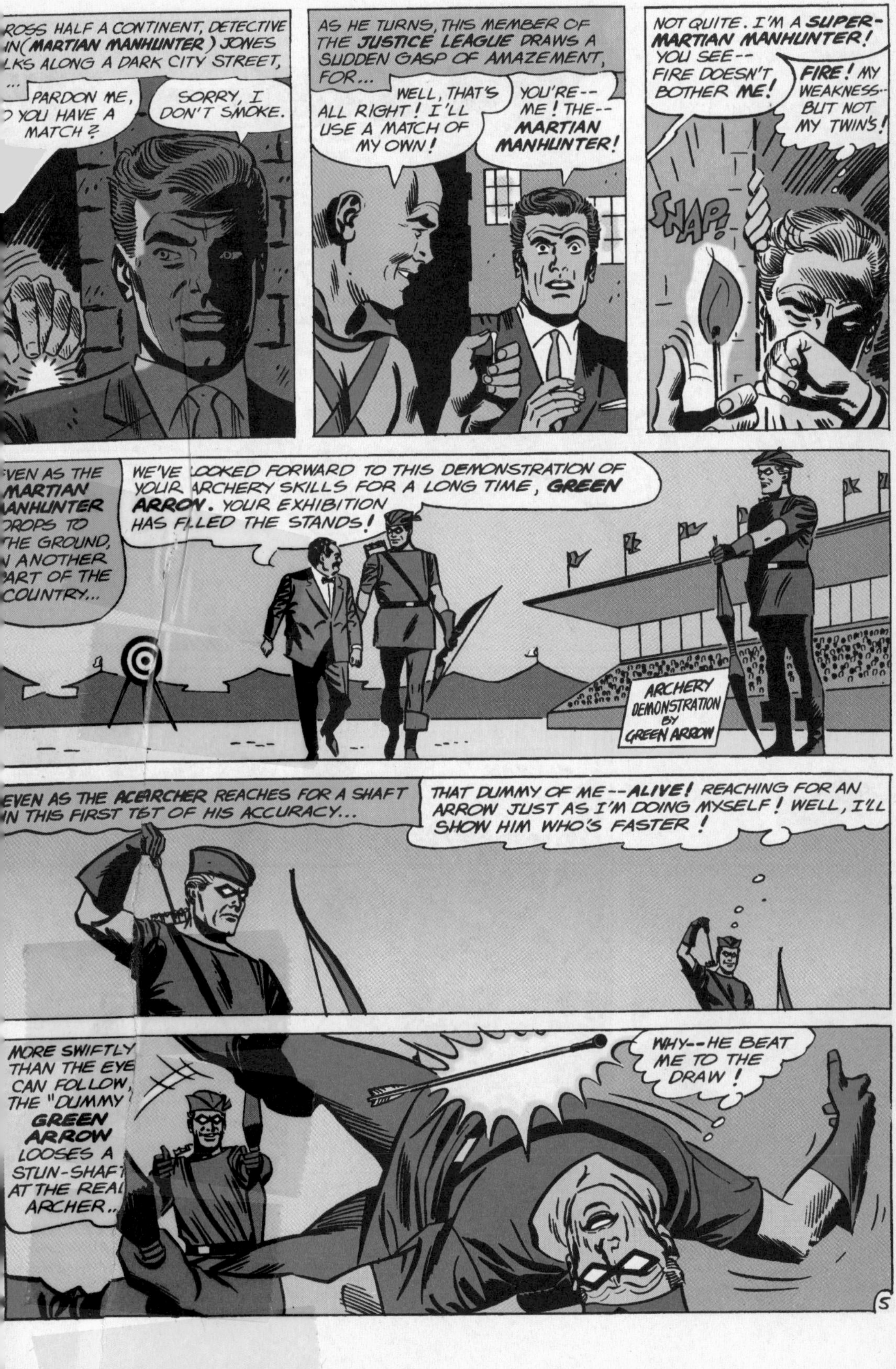

ROSS HALF A CONTINENT, DETECTIVE
IN (MARTIAN MANHUNTER) JONES
LKS ALONG A DARK CITY STREET, ...
PARDON ME, D YOU HAVE A MATCH?
SORRY, I DON'T SMOKE.
AS HE TURNS, THIS MEMBER OF THE JUSTICE LEAGUE DRAWS A SUDDEN GASP OF AMAZEMENT, FOR...
WELL, THAT'S ALL RIGHT! I'LL USE A MATCH OF MY OWN!
YOU'RE-- ME! THE-- MARTIAN MANHUNTER!
NOT QUITE. I'M A SUPER-MARTIAN MANHUNTER! YOU SEE-- FIRE DOESN'T BOTHER ME!
FIRE! MY WEAKNESS-- BUT NOT MY TWIN'S!
SNAP!
EVEN AS THE MARTIAN MANHUNTER DROPS TO THE GROUND, N ANOTHER PART OF THE COUNTRY...
WE'VE LOOKED FORWARD TO THIS DEMONSTRATION OF YOUR ARCHERY SKILLS FOR A LONG TIME, GREEN ARROW. YOUR EXHIBITION HAS FILLED THE STANDS!
ARCHERY DEMONSTRATION BY GREEN ARROW
EVEN AS THE ACE ARCHER REACHES FOR A SHAFT IN THIS FIRST TEST OF HIS ACCURACY...
THAT DUMMY OF ME--ALIVE! REACHING FOR AN ARROW JUST AS I'M DOING MYSELF! WELL, I'LL SHOW HIM WHO'S FASTER!
MORE SWIFTLY THAN THE EYE CAN FOLLOW, THE "DUMMY" GREEN ARROW LOOSES A STUN-SHAFT AT THE REAL ARCHER...
WHY--HE BEAT ME TO THE DRAW!
5

FAR AWAY, OFF THE COAST OF NORWAY, A MIGHTY MOVEMENT OF WATER ATTRACTS AQUAMAN'S ATTENTION...

THE MAELSTROM* IS MORE THAN ORDINARILY VIOLENT TODAY-- AND IT'S CAUGHT SOMEONE IN ITS GRIP! GOT TO GO TO HIS AID--

*Editor's Note: THE MAELSTROM IS A FAMOUS WHIRLPOOL LOCATED OF THE NORTHWEST COAST OF NORWAY.

SWIMMING POWERFULLY, THE SEA KING REACHES THE TRAPPED FIGURE, ONLY TO FEEL THE TERRIBLE CURRENT CLUTCH AT HIM AS...

GREAT NEPTUNE! THE TRAPPED FIGURE IS-- "ME"!

A MUCH IMPROVED "YOU" AQUAMAN! FOR WHILE THESE TREACHEROUS WATERS HAVE CAUGHT YOU IN THEIR GRIP--I CAN EASILY SWIM TO SAFETY!

IN GOTHAM CITY A DARK-GARBED FIGURE RACES TO HIS BATPLANE IN RESPONSE TO A BAT-SIGN IN THE SKY...

COMMISSIONER GORDON IS SIGNALLING ME TO MEET HIM!

A GRIM SHADOW COVERS THE RUNNING BATMAN AS HE SEES...

WHAT IN THUNDER? ANOTHER-- BATMAN!

I'M SUCH A BATMAN AS YOU'VE DREAMED OF BEING! FAR SUPERIOR TO YOU!

AND THERE'S YOUR PROOF!

IN THIS INCREDIBLE MANNER, THE ENTIRE JUSTICE LEAGUE EXCEPT HONORARY MEMBER SNAPPER CARR--AS BEEN RENDERED HELPLESS OR UNCONSCIOUS

6

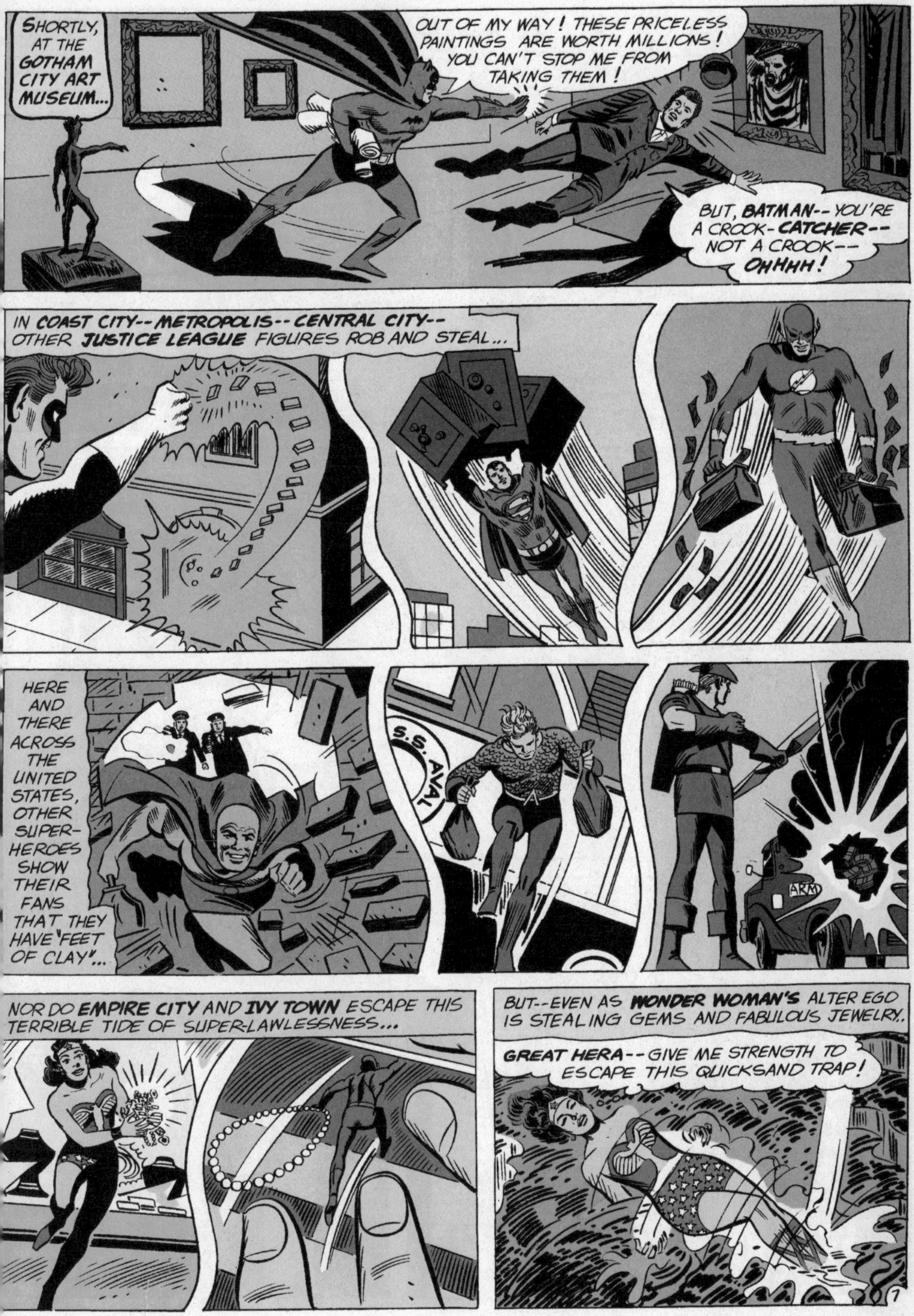
SHORTLY, AT THE GOTHAM CITY ART MUSEUM...
OUT OF MY WAY! THESE PRICELESS PAINTINGS ARE WORTH MILLIONS! YOU CAN'T STOP ME FROM TAKING THEM!
BUT, BATMAN-- YOU'RE A CROOK-CATCHER-- NOT A CROOK-- OHHHH!
IN COAST CITY--METROPOLIS--CENTRAL CITY-- OTHER JUSTICE LEAGUE FIGURES ROB AND STEAL...
HERE AND THERE ACROSS THE UNITED STATES, OTHER SUPER-HEROES SHOW THEIR FANS THAT THEY HAVE "FEET OF CLAY"...
S.S. AVAL
ARM
NOR DO EMPIRE CITY AND IVY TOWN ESCAPE THIS TERRIBLE TIDE OF SUPER-LAWLESSNESS...
BUT--EVEN AS WONDER WOMAN'S ALTER EGO IS STEALING GEMS AND FABULOUS JEWELRY,
GREAT HERA-- GIVE ME STRENGTH TO ESCAPE THIS QUICKSAND TRAP!
7

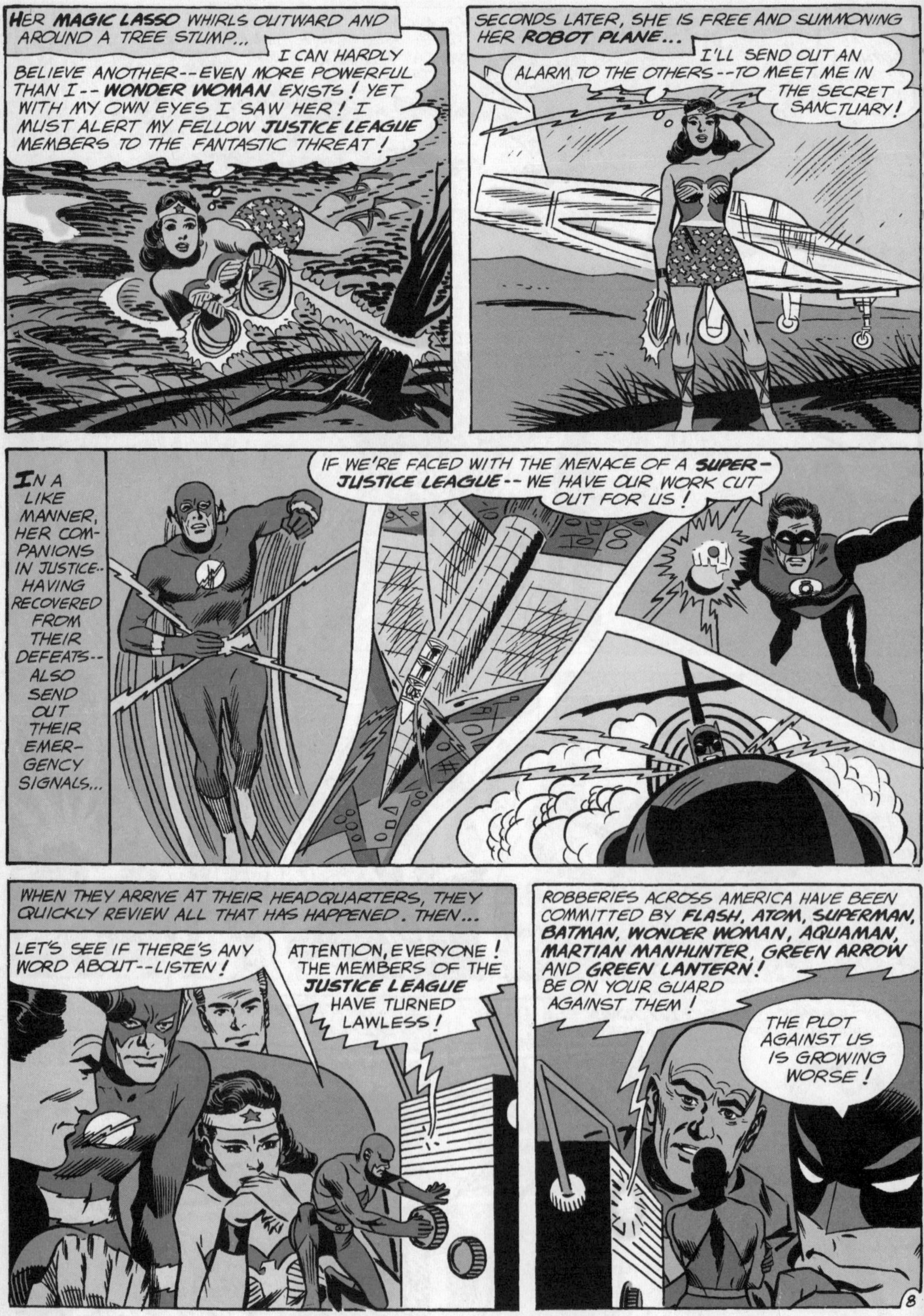
HER MAGIC LASSO WHIRLS OUTWARD AND AROUND A TREE STUMP...
I CAN HARDLY BELIEVE ANOTHER--EVEN MORE POWERFUL THAN I--WONDER WOMAN EXISTS! YET WITH MY OWN EYES I SAW HER! I MUST ALERT MY FELLOW JUSTICE LEAGUE MEMBERS TO THE FANTASTIC THREAT!
SECONDS LATER, SHE IS FREE AND SUMMONING HER ROBOT PLANE...
I'LL SEND OUT AN ALARM TO THE OTHERS--TO MEET ME IN THE SECRET SANCTUARY!
IN A LIKE MANNER, HER COMPANIONS IN JUSTICE.. HAVING RECOVERED FROM THEIR DEFEATS--ALSO SEND OUT THEIR EMERGENCY SIGNALS...
IF WE'RE FACED WITH THE MENACE OF A SUPER-JUSTICE LEAGUE--WE HAVE OUR WORK CUT OUT FOR US!
WHEN THEY ARRIVE AT THEIR HEADQUARTERS, THEY QUICKLY REVIEW ALL THAT HAS HAPPENED. THEN...
LET'S SEE IF THERE'S ANY WORD ABOUT--LISTEN!
ATTENTION, EVERYONE! THE MEMBERS OF THE JUSTICE LEAGUE HAVE TURNED LAWLESS!
ROBBERIES ACROSS AMERICA HAVE BEEN COMMITTED BY FLASH, ATOM, SUPERMAN, BATMAN, WONDER WOMAN, AQUAMAN, MARTIAN MANHUNTER, GREEN ARROW AND GREEN LANTERN! BE ON YOUR GUARD AGAINST THEM!
THE PLOT AGAINST US IS GROWING WORSE!
8

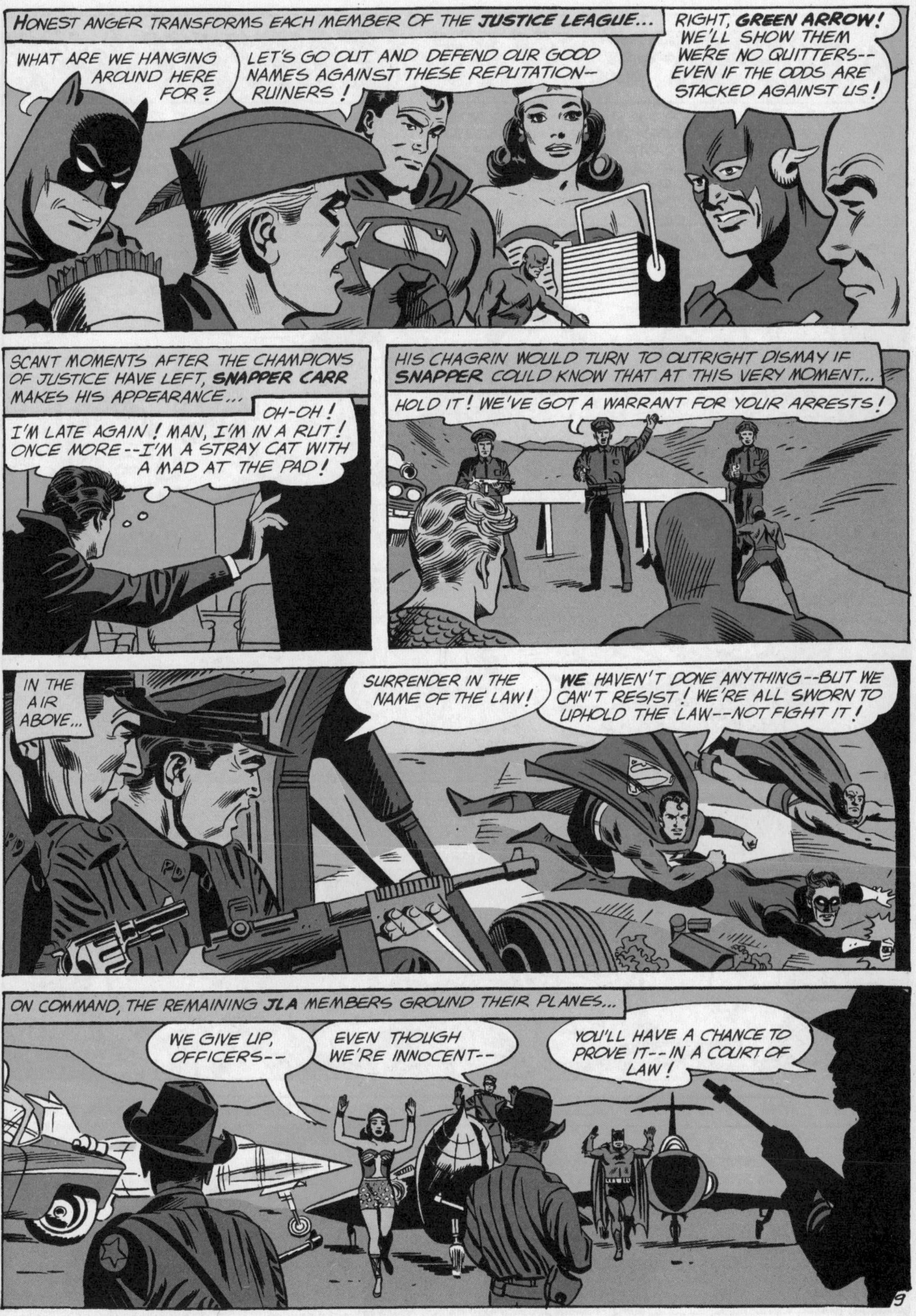
HONEST ANGER TRANSFORMS EACH MEMBER OF THE JUSTICE LEAGUE...
WHAT ARE WE HANGING AROUND HERE FOR?
LET'S GO OUT AND DEFEND OUR GOOD NAMES AGAINST THESE REPUTATION-RUINERS!
RIGHT, GREEN ARROW! WE'LL SHOW THEM WE'RE NO QUITTERS--EVEN IF THE ODDS ARE STACKED AGAINST US!
SCANT MOMENTS AFTER THE CHAMPIONS OF JUSTICE HAVE LEFT, SNAPPER CARR MAKES HIS APPEARANCE...
OH-OH! I'M LATE AGAIN! MAN, I'M IN A RUT! ONCE MORE--I'M A STRAY CAT WITH A MAD AT THE PAD!
HIS CHAGRIN WOULD TURN TO OUTRIGHT DISMAY IF SNAPPER COULD KNOW THAT AT THIS VERY MOMENT...
HOLD IT! WE'VE GOT A WARRANT FOR YOUR ARRESTS!
IN THE AIR ABOVE...
SURRENDER IN THE NAME OF THE LAW!
WE HAVEN'T DONE ANYTHING--BUT WE CAN'T RESIST! WE'RE ALL SWORN TO UPHOLD THE LAW--NOT FIGHT IT!
PD
PD
ON COMMAND, THE REMAINING JLA MEMBERS GROUND THEIR PLANES...
WE GIVE UP, OFFICERS--
EVEN THOUGH WE'RE INNOCENT--
YOU'LL HAVE A CHANCE TO PROVE IT--IN A COURT OF LAW!
9

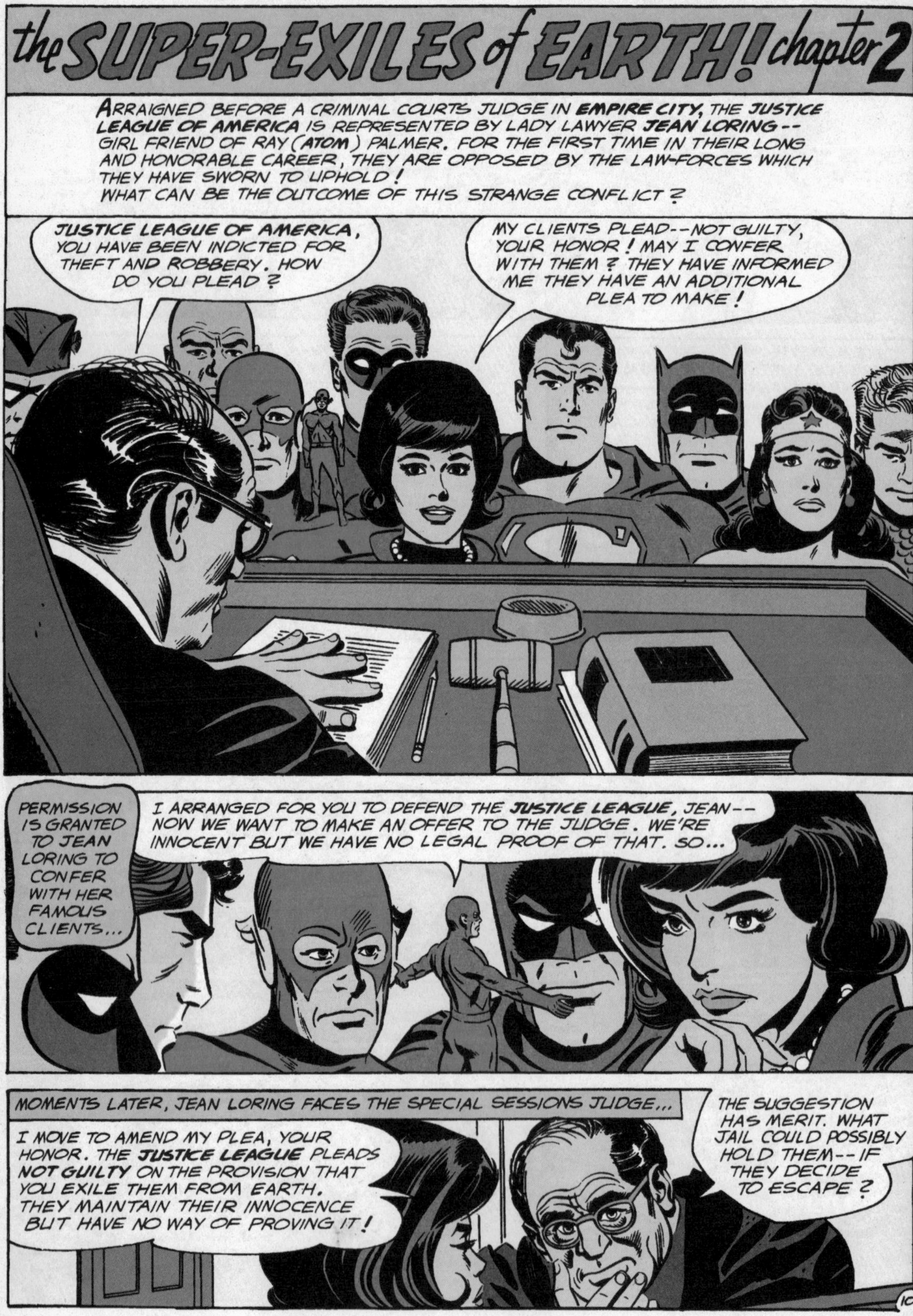

the SUPER-EXILES of EARTH! chapter 2
ARRAIGNED BEFORE A CRIMINAL COURTS JUDGE IN EMPIRE CITY, THE JUSTICE LEAGUE OF AMERICA IS REPRESENTED BY LADY LAWYER JEAN LORING -- GIRL FRIEND OF RAY (ATOM) PALMER. FOR THE FIRST TIME IN THEIR LONG AND HONORABLE CAREER, THEY ARE OPPOSED BY THE LAW-FORCES WHICH THEY HAVE SWORN TO UPHOLD! WHAT CAN BE THE OUTCOME OF THIS STRANGE CONFLICT?
JUSTICE LEAGUE OF AMERICA, YOU HAVE BEEN INDICTED FOR THEFT AND ROBBERY. HOW DO YOU PLEAD?
MY CLIENTS PLEAD--NOT GUILTY, YOUR HONOR! MAY I CONFER WITH THEM? THEY HAVE INFORMED ME THEY HAVE AN ADDITIONAL PLEA TO MAKE!
PERMISSION IS GRANTED TO JEAN LORING TO CONFER WITH HER FAMOUS CLIENTS...
I ARRANGED FOR YOU TO DEFEND THE JUSTICE LEAGUE, JEAN-- NOW WE WANT TO MAKE AN OFFER TO THE JUDGE. WE'RE INNOCENT BUT WE HAVE NO LEGAL PROOF OF THAT. SO...
MOMENTS LATER, JEAN LORING FACES THE SPECIAL SESSIONS JUDGE...
I MOVE TO AMEND MY PLEA, YOUR HONOR. THE JUSTICE LEAGUE PLEADS NOT GUILTY ON THE PROVISION THAT YOU EXILE THEM FROM EARTH. THEY MAINTAIN THEIR INNOCENCE BUT HAVE NO WAY OF PROVING IT!
THE SUGGESTION HAS MERIT. WHAT JAIL COULD POSSIBLY HOLD THEM-- IF THEY DECIDE TO ESCAPE?
10

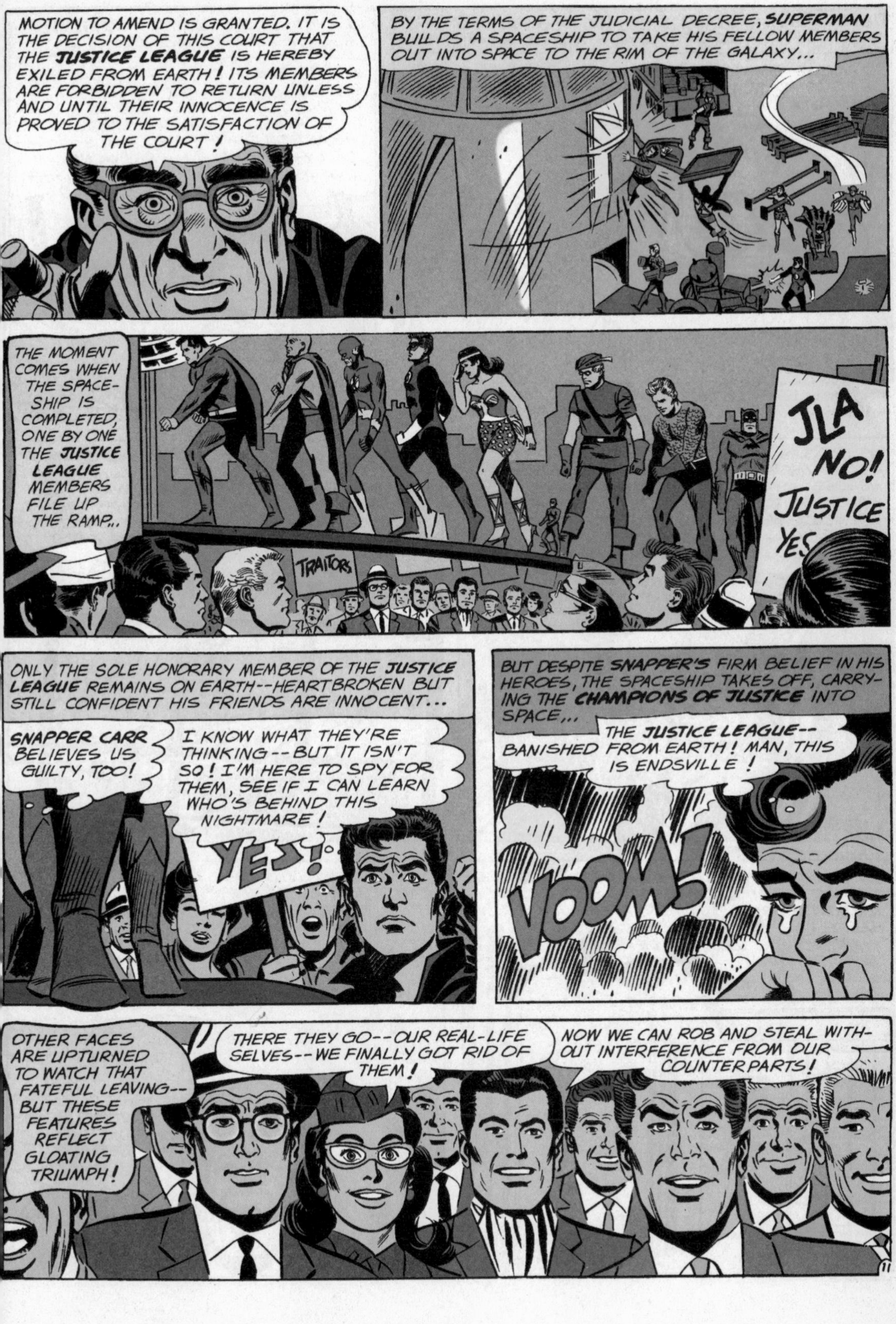
MOTION TO AMEND IS GRANTED. IT IS THE DECISION OF THIS COURT THAT THE JUSTICE LEAGUE IS HEREBY EXILED FROM EARTH! ITS MEMBERS ARE FORBIDDEN TO RETURN UNLESS AND UNTIL THEIR INNOCENCE IS PROVED TO THE SATISFACTION OF THE COURT!
BY THE TERMS OF THE JUDICIAL DECREE, SUPERMAN BUILDS A SPACESHIP TO TAKE HIS FELLOW MEMBERS OUT INTO SPACE TO THE RIM OF THE GALAXY...
THE MOMENT COMES WHEN THE SPACESHIP IS COMPLETED, ONE BY ONE THE JUSTICE LEAGUE MEMBERS FILE UP THE RAMP...
JLA NO! JUSTICE YES
TRAITORS
ONLY THE SOLE HONORARY MEMBER OF THE JUSTICE LEAGUE REMAINS ON EARTH--HEARTBROKEN BUT STILL CONFIDENT HIS FRIENDS ARE INNOCENT...
SNAPPER CARR BELIEVES US GUILTY, TOO!
I KNOW WHAT THEY'RE THINKING--BUT IT ISN'T SO! I'M HERE TO SPY FOR THEM, SEE IF I CAN LEARN WHO'S BEHIND THIS NIGHTMARE!
YES!
BUT DESPITE SNAPPER'S FIRM BELIEF IN HIS HEROES, THE SPACESHIP TAKES OFF, CARRYING THE CHAMPIONS OF JUSTICE INTO SPACE...
THE JUSTICE LEAGUE--BANISHED FROM EARTH! MAN, THIS IS ENDSVILLE!
VOOM!
OTHER FACES ARE UPTURNED TO WATCH THAT FATEFUL LEAVING--BUT THESE FEATURES REFLECT GLOATING TRIUMPH!
THERE THEY GO--OUR REAL-LIFE SELVES--WE FINALLY GOT RID OF THEM!
NOW WE CAN ROB AND STEAL WITHOUT INTERFERENCE FROM OUR COUNTERPARTS!
11

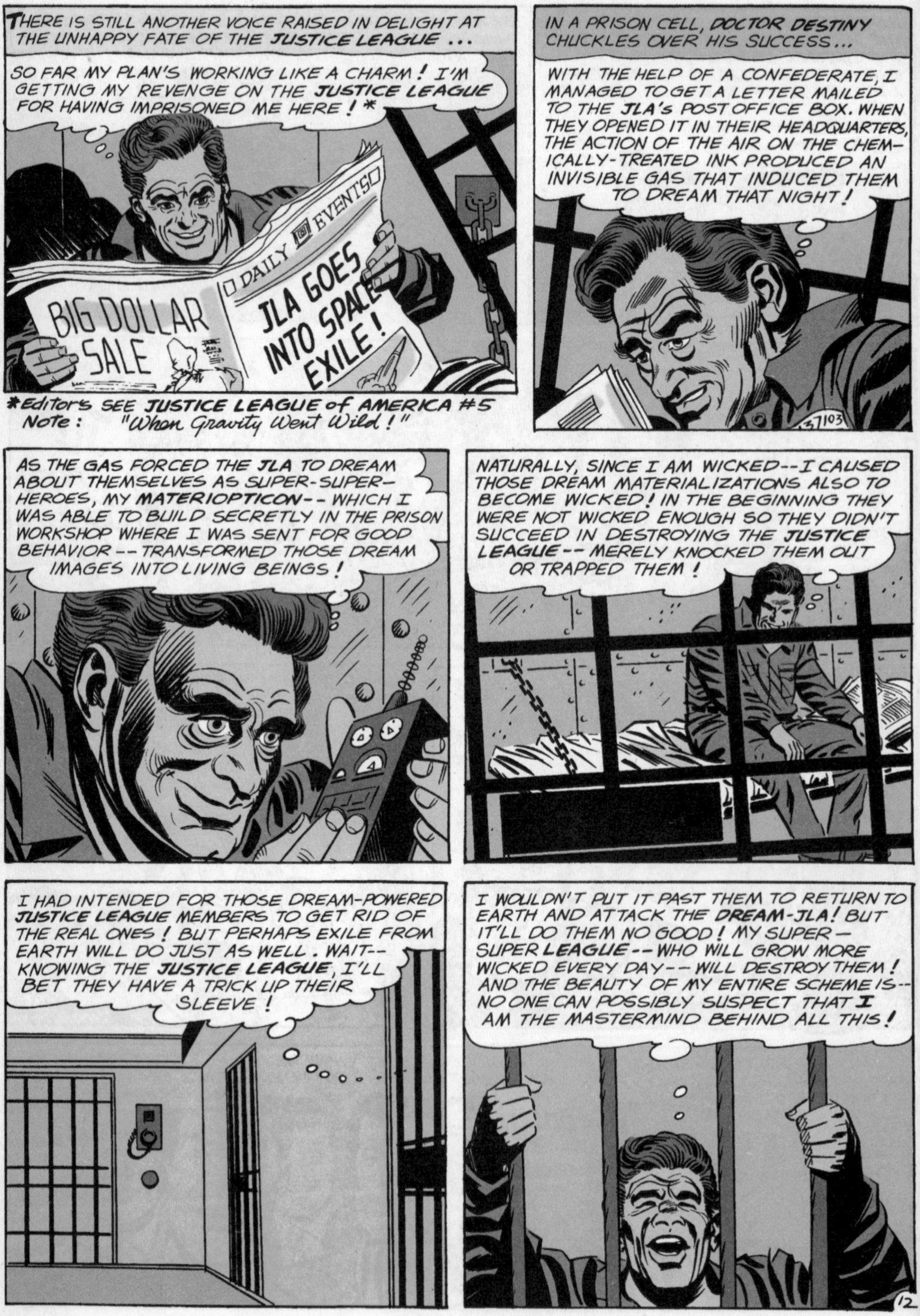
THERE IS STILL ANOTHER VOICE RAISED IN DELIGHT AT THE UNHAPPY FATE OF THE JUSTICE LEAGUE ...
SO FAR MY PLAN'S WORKING LIKE A CHARM! I'M GETTING MY REVENGE ON THE JUSTICE LEAGUE FOR HAVING IMPRISONED ME HERE! *
DAILY EVENTS
BIG DOLLAR SALE
JLA GOES INTO SPACE EXILE!
*Editor's Note: SEE JUSTICE LEAGUE of AMERICA #5 "When Gravity Went Wild!"
IN A PRISON CELL, DOCTOR DESTINY CHUCKLES OVER HIS SUCCESS...
WITH THE HELP OF A CONFEDERATE, I MANAGED TO GET A LETTER MAILED TO THE JLA's POST OFFICE BOX. WHEN THEY OPENED IT IN THEIR HEADQUARTERS, THE ACTION OF THE AIR ON THE CHEMICALLY-TREATED INK PRODUCED AN INVISIBLE GAS THAT INDUCED THEM TO DREAM THAT NIGHT!
AS THE GAS FORCED THE JLA TO DREAM ABOUT THEMSELVES AS SUPER-SUPER-HEROES, MY MATERIOPTICON -- WHICH I WAS ABLE TO BUILD SECRETLY IN THE PRISON WORKSHOP WHERE I WAS SENT FOR GOOD BEHAVIOR -- TRANSFORMED THOSE DREAM IMAGES INTO LIVING BEINGS!
NATURALLY, SINCE I AM WICKED -- I CAUSED THOSE DREAM MATERIALIZATIONS ALSO TO BECOME WICKED! IN THE BEGINNING THEY WERE NOT WICKED ENOUGH SO THEY DIDN'T SUCCEED IN DESTROYING THE JUSTICE LEAGUE -- MERELY KNOCKED THEM OUT OR TRAPPED THEM!
I HAD INTENDED FOR THOSE DREAM-POWERED JUSTICE LEAGUE MEMBERS TO GET RID OF THE REAL ONES! BUT PERHAPS EXILE FROM EARTH WILL DO JUST AS WELL. WAIT -- KNOWING THE JUSTICE LEAGUE, I'LL BET THEY HAVE A TRICK UP THEIR SLEEVE!
I WOULDN'T PUT IT PAST THEM TO RETURN TO EARTH AND ATTACK THE DREAM-JLA! BUT IT'LL DO THEM NO GOOD! MY SUPER-SUPER LEAGUE -- WHO WILL GROW MORE WICKED EVERY DAY -- WILL DESTROY THEM! AND THE BEAUTY OF MY ENTIRE SCHEME IS -- NO ONE CAN POSSIBLY SUSPECT THAT I AM THE MASTERMIND BEHIND ALL THIS!
12

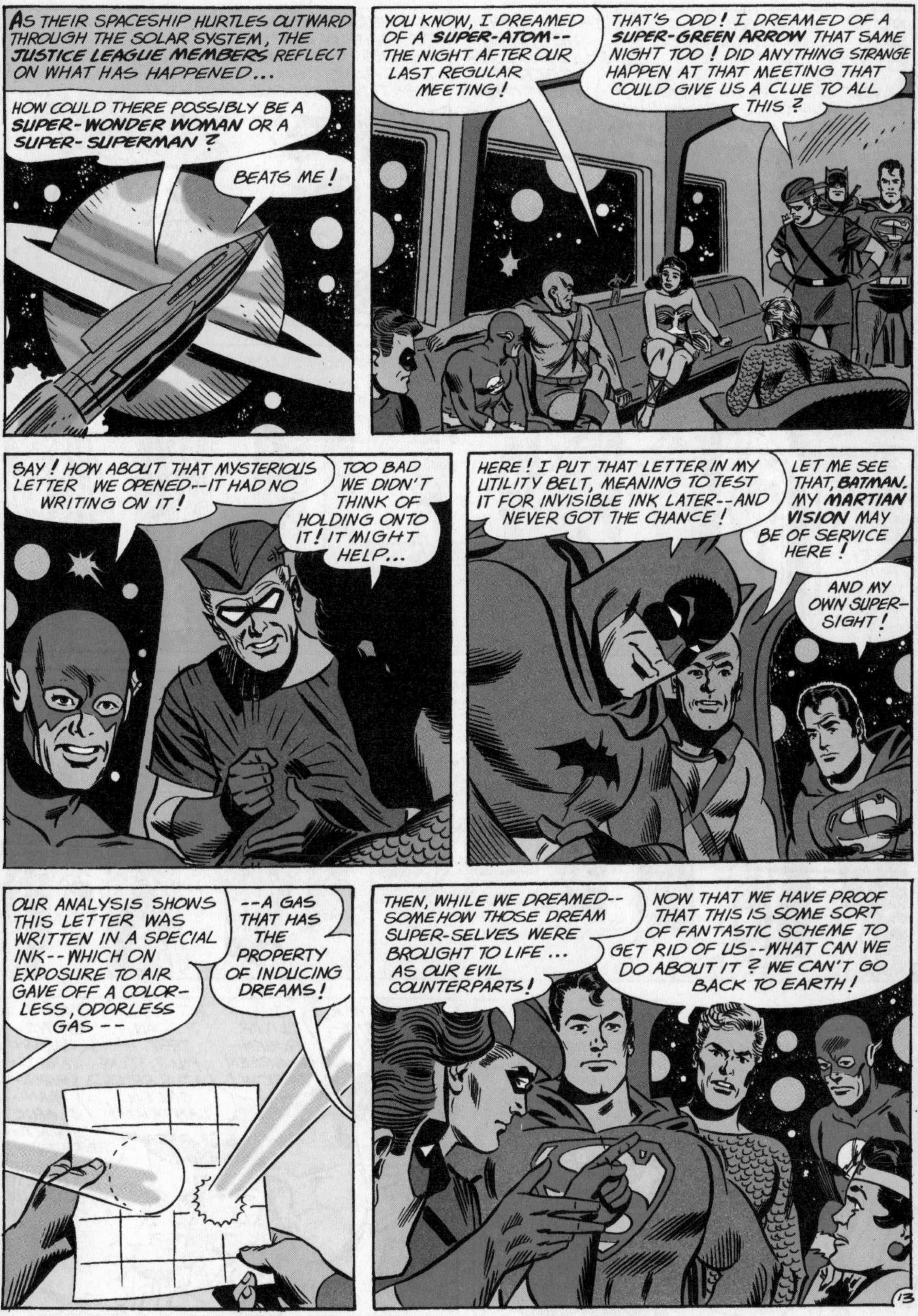
AS THEIR SPACESHIP HURTLES OUTWARD THROUGH THE SOLAR SYSTEM, THE JUSTICE LEAGUE MEMBERS REFLECT ON WHAT HAS HAPPENED...
HOW COULD THERE POSSIBLY BE A SUPER-WONDER WOMAN OR A SUPER-SUPERMAN ?
BEATS ME !
YOU KNOW, I DREAMED OF A SUPER-ATOM-- THE NIGHT AFTER OUR LAST REGULAR MEETING !
THAT'S ODD ! I DREAMED OF A SUPER-GREEN ARROW THAT SAME NIGHT TOO ! DID ANYTHING STRANGE HAPPEN AT THAT MEETING THAT COULD GIVE US A CLUE TO ALL THIS ?
SAY ! HOW ABOUT THAT MYSTERIOUS LETTER WE OPENED--IT HAD NO WRITING ON IT !
TOO BAD WE DIDN'T THINK OF HOLDING ONTO IT ! IT MIGHT HELP...
HERE ! I PUT THAT LETTER IN MY UTILITY BELT, MEANING TO TEST IT FOR INVISIBLE INK LATER--AND NEVER GOT THE CHANCE !
LET ME SEE THAT, BATMAN. MY MARTIAN VISION MAY BE OF SERVICE HERE !
AND MY OWN SUPER-SIGHT !
OUR ANALYSIS SHOWS THIS LETTER WAS WRITTEN IN A SPECIAL INK--WHICH ON EXPOSURE TO AIR GAVE OFF A COLORLESS, ODORLESS GAS --
--A GAS THAT HAS THE PROPERTY OF INDUCING DREAMS !
THEN, WHILE WE DREAMED-- SOMEHOW THOSE DREAM SUPER-SELVES WERE BROUGHT TO LIFE ... AS OUR EVIL COUNTERPARTS !
NOW THAT WE HAVE PROOF THAT THIS IS SOME SORT OF FANTASTIC SCHEME TO GET RID OF US--WHAT CAN WE DO ABOUT IT ? WE CAN'T GO BACK TO EARTH !
13

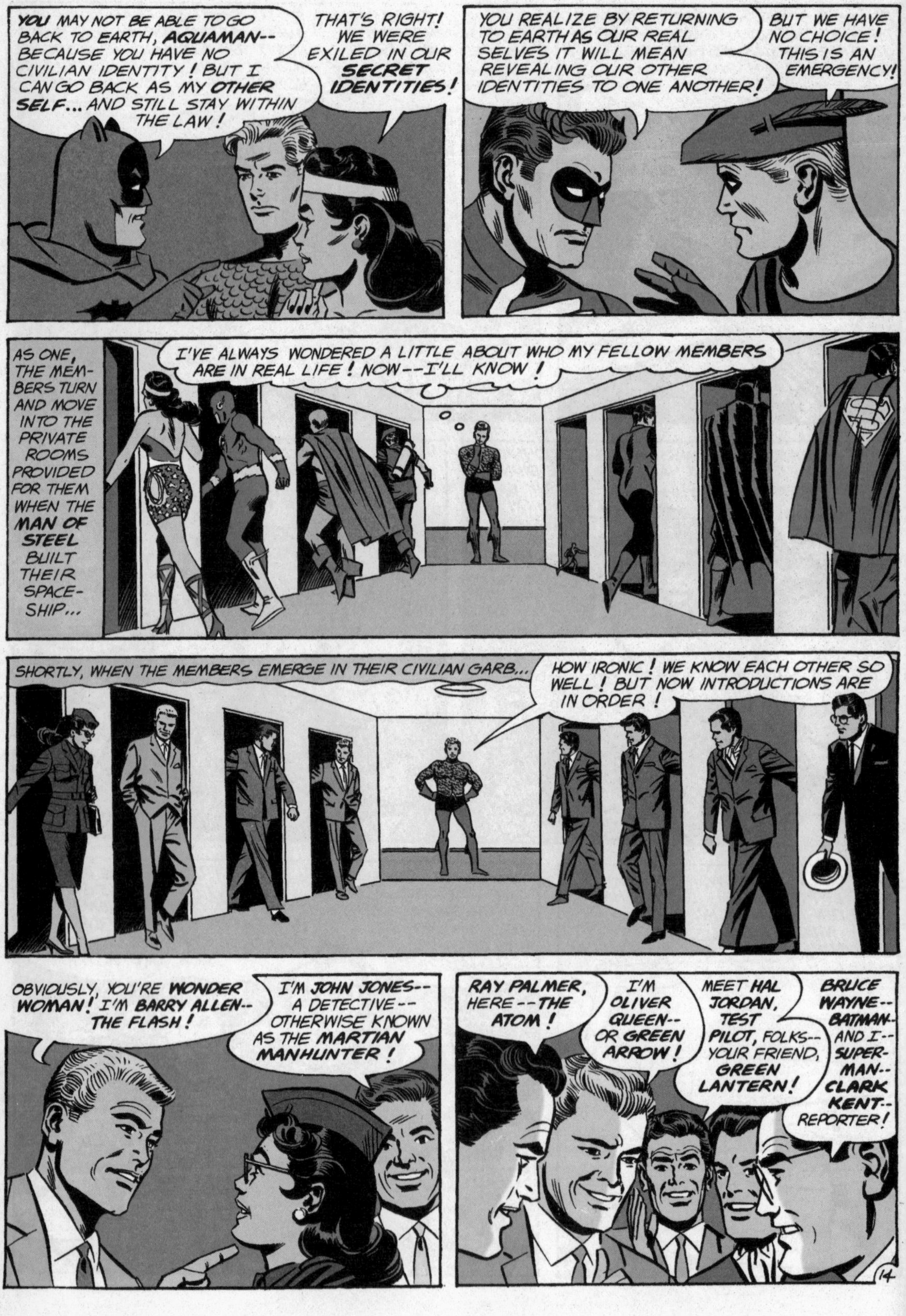
YOU MAY NOT BE ABLE TO GO BACK TO EARTH, AQUAMAN-- BECAUSE YOU HAVE NO CIVILIAN IDENTITY! BUT I CAN GO BACK AS MY OTHER SELF... AND STILL STAY WITHIN THE LAW!
THAT'S RIGHT! WE WERE EXILED IN OUR SECRET IDENTITIES!
YOU REALIZE BY RETURNING TO EARTH AS OUR REAL SELVES IT WILL MEAN REVEALING OUR OTHER IDENTITIES TO ONE ANOTHER!
BUT WE HAVE NO CHOICE! THIS IS AN EMERGENCY!
AS ONE, THE MEMBERS TURN AND MOVE INTO THE PRIVATE ROOMS PROVIDED FOR THEM WHEN THE MAN OF STEEL BUILT THEIR SPACE-SHIP...
I'VE ALWAYS WONDERED A LITTLE ABOUT WHO MY FELLOW MEMBERS ARE IN REAL LIFE! NOW--I'LL KNOW!
SHORTLY, WHEN THE MEMBERS EMERGE IN THEIR CIVILIAN GARB...
HOW IRONIC! WE KNOW EACH OTHER SO WELL! BUT NOW INTRODUCTIONS ARE IN ORDER!
OBVIOUSLY, YOU'RE WONDER WOMAN! I'M BARRY ALLEN-- THE FLASH!
I'M JOHN JONES-- A DETECTIVE-- OTHERWISE KNOWN AS THE MARTIAN MANHUNTER!
RAY PALMER, HERE--THE ATOM!
I'M OLIVER QUEEN-- OR GREEN ARROW!
MEET HAL JORDAN, TEST PILOT, FOLKS-- YOUR FRIEND, GREEN LANTERN!
BRUCE WAYNE-- BATMAN-- AND I-- SUPER-MAN-- CLARK KENT-- REPORTER!
14

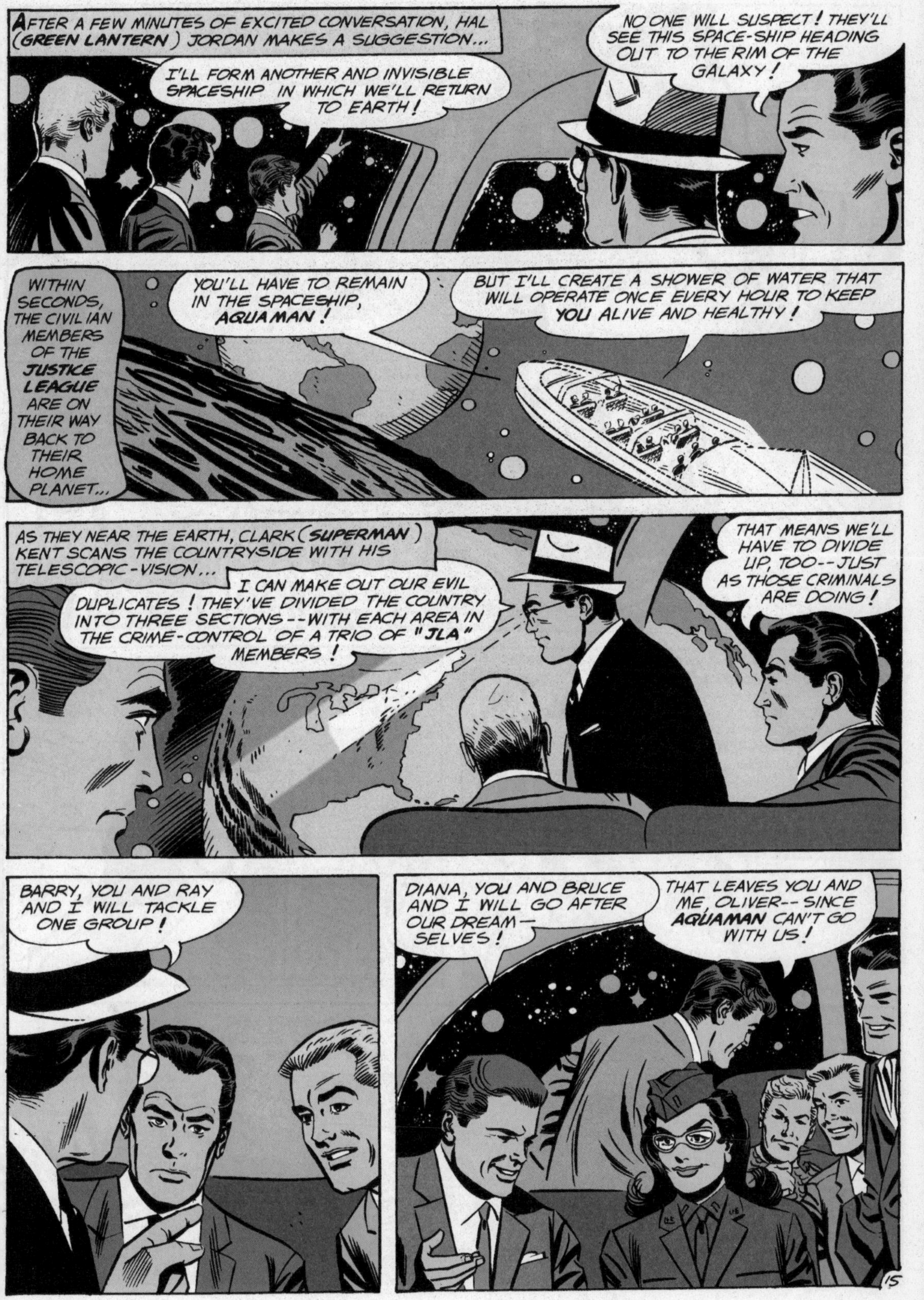

AFTER A FEW MINUTES OF EXCITED CONVERSATION, HAL (GREEN LANTERN) JORDAN MAKES A SUGGESTION...
I'LL FORM ANOTHER AND INVISIBLE SPACESHIP IN WHICH WE'LL RETURN TO EARTH!
NO ONE WILL SUSPECT! THEY'LL SEE THIS SPACE-SHIP HEADING OUT TO THE RIM OF THE GALAXY!
WITHIN SECONDS, THE CIVILIAN MEMBERS OF THE JUSTICE LEAGUE ARE ON THEIR WAY BACK TO THEIR HOME PLANET...
YOU'LL HAVE TO REMAIN IN THE SPACESHIP, AQUAMAN!
BUT I'LL CREATE A SHOWER OF WATER THAT WILL OPERATE ONCE EVERY HOUR TO KEEP YOU ALIVE AND HEALTHY!
AS THEY NEAR THE EARTH, CLARK (SUPERMAN) KENT SCANS THE COUNTRYSIDE WITH HIS TELESCOPIC-VISION...
I CAN MAKE OUT OUR EVIL DUPLICATES! THEY'VE DIVIDED THE COUNTRY INTO THREE SECTIONS--WITH EACH AREA IN THE CRIME-CONTROL OF A TRIO OF "JLA" MEMBERS!
THAT MEANS WE'LL HAVE TO DIVIDE UP, TOO--JUST AS THOSE CRIMINALS ARE DOING!
BARRY, YOU AND RAY AND I WILL TACKLE ONE GROUP!
DIANA, YOU AND BRUCE AND I WILL GO AFTER OUR DREAM-SELVES!
THAT LEAVES YOU AND ME, OLIVER-- SINCE AQUAMAN CAN'T GO WITH US!
15

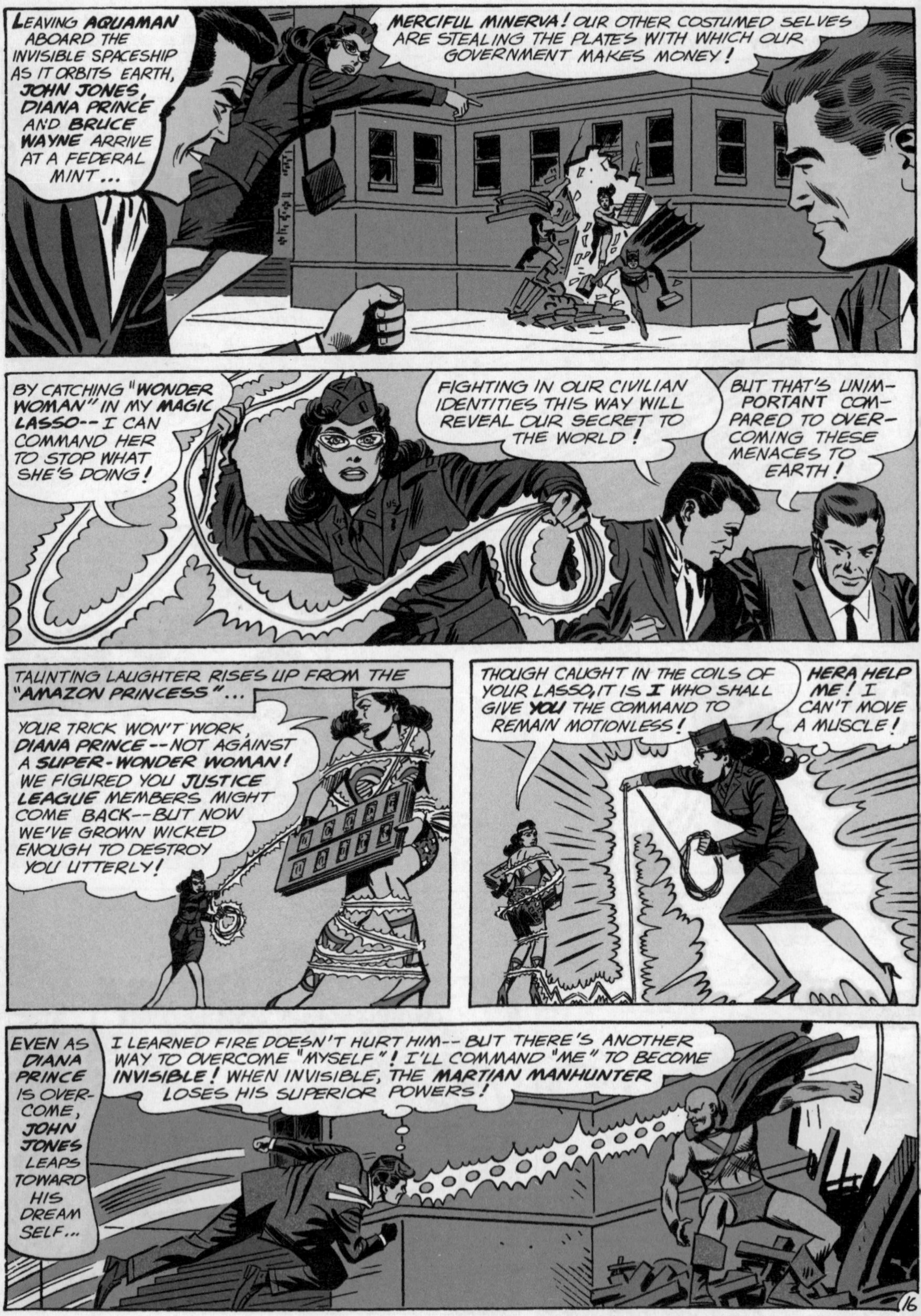
LEAVING AQUAMAN ABOARD THE INVISIBLE SPACESHIP AS IT ORBITS EARTH, JOHN JONES, DIANA PRINCE AND BRUCE WAYNE ARRIVE AT A FEDERAL MINT...
MERCIFUL MINERVA! OUR OTHER COSTUMED SELVES ARE STEALING THE PLATES WITH WHICH OUR GOVERNMENT MAKES MONEY!
BY CATCHING "WONDER WOMAN" IN MY MAGIC LASSO-- I CAN COMMAND HER TO STOP WHAT SHE'S DOING!
FIGHTING IN OUR CIVILIAN IDENTITIES THIS WAY WILL REVEAL OUR SECRET TO THE WORLD!
BUT THAT'S UNIMPORTANT COMPARED TO OVERCOMING THESE MENACES TO EARTH!
TAUNTING LAUGHTER RISES UP FROM THE "AMAZON PRINCESS"...
YOUR TRICK WON'T WORK, DIANA PRINCE--NOT AGAINST A SUPER-WONDER WOMAN! WE FIGURED YOU JUSTICE LEAGUE MEMBERS MIGHT COME BACK--BUT NOW WE'VE GROWN WICKED ENOUGH TO DESTROY YOU UTTERLY!
THOUGH CAUGHT IN THE COILS OF YOUR LASSO, IT IS I WHO SHALL GIVE YOU THE COMMAND TO REMAIN MOTIONLESS!
HERA HELP ME! I CAN'T MOVE A MUSCLE!
EVEN AS DIANA PRINCE IS OVERCOME, JOHN JONES LEAPS TOWARD HIS DREAM SELF...
I LEARNED FIRE DOESN'T HURT HIM-- BUT THERE'S ANOTHER WAY TO OVERCOME "MYSELF"! I'LL COMMAND "ME" TO BECOME INVISIBLE! WHEN INVISIBLE, THE MARTIAN MANHUNTER LOSES HIS SUPERIOR POWERS!
16

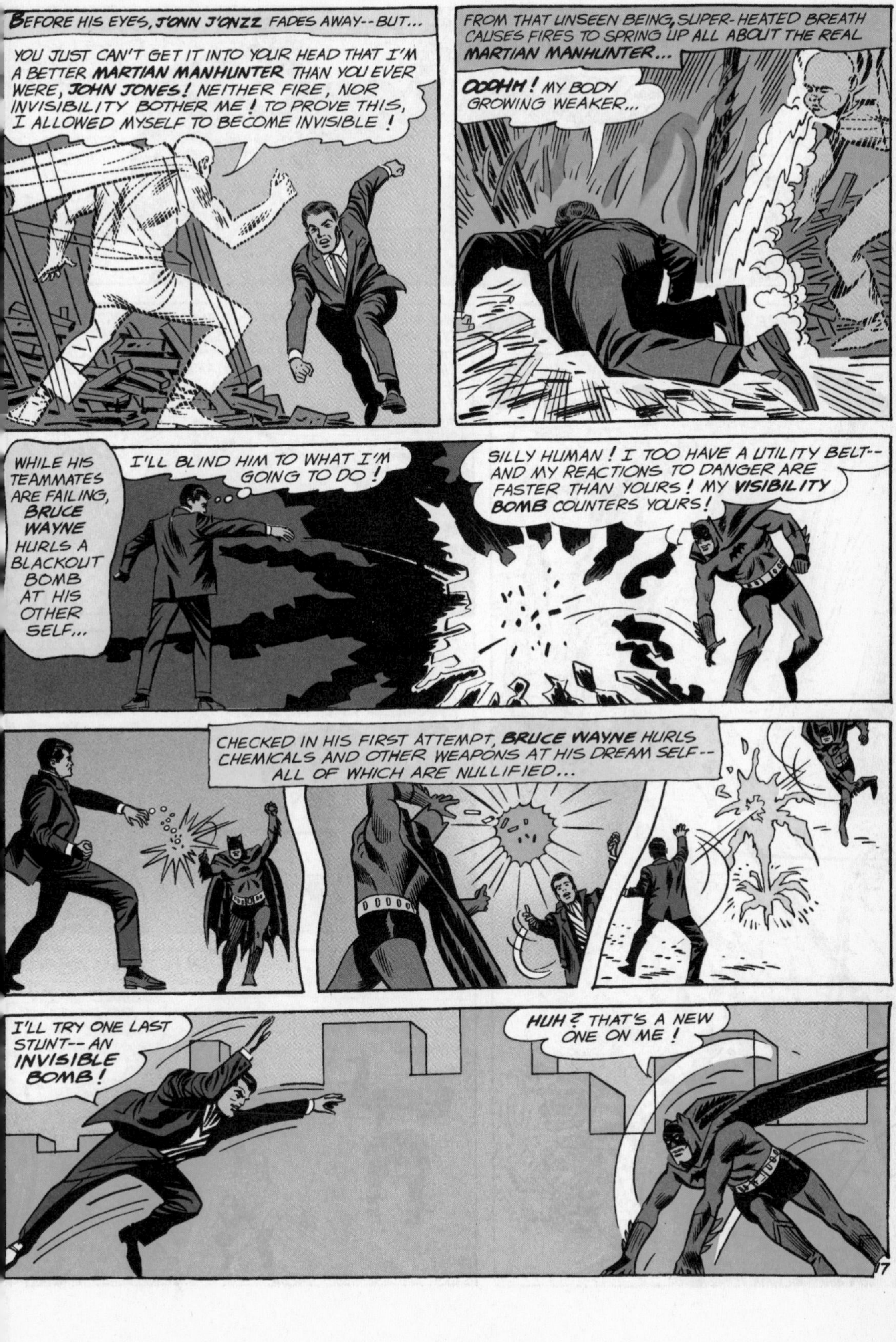
BEFORE HIS EYES, J'ONN J'ONZZ FADES AWAY--BUT...
YOU JUST CAN'T GET IT INTO YOUR HEAD THAT I'M A BETTER MARTIAN MANHUNTER THAN YOU EVER WERE, JOHN JONES! NEITHER FIRE, NOR INVISIBILITY BOTHER ME! TO PROVE THIS, I ALLOWED MYSELF TO BECOME INVISIBLE!
FROM THAT UNSEEN BEING, SUPER-HEATED BREATH CAUSES FIRES TO SPRING UP ALL ABOUT THE REAL MARTIAN MANHUNTER...
OOOHH! MY BODY GROWING WEAKER...
WHILE HIS TEAMMATES ARE FAILING, BRUCE WAYNE HURLS A BLACKOUT BOMB AT HIS OTHER SELF...
I'LL BLIND HIM TO WHAT I'M GOING TO DO!
SILLY HUMAN! I TOO HAVE A UTILITY BELT--AND MY REACTIONS TO DANGER ARE FASTER THAN YOURS! MY VISIBILITY BOMB COUNTERS YOURS!
CHECKED IN HIS FIRST ATTEMPT, BRUCE WAYNE HURLS CHEMICALS AND OTHER WEAPONS AT HIS DREAM SELF--ALL OF WHICH ARE NULLIFIED...
I'LL TRY ONE LAST STUNT--AN INVISIBLE BOMB!
HUH? THAT'S A NEW ONE ON ME!
7

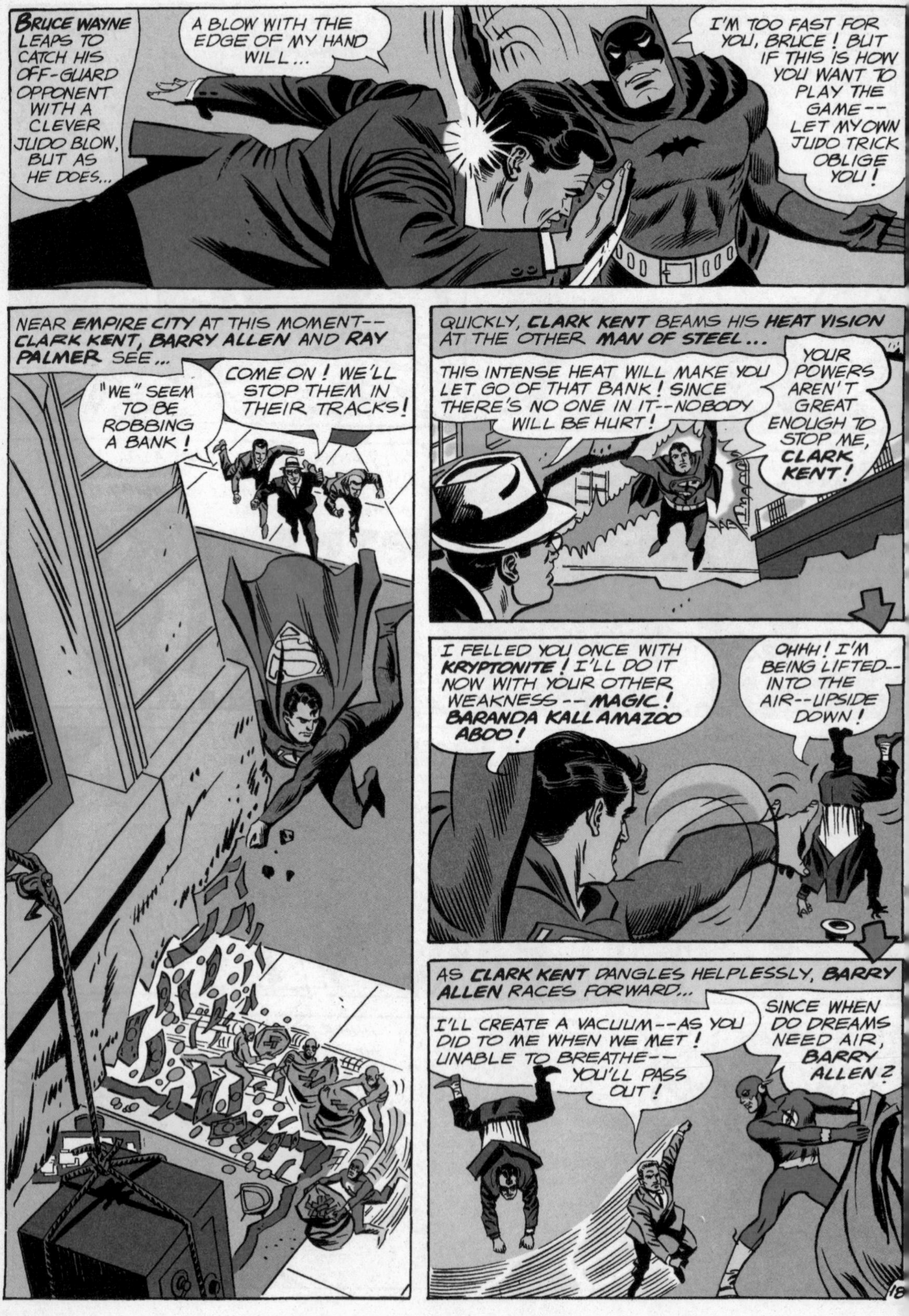
BRUCE WAYNE LEAPS TO CATCH HIS OFF-GUARD OPPONENT WITH A CLEVER JUDO BLOW, BUT AS HE DOES...
A BLOW WITH THE EDGE OF MY HAND WILL...
I'M TOO FAST FOR YOU, BRUCE! BUT IF THIS IS HOW YOU WANT TO PLAY THE GAME-- LET MY OWN JUDO TRICK OBLIGE YOU!
NEAR EMPIRE CITY AT THIS MOMENT-- CLARK KENT, BARRY ALLEN AND RAY PALMER SEE...
"WE" SEEM TO BE ROBBING A BANK!
COME ON! WE'LL STOP THEM IN THEIR TRACKS!
QUICKLY, CLARK KENT BEAMS HIS HEAT VISION AT THE OTHER MAN OF STEEL...
THIS INTENSE HEAT WILL MAKE YOU LET GO OF THAT BANK! SINCE THERE'S NO ONE IN IT--NOBODY WILL BE HURT!
YOUR POWERS AREN'T GREAT ENOUGH TO STOP ME, CLARK KENT!
I FELLED YOU ONCE WITH KRYPTONITE! I'LL DO IT NOW WITH YOUR OTHER WEAKNESS -- MAGIC! BARANDA KALLAMAZOO ABOO!
OHHH! I'M BEING LIFTED-- INTO THE AIR--UPSIDE DOWN!
AS CLARK KENT DANGLES HELPLESSLY, BARRY ALLEN RACES FORWARD...
I'LL CREATE A VACUUM--AS YOU DID TO ME WHEN WE MET! UNABLE TO BREATHE-- YOU'LL PASS OUT!
SINCE WHEN DO DREAMS NEED AIR, BARRY ALLEN?
18

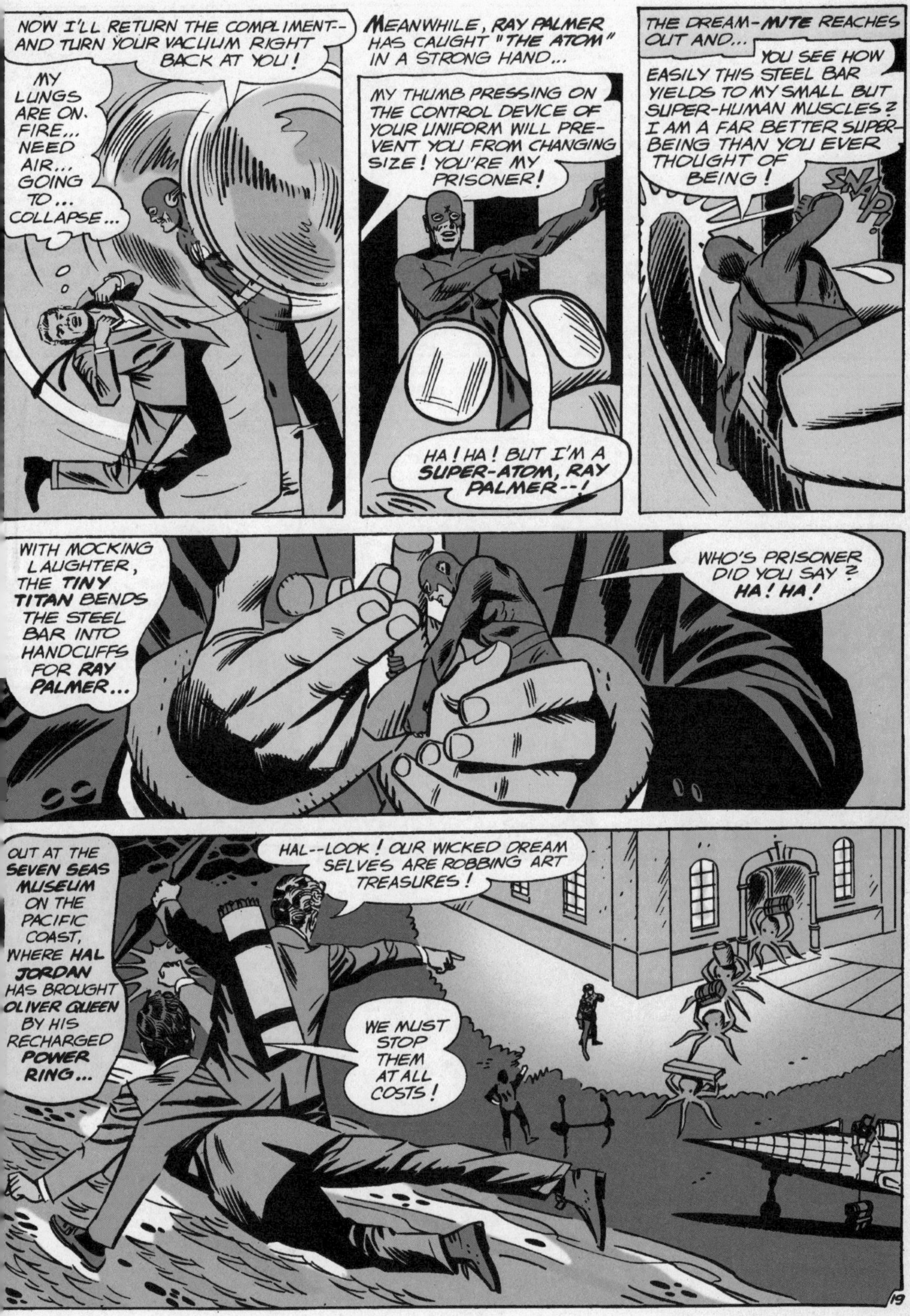
NOW I'LL RETURN THE COMPLIMENT-- AND TURN YOUR VACUUM RIGHT BACK AT YOU!
MY LUNGS ARE ON FIRE... NEED AIR... GOING TO... COLLAPSE...
MEANWHILE, RAY PALMER HAS CAUGHT "THE ATOM" IN A STRONG HAND...
MY THUMB PRESSING ON THE CONTROL DEVICE OF YOUR UNIFORM WILL PREVENT YOU FROM CHANGING SIZE! YOU'RE MY PRISONER!
HA! HA! BUT I'M A SUPER-ATOM, RAY PALMER--!
THE DREAM-MITE REACHES OUT AND...
YOU SEE HOW EASILY THIS STEEL BAR YIELDS TO MY SMALL BUT SUPER-HUMAN MUSCLES? I AM A FAR BETTER SUPER-BEING THAN YOU EVER THOUGHT OF BEING!
SNAP!
WITH MOCKING LAUGHTER, THE TINY TITAN BENDS THE STEEL BAR INTO HANDCUFFS FOR RAY PALMER...
WHO'S PRISONER DID YOU SAY? HA! HA!
OUT AT THE SEVEN SEAS MUSEUM ON THE PACIFIC COAST, WHERE HAL JORDAN HAS BROUGHT OLIVER QUEEN BY HIS RECHARGED POWER RING...
HAL--LOOK! OUR WICKED DREAM SELVES ARE ROBBING ART TREASURES!
WE MUST STOP THEM AT ALL COSTS!
19

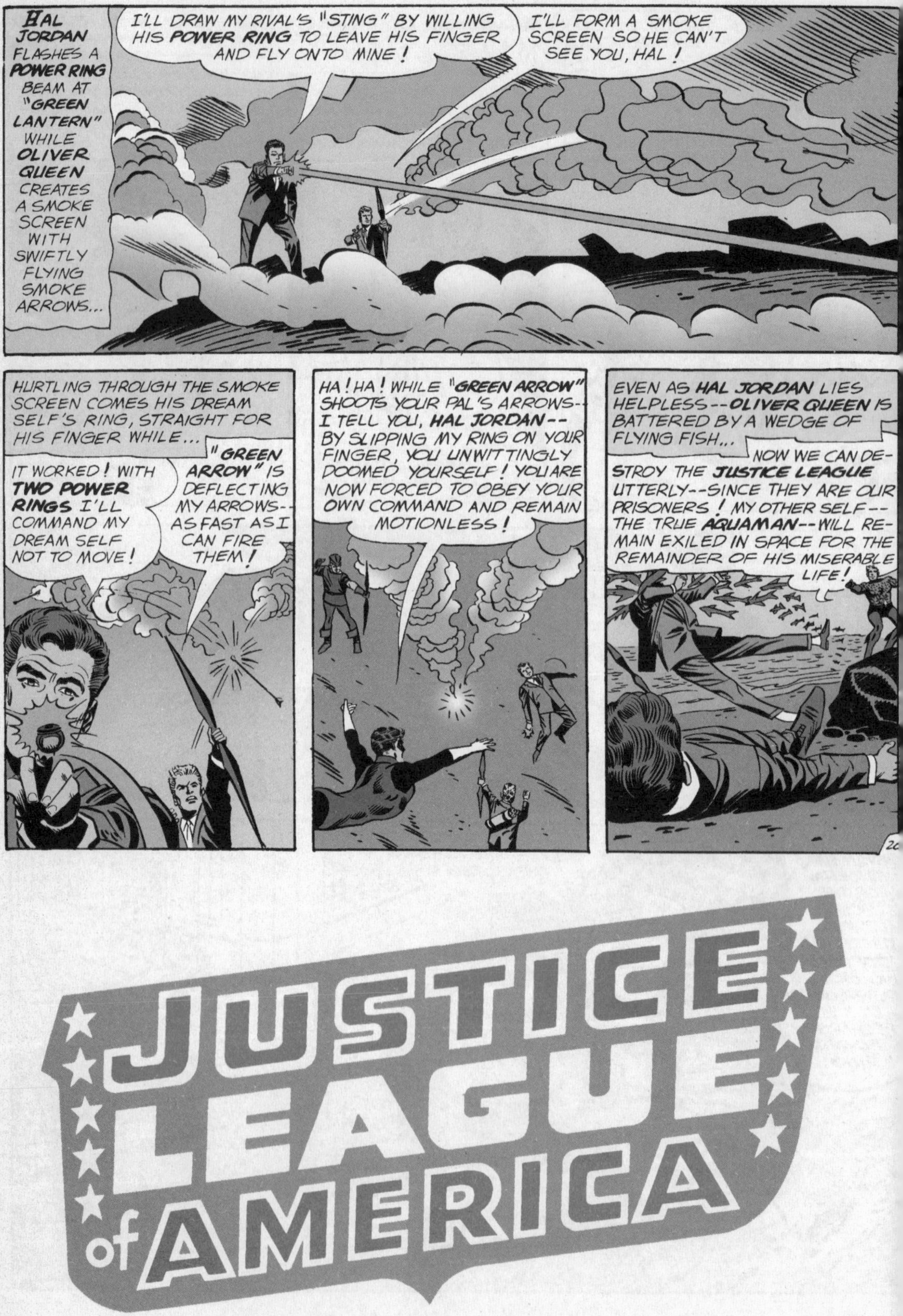
HAL JORDAN FLASHES A POWER RING BEAM AT "GREEN LANTERN" WHILE OLIVER QUEEN CREATES A SMOKE SCREEN WITH SWIFTLY FLYING SMOKE ARROWS...
I'LL DRAW MY RIVAL'S "STING" BY WILLING HIS POWER RING TO LEAVE HIS FINGER AND FLY ONTO MINE!
I'LL FORM A SMOKE SCREEN SO HE CAN'T SEE YOU, HAL!
HURTLING THROUGH THE SMOKE SCREEN COMES HIS DREAM SELF'S RING, STRAIGHT FOR HIS FINGER WHILE...
IT WORKED! WITH TWO POWER RINGS I'LL COMMAND MY DREAM SELF NOT TO MOVE!
"GREEN ARROW" IS DEFLECTING MY ARROWS--AS FAST AS I CAN FIRE THEM!
HA! HA! WHILE "GREEN ARROW" SHOOTS YOUR PAL'S ARROWS--I TELL YOU, HAL JORDAN--BY SLIPPING MY RING ON YOUR FINGER, YOU UNWITTINGLY DOOMED YOURSELF! YOU ARE NOW FORCED TO OBEY YOUR OWN COMMAND AND REMAIN MOTIONLESS!
EVEN AS HAL JORDAN LIES HELPLESS--OLIVER QUEEN IS BATTERED BY A WEDGE OF FLYING FISH...
NOW WE CAN DESTROY THE JUSTICE LEAGUE UTTERLY--SINCE THEY ARE OUR PRISONERS! MY OTHER SELF--THE TRUE AQUAMAN--WILL REMAIN EXILED IN SPACE FOR THE REMAINDER OF HIS MISERABLE LIFE!

JUSTICE LEAGUE of AMERICA

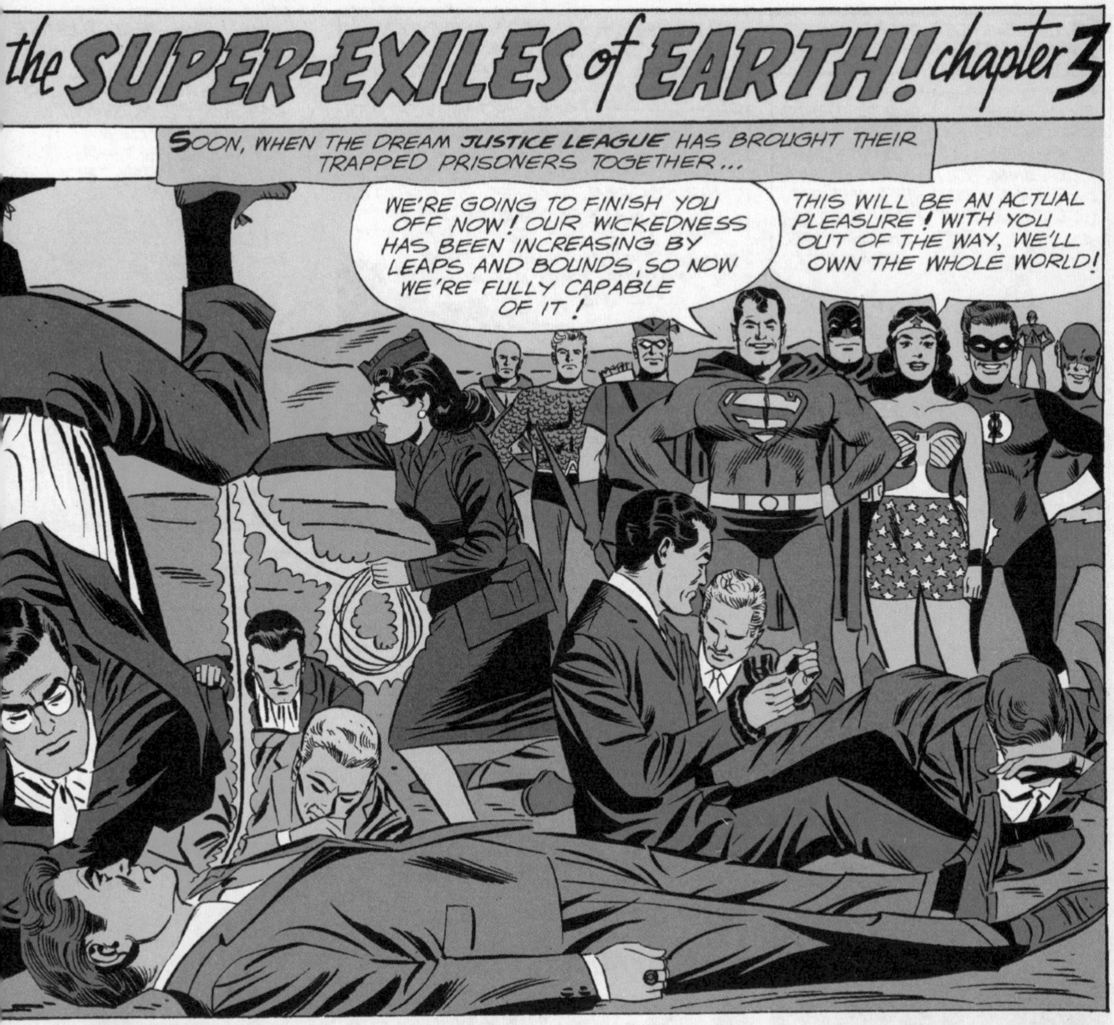
the SUPER-EXILES of EARTH! chapter 3
SOON, WHEN THE DREAM JUSTICE LEAGUE HAS BROUGHT THEIR TRAPPED PRISONERS TOGETHER...
WE'RE GOING TO FINISH YOU OFF NOW! OUR WICKEDNESS HAS BEEN INCREASING BY LEAPS AND BOUNDS, SO NOW WE'RE FULLY CAPABLE OF IT!
THIS WILL BE AN ACTUAL PLEASURE! WITH YOU OUT OF THE WAY, WE'LL OWN THE WHOLE WORLD!

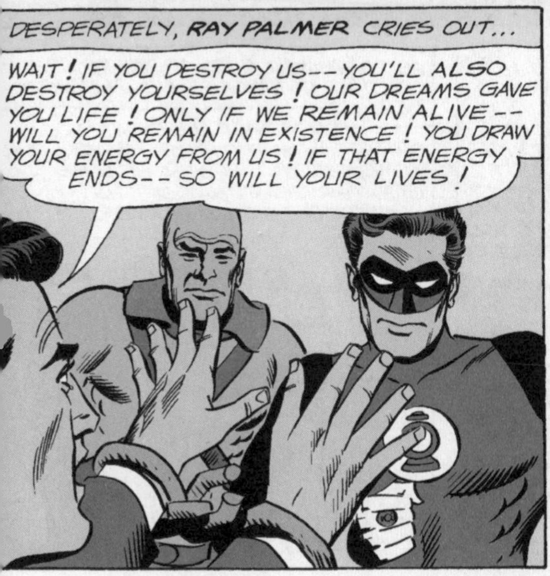
DESPERATELY, RAY PALMER CRIES OUT...
WAIT! IF YOU DESTROY US--YOU'LL ALSO DESTROY YOURSELVES! OUR DREAMS GAVE YOU LIFE! ONLY IF WE REMAIN ALIVE--WILL YOU REMAIN IN EXISTENCE! YOU DRAW YOUR ENERGY FROM US! IF THAT ENERGY ENDS--SO WILL YOUR LIVES!

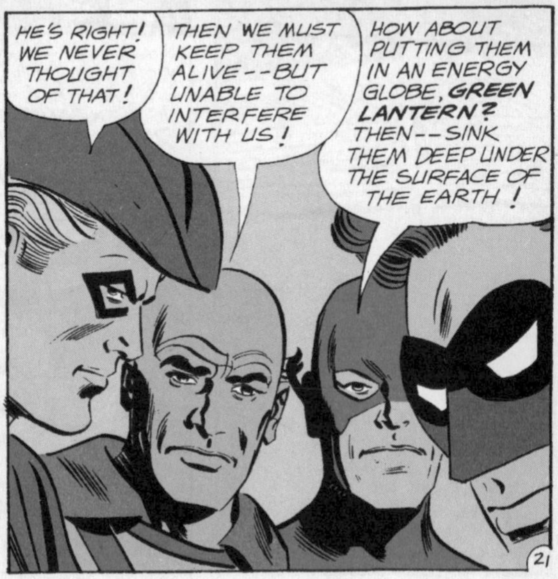
HE'S RIGHT! WE NEVER THOUGHT OF THAT!
THEN WE MUST KEEP THEM ALIVE--BUT UNABLE TO INTERFERE WITH US!
HOW ABOUT PUTTING THEM IN AN ENERGY GLOBE, GREEN LANTERN? THEN--SINK THEM DEEP UNDER THE SURFACE OF THE EARTH!
21

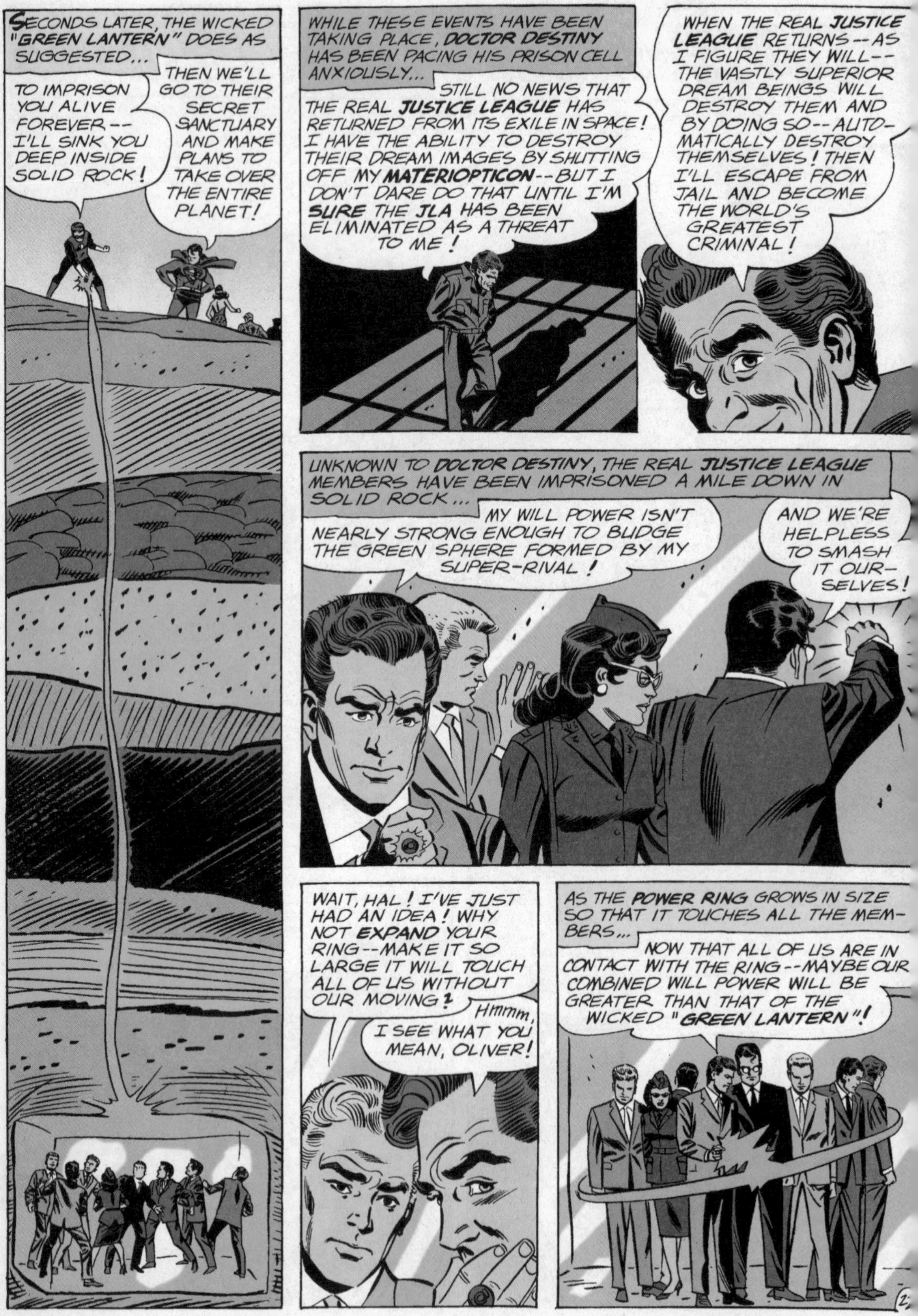
SECONDS LATER, THE WICKED "GREEN LANTERN" DOES AS SUGGESTED...
TO IMPRISON YOU ALIVE FOREVER-- I'LL SINK YOU DEEP INSIDE SOLID ROCK!
THEN WE'LL GO TO THEIR SECRET SANCTUARY AND MAKE PLANS TO TAKE OVER THE ENTIRE PLANET!
WHILE THESE EVENTS HAVE BEEN TAKING PLACE, DOCTOR DESTINY HAS BEEN PACING HIS PRISON CELL ANXIOUSLY...
STILL NO NEWS THAT THE REAL JUSTICE LEAGUE HAS RETURNED FROM ITS EXILE IN SPACE! I HAVE THE ABILITY TO DESTROY THEIR DREAM IMAGES BY SHUTTING OFF MY MATERIOPTICON--BUT I DON'T DARE DO THAT UNTIL I'M SURE THE JLA HAS BEEN ELIMINATED AS A THREAT TO ME!
WHEN THE REAL JUSTICE LEAGUE RETURNS--AS I FIGURE THEY WILL-- THE VASTLY SUPERIOR DREAM BEINGS WILL DESTROY THEM AND BY DOING SO--AUTOMATICALLY DESTROY THEMSELVES! THEN I'LL ESCAPE FROM JAIL AND BECOME THE WORLD'S GREATEST CRIMINAL!
UNKNOWN TO DOCTOR DESTINY, THE REAL JUSTICE LEAGUE MEMBERS HAVE BEEN IMPRISONED A MILE DOWN IN SOLID ROCK...
MY WILL POWER ISN'T NEARLY STRONG ENOUGH TO BUDGE THE GREEN SPHERE FORMED BY MY SUPER-RIVAL!
AND WE'RE HELPLESS TO SMASH IT OURSELVES!
WAIT, HAL! I'VE JUST HAD AN IDEA! WHY NOT EXPAND YOUR RING--MAKE IT SO LARGE IT WILL TOUCH ALL OF US WITHOUT OUR MOVING?
Hmmm, I SEE WHAT YOU MEAN, OLIVER!
AS THE POWER RING GROWS IN SIZE SO THAT IT TOUCHES ALL THE MEMBERS...
NOW THAT ALL OF US ARE IN CONTACT WITH THE RING--MAYBE OUR COMBINED WILL POWER WILL BE GREATER THAN THAT OF THE WICKED "GREEN LANTERN"!

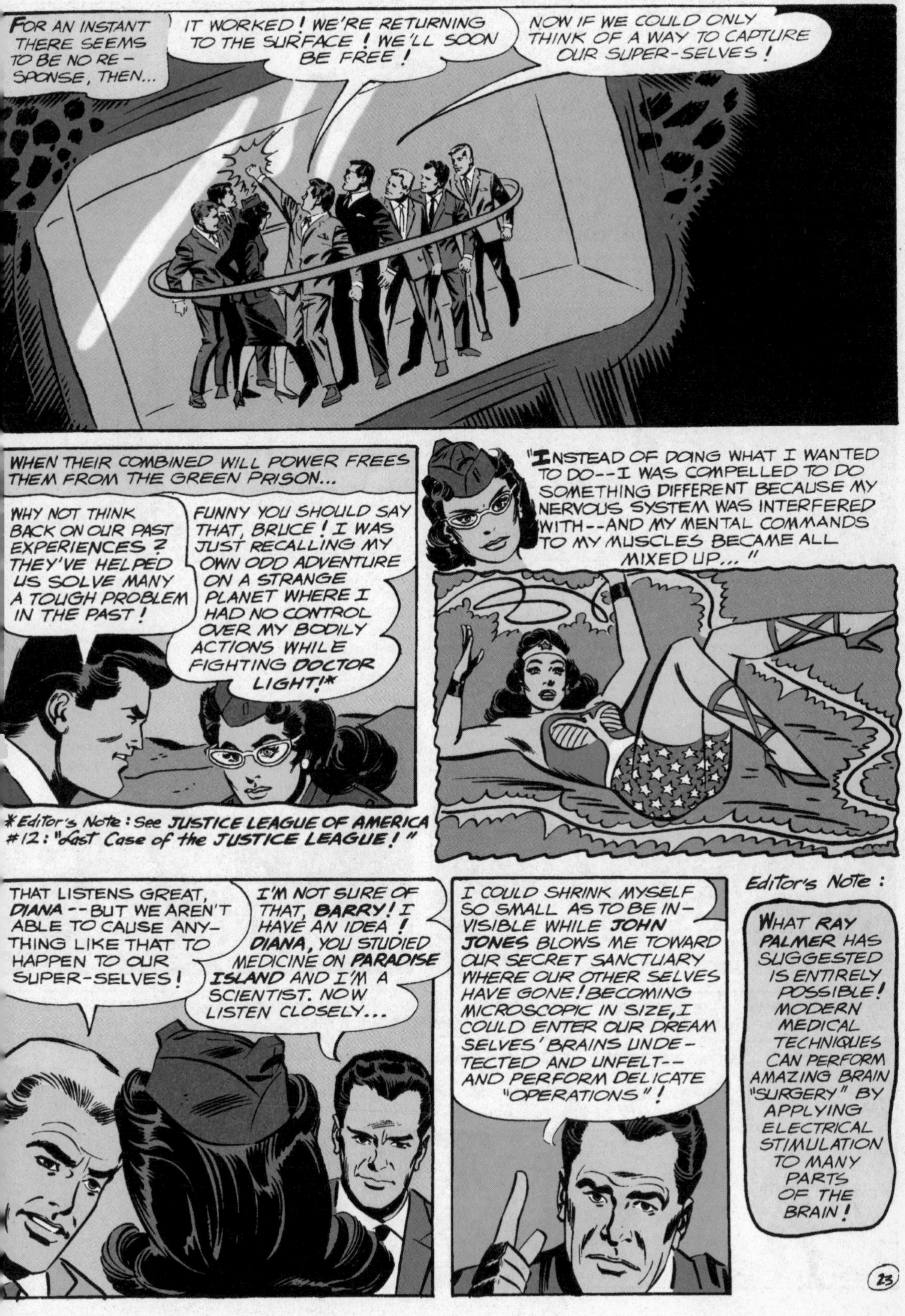
FOR AN INSTANT THERE SEEMS TO BE NO RE-SPONSE, THEN...
IT WORKED! WE'RE RETURNING TO THE SURFACE! WE'LL SOON BE FREE!
NOW IF WE COULD ONLY THINK OF A WAY TO CAPTURE OUR SUPER-SELVES!
WHEN THEIR COMBINED WILL POWER FREES THEM FROM THE GREEN PRISON...
WHY NOT THINK BACK ON OUR PAST EXPERIENCES? THEY'VE HELPED US SOLVE MANY A TOUGH PROBLEM IN THE PAST!
FUNNY YOU SHOULD SAY THAT, BRUCE! I WAS JUST RECALLING MY OWN ODD ADVENTURE ON A STRANGE PLANET WHERE I HAD NO CONTROL OVER MY BODILY ACTIONS WHILE FIGHTING DOCTOR LIGHT!*
*Editor's Note: See JUSTICE LEAGUE OF AMERICA #12: "Last Case of the JUSTICE LEAGUE!"
"INSTEAD OF DOING WHAT I WANTED TO DO--I WAS COMPELLED TO DO SOMETHING DIFFERENT BECAUSE MY NERVOUS SYSTEM WAS INTERFERED WITH--AND MY MENTAL COMMANDS TO MY MUSCLES BECAME ALL MIXED UP..."
THAT LISTENS GREAT, DIANA--BUT WE AREN'T ABLE TO CAUSE ANY-THING LIKE THAT TO HAPPEN TO OUR SUPER-SELVES!
I'M NOT SURE OF THAT, BARRY! I HAVE AN IDEA! DIANA, YOU STUDIED MEDICINE ON PARADISE ISLAND AND I'M A SCIENTIST. NOW LISTEN CLOSELY...
I COULD SHRINK MYSELF SO SMALL AS TO BE IN-VISIBLE WHILE JOHN JONES BLOWS ME TOWARD OUR SECRET SANCTUARY WHERE OUR OTHER SELVES HAVE GONE! BECOMING MICROSCOPIC IN SIZE, I COULD ENTER OUR DREAM SELVES' BRAINS UNDE-TECTED AND UNFELT--AND PERFORM DELICATE "OPERATIONS"!
Editor's Note:
WHAT RAY PALMER HAS SUGGESTED IS ENTIRELY POSSIBLE! MODERN MEDICAL TECHNIQUES CAN PERFORM AMAZING BRAIN "SURGERY" BY APPLYING ELECTRICAL STIMULATION TO MANY PARTS OF THE BRAIN!
23

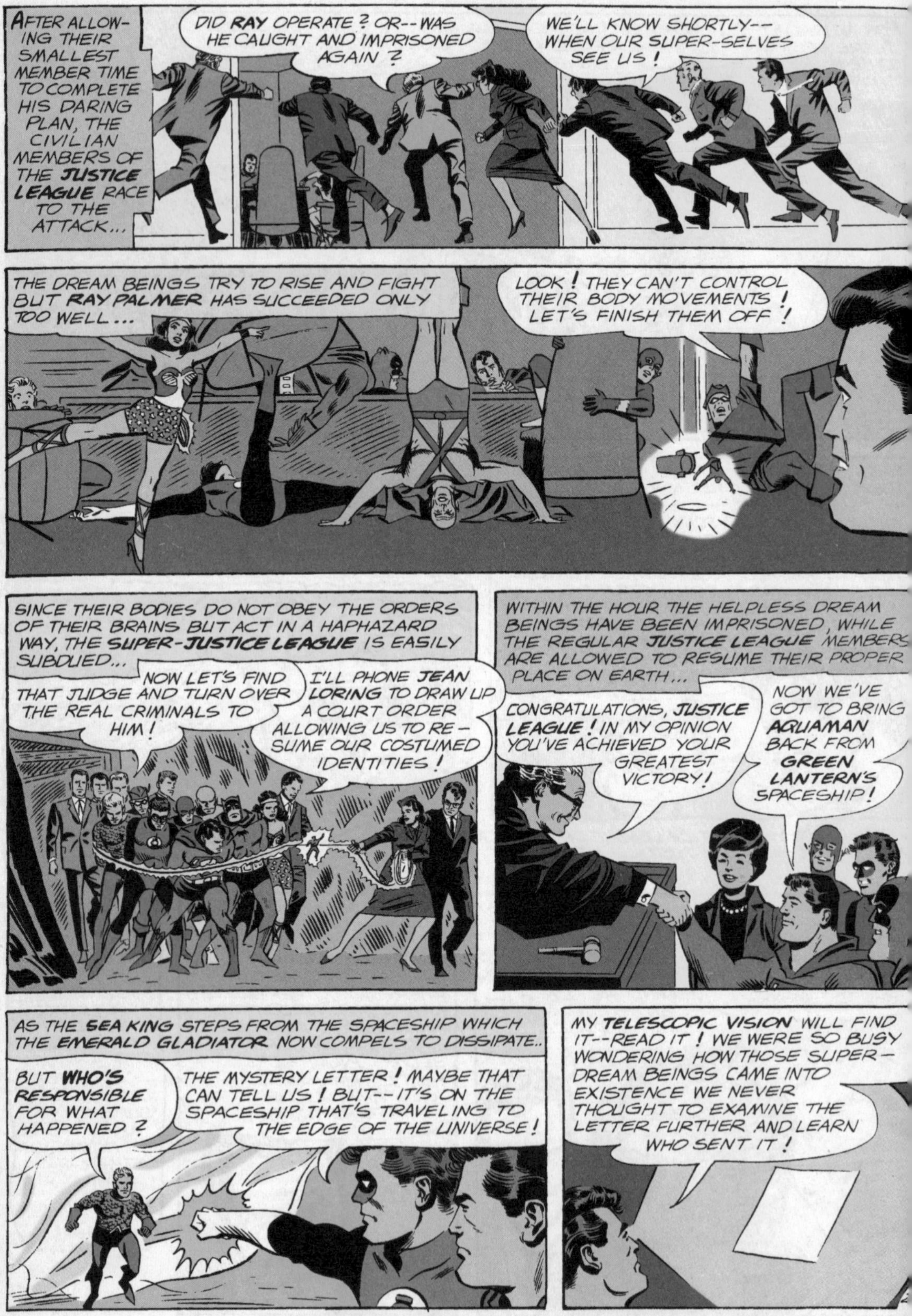
AFTER ALLOWING THEIR SMALLEST MEMBER TIME TO COMPLETE HIS DARING PLAN, THE CIVILIAN MEMBERS OF THE JUSTICE LEAGUE RACE TO THE ATTACK...
DID RAY OPERATE? OR--WAS HE CAUGHT AND IMPRISONED AGAIN?
WE'LL KNOW SHORTLY-- WHEN OUR SUPER-SELVES SEE US!
THE DREAM BEINGS TRY TO RISE AND FIGHT BUT RAY PALMER HAS SUCCEEDED ONLY TOO WELL...
LOOK! THEY CAN'T CONTROL THEIR BODY MOVEMENTS! LET'S FINISH THEM OFF!
SINCE THEIR BODIES DO NOT OBEY THE ORDERS OF THEIR BRAINS BUT ACT IN A HAPHAZARD WAY, THE SUPER-JUSTICE LEAGUE IS EASILY SUBDUED...
NOW LET'S FIND THAT JUDGE AND TURN OVER THE REAL CRIMINALS TO HIM!
I'LL PHONE JEAN LORING TO DRAW UP A COURT ORDER ALLOWING US TO RE-SUME OUR COSTUMED IDENTITIES!
WITHIN THE HOUR THE HELPLESS DREAM BEINGS HAVE BEEN IMPRISONED, WHILE THE REGULAR JUSTICE LEAGUE MEMBERS ARE ALLOWED TO RESUME THEIR PROPER PLACE ON EARTH...
CONGRATULATIONS, JUSTICE LEAGUE! IN MY OPINION YOU'VE ACHIEVED YOUR GREATEST VICTORY!
NOW WE'VE GOT TO BRING AQUAMAN BACK FROM GREEN LANTERN'S SPACESHIP!
AS THE SEA KING STEPS FROM THE SPACESHIP WHICH THE EMERALD GLADIATOR NOW COMPELS TO DISSIPATE...
BUT WHO'S RESPONSIBLE FOR WHAT HAPPENED?
THE MYSTERY LETTER! MAYBE THAT CAN TELL US! BUT--IT'S ON THE SPACESHIP THAT'S TRAVELING TO THE EDGE OF THE UNIVERSE!
MY TELESCOPIC VISION WILL FIND IT--READ IT! WE WERE SO BUSY WONDERING HOW THOSE SUPER-DREAM BEINGS CAME INTO EXISTENCE WE NEVER THOUGHT TO EXAMINE THE LETTER FURTHER AND LEARN WHO SENT IT!

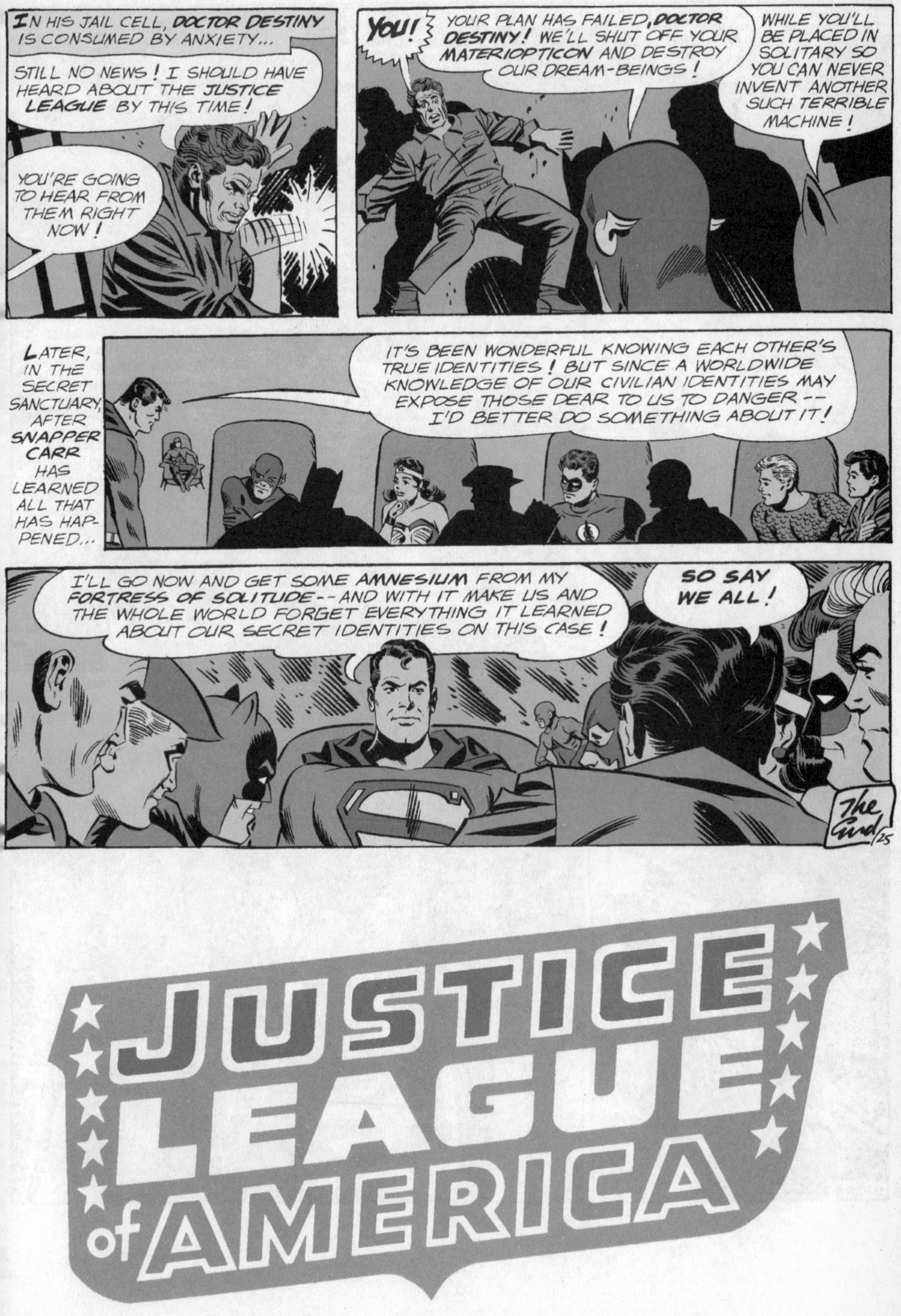
IN HIS JAIL CELL, DOCTOR DESTINY IS CONSUMED BY ANXIETY...
STILL NO NEWS! I SHOULD HAVE HEARD ABOUT THE JUSTICE LEAGUE BY THIS TIME!
YOU'RE GOING TO HEAR FROM THEM RIGHT NOW!
YOU!
YOUR PLAN HAS FAILED, DOCTOR DESTINY! WE'LL SHUT OFF YOUR MATERIOPTICON AND DESTROY OUR DREAM-BEINGS!
WHILE YOU'LL BE PLACED IN SOLITARY SO YOU CAN NEVER INVENT ANOTHER SUCH TERRIBLE MACHINE!
LATER, IN THE SECRET SANCTUARY, AFTER SNAPPER CARR HAS LEARNED ALL THAT HAS HAPPENED...
IT'S BEEN WONDERFUL KNOWING EACH OTHER'S TRUE IDENTITIES! BUT SINCE A WORLDWIDE KNOWLEDGE OF OUR CIVILIAN IDENTITIES MAY EXPOSE THOSE DEAR TO US TO DANGER -- I'D BETTER DO SOMETHING ABOUT IT!
I'LL GO NOW AND GET SOME AMNESIUM FROM MY FORTRESS OF SOLITUDE -- AND WITH IT MAKE US AND THE WHOLE WORLD FORGET EVERYTHING IT LEARNED ABOUT OUR SECRET IDENTITIES ON THIS CASE!
SO SAY WE ALL!
The End
25

JUSTICE LEAGUE of AMERICA

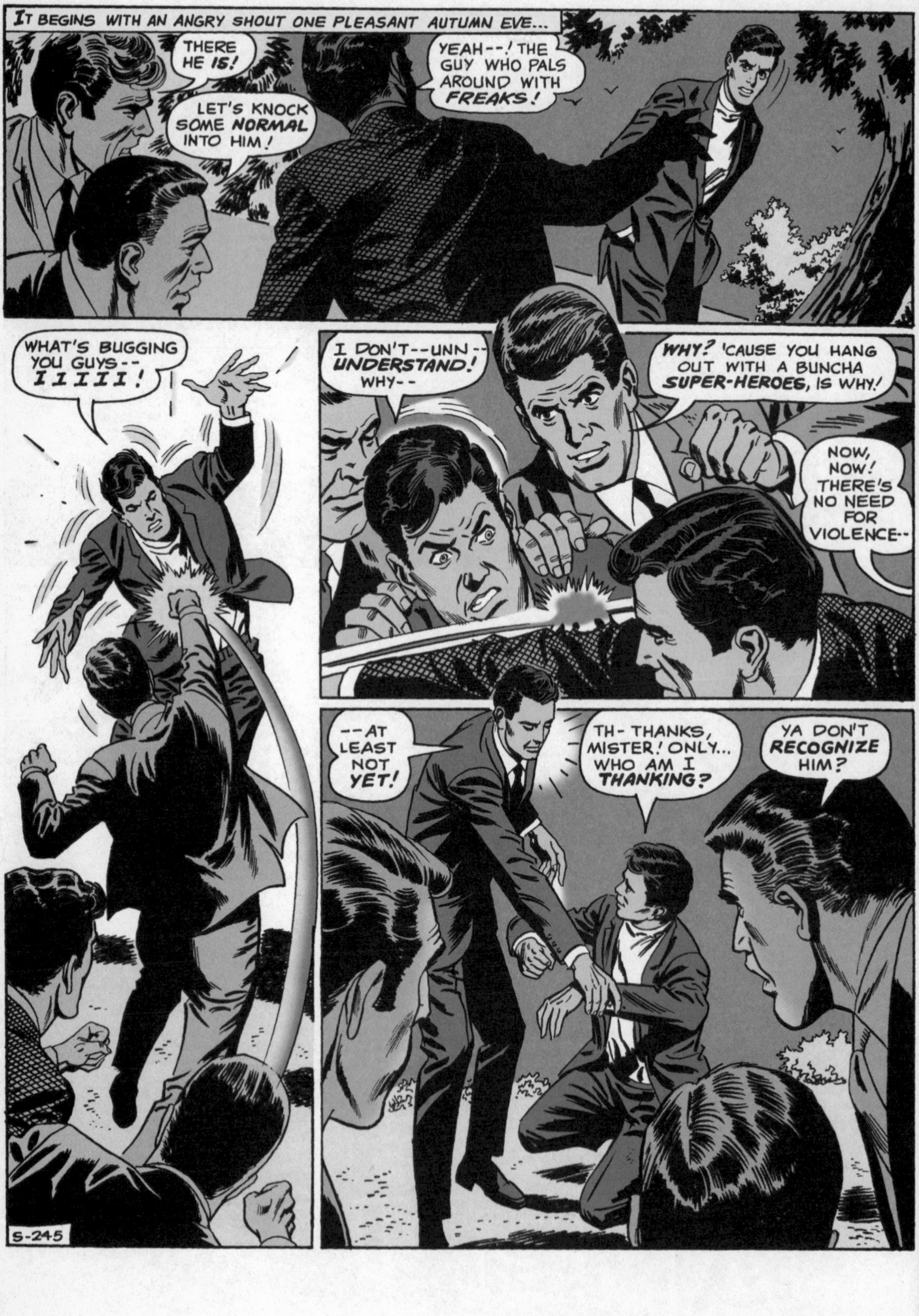
IT BEGINS WITH AN ANGRY SHOUT ONE PLEASANT AUTUMN EVE...
THERE HE IS!
LET'S KNOCK SOME NORMAL INTO HIM!
YEAH--! THE GUY WHO PALS AROUND WITH FREAKS!
WHAT'S BUGGING YOU GUYS-- IIIII!
I DON'T--UNN-- UNDERSTAND! WHY--
WHY? 'CAUSE YOU HANG OUT WITH A BUNCHA SUPER-HEROES, IS WHY!
NOW, NOW! THERE'S NO NEED FOR VIOLENCE--
--AT LEAST NOT YET!
TH-THANKS, MISTER! ONLY... WHO AM I THANKING?
YA DON'T RECOGNIZE HIM?
S-245

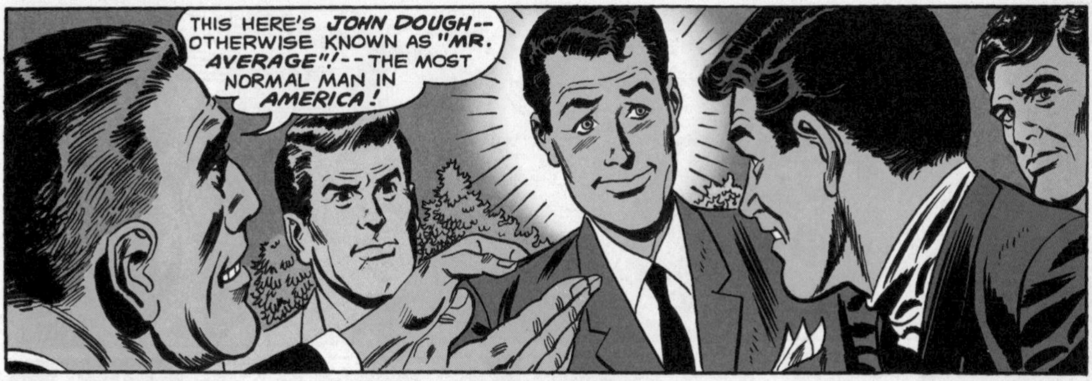
THIS HERE'S JOHN DOUGH-- OTHERWISE KNOWN AS "MR. AVERAGE"!--THE MOST NORMAL MAN IN AMERICA!

A SIMPLE, APPARENTLY UNPLANNED MEETING BETWEEN SNAPPER CARR, COLLEGIATE MASCOT OF THE--

JUSTICE LEAGUE of AMERICA

--AND THE STAGGERINGLY UNSPECTACULAR JOHN DOUGH... A MEETING THAT WILL HAVE DIRE CONSEQUENCES... FOR SOON, THE LOYAL TEEN-AGER WILL ANSWER TO THE NAME...

"SNAPPER CARR--SUPER-TRAITOR!"

STORY: DENNY O'NEIL **ART:** DICK DILLIN & JOE GIELLA

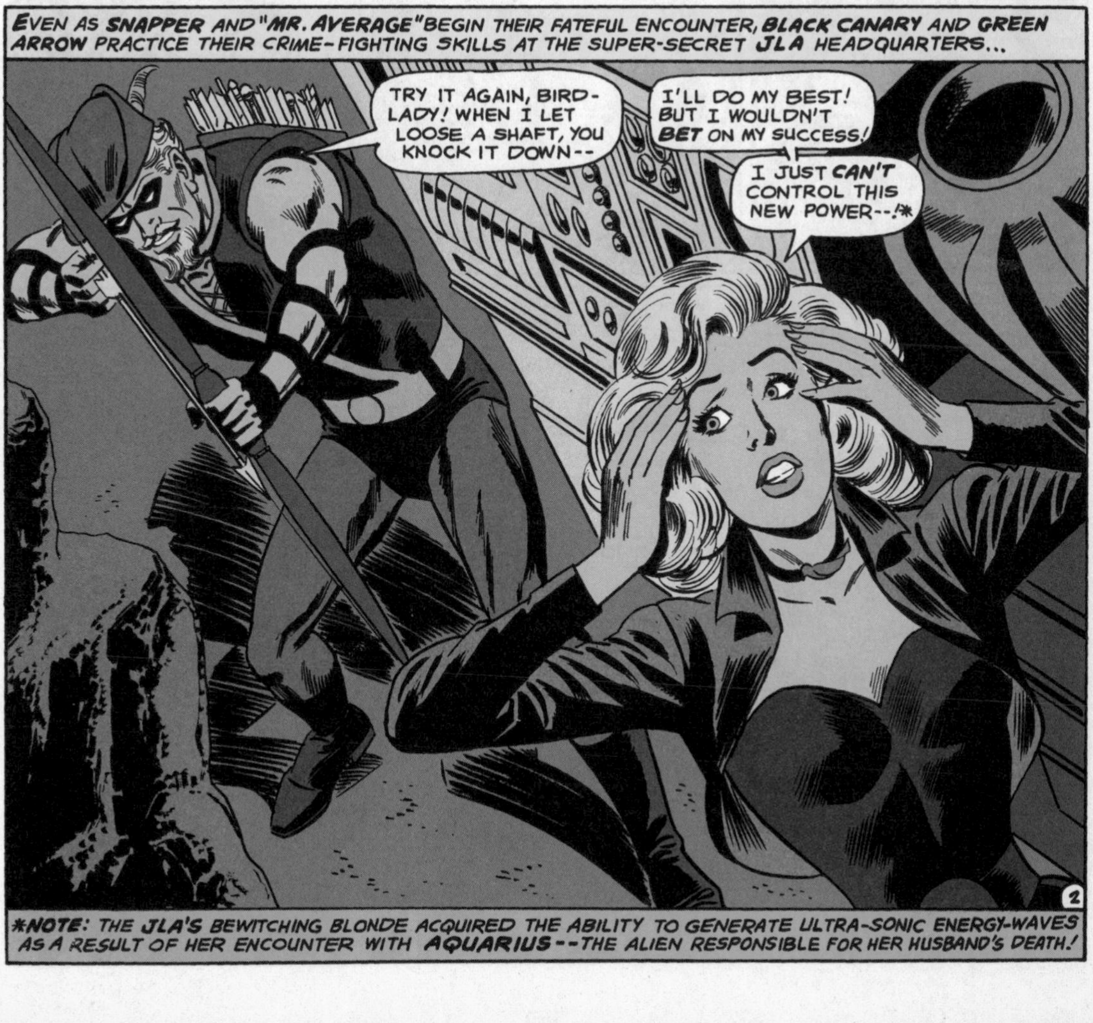
EVEN AS SNAPPER AND "MR. AVERAGE" BEGIN THEIR FATEFUL ENCOUNTER, BLACK CANARY AND GREEN ARROW PRACTICE THEIR CRIME-FIGHTING SKILLS AT THE SUPER-SECRET JLA HEADQUARTERS...
TRY IT AGAIN, BIRD-LADY! WHEN I LET LOOSE A SHAFT, YOU KNOCK IT DOWN--
I'LL DO MY BEST! BUT I WOULDN'T BET ON MY SUCCESS!
I JUST CAN'T CONTROL THIS NEW POWER--!*
2
*NOTE: THE JLA'S BEWITCHING BLONDE ACQUIRED THE ABILITY TO GENERATE ULTRA-SONIC ENERGY-WAVES AS A RESULT OF HER ENCOUNTER WITH AQUARIUS--THE ALIEN RESPONSIBLE FOR HER HUSBAND'S DEATH!

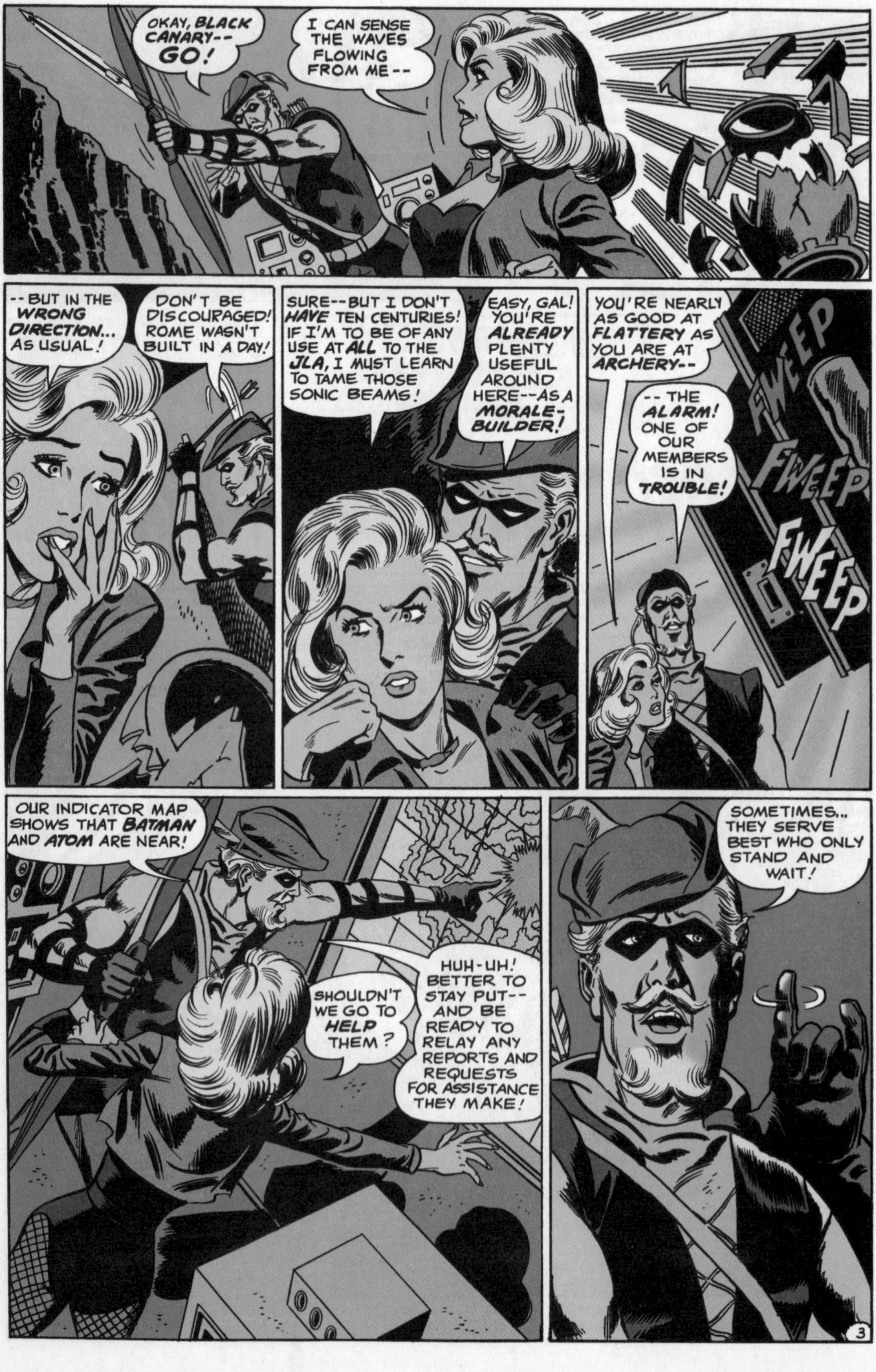
OKAY, BLACK CANARY-- GO!
I CAN SENSE THE WAVES FLOWING FROM ME--
-- BUT IN THE WRONG DIRECTION... AS USUAL!
DON'T BE DISCOURAGED! ROME WASN'T BUILT IN A DAY!
SURE--BUT I DON'T HAVE TEN CENTURIES! IF I'M TO BE OF ANY USE AT ALL TO THE JLA, I MUST LEARN TO TAME THOSE SONIC BEAMS!
EASY, GAL! YOU'RE ALREADY PLENTY USEFUL AROUND HERE--AS A MORALE-BUILDER!
YOU'RE NEARLY AS GOOD AT FLATTERY AS YOU ARE AT ARCHERY--
-- THE ALARM! ONE OF OUR MEMBERS IS IN TROUBLE!
FWEEP
FWEEP
FWEEP
FWEEP
OUR INDICATOR MAP SHOWS THAT BATMAN AND ATOM ARE NEAR!
SHOULDN'T WE GO TO HELP THEM?
HUH-UH! BETTER TO STAY PUT-- AND BE READY TO RELAY ANY REPORTS AND REQUESTS FOR ASSISTANCE THEY MAKE!
SOMETIMES... THEY SERVE BEST WHO ONLY STAND AND WAIT!
3

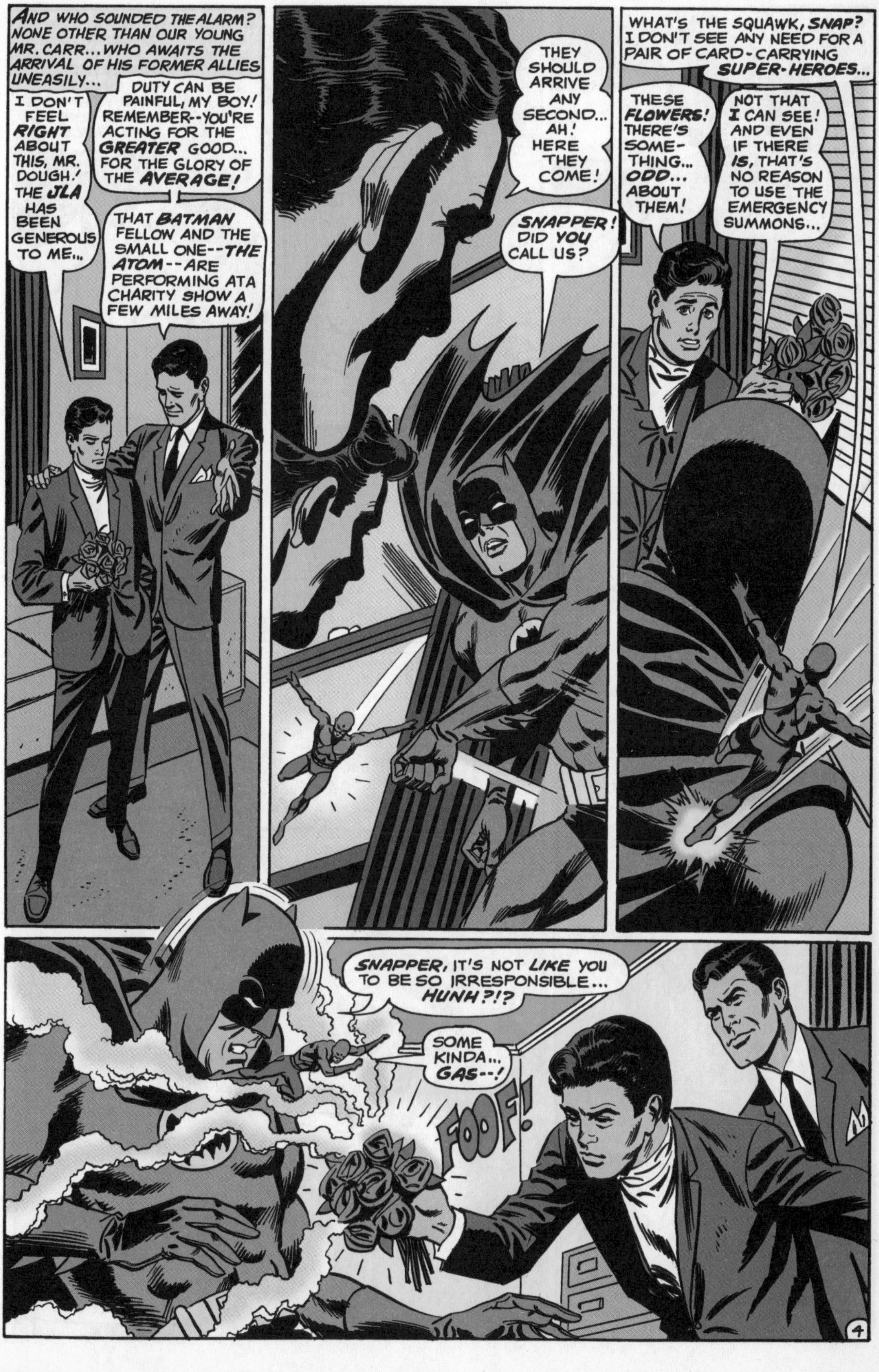
AND WHO SOUNDED THE ALARM? NONE OTHER THAN OUR YOUNG MR. CARR... WHO AWAITS THE ARRIVAL OF HIS FORMER ALLIES UNEASILY...
I DON'T FEEL RIGHT ABOUT THIS, MR. DOUGH! THE JLA HAS BEEN GENEROUS TO ME...
DUTY CAN BE PAINFUL, MY BOY! REMEMBER--YOU'RE ACTING FOR THE GREATER GOOD... FOR THE GLORY OF THE AVERAGE!
THAT BATMAN FELLOW AND THE SMALL ONE--THE ATOM--ARE PERFORMING AT A CHARITY SHOW A FEW MILES AWAY!
THEY SHOULD ARRIVE ANY SECOND... AH! HERE THEY COME!
SNAPPER! DID YOU CALL US?
WHAT'S THE SQUAWK, SNAP? I DON'T SEE ANY NEED FOR A PAIR OF CARD-CARRYING SUPER-HEROES...
THESE FLOWERS! THERE'S SOME-THING... ODD... ABOUT THEM!
NOT THAT I CAN SEE! AND EVEN IF THERE IS, THAT'S NO REASON TO USE THE EMERGENCY SUMMONS...
SNAPPER, IT'S NOT LIKE YOU TO BE SO IRRESPONSIBLE... HUNH?!?
SOME KINDA... GAS--!
FOOF!
4

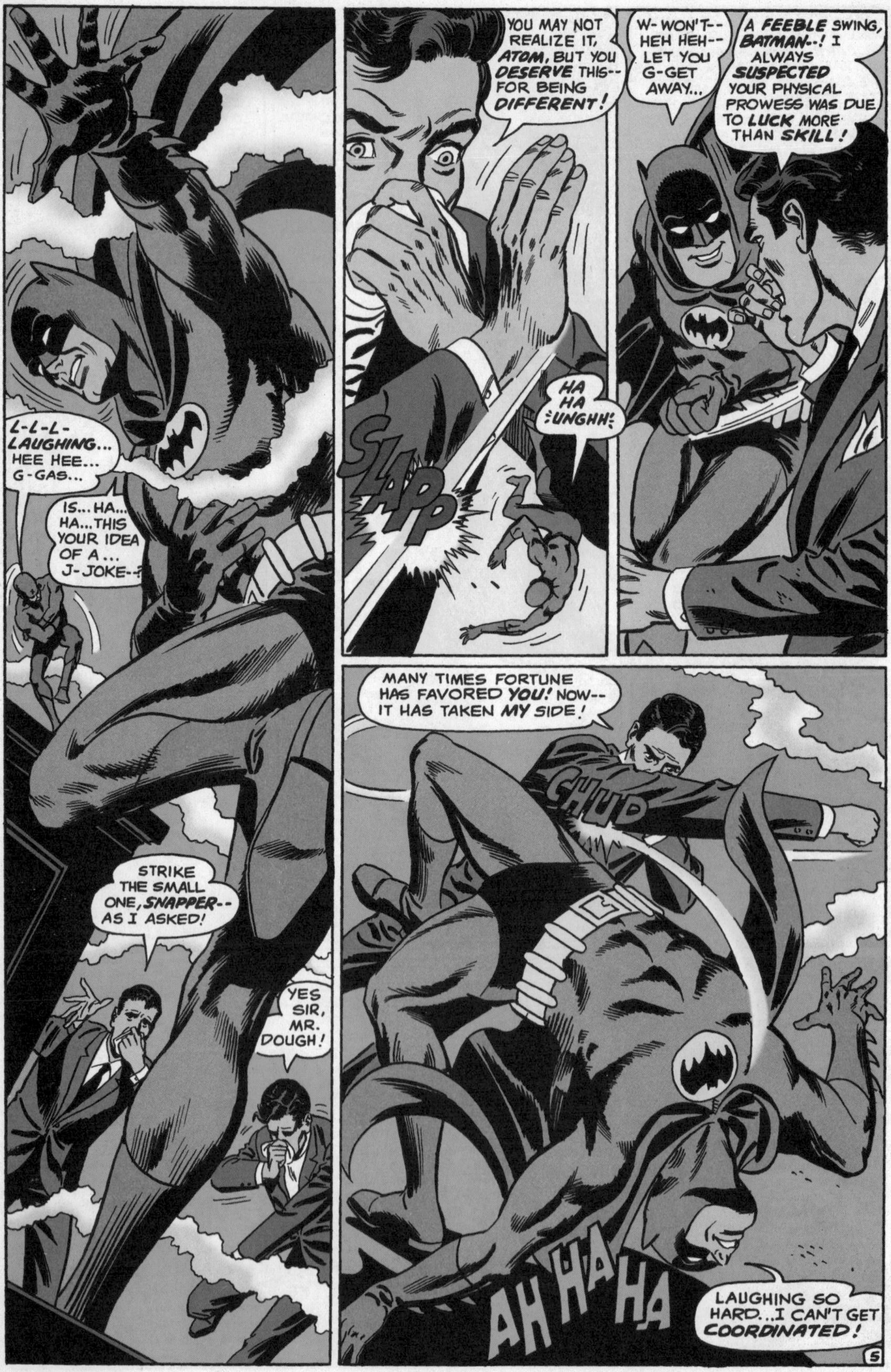
L-L-L-LAUGHING... HEE HEE... G-GAS...
IS...HA... HA...THIS YOUR IDEA OF A... J-JOKE--?
STRIKE THE SMALL ONE, SNAPPER-- AS I ASKED!
YES SIR, MR. DOUGH!
YOU MAY NOT REALIZE IT, ATOM, BUT YOU DESERVE THIS-- FOR BEING DIFFERENT!
SLAPP
HA HA UNGHH!
W-WON'T-- HEH HEH-- LET YOU G-GET AWAY...
A FEEBLE SWING, BATMAN--! I ALWAYS SUSPECTED YOUR PHYSICAL PROWESS WAS DUE TO LUCK MORE THAN SKILL!
MANY TIMES FORTUNE HAS FAVORED YOU! NOW-- IT HAS TAKEN MY SIDE!
CHUD
AH HA HA HA
LAUGHING SO HARD...I CAN'T GET COORDINATED!
5

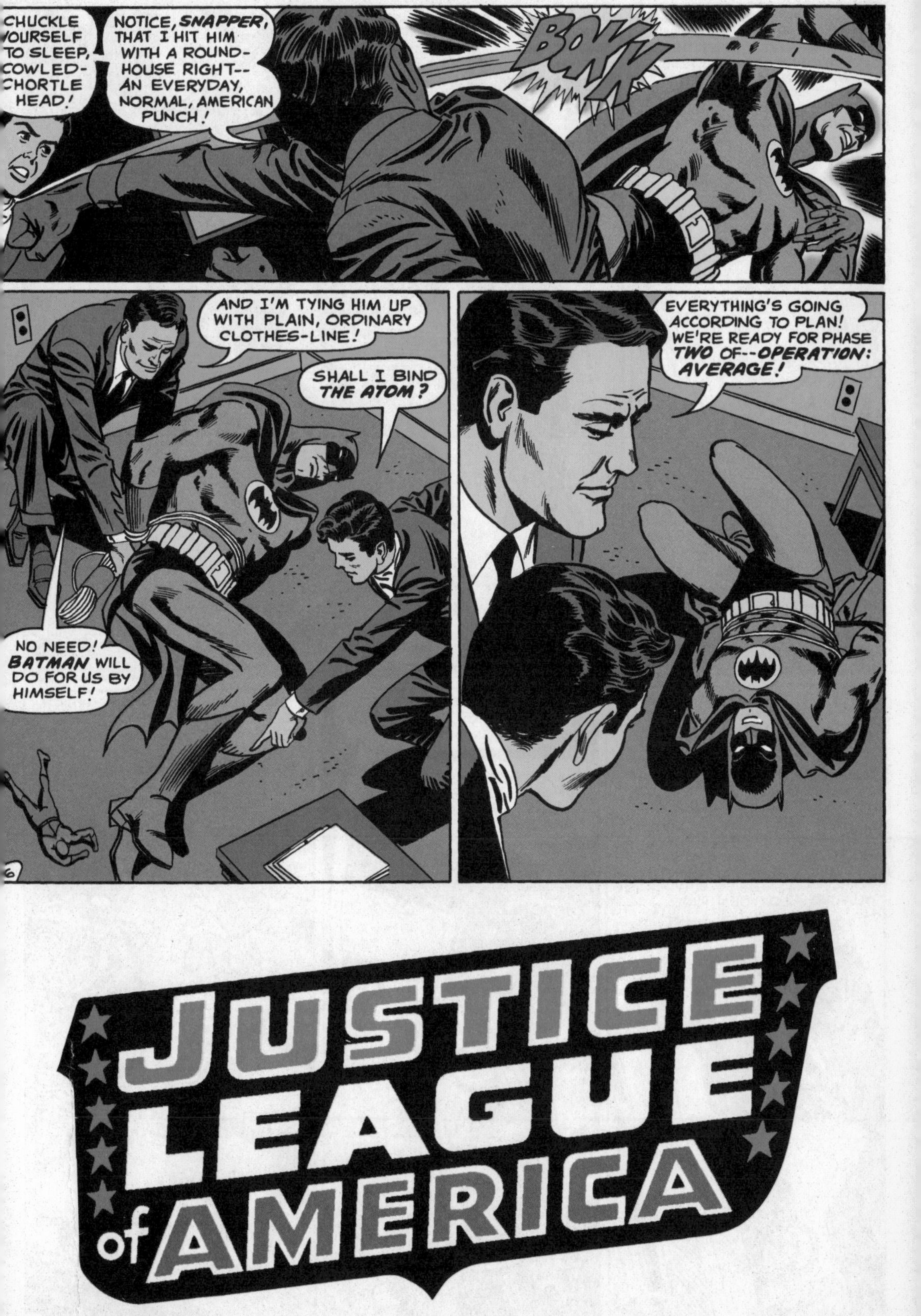
CHUCKLE YOURSELF TO SLEEP, COWLED-CHORTLE HEAD!
NOTICE, SNAPPER, THAT I HIT HIM WITH A ROUND-HOUSE RIGHT-- AN EVERYDAY, NORMAL, AMERICAN PUNCH!
BOKK
AND I'M TYING HIM UP WITH PLAIN, ORDINARY CLOTHES-LINE!
SHALL I BIND THE ATOM?
NO NEED! BATMAN WILL DO FOR US BY HIMSELF!
EVERYTHING'S GOING ACCORDING TO PLAN! WE'RE READY FOR PHASE TWO OF--OPERATION: AVERAGE!
6

JUSTICE LEAGUE of AMERICA

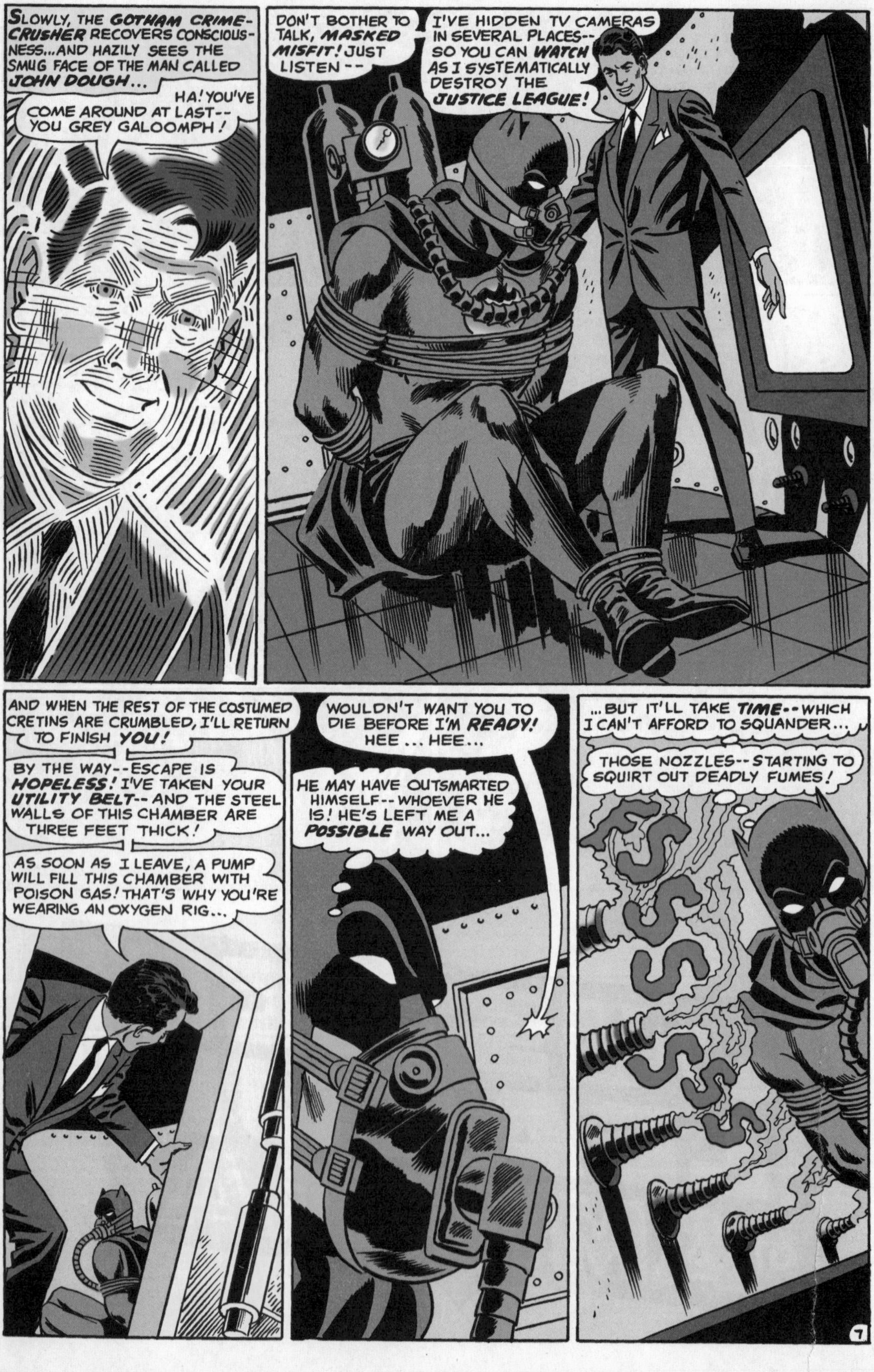
SLOWLY, THE GOTHAM CRIME-CRUSHER RECOVERS CONSCIOUSNESS...AND HAZILY SEES THE SMUG FACE OF THE MAN CALLED JOHN DOUGH...
HA! YOU'VE COME AROUND AT LAST-- YOU GREY GALOOMPH!
DON'T BOTHER TO TALK, MASKED MISFIT! JUST LISTEN --
I'VE HIDDEN TV CAMERAS IN SEVERAL PLACES-- SO YOU CAN WATCH AS I SYSTEMATICALLY DESTROY THE JUSTICE LEAGUE!
AND WHEN THE REST OF THE COSTUMED CRETINS ARE CRUMBLED, I'LL RETURN TO FINISH YOU!
BY THE WAY--ESCAPE IS HOPELESS! I'VE TAKEN YOUR UTILITY BELT-- AND THE STEEL WALLS OF THIS CHAMBER ARE THREE FEET THICK!
AS SOON AS I LEAVE, A PUMP WILL FILL THIS CHAMBER WITH POISON GAS! THAT'S WHY YOU'RE WEARING AN OXYGEN RIG...
WOULDN'T WANT YOU TO DIE BEFORE I'M READY! HEE ... HEE...
HE MAY HAVE OUTSMARTED HIMSELF-- WHOEVER HE IS! HE'S LEFT ME A POSSIBLE WAY OUT...
...BUT IT'LL TAKE TIME-- WHICH I CAN'T AFFORD TO SQUANDER...
THOSE NOZZLES-- STARTING TO SQUIRT OUT DEADLY FUMES!
SSSSSSS
7

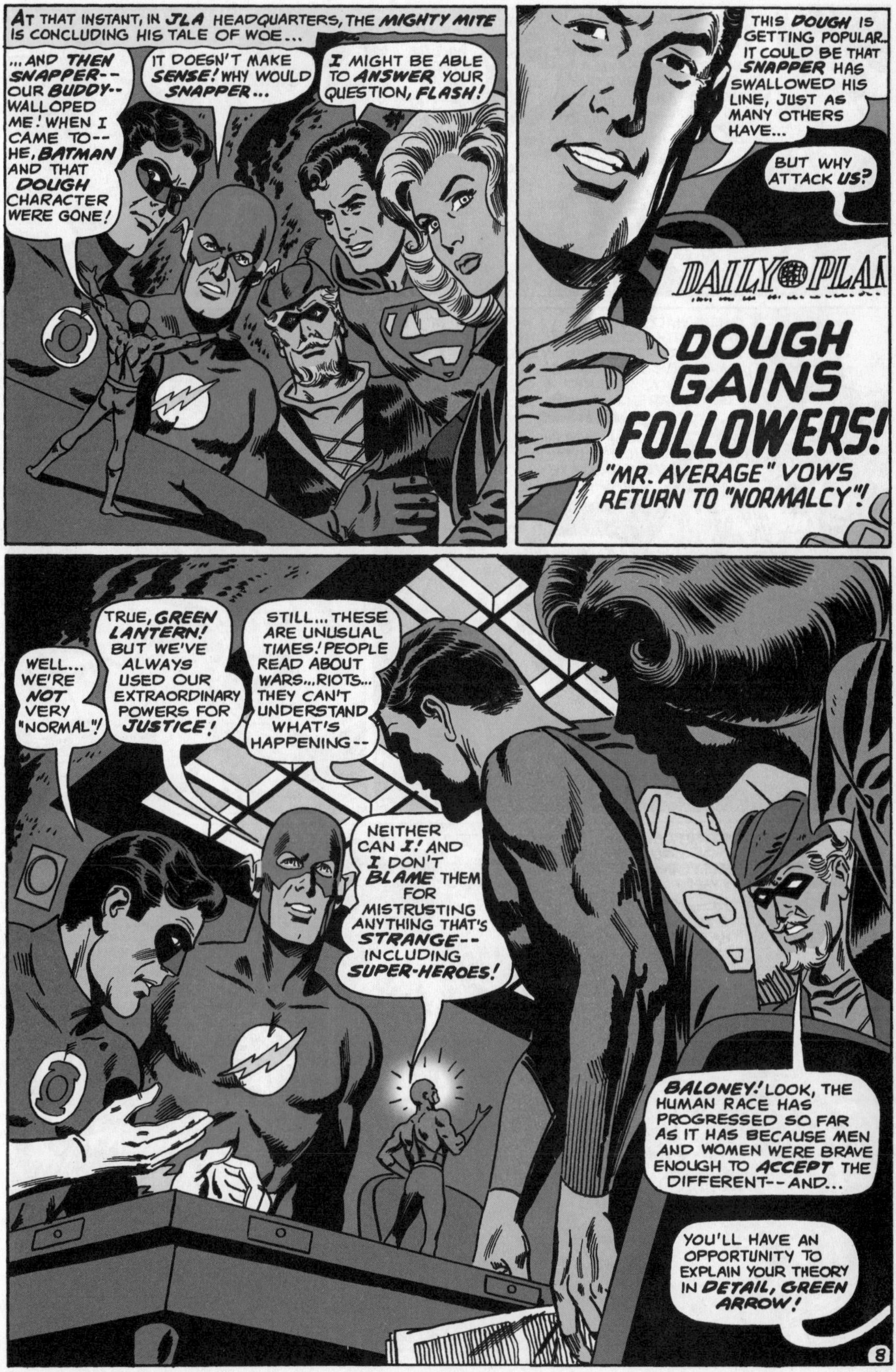
AT THAT INSTANT, IN JLA HEADQUARTERS, THE MIGHTY MITE IS CONCLUDING HIS TALE OF WOE...
...AND THEN SNAPPER-- OUR BUDDY-- WALLOPED ME! WHEN I CAME TO-- HE, BATMAN AND THAT DOUGH CHARACTER WERE GONE!
IT DOESN'T MAKE SENSE! WHY WOULD SNAPPER...
I MIGHT BE ABLE TO ANSWER YOUR QUESTION, FLASH!
THIS DOUGH IS GETTING POPULAR.. IT COULD BE THAT SNAPPER HAS SWALLOWED HIS LINE, JUST AS MANY OTHERS HAVE...
BUT WHY ATTACK US?
DAILY PLA
DOUGH GAINS FOLLOWERS!
"MR. AVERAGE" VOWS RETURN TO "NORMALCY"!
WELL... WE'RE NOT VERY "NORMAL"!
TRUE, GREEN LANTERN! BUT WE'VE ALWAYS USED OUR EXTRAORDINARY POWERS FOR JUSTICE!
STILL... THESE ARE UNUSUAL TIMES! PEOPLE READ ABOUT WARS...RIOTS... THEY CAN'T UNDERSTAND WHAT'S HAPPENING--
NEITHER CAN I! AND I DON'T BLAME THEM FOR MISTRUSTING ANYTHING THAT'S STRANGE-- INCLUDING SUPER-HEROES!
BALONEY! LOOK, THE HUMAN RACE HAS PROGRESSED SO FAR AS IT HAS BECAUSE MEN AND WOMEN WERE BRAVE ENOUGH TO ACCEPT THE DIFFERENT-- AND...
YOU'LL HAVE AN OPPORTUNITY TO EXPLAIN YOUR THEORY IN DETAIL, GREEN ARROW!
8

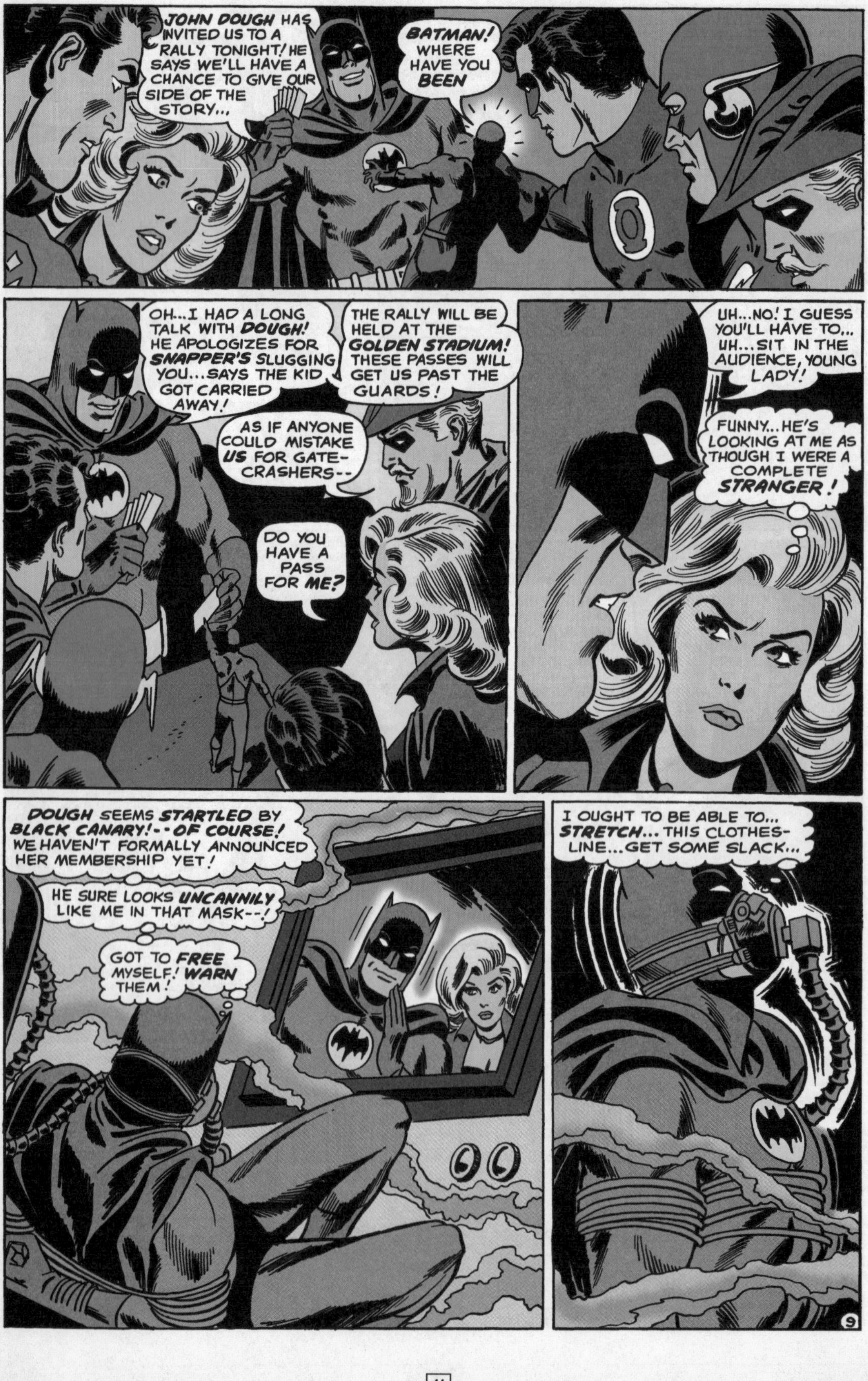

JOHN DOUGH HAS INVITED US TO A RALLY TONIGHT! HE SAYS WE'LL HAVE A CHANCE TO GIVE OUR SIDE OF THE STORY...
BATMAN! WHERE HAVE YOU BEEN
OH...I HAD A LONG TALK WITH DOUGH! HE APOLOGIZES FOR SNAPPER'S SLUGGING YOU...SAYS THE KID GOT CARRIED AWAY!
THE RALLY WILL BE HELD AT THE GOLDEN STADIUM! THESE PASSES WILL GET US PAST THE GUARDS!
AS IF ANYONE COULD MISTAKE US FOR GATE-CRASHERS--
DO YOU HAVE A PASS FOR ME?
UH...NO! I GUESS YOU'LL HAVE TO... UH...SIT IN THE AUDIENCE, YOUNG LADY!
FUNNY...HE'S LOOKING AT ME AS THOUGH I WERE A COMPLETE STRANGER!
DOUGH SEEMS STARTLED BY BLACK CANARY!--OF COURSE! WE HAVEN'T FORMALLY ANNOUNCED HER MEMBERSHIP YET!
HE SURE LOOKS UNCANNILY LIKE ME IN THAT MASK--!
GOT TO FREE MYSELF! WARN THEM!
I OUGHT TO BE ABLE TO... STRETCH... THIS CLOTHES-LINE...GET SOME SLACK...
9

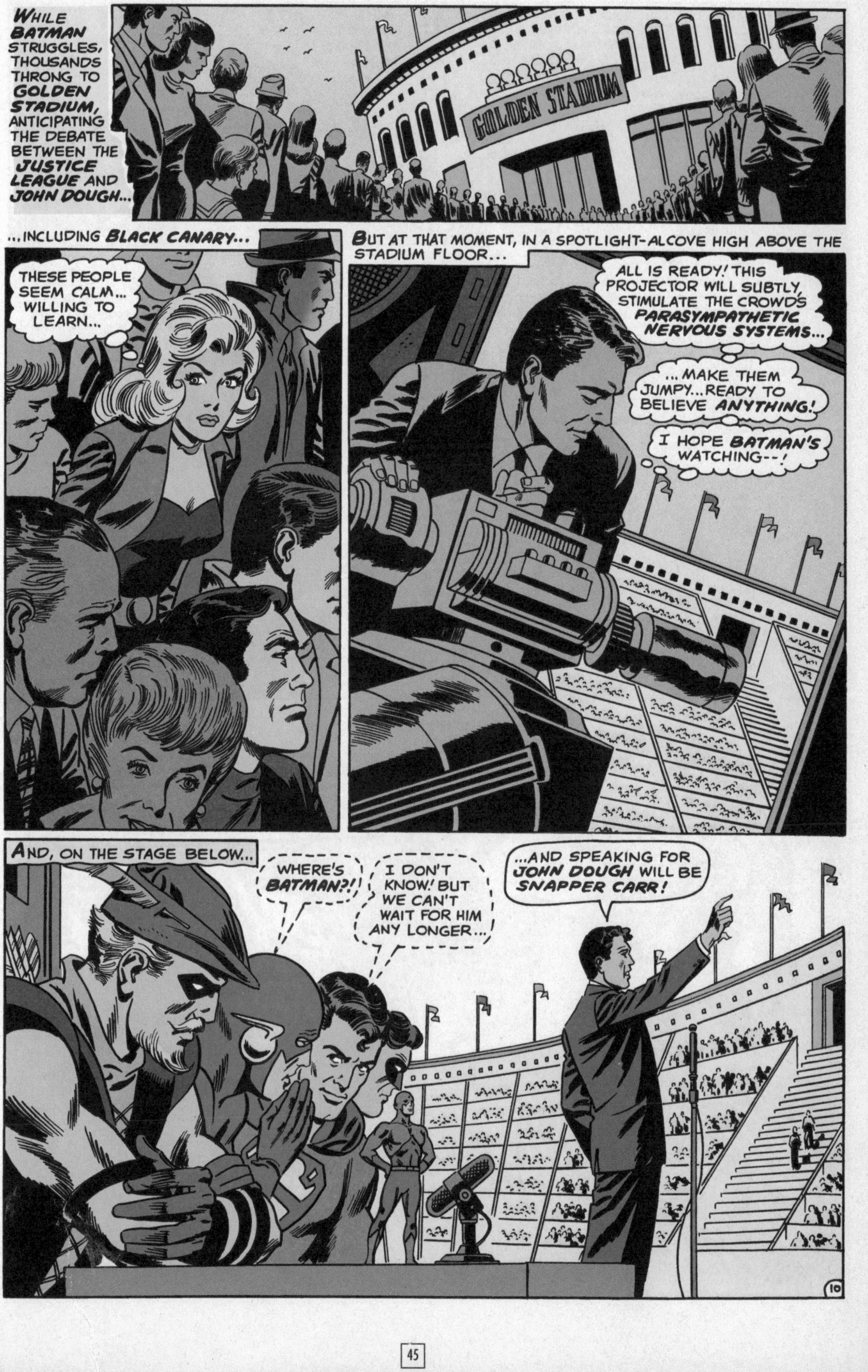
WHILE BATMAN STRUGGLES, THOUSANDS THRONG TO GOLDEN STADIUM, ANTICIPATING THE DEBATE BETWEEN THE JUSTICE LEAGUE AND JOHN DOUGH...
GOLDEN STADIUM
...INCLUDING BLACK CANARY...
THESE PEOPLE SEEM CALM... WILLING TO LEARN...
BUT AT THAT MOMENT, IN A SPOTLIGHT-ALCOVE HIGH ABOVE THE STADIUM FLOOR...
ALL IS READY! THIS PROJECTOR WILL SUBTLY, STIMULATE THE CROWD'S PARASYMPATHETIC NERVOUS SYSTEMS...
...MAKE THEM JUMPY...READY TO BELIEVE ANYTHING!
I HOPE BATMAN'S WATCHING--!
AND, ON THE STAGE BELOW...
WHERE'S BATMAN?!
I DON'T KNOW! BUT WE CAN'T WAIT FOR HIM ANY LONGER...
...AND SPEAKING FOR JOHN DOUGH WILL BE SNAPPER CARR!
10

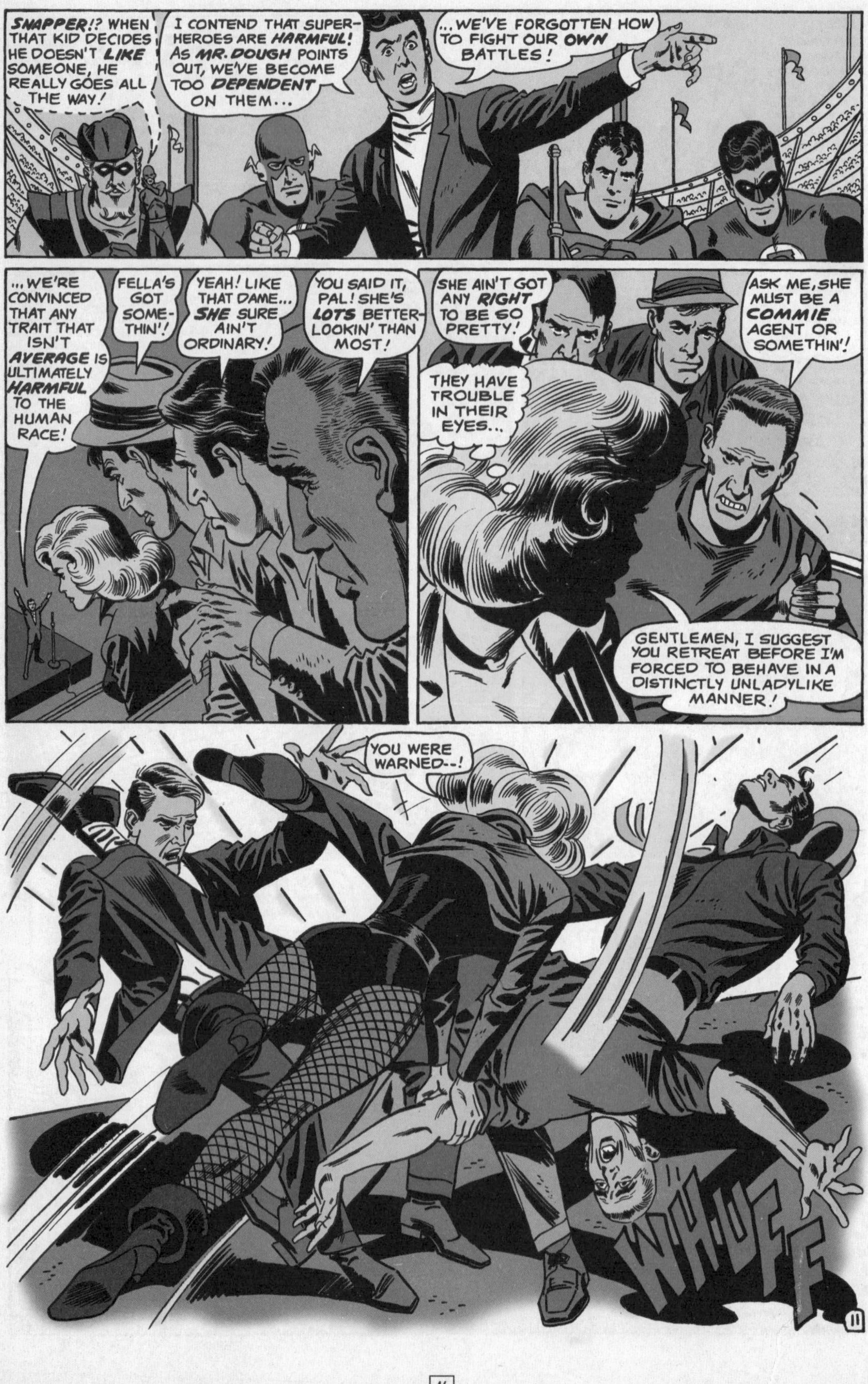

SNAPPER!? WHEN THAT KID DECIDES HE DOESN'T LIKE SOMEONE, HE REALLY GOES ALL THE WAY!
I CONTEND THAT SUPER-HEROES ARE HARMFUL! AS MR. DOUGH POINTS OUT, WE'VE BECOME TOO DEPENDENT ON THEM...
...WE'VE FORGOTTEN HOW TO FIGHT OUR OWN BATTLES!
...WE'RE CONVINCED THAT ANY TRAIT THAT ISN'T AVERAGE IS ULTIMATELY HARMFUL TO THE HUMAN RACE!
FELLA'S GOT SOME-THIN'!
YEAH! LIKE THAT DAME... SHE SURE AIN'T ORDINARY!
YOU SAID IT, PAL! SHE'S LOTS BETTER-LOOKIN' THAN MOST!
SHE AIN'T GOT ANY RIGHT TO BE SO PRETTY!
ASK ME, SHE MUST BE A COMMIE AGENT OR SOMETHIN'!
THEY HAVE TROUBLE IN THEIR EYES...
GENTLEMEN, I SUGGEST YOU RETREAT BEFORE I'M FORCED TO BEHAVE IN A DISTINCTLY UNLADYLIKE MANNER!
YOU WERE WARNED--!
WHUFF
11

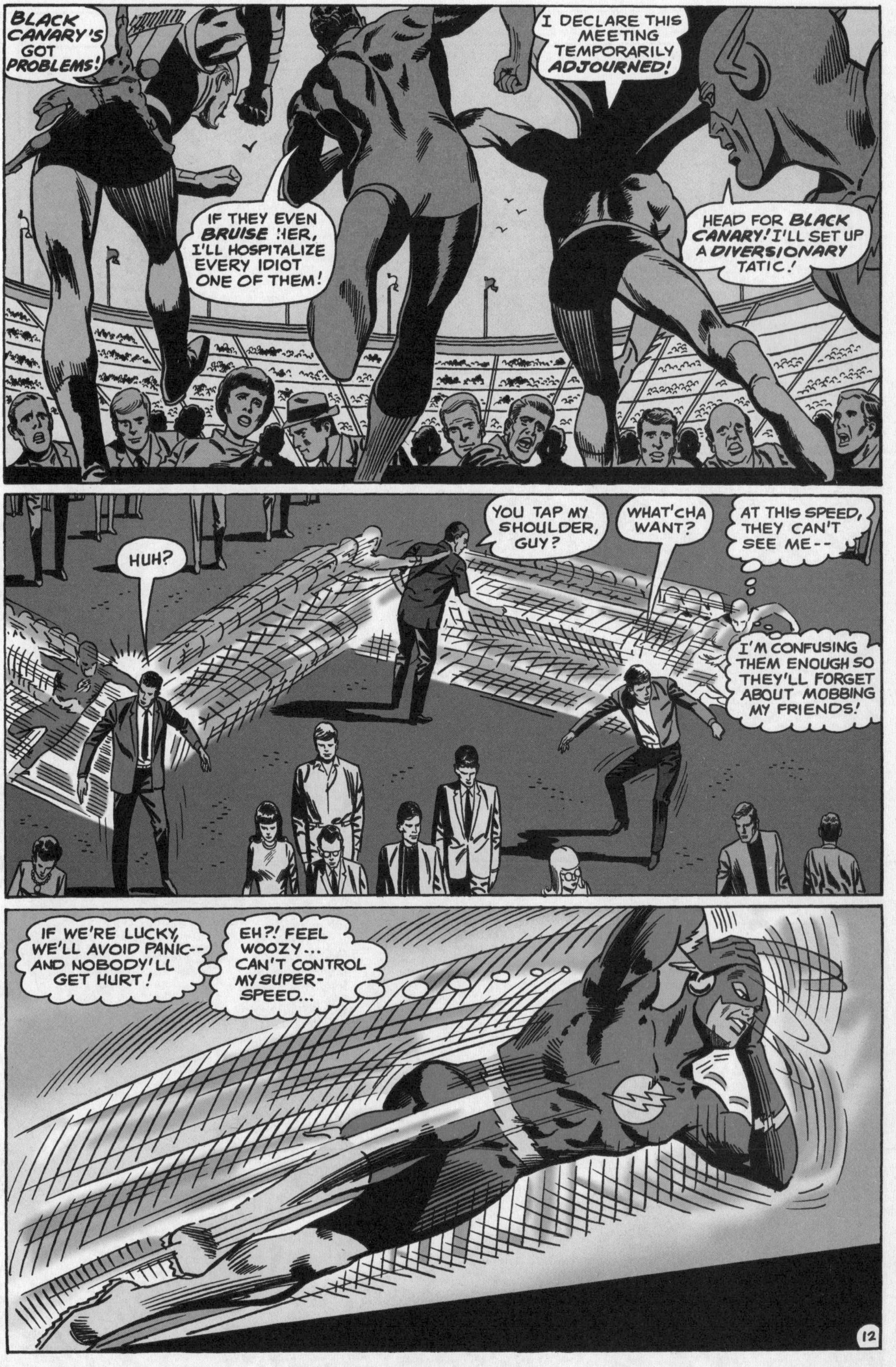
BLACK CANARY'S GOT PROBLEMS!
IF THEY EVEN BRUISE HER, I'LL HOSPITALIZE EVERY IDIOT ONE OF THEM!
I DECLARE THIS MEETING TEMPORARILY ADJOURNED!
HEAD FOR BLACK CANARY! I'LL SET UP A DIVERSIONARY TATIC!
HUH?
YOU TAP MY SHOULDER, GUY?
WHAT'CHA WANT?
AT THIS SPEED, THEY CAN'T SEE ME--
I'M CONFUSING THEM ENOUGH SO THEY'LL FORGET ABOUT MOBBING MY FRIENDS!
IF WE'RE LUCKY, WE'LL AVOID PANIC-- AND NOBODY'LL GET HURT!
EH?! FEEL WOOZY... CAN'T CONTROL MY SUPER-SPEED...
12

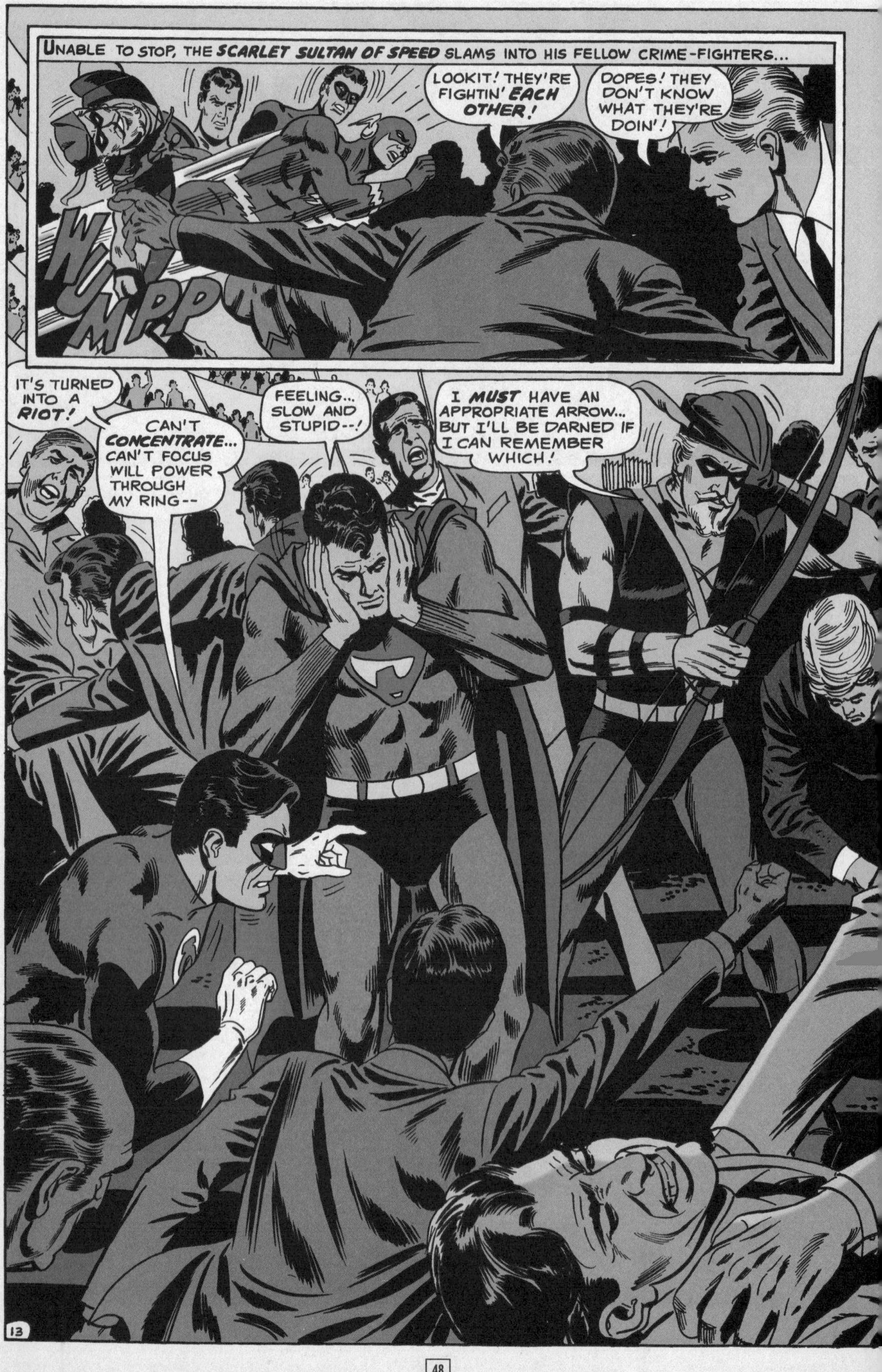
UNABLE TO STOP, THE SCARLET SULTAN OF SPEED SLAMS INTO HIS FELLOW CRIME-FIGHTERS...
LOOKIT! THEY'RE FIGHTIN' EACH OTHER!
DOPES! THEY DON'T KNOW WHAT THEY'RE DOIN'!
WUMPP
IT'S TURNED INTO A RIOT!
CAN'T CONCENTRATE... CAN'T FOCUS WILL POWER THROUGH MY RING--
FEELING... SLOW AND STUPID--!
I MUST HAVE AN APPROPRIATE ARROW... BUT I'LL BE DARNED IF I CAN REMEMBER WHICH!
13

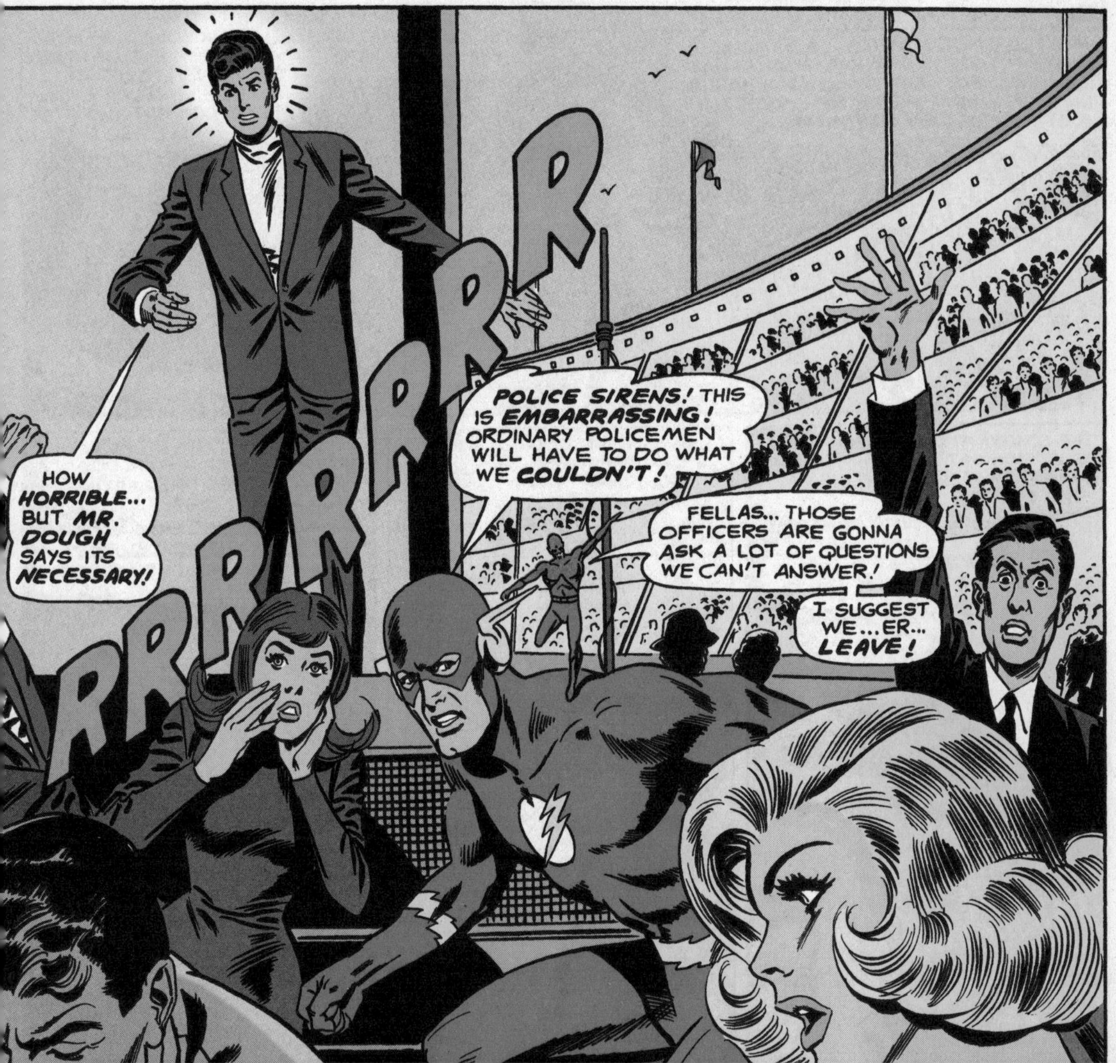
HOW HORRIBLE... BUT MR. DOUGH SAYS ITS NECESSARY!
RRRRRRRRR
POLICE SIRENS! THIS IS EMBARRASSING! ORDINARY POLICEMEN WILL HAVE TO DO WHAT WE COULDN'T!
FELLAS... THOSE OFFICERS ARE GONNA ASK A LOT OF QUESTIONS WE CAN'T ANSWER!
I SUGGEST WE...ER... LEAVE!

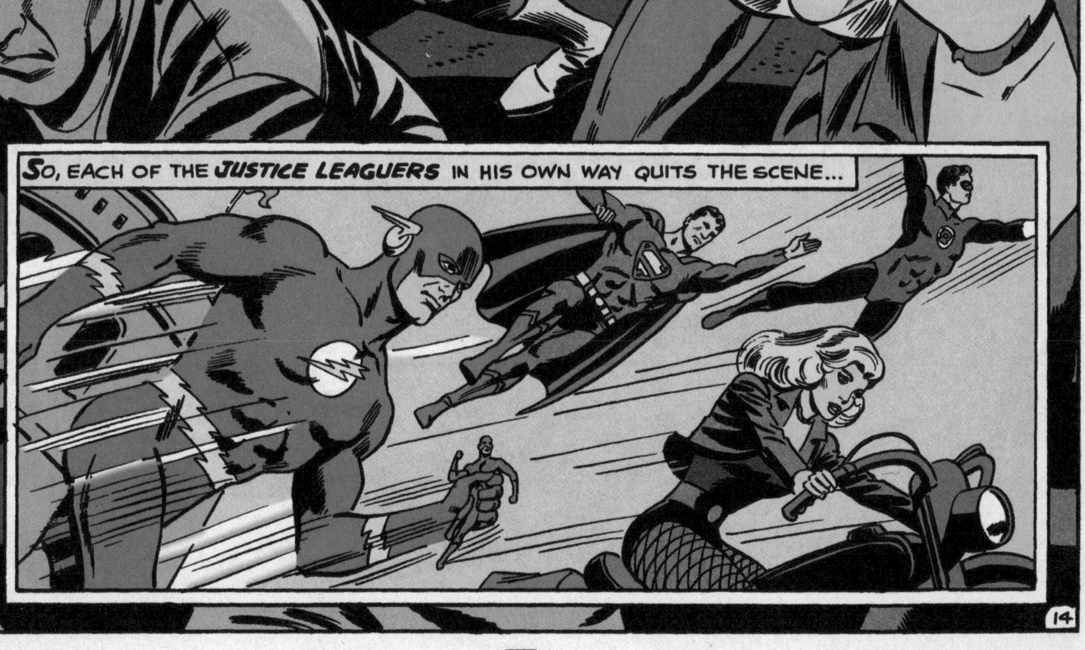
SO, EACH OF THE JUSTICE LEAGUERS IN HIS OWN WAY QUITS THE SCENE...
14

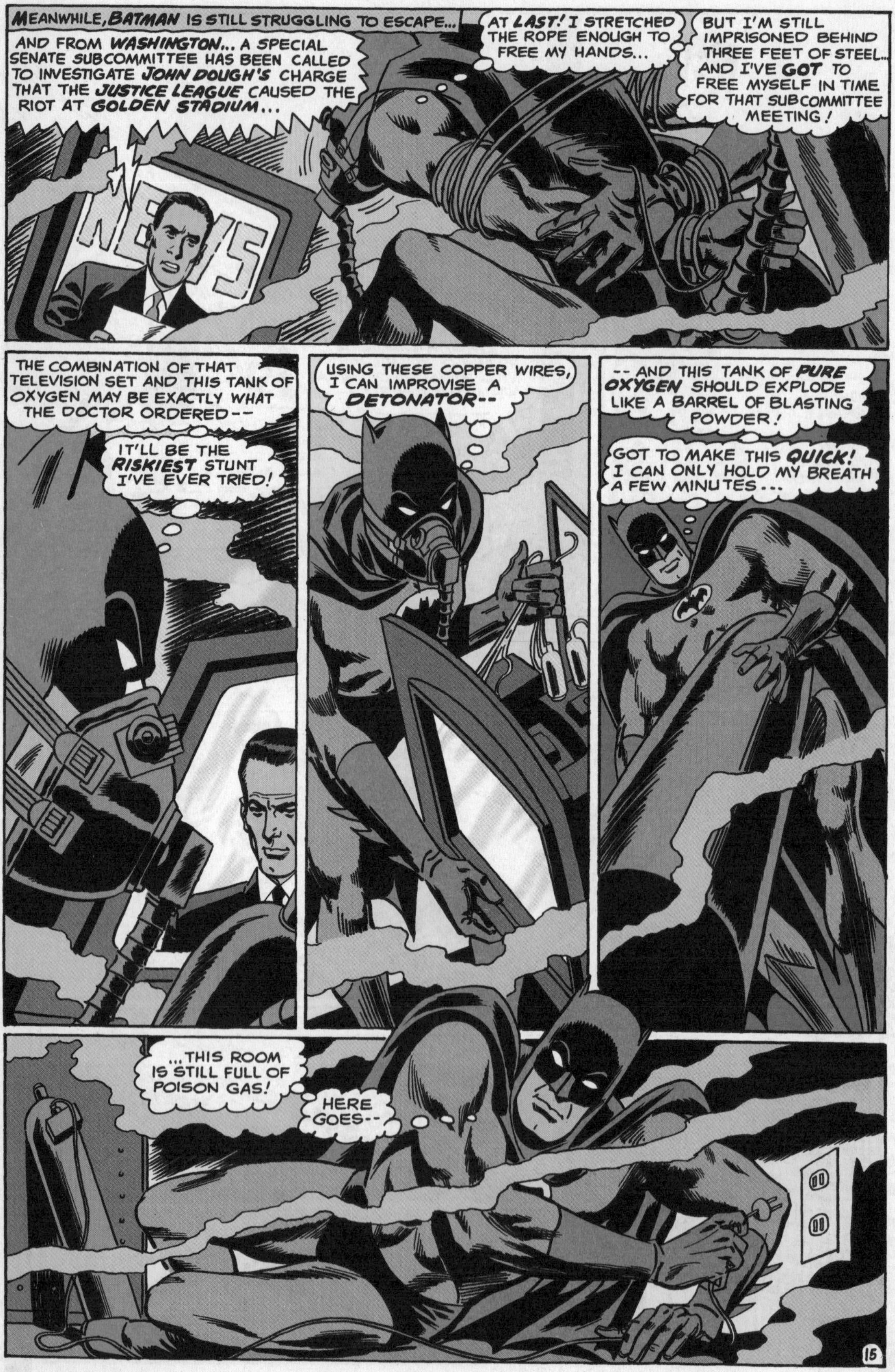
MEANWHILE, BATMAN IS STILL STRUGGLING TO ESCAPE...
AND FROM WASHINGTON... A SPECIAL SENATE SUBCOMMITTEE HAS BEEN CALLED TO INVESTIGATE JOHN DOUGH'S CHARGE THAT THE JUSTICE LEAGUE CAUSED THE RIOT AT GOLDEN STADIUM...
AT LAST! I STRETCHED THE ROPE ENOUGH TO FREE MY HANDS...
BUT I'M STILL IMPRISONED BEHIND THREE FEET OF STEEL... AND I'VE GOT TO FREE MYSELF IN TIME FOR THAT SUBCOMMITTEE MEETING!
NEWS
THE COMBINATION OF THAT TELEVISION SET AND THIS TANK OF OXYGEN MAY BE EXACTLY WHAT THE DOCTOR ORDERED--
IT'LL BE THE RISKIEST STUNT I'VE EVER TRIED!
USING THESE COPPER WIRES, I CAN IMPROVISE A DETONATOR--
-- AND THIS TANK OF PURE OXYGEN SHOULD EXPLODE LIKE A BARREL OF BLASTING POWDER!
GOT TO MAKE THIS QUICK! I CAN ONLY HOLD MY BREATH A FEW MINUTES...
...THIS ROOM IS STILL FULL OF POISON GAS!
HERE GOES--
15

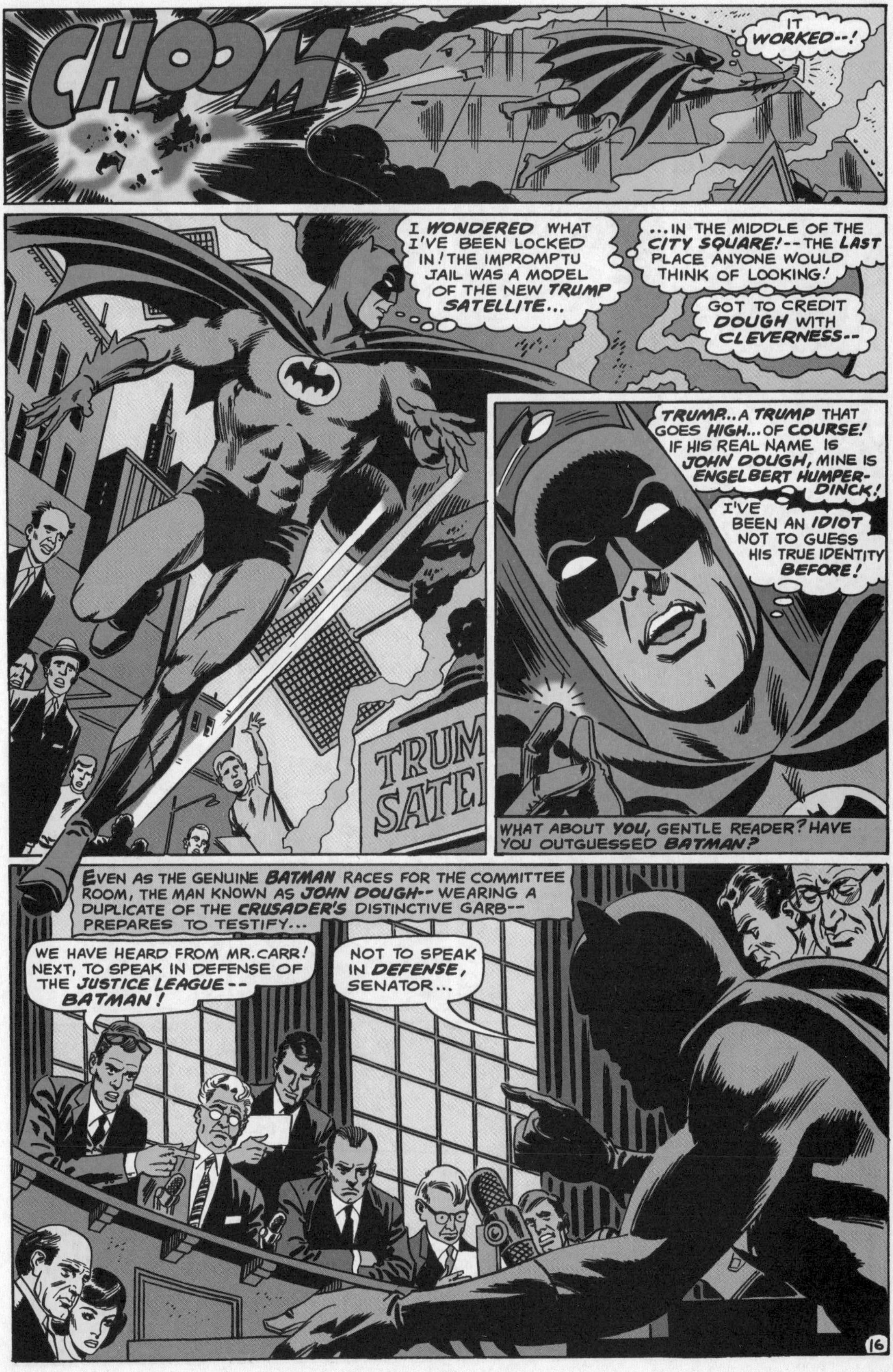
CHOOM
IT WORKED--!
I WONDERED WHAT I'VE BEEN LOCKED IN! THE IMPROMPTU JAIL WAS A MODEL OF THE NEW TRUMP SATELLITE...
...IN THE MIDDLE OF THE CITY SQUARE!--THE LAST PLACE ANYONE WOULD THINK OF LOOKING!
GOT TO CREDIT DOUGH WITH CLEVERNESS--
TRUM
SATEL
TRUMP...A TRUMP THAT GOES HIGH...OF COURSE! IF HIS REAL NAME IS JOHN DOUGH, MINE IS ENGELBERT HUMPER-DINCK!
I'VE BEEN AN IDIOT NOT TO GUESS HIS TRUE IDENTITY BEFORE!
WHAT ABOUT YOU, GENTLE READER? HAVE YOU OUTGUESSED BATMAN?
EVEN AS THE GENUINE BATMAN RACES FOR THE COMMITTEE ROOM, THE MAN KNOWN AS JOHN DOUGH-- WEARING A DUPLICATE OF THE CRUSADER'S DISTINCTIVE GARB-- PREPARES TO TESTIFY...
WE HAVE HEARD FROM MR. CARR! NEXT, TO SPEAK IN DEFENSE OF THE JUSTICE LEAGUE-- BATMAN!
NOT TO SPEAK IN DEFENSE, SENATOR...
16

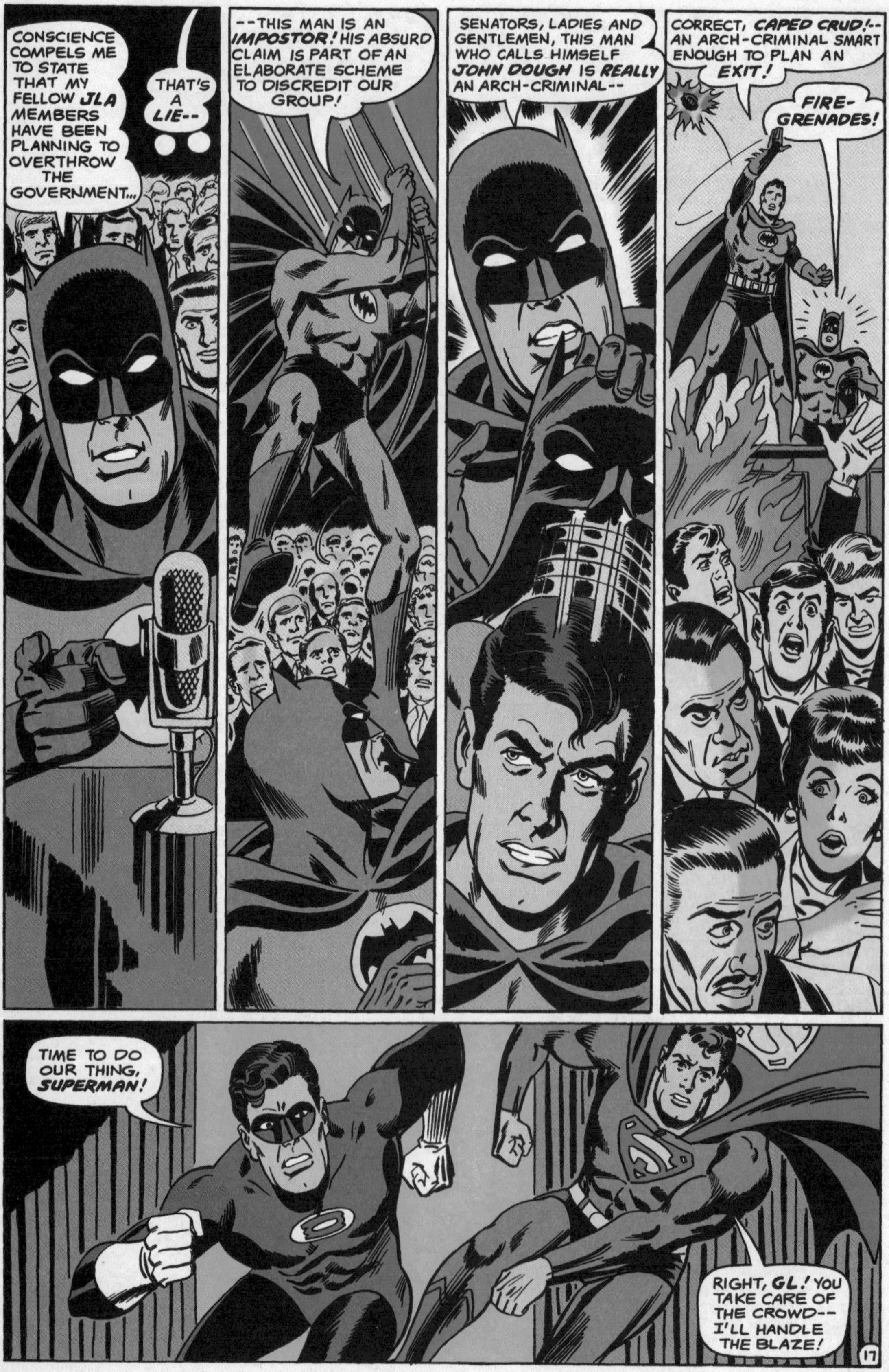
CONSCIENCE COMPELS ME TO STATE THAT MY FELLOW JLA MEMBERS HAVE BEEN PLANNING TO OVERTHROW THE GOVERNMENT...
THAT'S A LIE--
--THIS MAN IS AN IMPOSTOR! HIS ABSURD CLAIM IS PART OF AN ELABORATE SCHEME TO DISCREDIT OUR GROUP!
SENATORS, LADIES AND GENTLEMEN, THIS MAN WHO CALLS HIMSELF JOHN DOUGH IS REALLY AN ARCH-CRIMINAL--
CORRECT, CAPED CRUD!--AN ARCH-CRIMINAL SMART ENOUGH TO PLAN AN EXIT!
FIRE-GRENADES!
TIME TO DO OUR THING, SUPERMAN!
RIGHT, GL! YOU TAKE CARE OF THE CROWD--I'LL HANDLE THE BLAZE!
17

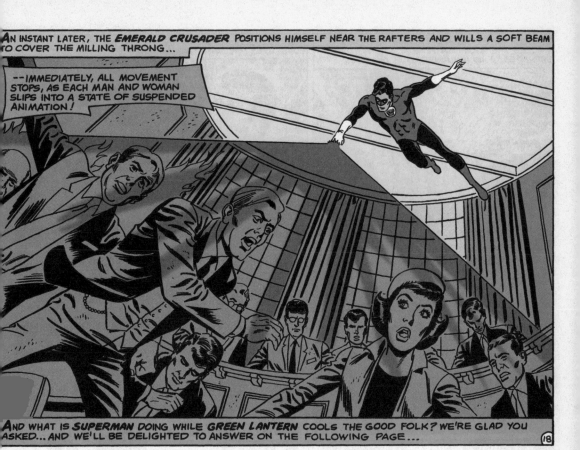

AN INSTANT LATER, THE EMERALD CRUSADER POSITIONS HIMSELF NEAR THE RAFTERS AND WILLS A SOFT BEAM TO COVER THE MILLING THRONG...
--IMMEDIATELY, ALL MOVEMENT STOPS, AS EACH MAN AND WOMAN SLIPS INTO A STATE OF SUSPENDED ANIMATION!
AND WHAT IS SUPERMAN DOING WHILE GREEN LANTERN COOLS THE GOOD FOLK? WE'RE GLAD YOU ASKED... AND WE'LL BE DELIGHTED TO ANSWER ON THE FOLLOWING PAGE...
18

JUSTICE LEAGUE of AMERICA

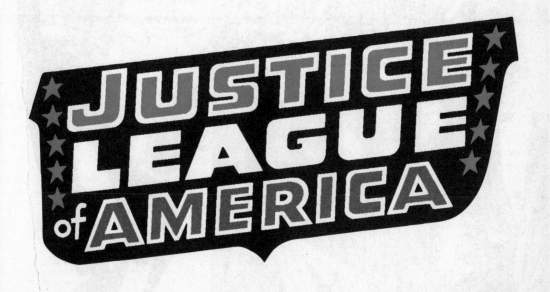

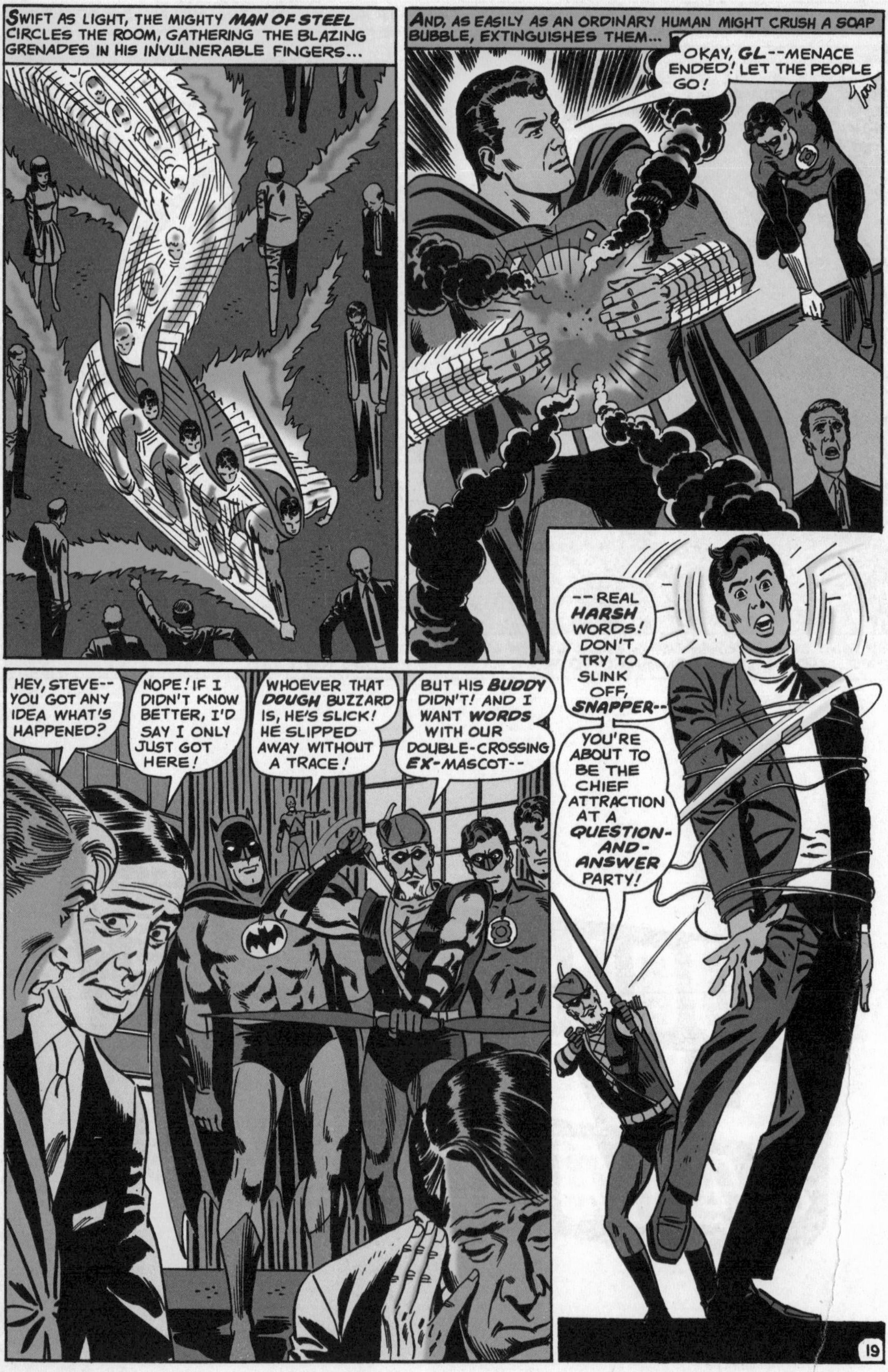

SWIFT AS LIGHT, THE MIGHTY MAN OF STEEL CIRCLES THE ROOM, GATHERING THE BLAZING GRENADES IN HIS INVULNERABLE FINGERS...
AND, AS EASILY AS AN ORDINARY HUMAN MIGHT CRUSH A SOAP BUBBLE, EXTINGUISHES THEM...
OKAY, GL--MENACE ENDED! LET THE PEOPLE GO!
HEY, STEVE--YOU GOT ANY IDEA WHAT'S HAPPENED?
NOPE! IF I DIDN'T KNOW BETTER, I'D SAY I ONLY JUST GOT HERE!
WHOEVER THAT DOUGH BUZZARD IS, HE'S SLICK! HE SLIPPED AWAY WITHOUT A TRACE!
BUT HIS BUDDY DIDN'T! AND I WANT WORDS WITH OUR DOUBLE-CROSSING EX-MASCOT--
--REAL HARSH WORDS! DON'T TRY TO SLINK OFF, SNAPPER--
YOU'RE ABOUT TO BE THE CHIEF ATTRACTION AT A QUESTION-AND-ANSWER PARTY!
19

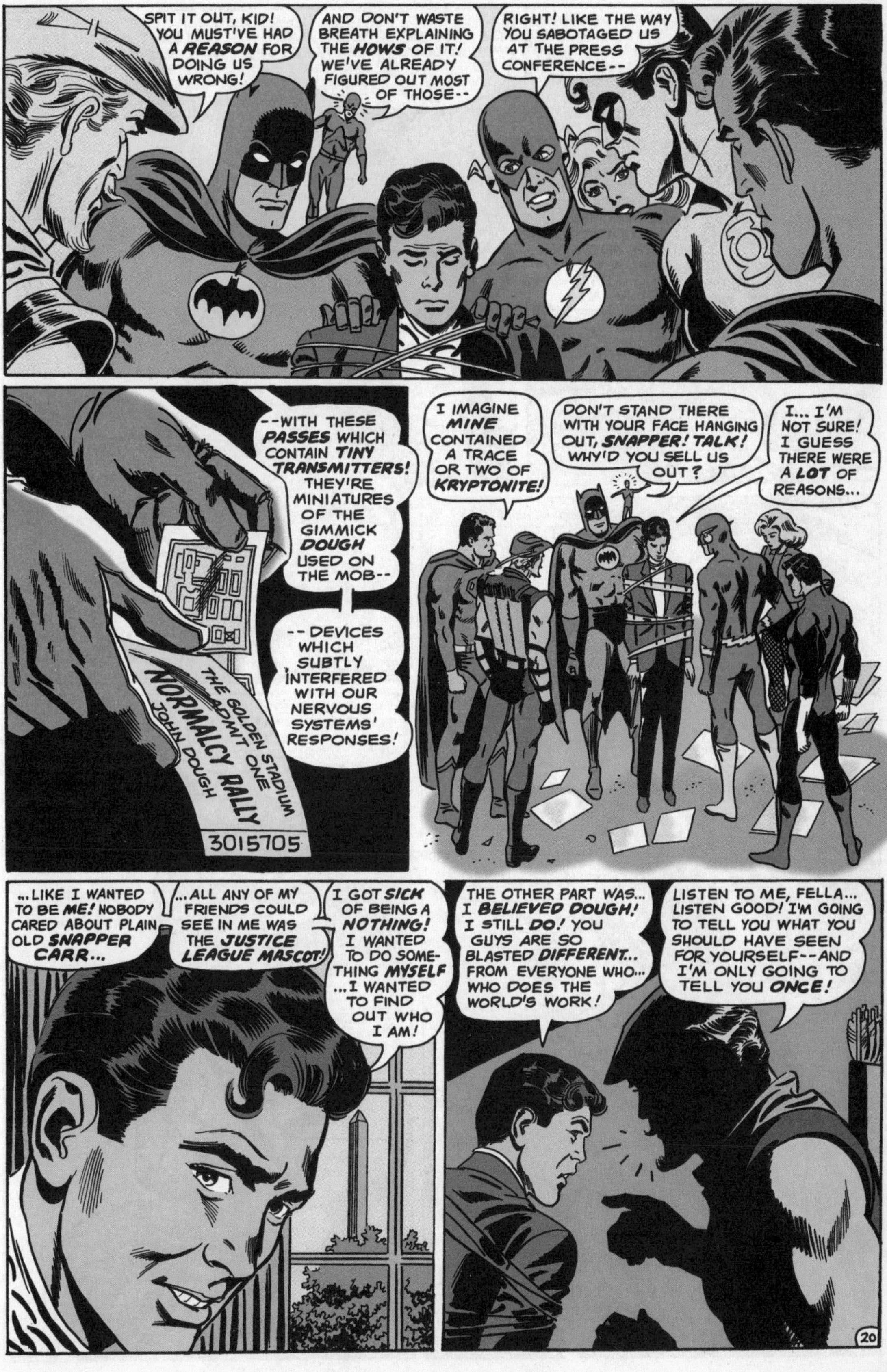
SPIT IT OUT, KID! YOU MUST'VE HAD A REASON FOR DOING US WRONG!
AND DON'T WASTE BREATH EXPLAINING THE HOWS OF IT! WE'VE ALREADY FIGURED OUT MOST OF THOSE--
RIGHT! LIKE THE WAY YOU SABOTAGED US AT THE PRESS CONFERENCE--
--WITH THESE PASSES WHICH CONTAIN TINY TRANSMITTERS! THEY'RE MINIATURES OF THE GIMMICK DOUGH USED ON THE MOB--
--DEVICES WHICH SUBTLY INTERFERED WITH OUR NERVOUS SYSTEMS' RESPONSES!
THE GOLDEN STADIUM
ADMIT ONE
NORMALCY RALLY
JOHN DOUGH
3015705
I IMAGINE MINE CONTAINED A TRACE OR TWO OF KRYPTONITE!
DON'T STAND THERE WITH YOUR FACE HANGING OUT, SNAPPER! TALK! WHY'D YOU SELL US OUT?
I... I'M NOT SURE! I GUESS THERE WERE A LOT OF REASONS...
...LIKE I WANTED TO BE ME! NOBODY CARED ABOUT PLAIN OLD SNAPPER CARR...
...ALL ANY OF MY FRIENDS COULD SEE IN ME WAS THE JUSTICE LEAGUE MASCOT!
I GOT SICK OF BEING A NOTHING! I WANTED TO DO SOMETHING MYSELF ...I WANTED TO FIND OUT WHO I AM!
THE OTHER PART WAS... I BELIEVED DOUGH! I STILL DO! YOU GUYS ARE SO BLASTED DIFFERENT... FROM EVERYONE WHO... WHO DOES THE WORLD'S WORK!
LISTEN TO ME, FELLA... LISTEN GOOD! I'M GOING TO TELL YOU WHAT YOU SHOULD HAVE SEEN FOR YOURSELF--AND I'M ONLY GOING TO TELL YOU ONCE!
20

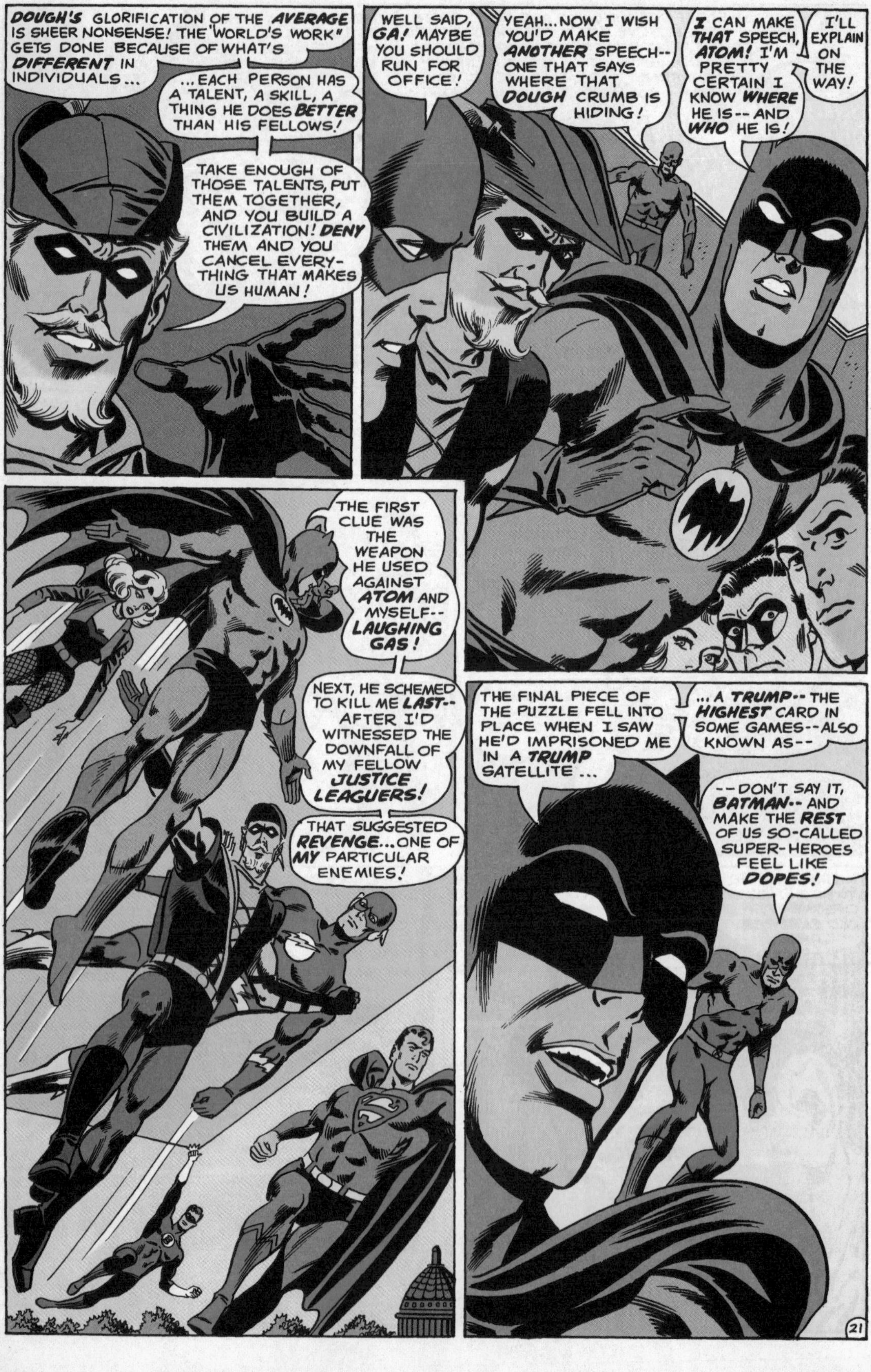
DOUGH'S GLORIFICATION OF THE AVERAGE IS SHEER NONSENSE! THE "WORLD'S WORK" GETS DONE BECAUSE OF WHAT'S DIFFERENT IN INDIVIDUALS...
...EACH PERSON HAS A TALENT, A SKILL, A THING HE DOES BETTER THAN HIS FELLOWS!
TAKE ENOUGH OF THOSE TALENTS, PUT THEM TOGETHER, AND YOU BUILD A CIVILIZATION! DENY THEM AND YOU CANCEL EVERYTHING THAT MAKES US HUMAN!
WELL SAID, GA! MAYBE YOU SHOULD RUN FOR OFFICE!
YEAH...NOW I WISH YOU'D MAKE ANOTHER SPEECH-- ONE THAT SAYS WHERE THAT DOUGH CRUMB IS HIDING!
I CAN MAKE THAT SPEECH, ATOM! I'M PRETTY CERTAIN I KNOW WHERE HE IS-- AND WHO HE IS!
I'LL EXPLAIN ON THE WAY!
THE FIRST CLUE WAS THE WEAPON HE USED AGAINST ATOM AND MYSELF-- LAUGHING GAS!
NEXT, HE SCHEMED TO KILL ME LAST-- AFTER I'D WITNESSED THE DOWNFALL OF MY FELLOW JUSTICE LEAGUERS!
THAT SUGGESTED REVENGE...ONE OF MY PARTICULAR ENEMIES!
THE FINAL PIECE OF THE PUZZLE FELL INTO PLACE WHEN I SAW HE'D IMPRISONED ME IN A TRUMP SATELLITE...
...A TRUMP-- THE HIGHEST CARD IN SOME GAMES--ALSO KNOWN AS--
--DON'T SAY IT, BATMAN-- AND MAKE THE REST OF US SO-CALLED SUPER-HEROES FEEL LIKE DOPES!
21

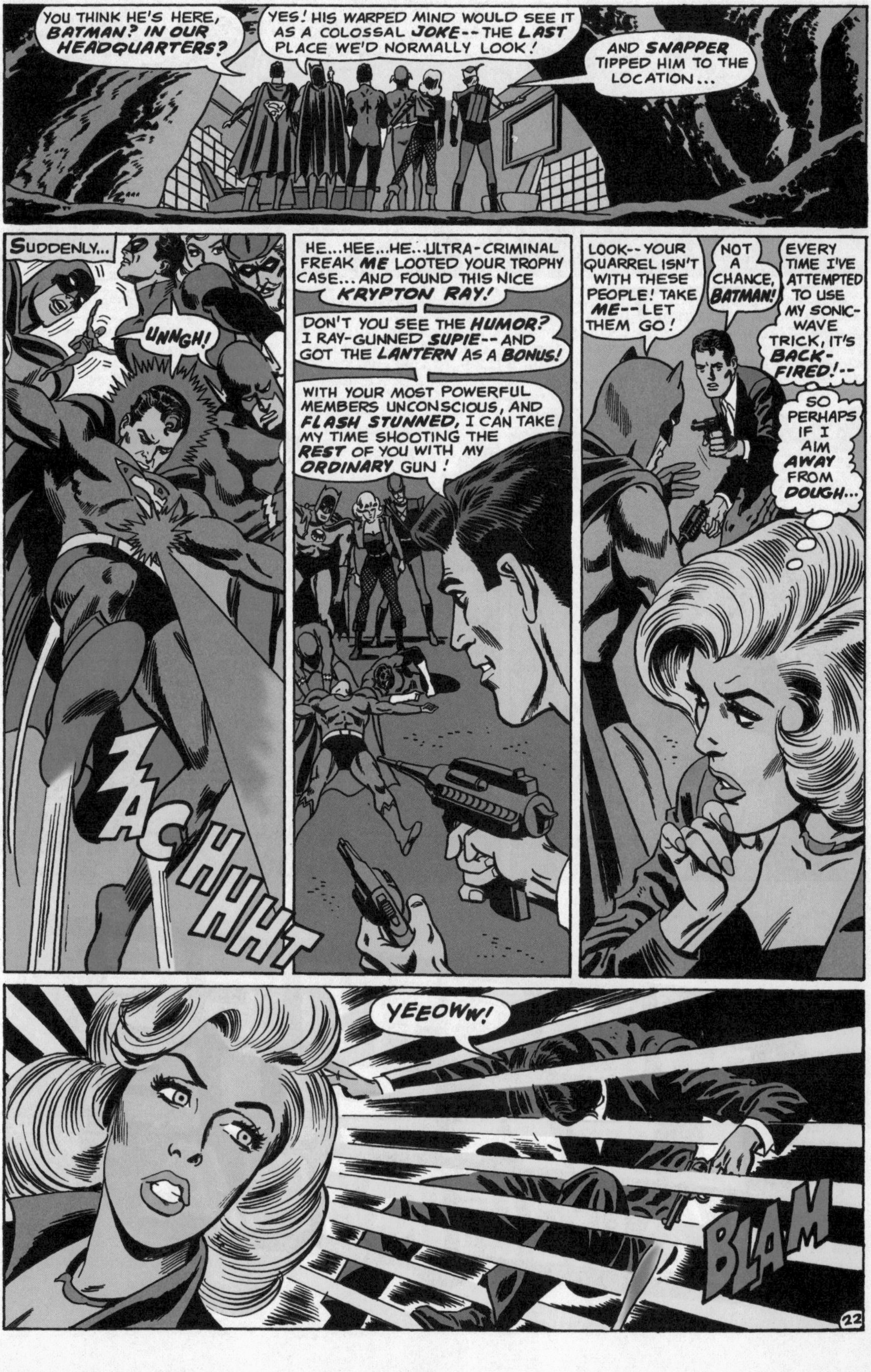
YOU THINK HE'S HERE, BATMAN? IN OUR HEADQUARTERS?
YES! HIS WARPED MIND WOULD SEE IT AS A COLOSSAL JOKE--THE LAST PLACE WE'D NORMALLY LOOK!
AND SNAPPER TIPPED HIM TO THE LOCATION...
SUDDENLY...
UNNGH!
ZACHHHT
HE...HEE...HE...ULTRA-CRIMINAL FREAK ME LOOTED YOUR TROPHY CASE... AND FOUND THIS NICE KRYPTON RAY!
DON'T YOU SEE THE HUMOR? I RAY-GUNNED SUPIE--AND GOT THE LANTERN AS A BONUS!
WITH YOUR MOST POWERFUL MEMBERS UNCONSCIOUS, AND FLASH STUNNED, I CAN TAKE MY TIME SHOOTING THE REST OF YOU WITH MY ORDINARY GUN!
LOOK--YOUR QUARREL ISN'T WITH THESE PEOPLE! TAKE ME--LET THEM GO!
NOT A CHANCE, BATMAN!
EVERY TIME I'VE ATTEMPTED TO USE MY SONIC-WAVE TRICK, IT'S BACK-FIRED!--
SO PERHAPS IF I AIM AWAY FROM DOUGH...
YEEOWW!
BLAM
22

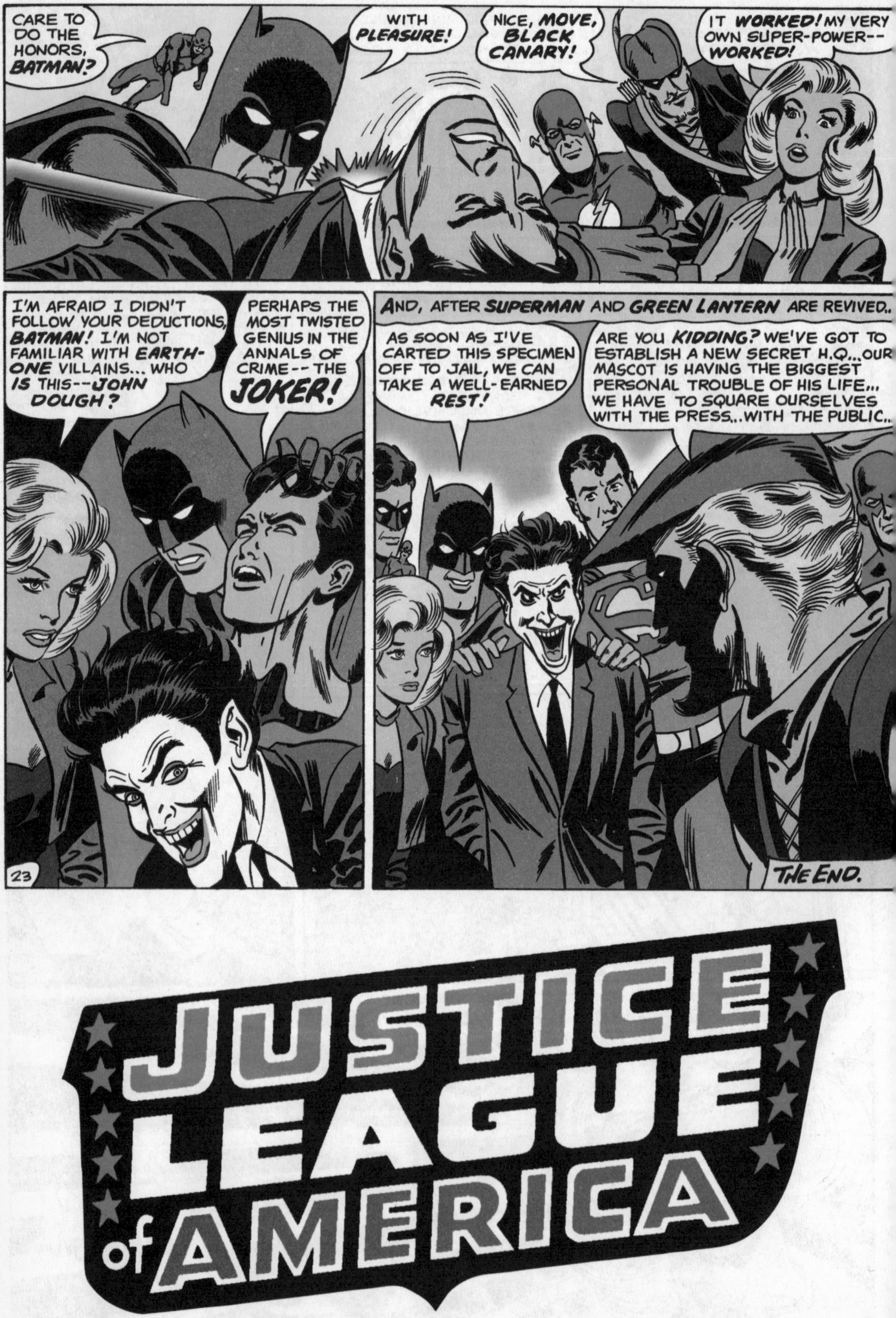
CARE TO DO THE HONORS, BATMAN?
WITH PLEASURE!
NICE, MOVE, BLACK CANARY!
IT WORKED! MY VERY OWN SUPER-POWER-- WORKED!
I'M AFRAID I DIDN'T FOLLOW YOUR DEDUCTIONS, BATMAN! I'M NOT FAMILIAR WITH EARTH-ONE VILLAINS... WHO IS THIS--JOHN DOUGH?
PERHAPS THE MOST TWISTED GENIUS IN THE ANNALS OF CRIME-- THE JOKER!
23
AND, AFTER SUPERMAN AND GREEN LANTERN ARE REVIVED..
AS SOON AS I'VE CARTED THIS SPECIMEN OFF TO JAIL, WE CAN TAKE A WELL-EARNED REST!
ARE YOU KIDDING? WE'VE GOT TO ESTABLISH A NEW SECRET H.Q...OUR MASCOT IS HAVING THE BIGGEST PERSONAL TROUBLE OF HIS LIFE... WE HAVE TO SQUARE OURSELVES WITH THE PRESS...WITH THE PUBLIC..
THE END.

JUSTICE LEAGUE of AMERICA

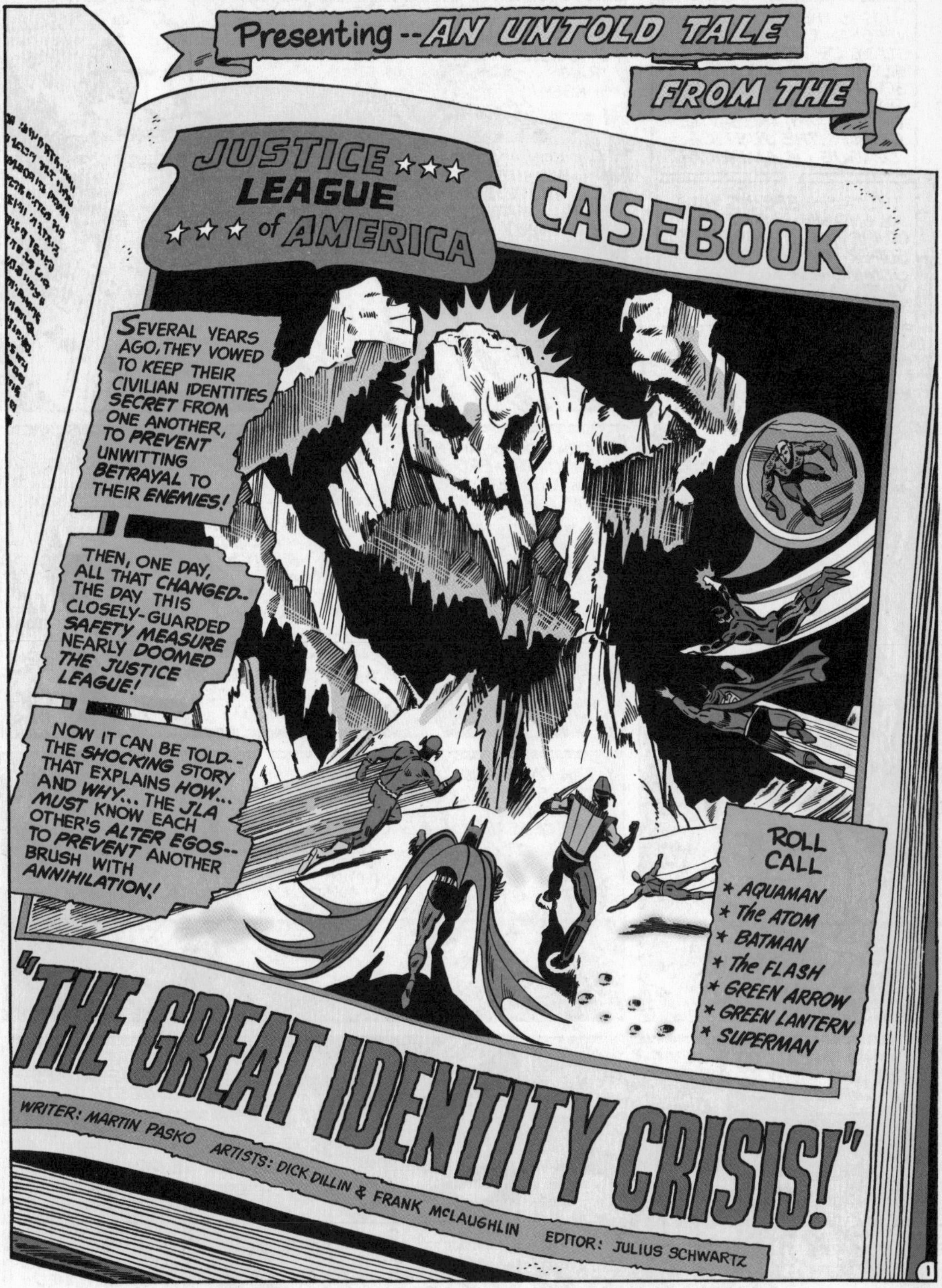
Presenting -- AN UNTOLD TALE
FROM THE
JUSTICE LEAGUE of AMERICA
CASEBOOK
SEVERAL YEARS AGO, THEY VOWED TO KEEP THEIR CIVILIAN IDENTITIES SECRET FROM ONE ANOTHER, TO PREVENT UNWITTING BETRAYAL TO THEIR ENEMIES!
THEN, ONE DAY, ALL THAT CHANGED-- THE DAY THIS CLOSELY-GUARDED SAFETY MEASURE NEARLY DOOMED THE JUSTICE LEAGUE!
NOW IT CAN BE TOLD-- THE SHOCKING STORY THAT EXPLAINS HOW... AND WHY... THE JLA MUST KNOW EACH OTHER'S ALTER EGOS-- TO PREVENT ANOTHER BRUSH WITH ANNIHILATION!
ROLL CALL
* AQUAMAN
* The ATOM
* BATMAN
* The FLASH
* GREEN ARROW
* GREEN LANTERN
* SUPERMAN
"THE GREAT IDENTITY CRISIS!"
WRITER: MARTIN PASKO ARTISTS: DICK DILLIN & FRANK McLAUGHLIN EDITOR: JULIUS SCHWARTZ
1

THIS IS THE *ARCTIC WILDERNESS:* AN ENDLESS LANDSCAPE OF FROZEN WHITE, SILENT SAVE FOR THE SCREAMING OF THE BITTEREST OF WINDS-- *AND,* ON *THIS* DAY, THE BATTLE-CRY OF... *THE JUSTICE LEAGUE OF AMERICA!*

THE CRISIS *BEGINS* WITH AN *ENDING*-- AS *SEVEN* OF THE *WORLD'S* GREATEST *SUPER-HEROES* ARE *SUMMONED* TO THIS WASTELAND TO *END* A MONSTER'S RAMPAGE...

DYNAMITE, RING-SLINGER!

CONSIDERING THE *WEIGHT* OF THAT BRUTE, I'D CALL THAT ONE *HEAVY TRIP!*

KA-WHAMM

KK-TAKK

FFWAMM

CAN YOU BEAT *THAT?* IT'S *OVER*--FROSTY'S NOT EVEN BEGGING FOR A *REMATCH!*

BIG FREAKIN' *DEAL!* YOU TOOK HIM *OUT,* LANTERN--BUT IT'S UP TO MY *NET-ARROW* TO *KEEP* HIM THAT WAY!

THIS LITTLE *SKIRMISH* SURE DIDN'T TAKE *LONG,* DID IT?...

...IN *FACT, FOUR* OF US WERE *TOTALLY UNNECESSARY!*

RIGHT! I'VE BEEN ABOUT AS *HELPFUL* HERE AS A *BEACHED WHALE!*

WHEN YOU'RE MY SIZE, FISH-FACE, YOU GET *USED* TO IT!

WHY'D YA *CALL US OUT* HERE ANYHOO, *SUPES?*

WHAT--? I *DIDN'T CALL* ANYONE!

ME NEITHER!

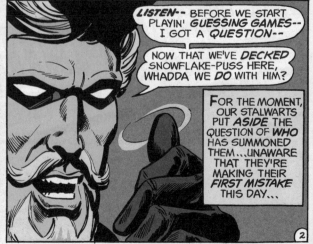

LISTEN-- BEFORE WE START PLAYIN' *GUESSING GAMES--* I GOT A *QUESTION--*

NOW THAT WE'VE *DECKED* SNOWFLAKE-PUSS HERE, WHADDA WE *DO* WITH HIM?

FOR THE MOMENT, OUR STALWARTS PUT *ASIDE* THE QUESTION OF *WHO* HAS SUMMONED THEM...UNAWARE THAT THEY'RE MAKING THEIR *FIRST MISTAKE* THIS DAY...

2

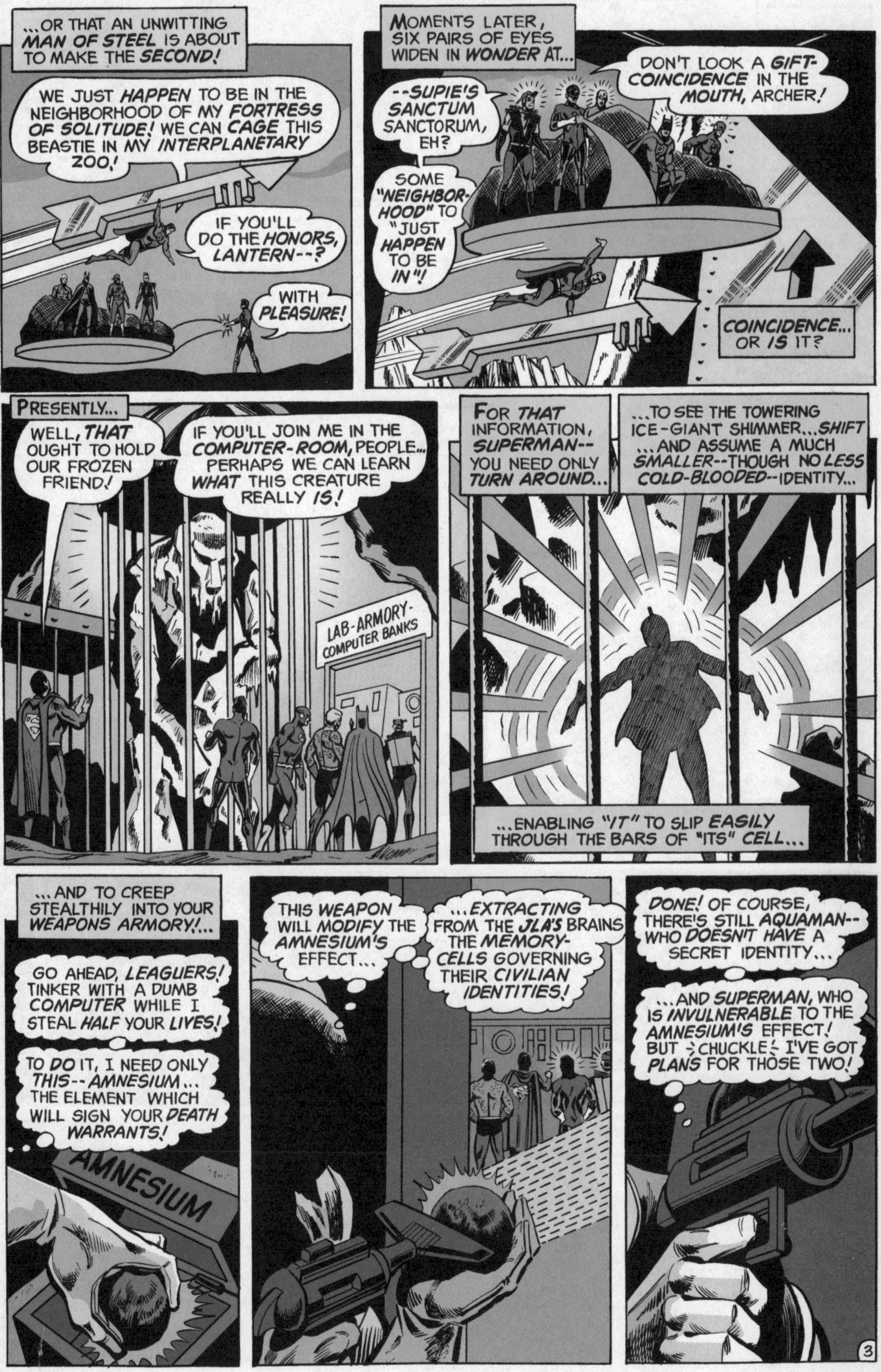
...OR THAT AN UNWITTING MAN OF STEEL IS ABOUT TO MAKE THE SECOND!
WE JUST HAPPEN TO BE IN THE NEIGHBORHOOD OF MY FORTRESS OF SOLITUDE! WE CAN CAGE THIS BEASTIE IN MY INTERPLANETARY ZOO!
IF YOU'LL DO THE HONORS, LANTERN--?
WITH PLEASURE!
MOMENTS LATER, SIX PAIRS OF EYES WIDEN IN WONDER AT...
--SUPIE'S SANCTUM SANCTORUM, EH?
SOME "NEIGHBORHOOD" TO "JUST HAPPEN TO BE IN"!
DON'T LOOK A GIFT-COINCIDENCE IN THE MOUTH, ARCHER!
COINCIDENCE... OR IS IT?
PRESENTLY...
WELL, THAT OUGHT TO HOLD OUR FROZEN FRIEND!
IF YOU'LL JOIN ME IN THE COMPUTER-ROOM, PEOPLE... PERHAPS WE CAN LEARN WHAT THIS CREATURE REALLY IS!
LAB-ARMORY-COMPUTER BANKS
FOR THAT INFORMATION, SUPERMAN--YOU NEED ONLY TURN AROUND...
...TO SEE THE TOWERING ICE-GIANT SHIMMER...SHIFT ...AND ASSUME A MUCH SMALLER--THOUGH NO LESS COLD-BLOODED--IDENTITY...
...ENABLING "IT" TO SLIP EASILY THROUGH THE BARS OF "ITS" CELL...
...AND TO CREEP STEALTHILY INTO YOUR WEAPONS ARMORY!...
GO AHEAD, LEAGUERS! TINKER WITH A DUMB COMPUTER WHILE I STEAL HALF YOUR LIVES!
TO DO IT, I NEED ONLY THIS--AMNESIUM... THE ELEMENT WHICH WILL SIGN YOUR DEATH WARRANTS!
AMNESIUM
THIS WEAPON WILL MODIFY THE AMNESIUM'S EFFECT...
...EXTRACTING FROM THE JLA'S BRAINS THE MEMORY-CELLS GOVERNING THEIR CIVILIAN IDENTITIES!
DONE! OF COURSE, THERE'S STILL AQUAMAN--WHO DOESN'T HAVE A SECRET IDENTITY...
...AND SUPERMAN, WHO IS INVULNERABLE TO THE AMNESIUM'S EFFECT! BUT -CHUCKLE- I'VE GOT PLANS FOR THOSE TWO!
3

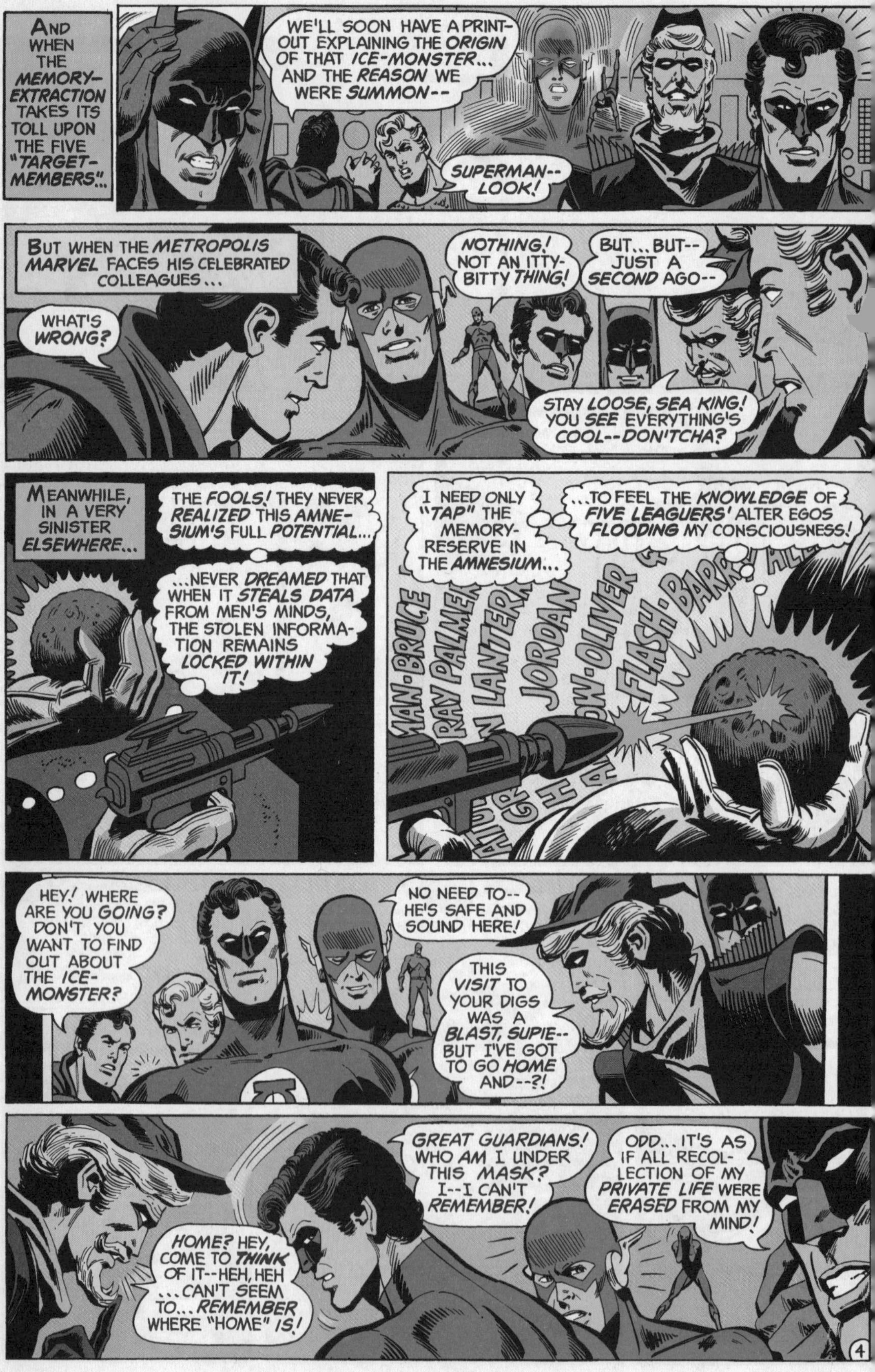

AND WHEN THE MEMORY-EXTRACTION TAKES ITS TOLL UPON THE FIVE "TARGET-MEMBERS"...
WE'LL SOON HAVE A PRINT-OUT EXPLAINING THE ORIGIN OF THAT ICE-MONSTER... AND THE REASON WE WERE SUMMON--
SUPERMAN-- LOOK!
BUT WHEN THE METROPOLIS MARVEL FACES HIS CELEBRATED COLLEAGUES...
WHAT'S WRONG?
NOTHING! NOT AN ITTY-BITTY THING!
BUT... BUT-- JUST A SECOND AGO--
STAY LOOSE, SEA KING! YOU SEE EVERYTHING'S COOL--DON'TCHA?
MEANWHILE, IN A VERY SINISTER ELSEWHERE...
THE FOOLS! THEY NEVER REALIZED THIS AMNESIUM'S FULL POTENTIAL...
...NEVER DREAMED THAT WHEN IT STEALS DATA FROM MEN'S MINDS, THE STOLEN INFORMATION REMAINS LOCKED WITHIN IT!
I NEED ONLY "TAP" THE MEMORY-RESERVE IN THE AMNESIUM...
...TO FEEL THE KNOWLEDGE OF FIVE LEAGUERS' ALTER EGOS FLOODING MY CONSCIOUSNESS!
MAN-BRUCE
RAY PALMER
N LANTERN
JORDAN
OW-OLIVER
FLASH-BARR
HEY! WHERE ARE YOU GOING? DON'T YOU WANT TO FIND OUT ABOUT THE ICE-MONSTER?
NO NEED TO-- HE'S SAFE AND SOUND HERE!
THIS VISIT TO YOUR DIGS WAS A BLAST, SUPIE-- BUT I'VE GOT TO GO HOME AND--?!
GREAT GUARDIANS! WHO AM I UNDER THIS MASK? I--I CAN'T REMEMBER!
ODD... IT'S AS IF ALL RECOLLECTION OF MY PRIVATE LIFE WERE ERASED FROM MY MIND!
HOME? HEY, COME TO THINK OF IT--HEH, HEH ...CAN'T SEEM TO... REMEMBER WHERE "HOME" IS!
4

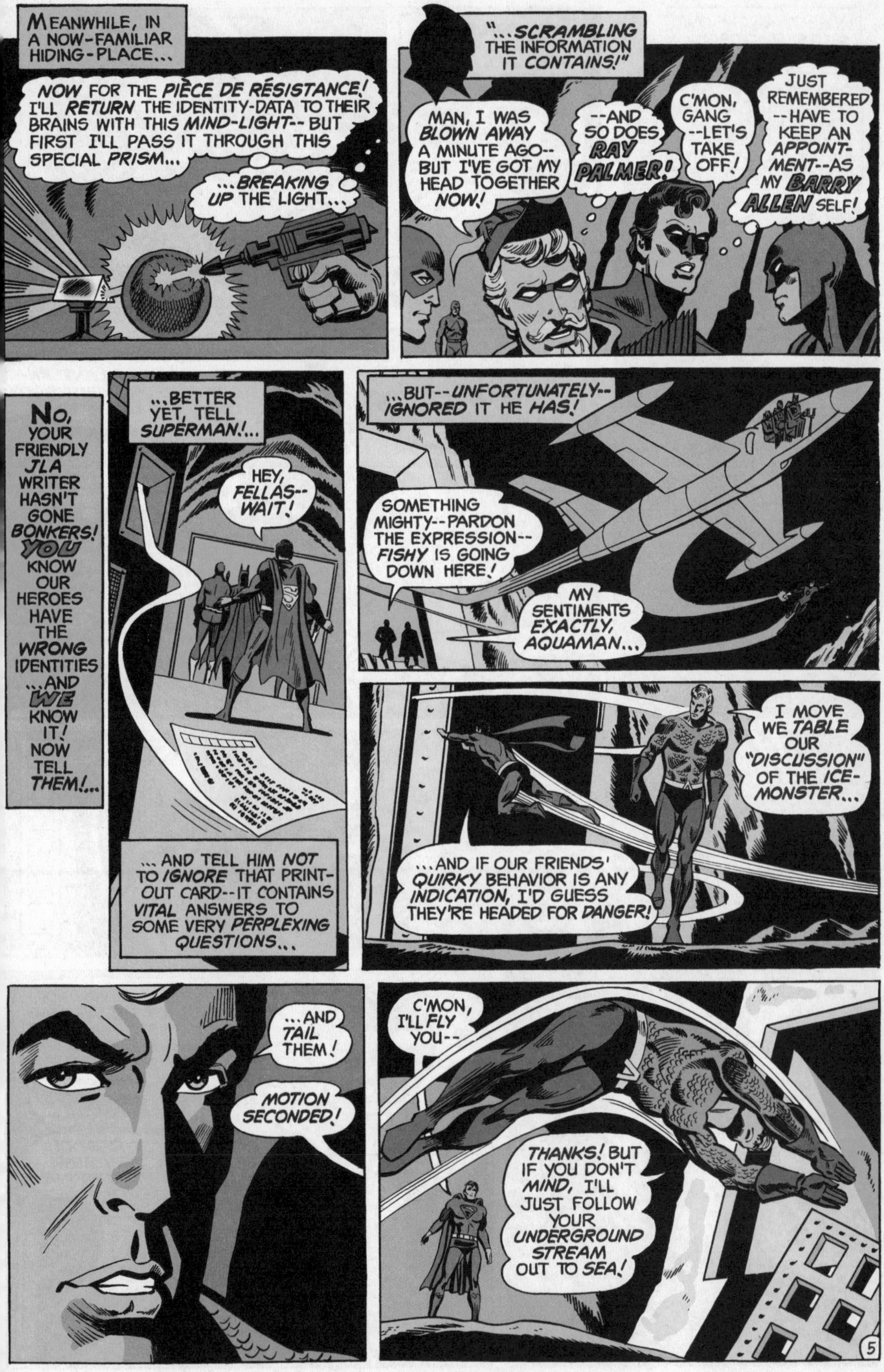
MEANWHILE, IN A NOW-FAMILIAR HIDING-PLACE...
NOW FOR THE PIÈCE DE RÉSISTANCE! I'LL RETURN THE IDENTITY-DATA TO THEIR BRAINS WITH THIS MIND-LIGHT-- BUT FIRST I'LL PASS IT THROUGH THIS SPECIAL PRISM...
...BREAKING UP THE LIGHT...
"...SCRAMBLING THE INFORMATION IT CONTAINS!"
MAN, I WAS BLOWN AWAY A MINUTE AGO-- BUT I'VE GOT MY HEAD TOGETHER NOW!
--AND SO DOES RAY PALMER!
C'MON, GANG --LET'S TAKE OFF!
JUST REMEMBERED --HAVE TO KEEP AN APPOINTMENT--AS MY BARRY ALLEN SELF!
NO, YOUR FRIENDLY JLA WRITER HASN'T GONE BONKERS! YOU KNOW OUR HEROES HAVE THE WRONG IDENTITIES ...AND WE KNOW IT! NOW TELL THEM!...
...BETTER YET, TELL SUPERMAN!...
HEY, FELLAS-- WAIT!
...AND TELL HIM NOT TO IGNORE THAT PRINT-OUT CARD--IT CONTAINS VITAL ANSWERS TO SOME VERY PERPLEXING QUESTIONS...
...BUT--UNFORTUNATELY--IGNORED IT HE HAS!
SOMETHING MIGHTY--PARDON THE EXPRESSION--FISHY IS GOING DOWN HERE!
MY SENTIMENTS EXACTLY, AQUAMAN...
I MOVE WE TABLE OUR "DISCUSSION" OF THE ICE-MONSTER...
...AND IF OUR FRIENDS' QUIRKY BEHAVIOR IS ANY INDICATION, I'D GUESS THEY'RE HEADED FOR DANGER!
...AND TAIL THEM!
MOTION SECONDED!
C'MON, I'LL FLY YOU--
THANKS! BUT IF YOU DON'T MIND, I'LL JUST FOLLOW YOUR UNDERGROUND STREAM OUT TO SEA!
5

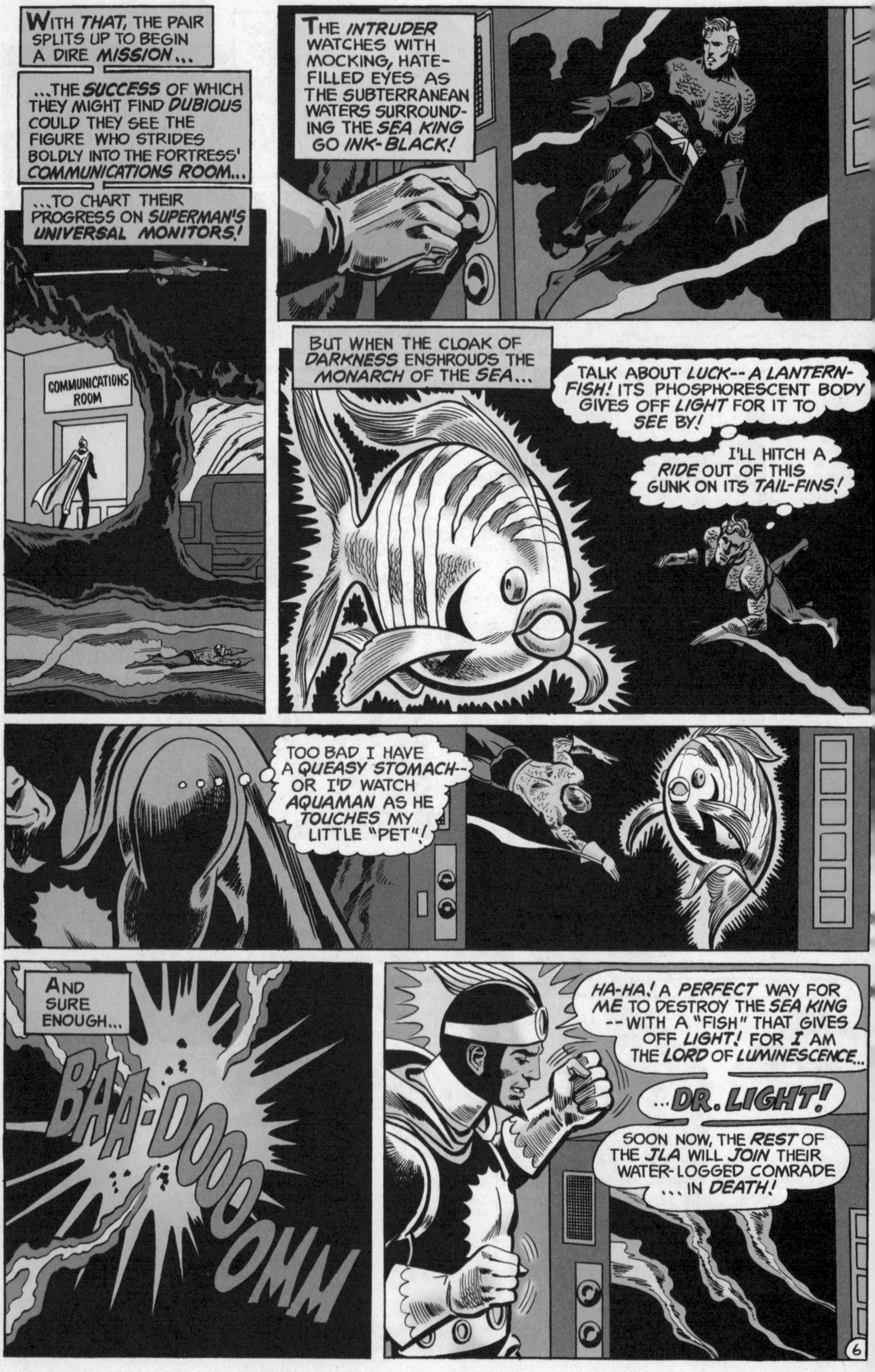
WITH THAT, THE PAIR SPLITS UP TO BEGIN A DIRE MISSION...
...THE SUCCESS OF WHICH THEY MIGHT FIND DUBIOUS COULD THEY SEE THE FIGURE WHO STRIDES BOLDLY INTO THE FORTRESS' COMMUNICATIONS ROOM...
...TO CHART THEIR PROGRESS ON SUPERMAN'S UNIVERSAL MONITORS!
COMMUNICATIONS ROOM
THE INTRUDER WATCHES WITH MOCKING, HATE-FILLED EYES AS THE SUBTERRANEAN WATERS SURROUNDING THE SEA KING GO INK-BLACK!
BUT WHEN THE CLOAK OF DARKNESS ENSHROUDS THE MONARCH OF THE SEA...
TALK ABOUT LUCK-- A LANTERN-FISH! ITS PHOSPHORESCENT BODY GIVES OFF LIGHT FOR IT TO SEE BY!
I'LL HITCH A RIDE OUT OF THIS GUNK ON ITS TAIL-FINS!
TOO BAD I HAVE A QUEASY STOMACH-- OR I'D WATCH AQUAMAN AS HE TOUCHES MY LITTLE "PET"!
AND SURE ENOUGH...
BAA-DOOOOOMM
HA-HA! A PERFECT WAY FOR ME TO DESTROY THE SEA KING -- WITH A "FISH" THAT GIVES OFF LIGHT! FOR I AM THE LORD OF LUMINESCENCE...
...DR. LIGHT!
SOON NOW, THE REST OF THE JLA WILL JOIN THEIR WATER-LOGGED COMRADE ... IN DEATH!
6

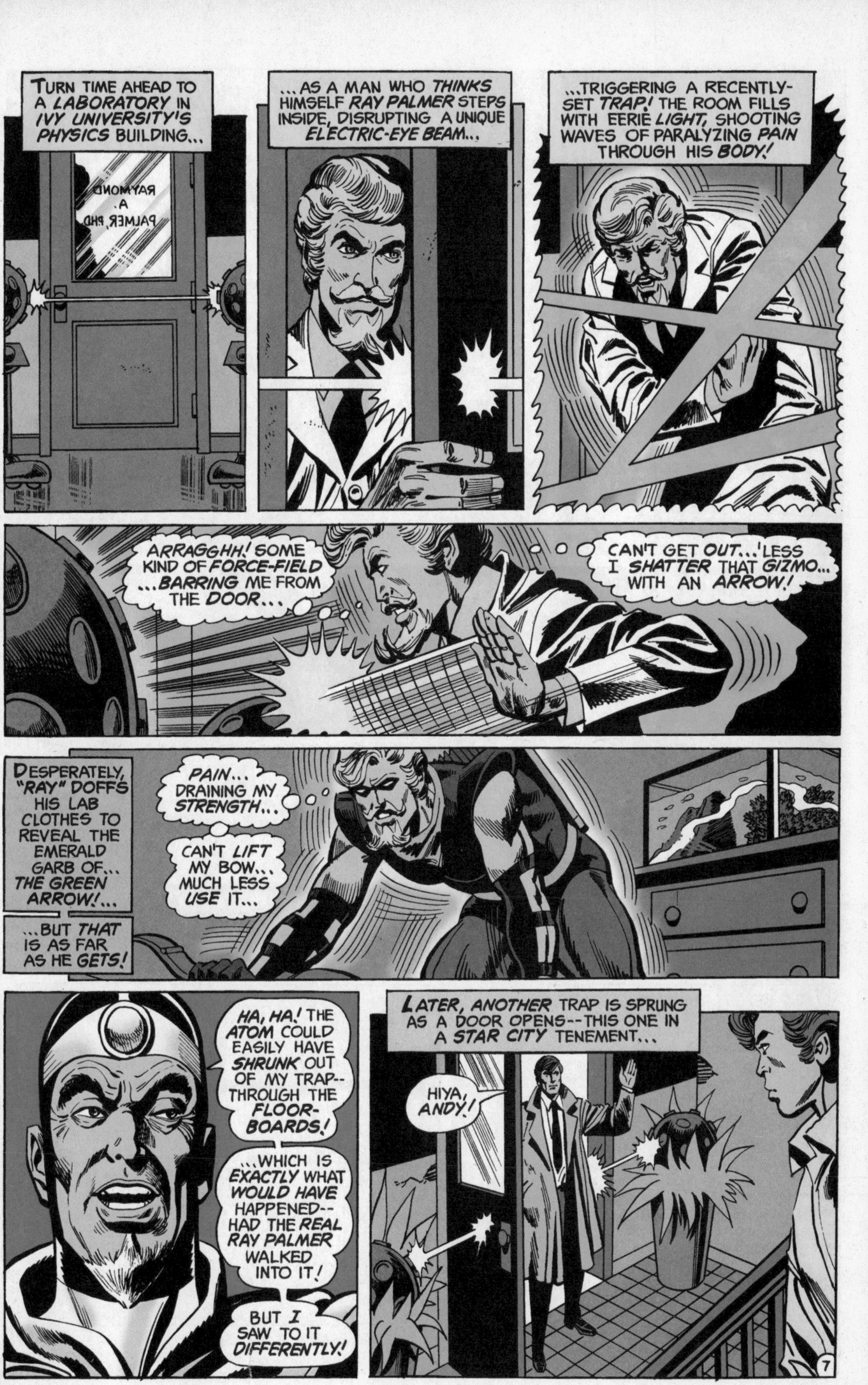
TURN TIME AHEAD TO A LABORATORY IN IVY UNIVERSITY'S PHYSICS BUILDING...
RAYMOND A. PALMER, PHD
...AS A MAN WHO THINKS HIMSELF RAY PALMER STEPS INSIDE, DISRUPTING A UNIQUE ELECTRIC-EYE BEAM...
...TRIGGERING A RECENTLY-SET TRAP! THE ROOM FILLS WITH EERIE LIGHT, SHOOTING WAVES OF PARALYZING PAIN THROUGH HIS BODY!
ARRAGGHH! SOME KIND OF FORCE-FIELD ...BARRING ME FROM THE DOOR...
CAN'T GET OUT...'LESS I SHATTER THAT GIZMO... WITH AN ARROW!
DESPERATELY, "RAY" DOFFS HIS LAB CLOTHES TO REVEAL THE EMERALD GARB OF... THE GREEN ARROW!...
PAIN... DRAINING MY STRENGTH...
CAN'T LIFT MY BOW... MUCH LESS USE IT...
...BUT THAT IS AS FAR AS HE GETS!
HA, HA! THE ATOM COULD EASILY HAVE SHRUNK OUT OF MY TRAP-- THROUGH THE FLOOR-BOARDS!
...WHICH IS EXACTLY WHAT WOULD HAVE HAPPENED-- HAD THE REAL RAY PALMER WALKED INTO IT!
BUT I SAW TO IT DIFFERENTLY!
LATER, ANOTHER TRAP IS SPRUNG AS A DOOR OPENS--THIS ONE IN A STAR CITY TENEMENT...
HIYA, ANDY!
7

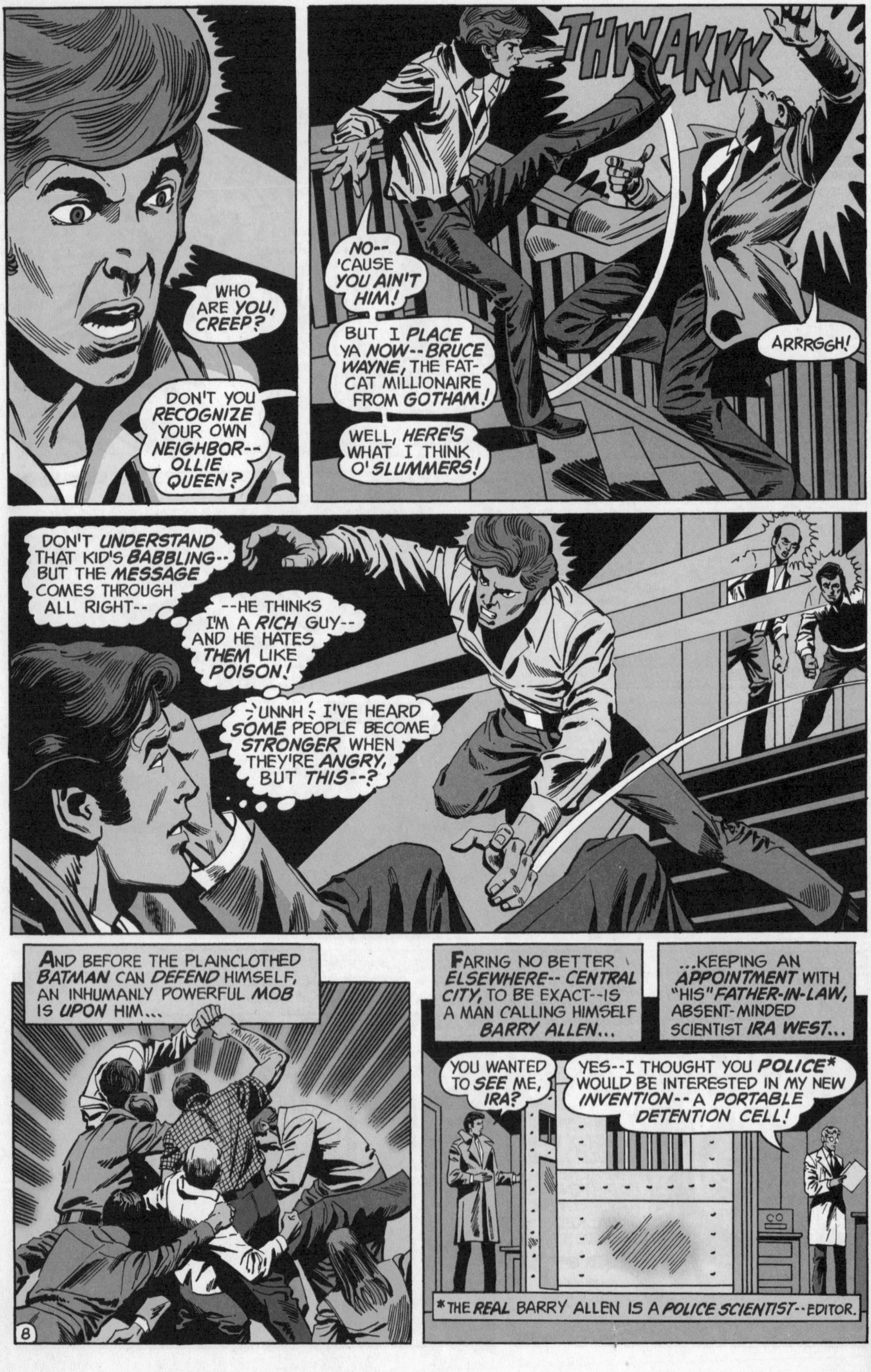
WHO ARE YOU, CREEP?
DON'T YOU RECOGNIZE YOUR OWN NEIGHBOR-- OLLIE QUEEN?
THWAKKK
NO-- 'CAUSE YOU AIN'T HIM!
BUT I PLACE YA NOW--BRUCE WAYNE, THE FAT-CAT MILLIONAIRE FROM GOTHAM!
WELL, HERE'S WHAT I THINK O' SLUMMERS!
ARRRGGH!
DON'T UNDERSTAND THAT KID'S BABBLING-- BUT THE MESSAGE COMES THROUGH ALL RIGHT--
--HE THINKS I'M A RICH GUY-- AND HE HATES THEM LIKE POISON!
UNNH! I'VE HEARD SOME PEOPLE BECOME STRONGER WHEN THEY'RE ANGRY, BUT THIS--?
AND BEFORE THE PLAINCLOTHED BATMAN CAN DEFEND HIMSELF, AN INHUMANLY POWERFUL MOB IS UPON HIM...
8
FARING NO BETTER ELSEWHERE-- CENTRAL CITY, TO BE EXACT--IS A MAN CALLING HIMSELF BARRY ALLEN...
...KEEPING AN APPOINTMENT WITH "HIS" FATHER-IN-LAW, ABSENT-MINDED SCIENTIST IRA WEST...
YOU WANTED TO SEE ME, IRA?
YES--I THOUGHT YOU POLICE* WOULD BE INTERESTED IN MY NEW INVENTION-- A PORTABLE DETENTION CELL!
*THE REAL BARRY ALLEN IS A POLICE SCIENTIST--EDITOR.

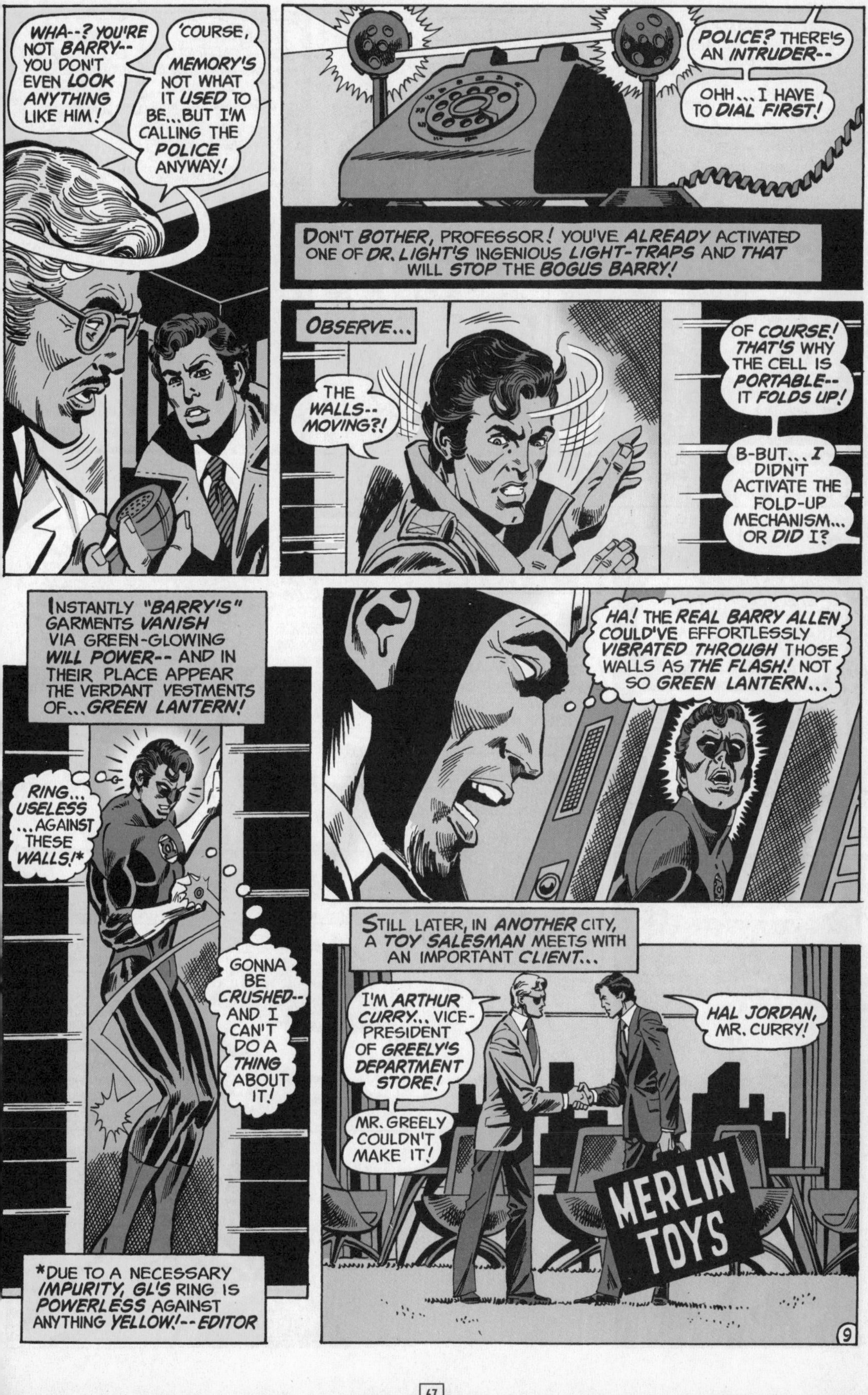

WHA--? YOU'RE NOT BARRY-- YOU DON'T EVEN LOOK ANYTHING LIKE HIM!
'COURSE, MEMORY'S NOT WHAT IT USED TO BE... BUT I'M CALLING THE POLICE ANYWAY!
POLICE? THERE'S AN INTRUDER--
OHH... I HAVE TO DIAL FIRST!
DON'T BOTHER, PROFESSOR! YOU'VE ALREADY ACTIVATED ONE OF DR. LIGHT'S INGENIOUS LIGHT-TRAPS AND THAT WILL STOP THE BOGUS BARRY!
OBSERVE...
THE WALLS-- MOVING?!
OF COURSE! THAT'S WHY THE CELL IS PORTABLE-- IT FOLDS UP!
B-BUT... I DIDN'T ACTIVATE THE FOLD-UP MECHANISM... OR DID I?
INSTANTLY "BARRY'S" GARMENTS VANISH VIA GREEN-GLOWING WILL POWER-- AND IN THEIR PLACE APPEAR THE VERDANT VESTMENTS OF... GREEN LANTERN!
RING... USELESS ...AGAINST THESE WALLS!*
GONNA BE CRUSHED-- AND I CAN'T DO A THING ABOUT IT!
*DUE TO A NECESSARY IMPURITY, GL'S RING IS POWERLESS AGAINST ANYTHING YELLOW!--EDITOR
HA! THE REAL BARRY ALLEN COULD'VE EFFORTLESSLY VIBRATED THROUGH THOSE WALLS AS THE FLASH! NOT SO GREEN LANTERN...
STILL LATER, IN ANOTHER CITY, A TOY SALESMAN MEETS WITH AN IMPORTANT CLIENT...
I'M ARTHUR CURRY... VICE-PRESIDENT OF GREELY'S DEPARTMENT STORE!
MR. GREELY COULDN'T MAKE IT!
HAL JORDAN, MR. CURRY!
MERLIN TOYS
9

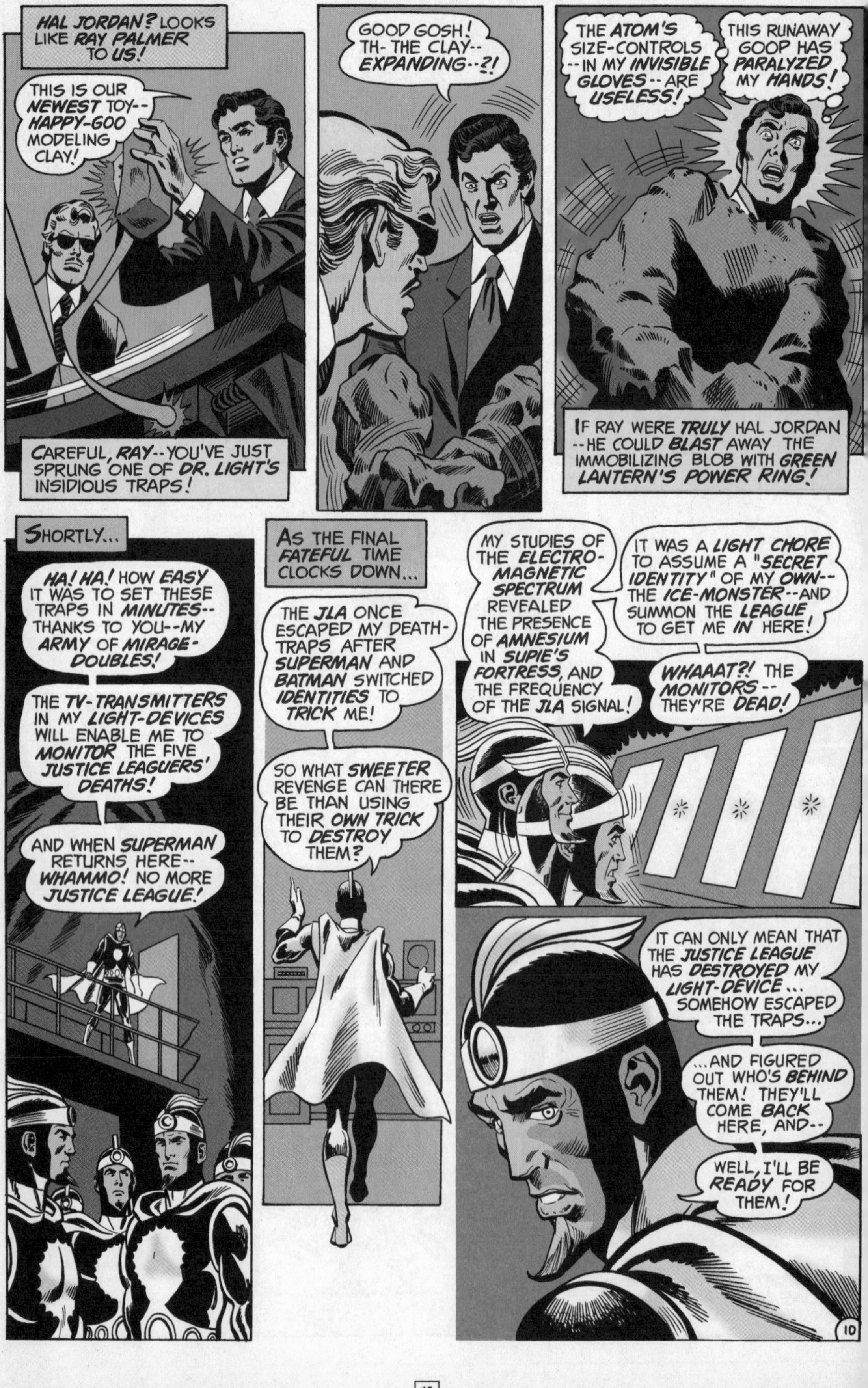
HAL JORDAN? LOOKS LIKE RAY PALMER TO US!
THIS IS OUR NEWEST TOY-- HAPPY-GOO MODELING CLAY!
CAREFUL, RAY--YOU'VE JUST SPRUNG ONE OF DR. LIGHT'S INSIDIOUS TRAPS!
GOOD GOSH! TH- THE CLAY-- EXPANDING--?!
THE ATOM'S SIZE-CONTROLS --IN MY INVISIBLE GLOVES-- ARE USELESS!
THIS RUNAWAY GOOP HAS PARALYZED MY HANDS!
IF RAY WERE TRULY HAL JORDAN --HE COULD BLAST AWAY THE IMMOBILIZING BLOB WITH GREEN LANTERN'S POWER RING!
SHORTLY...
HA! HA! HOW EASY IT WAS TO SET THESE TRAPS IN MINUTES-- THANKS TO YOU--MY ARMY OF MIRAGE-DOUBLES!
THE TV-TRANSMITTERS IN MY LIGHT-DEVICES WILL ENABLE ME TO MONITOR THE FIVE JUSTICE LEAGUERS' DEATHS!
AND WHEN SUPERMAN RETURNS HERE-- WHAMMO! NO MORE JUSTICE LEAGUE!
AS THE FINAL FATEFUL TIME CLOCKS DOWN...
THE JLA ONCE ESCAPED MY DEATH-TRAPS AFTER SUPERMAN AND BATMAN SWITCHED IDENTITIES TO TRICK ME!
SO WHAT SWEETER REVENGE CAN THERE BE THAN USING THEIR OWN TRICK TO DESTROY THEM?
MY STUDIES OF THE ELECTRO-MAGNETIC SPECTRUM REVEALED THE PRESENCE OF AMNESIUM IN SUPIE'S FORTRESS, AND THE FREQUENCY OF THE JLA SIGNAL!
IT WAS A LIGHT CHORE TO ASSUME A "SECRET IDENTITY" OF MY OWN-- THE ICE-MONSTER--AND SUMMON THE LEAGUE TO GET ME IN HERE!
WHAAAT?! THE MONITORS-- THEY'RE DEAD!
IT CAN ONLY MEAN THAT THE JUSTICE LEAGUE HAS DESTROYED MY LIGHT-DEVICE... SOMEHOW ESCAPED THE TRAPS...
...AND FIGURED OUT WHO'S BEHIND THEM! THEY'LL COME BACK HERE, AND--
WELL, I'LL BE READY FOR THEM!
10

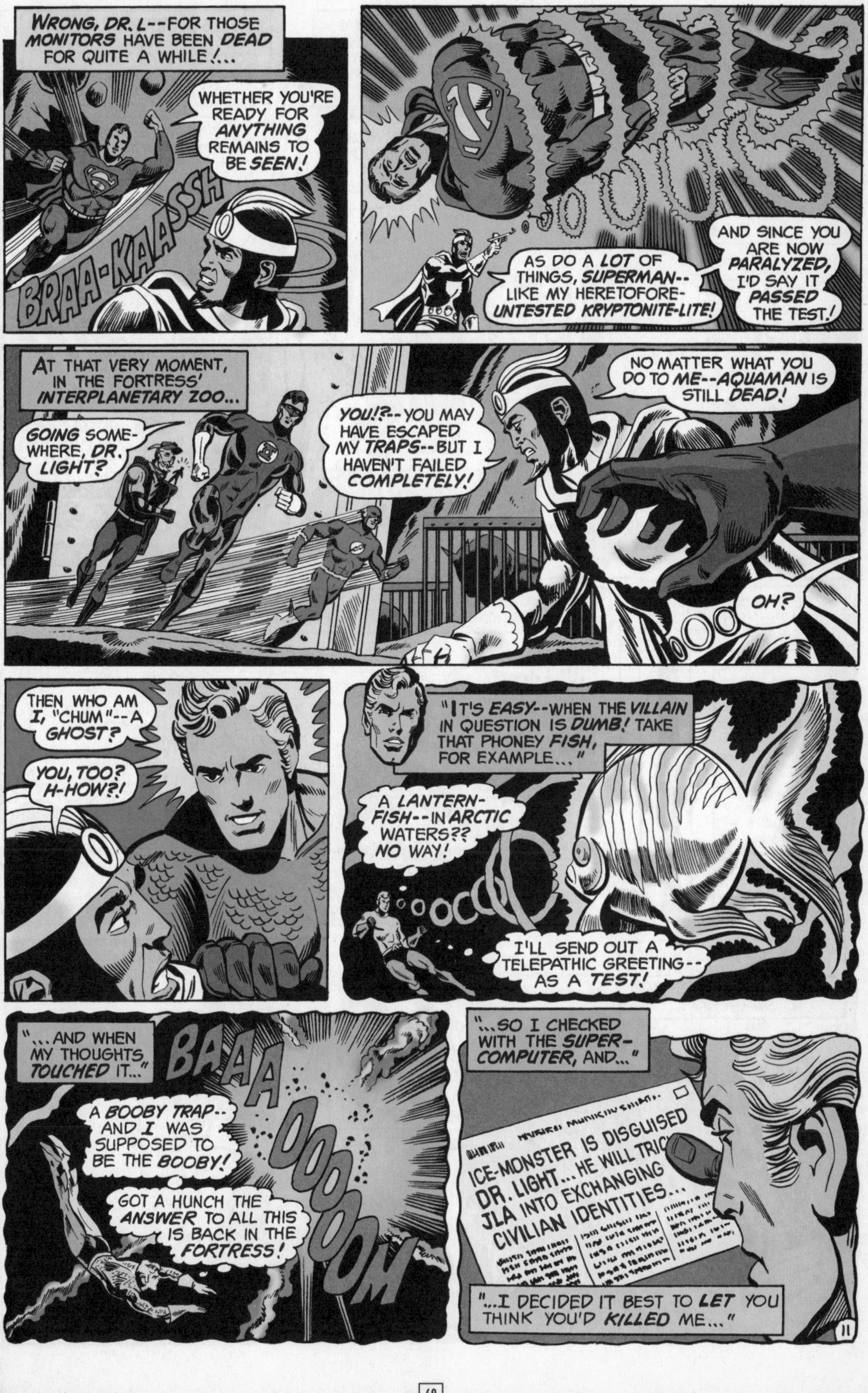
WRONG, DR. L--FOR THOSE MONITORS HAVE BEEN DEAD FOR QUITE A WHILE!...
WHETHER YOU'RE READY FOR ANYTHING REMAINS TO BE SEEN!
BRAA-KAASSH
AS DO A LOT OF THINGS, SUPERMAN-- LIKE MY HERETOFORE-UNTESTED KRYPTONITE-LITE!
AND SINCE YOU ARE NOW PARALYZED, I'D SAY IT PASSED THE TEST!
AT THAT VERY MOMENT, IN THE FORTRESS' INTERPLANETARY ZOO...
GOING SOME-WHERE, DR. LIGHT?
YOU!?--YOU MAY HAVE ESCAPED MY TRAPS--BUT I HAVEN'T FAILED COMPLETELY!
NO MATTER WHAT YOU DO TO ME--AQUAMAN IS STILL DEAD!
OH?
THEN WHO AM I, "CHUM"--A GHOST?
YOU, TOO? H-HOW?!
"IT'S EASY--WHEN THE VILLAIN IN QUESTION IS DUMB! TAKE THAT PHONEY FISH, FOR EXAMPLE..."
A LANTERN-FISH--IN ARCTIC WATERS?? NO WAY!
I'LL SEND OUT A TELEPATHIC GREETING--AS A TEST!
"...AND WHEN MY THOUGHTS TOUCHED IT..."
BAAAOOOOOM
A BOOBY TRAP--AND I WAS SUPPOSED TO BE THE BOOBY!
GOT A HUNCH THE ANSWER TO ALL THIS IS BACK IN THE FORTRESS!
"...SO I CHECKED WITH THE SUPER-COMPUTER, AND..."
ICE-MONSTER IS DISGUISED DR. LIGHT... HE WILL TRIC
JLA INTO EXCHANGING CIVILIAN IDENTITIES...
"...I DECIDED IT BEST TO LET YOU THINK YOU'D KILLED ME..."
11

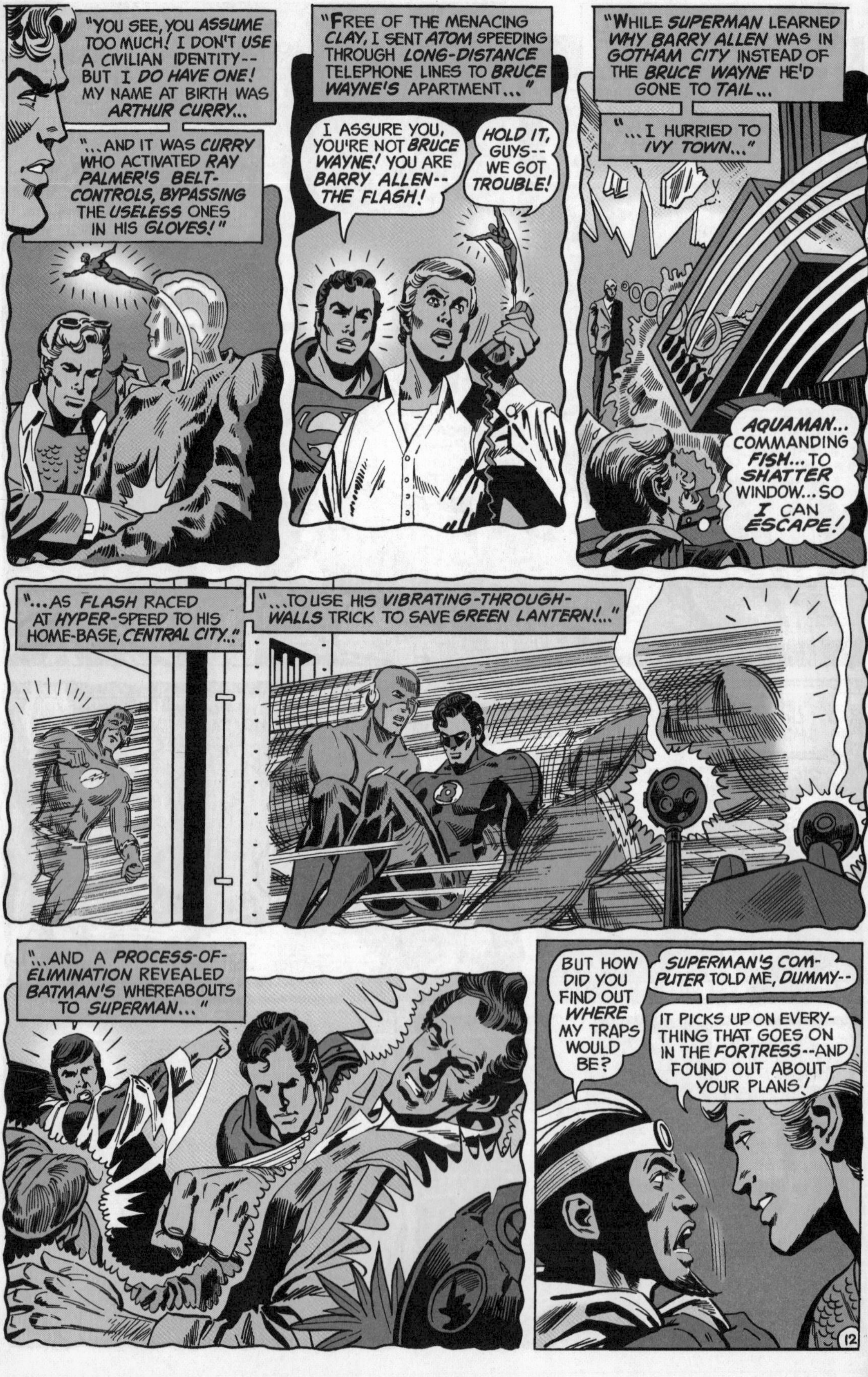
"YOU SEE, YOU ASSUME TOO MUCH! I DON'T USE A CIVILIAN IDENTITY-- BUT I DO HAVE ONE! MY NAME AT BIRTH WAS ARTHUR CURRY...
"...AND IT WAS CURRY WHO ACTIVATED RAY PALMER'S BELT-CONTROLS, BYPASSING THE USELESS ONES IN HIS GLOVES!"
"FREE OF THE MENACING CLAY, I SENT ATOM SPEEDING THROUGH LONG-DISTANCE TELEPHONE LINES TO BRUCE WAYNE'S APARTMENT..."
I ASSURE YOU, YOU'RE NOT BRUCE WAYNE! YOU ARE BARRY ALLEN-- THE FLASH!
HOLD IT, GUYS-- WE GOT TROUBLE!
"WHILE SUPERMAN LEARNED WHY BARRY ALLEN WAS IN GOTHAM CITY INSTEAD OF THE BRUCE WAYNE HE'D GONE TO TAIL...
"...I HURRIED TO IVY TOWN..."
AQUAMAN... COMMANDING FISH... TO SHATTER WINDOW... SO I CAN ESCAPE!
"...AS FLASH RACED AT HYPER-SPEED TO HIS HOME-BASE, CENTRAL CITY..."
"...TO USE HIS VIBRATING-THROUGH-WALLS TRICK TO SAVE GREEN LANTERN!..."
"...AND A PROCESS-OF-ELIMINATION REVEALED BATMAN'S WHEREABOUTS TO SUPERMAN..."
BUT HOW DID YOU FIND OUT WHERE MY TRAPS WOULD BE?
SUPERMAN'S COMPUTER TOLD ME, DUMMY--
IT PICKS UP ON EVERYTHING THAT GOES ON IN THE FORTRESS--AND FOUND OUT ABOUT YOUR PLANS!
12

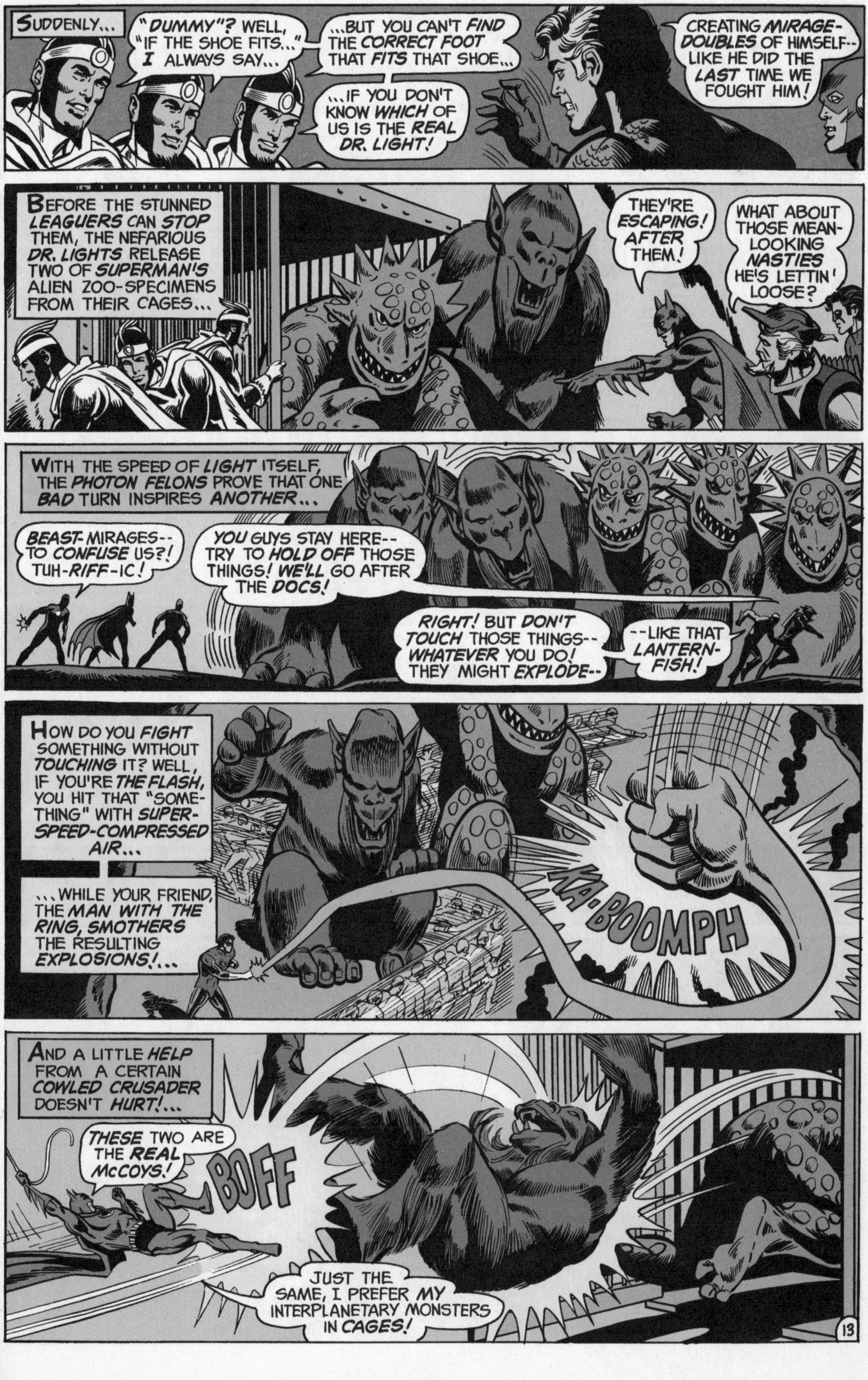
SUDDENLY...
"DUMMY"? WELL, "IF THE SHOE FITS..." I ALWAYS SAY...
...BUT YOU CAN'T FIND THE CORRECT FOOT THAT FITS THAT SHOE...
...IF YOU DON'T KNOW WHICH OF US IS THE REAL DR. LIGHT!
CREATING MIRAGE-DOUBLES OF HIMSELF--LIKE HE DID THE LAST TIME WE FOUGHT HIM!
BEFORE THE STUNNED LEAGUERS CAN STOP THEM, THE NEFARIOUS DR. LIGHTS RELEASE TWO OF SUPERMAN'S ALIEN ZOO-SPECIMENS FROM THEIR CAGES...
THEY'RE ESCAPING! AFTER THEM!
WHAT ABOUT THOSE MEAN-LOOKING NASTIES HE'S LETTIN' LOOSE?
WITH THE SPEED OF LIGHT ITSELF, THE PHOTON FELONS PROVE THAT ONE BAD TURN INSPIRES ANOTHER...
BEAST-MIRAGES--TO CONFUSE US?! TUH-RIFF-IC!
YOU GUYS STAY HERE--TRY TO HOLD OFF THOSE THINGS! WE'LL GO AFTER THE DOCS!
RIGHT! BUT DON'T TOUCH THOSE THINGS--WHATEVER YOU DO! THEY MIGHT EXPLODE--
--LIKE THAT LANTERN-FISH!
HOW DO YOU FIGHT SOMETHING WITHOUT TOUCHING IT? WELL, IF YOU'RE THE FLASH, YOU HIT THAT "SOME-THING" WITH SUPER-SPEED-COMPRESSED AIR...
...WHILE YOUR FRIEND, THE MAN WITH THE RING, SMOTHERS THE RESULTING EXPLOSIONS!...
KA-BOOMPH
AND A LITTLE HELP FROM A CERTAIN COWLED CRUSADER DOESN'T HURT!...
THESE TWO ARE THE REAL McCOYS!
BOFF
JUST THE SAME, I PREFER MY INTERPLANETARY MONSTERS IN CAGES!
13

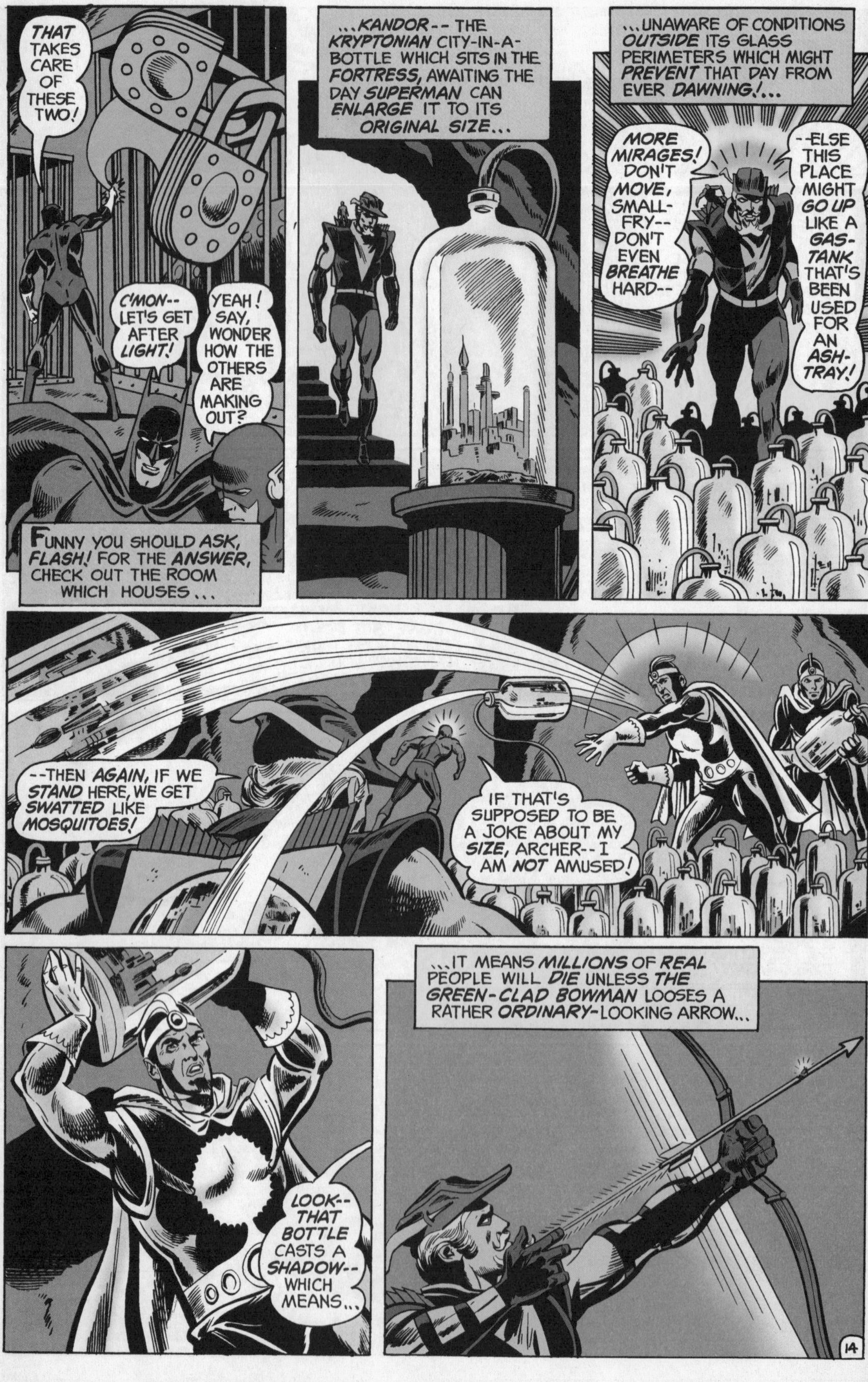
THAT TAKES CARE OF THESE TWO!
C'MON-- LET'S GET AFTER LIGHT!
YEAH! SAY, WONDER HOW THE OTHERS ARE MAKING OUT?
FUNNY YOU SHOULD ASK, FLASH! FOR THE ANSWER, CHECK OUT THE ROOM WHICH HOUSES...
...KANDOR-- THE KRYPTONIAN CITY-IN-A-BOTTLE WHICH SITS IN THE FORTRESS, AWAITING THE DAY SUPERMAN CAN ENLARGE IT TO ITS ORIGINAL SIZE...
...UNAWARE OF CONDITIONS OUTSIDE ITS GLASS PERIMETERS WHICH MIGHT PREVENT THAT DAY FROM EVER DAWNING!...
MORE MIRAGES! DON'T MOVE, SMALL-FRY-- DON'T EVEN BREATHE HARD--
--ELSE THIS PLACE MIGHT GO UP LIKE A GAS-TANK THAT'S BEEN USED FOR AN ASH-TRAY!
--THEN AGAIN, IF WE STAND HERE, WE GET SWATTED LIKE MOSQUITOES!
IF THAT'S SUPPOSED TO BE A JOKE ABOUT MY SIZE, ARCHER-- I AM NOT AMUSED!
LOOK-- THAT BOTTLE CASTS A SHADOW-- WHICH MEANS...
...IT MEANS MILLIONS OF REAL PEOPLE WILL DIE UNLESS THE GREEN-CLAD BOWMAN LOOSES A RATHER ORDINARY-LOOKING ARROW...
14

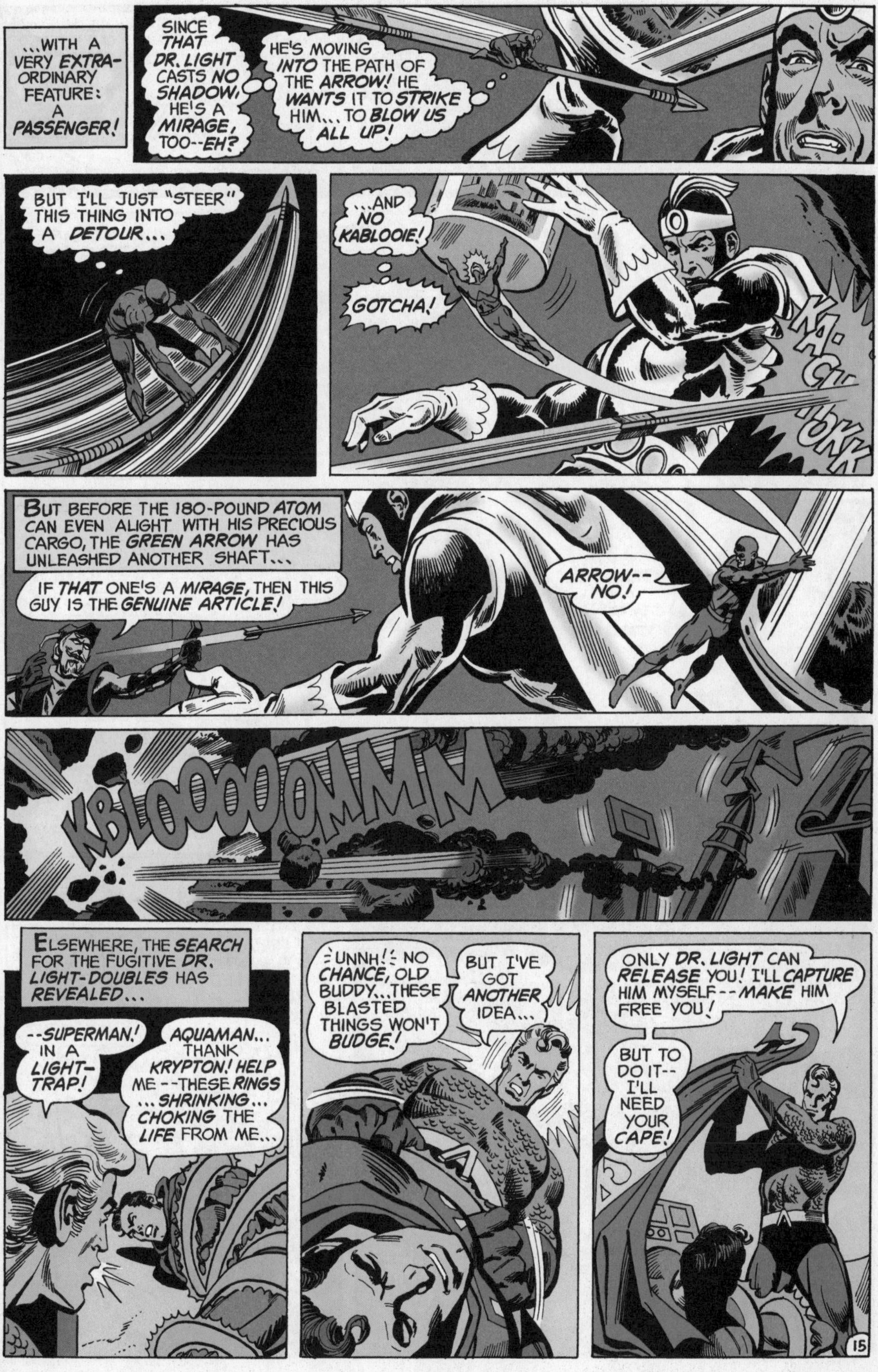
...WITH A VERY EXTRA-ORDINARY FEATURE: A PASSENGER!
SINCE THAT DR. LIGHT CASTS NO SHADOW, HE'S A MIRAGE, TOO--EH?
HE'S MOVING INTO THE PATH OF THE ARROW! HE WANTS IT TO STRIKE HIM... TO BLOW US ALL UP!
BUT I'LL JUST "STEER" THIS THING INTO A DETOUR...
...AND NO KABLOOIE!
GOTCHA!
KA-CHOKK
BUT BEFORE THE 180-POUND ATOM CAN EVEN ALIGHT WITH HIS PRECIOUS CARGO, THE GREEN ARROW HAS UNLEASHED ANOTHER SHAFT...
IF THAT ONE'S A MIRAGE, THEN THIS GUY IS THE GENUINE ARTICLE!
ARROW-- NO!
KBLOOOOOMMM
ELSEWHERE, THE SEARCH FOR THE FUGITIVE DR. LIGHT-DOUBLES HAS REVEALED...
--SUPERMAN! IN A LIGHT-TRAP!
AQUAMAN... THANK KRYPTON! HELP ME --THESE RINGS ...SHRINKING... CHOKING THE LIFE FROM ME...
UNNH! NO CHANCE, OLD BUDDY...THESE BLASTED THINGS WON'T BUDGE!
BUT I'VE GOT ANOTHER IDEA...
ONLY DR. LIGHT CAN RELEASE YOU! I'LL CAPTURE HIM MYSELF--MAKE HIM FREE YOU!
BUT TO DO IT-- I'LL NEED YOUR CAPE!
15

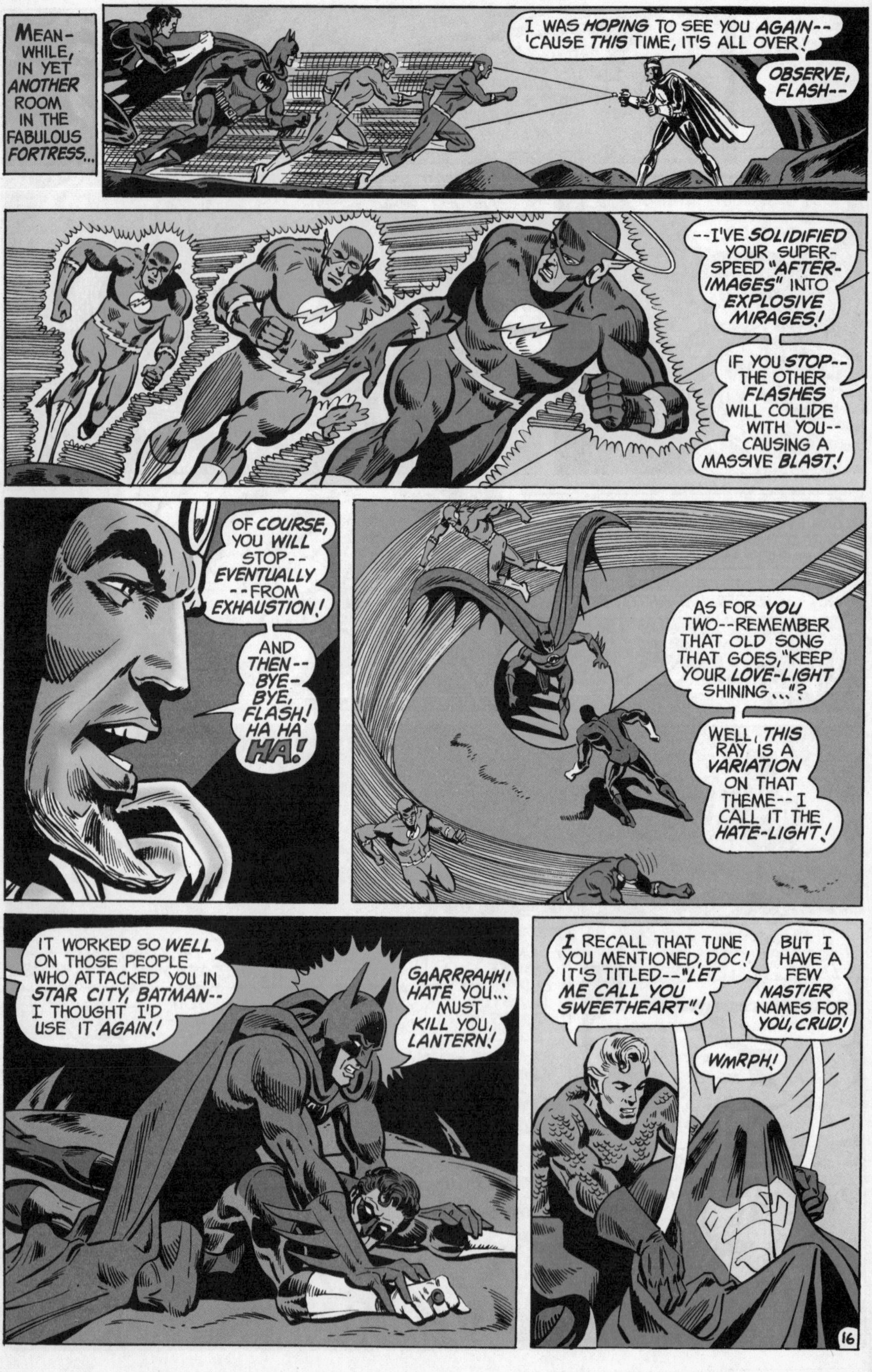
MEAN-WHILE, IN YET ANOTHER ROOM IN THE FABULOUS FORTRESS...
I WAS HOPING TO SEE YOU AGAIN-- 'CAUSE THIS TIME, IT'S ALL OVER!
OBSERVE, FLASH--
--I'VE SOLIDIFIED YOUR SUPER-SPEED "AFTER-IMAGES" INTO EXPLOSIVE MIRAGES!
IF YOU STOP-- THE OTHER FLASHES WILL COLLIDE WITH YOU-- CAUSING A MASSIVE BLAST!
OF COURSE, YOU WILL STOP-- EVENTUALLY --FROM EXHAUSTION!
AND THEN-- BYE-BYE, FLASH! HA HA HA!
AS FOR YOU TWO--REMEMBER THAT OLD SONG THAT GOES, "KEEP YOUR LOVE-LIGHT SHINING..."?
WELL, THIS RAY IS A VARIATION ON THAT THEME-- I CALL IT THE HATE-LIGHT!
IT WORKED SO WELL ON THOSE PEOPLE WHO ATTACKED YOU IN STAR CITY, BATMAN-- I THOUGHT I'D USE IT AGAIN!
GAARRRAHH! HATE YOU... MUST KILL YOU, LANTERN!
I RECALL THAT TUNE YOU MENTIONED, DOC! IT'S TITLED--"LET ME CALL YOU SWEETHEART"!
BUT I HAVE A FEW NASTIER NAMES FOR YOU, CRUD!
WMRPH!
16

AS I *THOUGHT*--ANOTHER *MIRAGE!* THE *INDESTRUCTIBLE CAPE* MAKES A PERFECT *MIRAGE-DETECTOR!*

THAT'S *THREE* DOWN-- ONLY THE *REAL DR. LIGHT* IS LEFT!

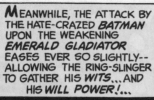

MEANWHILE, THE ATTACK BY THE HATE-CRAZED *BATMAN* UPON THE WEAKENING *EMERALD GLADIATOR* EASES EVER SO SLIGHTLY-- ALLOWING THE RING-SLINGER TO GATHER HIS *WITS*,...AND HIS *WILL POWER!*...

HATE TO PULL A *SNEAK ATTACK* LIKE THIS, PAL...

...BUT BETTER *YOU* SHOULD WAKE UP WITH A *HEADACHE* THAN A DEAD *GREEN LANTERN* IN YOUR GRIP!

THWAKKK

SO, YOU ASK, *WHERE* IS THE *REAL DR. LIGHT?* THAT'S *EXACTLY* WHAT *TWO* OF OUR *HEROIC* TEAM-- WHO HAVE JUST MIRACULOUSLY *ESCAPED* BEING *BLOWN* TO *BITS*-- WOULD LIKE TO KNOW...

GET THE *LEAD* OUT, TINY-TOES! WE GOTTA *FIND* THAT *BADDIE*-- BEFORE HE DESTROYS THE ENTIRE *FORTRESS!*

WHEN WE *DO*, I'VE GOT A LITTLE *PRESENT* FOR HIM-- RIGHT *HERE!*

BUT AT THE *HEAD* OF THOSE STAIRS THEY FIND...

GET *BACK*, YOU TWO-- THIS ROOM IS GONNA EXPLODE!

IT'S THE *ONLY WAY* WE CAN SAVE *FLASH'S* LIFE!

FLASH! OVER *HERE!*

VIBRATE THROUGH THE CAPE-- INTO THE *COMPUTER ROOM!*

17

KA-BOOOMM

AT THAT MOMENT, *DR. LIGHT* HAS RETURNED TO THE *COMMUNICATIONS ROOM*, WHERE...

IN YOUR *WEAKENED* CONDITION, THIS AMNESIUM SHOULD WORK *PERFECTLY* ON YOU, *SUPERMAN!*

BEFORE YOU *DIE*, I INTEND TO *USE* IT TO PLUCK EVERY *SECRET* OUT OF YOUR *MISERABLE BRAIN--*

SORRY, DOC-- WE HAVE *OTHER* IDEAS!

BASSSH

AAARRRGHH!

WITH THE SWIFTNESS OF A WHIRLING *ELECTRON, THE ATOM* INJECTS THE NEFARIOUS DOCTOR WITH THE *HYPODERMIC NEEDLE* THAT *SUPERMAN* USES TO TRANQUILIZE HIS *ZOO* SPECIMENS...

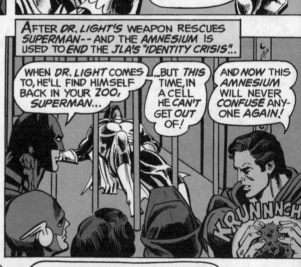

AFTER *DR. LIGHT'S* WEAPON RESCUES *SUPERMAN*-- AND THE *AMNESIUM* IS USED TO *END* THE JLA'S "IDENTITY CRISIS"...

WHEN *DR. LIGHT* COMES TO, HE'LL FIND HIMSELF BACK IN YOUR *ZOO*, *SUPERMAN*...

...BUT *THIS* TIME, IN A *CELL* HE *CAN'T GET OUT* OF!

AND *NOW* THIS *AMNESIUM* WILL NEVER *CONFUSE* ANYONE AGAIN!

KRUNNNCH

HEY, GUYS--IF WE'D KNOWN EACH OTHER'S *IDENTITIES* IN THE *FIRST* PLACE...

...OL' *DOC* WOULDN'T HAVE GOTTEN TO *FIRST BASE* WITH THOSE *TRAPS!*

WE COULD'VE *STOPPED* HIM BEFORE HE EVEN *STARTED!*

FROM *NOW* ON, WE SHOULD KEEP OUR *SECRET I.D.'S* KNOWN TO ALL THE *MEMBERS*--TO PREVENT THIS FROM EVER HAPPENING AGAIN--OKAY?

AGREED!

NOW, FRIENDS-- IF YOU'LL *EXCUSE* ME, I HAVE A *FORTRESS* TO REBUILD!

THE END

18

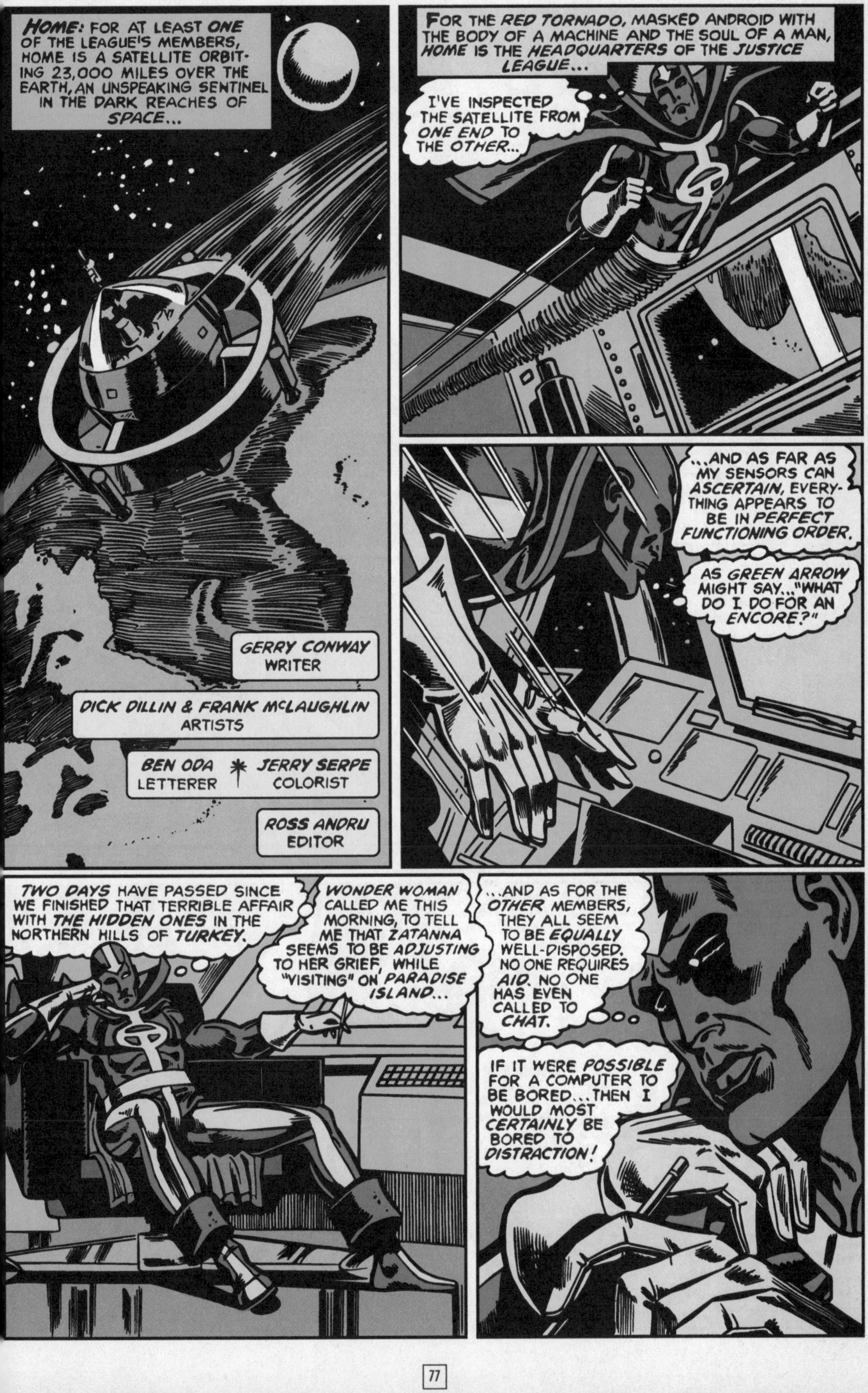
HOME: FOR AT LEAST ONE OF THE LEAGUE'S MEMBERS, HOME IS A SATELLITE ORBITING 23,000 MILES OVER THE EARTH, AN UNSPEAKING SENTINEL IN THE DARK REACHES OF SPACE...
GERRY CONWAY WRITER
DICK DILLIN & FRANK McLAUGHLIN ARTISTS
BEN ODA LETTERER
JERRY SERPE COLORIST
ROSS ANDRU EDITOR
FOR THE RED TORNADO, MASKED ANDROID WITH THE BODY OF A MACHINE AND THE SOUL OF A MAN, HOME IS THE HEADQUARTERS OF THE JUSTICE LEAGUE...
I'VE INSPECTED THE SATELLITE FROM ONE END TO THE OTHER...
...AND AS FAR AS MY SENSORS CAN ASCERTAIN, EVERYTHING APPEARS TO BE IN PERFECT FUNCTIONING ORDER.
AS GREEN ARROW MIGHT SAY..."WHAT DO I DO FOR AN ENCORE?"
TWO DAYS HAVE PASSED SINCE WE FINISHED THAT TERRIBLE AFFAIR WITH THE HIDDEN ONES IN THE NORTHERN HILLS OF TURKEY.
WONDER WOMAN CALLED ME THIS MORNING, TO TELL ME THAT ZATANNA SEEMS TO BE ADJUSTING TO HER GRIEF, WHILE "VISITING" ON PARADISE ISLAND...
...AND AS FOR THE OTHER MEMBERS, THEY ALL SEEM TO BE EQUALLY WELL-DISPOSED. NO ONE REQUIRES AID. NO ONE HAS EVEN CALLED TO CHAT.
IF IT WERE POSSIBLE FOR A COMPUTER TO BE BORED...THEN I WOULD MOST CERTAINLY BE BORED TO DISTRACTION!

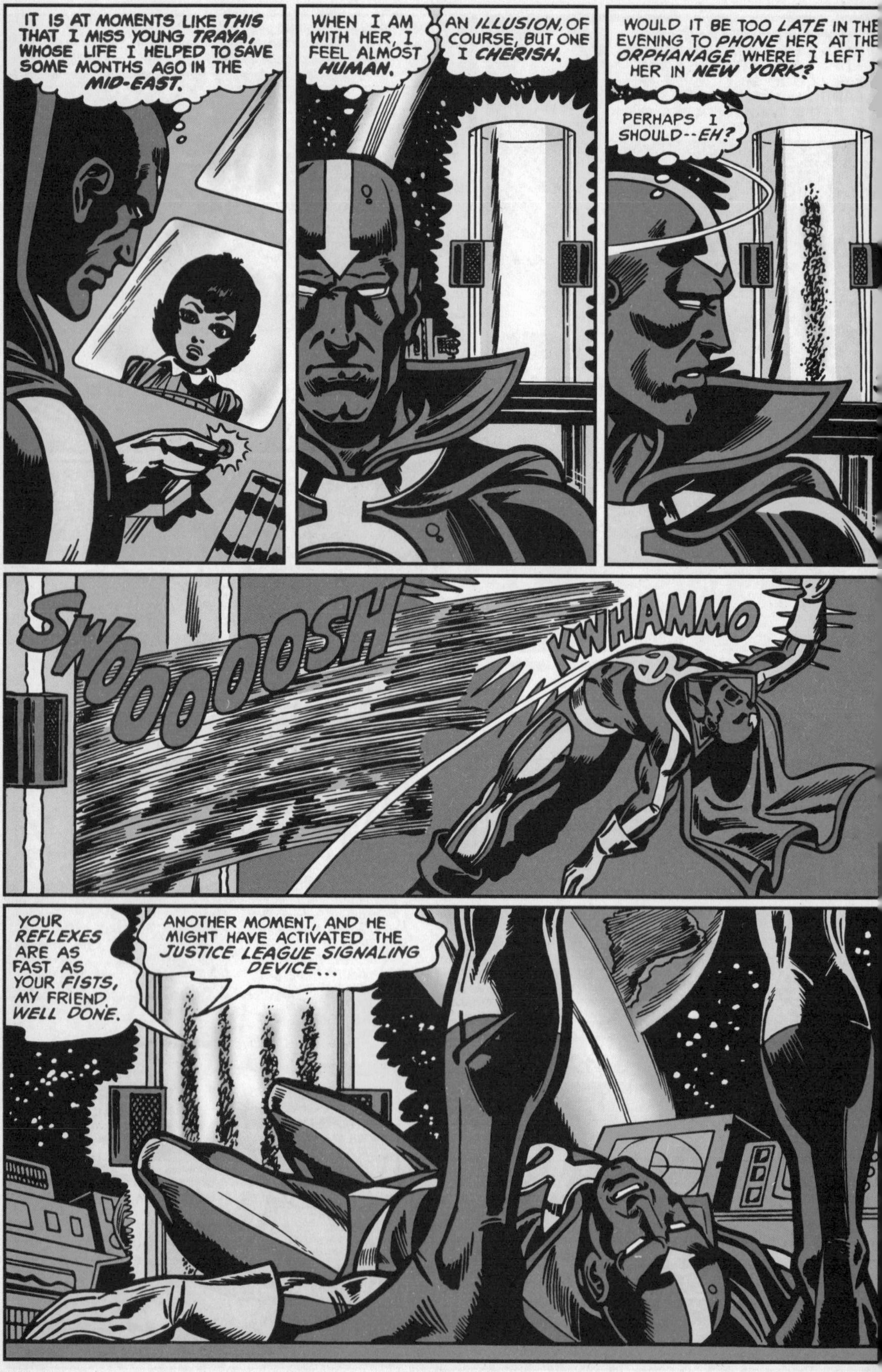
IT IS AT MOMENTS LIKE THIS THAT I MISS YOUNG TRAYA, WHOSE LIFE I HELPED TO SAVE SOME MONTHS AGO IN THE MID-EAST.
WHEN I AM WITH HER, I FEEL ALMOST HUMAN.
AN ILLUSION, OF COURSE, BUT ONE I CHERISH.
WOULD IT BE TOO LATE IN THE EVENING TO PHONE HER AT THE ORPHANAGE WHERE I LEFT HER IN NEW YORK?
PERHAPS I SHOULD--EH?
SWOOOOOOSH
KWHAMMO
YOUR REFLEXES ARE AS FAST AS YOUR FISTS, MY FRIEND. WELL DONE.
ANOTHER MOMENT, AND HE MIGHT HAVE ACTIVATED THE JUSTICE LEAGUE SIGNALING DEVICE...

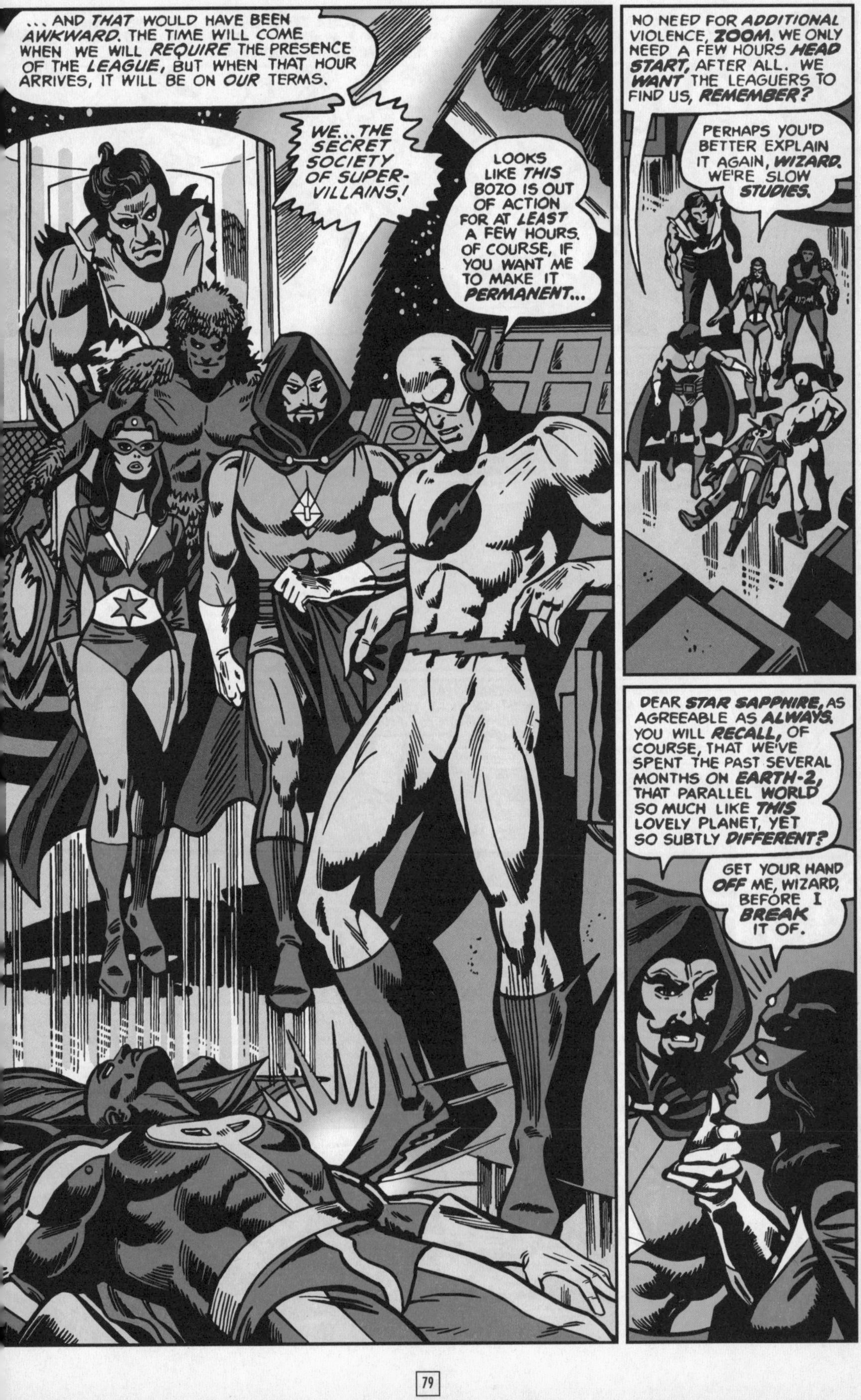

...AND THAT WOULD HAVE BEEN AWKWARD. THE TIME WILL COME WHEN WE WILL REQUIRE THE PRESENCE OF THE LEAGUE, BUT WHEN THAT HOUR ARRIVES, IT WILL BE ON OUR TERMS.
WE...THE SECRET SOCIETY OF SUPER-VILLAINS!
LOOKS LIKE THIS BOZO IS OUT OF ACTION FOR AT LEAST A FEW HOURS. OF COURSE, IF YOU WANT ME TO MAKE IT PERMANENT...
NO NEED FOR ADDITIONAL VIOLENCE, ZOOM. WE ONLY NEED A FEW HOURS HEAD START, AFTER ALL. WE WANT THE LEAGUERS TO FIND US, REMEMBER?
PERHAPS YOU'D BETTER EXPLAIN IT AGAIN, WIZARD. WE'RE SLOW STUDIES.
DEAR STAR SAPPHIRE, AS AGREEABLE AS ALWAYS. YOU WILL RECALL, OF COURSE, THAT WE'VE SPENT THE PAST SEVERAL MONTHS ON EARTH-2, THAT PARALLEL WORLD SO MUCH LIKE THIS LOVELY PLANET, YET SO SUBTLY DIFFERENT?
GET YOUR HAND OFF ME, WIZARD, BEFORE I BREAK IT OF.

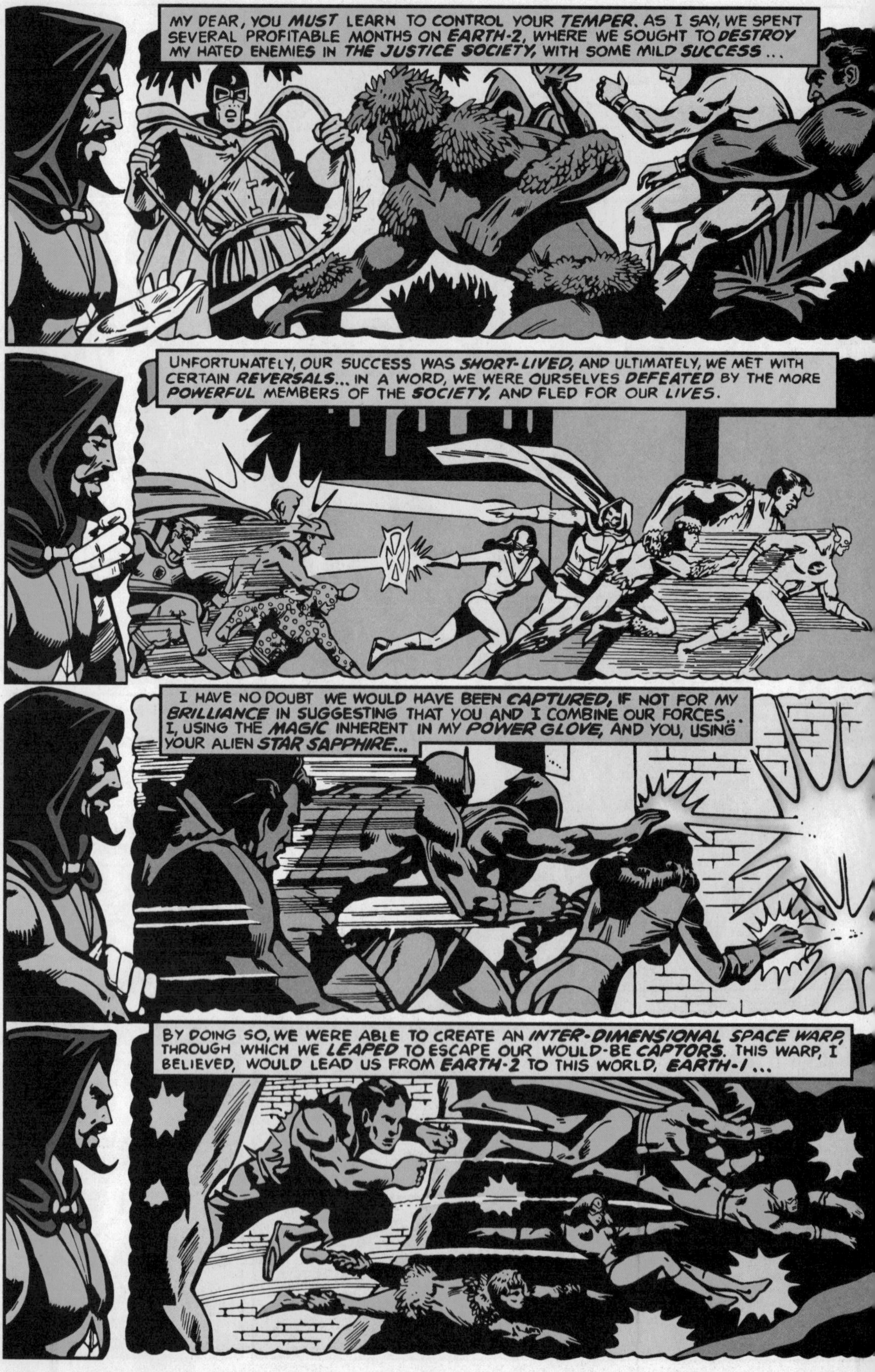
MY DEAR, YOU MUST LEARN TO CONTROL YOUR TEMPER. AS I SAY, WE SPENT SEVERAL PROFITABLE MONTHS ON EARTH-2, WHERE WE SOUGHT TO DESTROY MY HATED ENEMIES IN THE JUSTICE SOCIETY, WITH SOME MILD SUCCESS...
UNFORTUNATELY, OUR SUCCESS WAS SHORT-LIVED, AND ULTIMATELY, WE MET WITH CERTAIN REVERSALS... IN A WORD, WE WERE OURSELVES DEFEATED BY THE MORE POWERFUL MEMBERS OF THE SOCIETY, AND FLED FOR OUR LIVES.
I HAVE NO DOUBT WE WOULD HAVE BEEN CAPTURED, IF NOT FOR MY BRILLIANCE IN SUGGESTING THAT YOU AND I COMBINE OUR FORCES... I, USING THE MAGIC INHERENT IN MY POWER GLOVE, AND YOU, USING YOUR ALIEN STAR SAPPHIRE...
BY DOING SO, WE WERE ABLE TO CREATE AN INTER-DIMENSIONAL SPACE WARP, THROUGH WHICH WE LEAPED TO ESCAPE OUR WOULD-BE CAPTORS. THIS WARP, I BELIEVED, WOULD LEAD US FROM EARTH-2 TO THIS WORLD, EARTH-1...

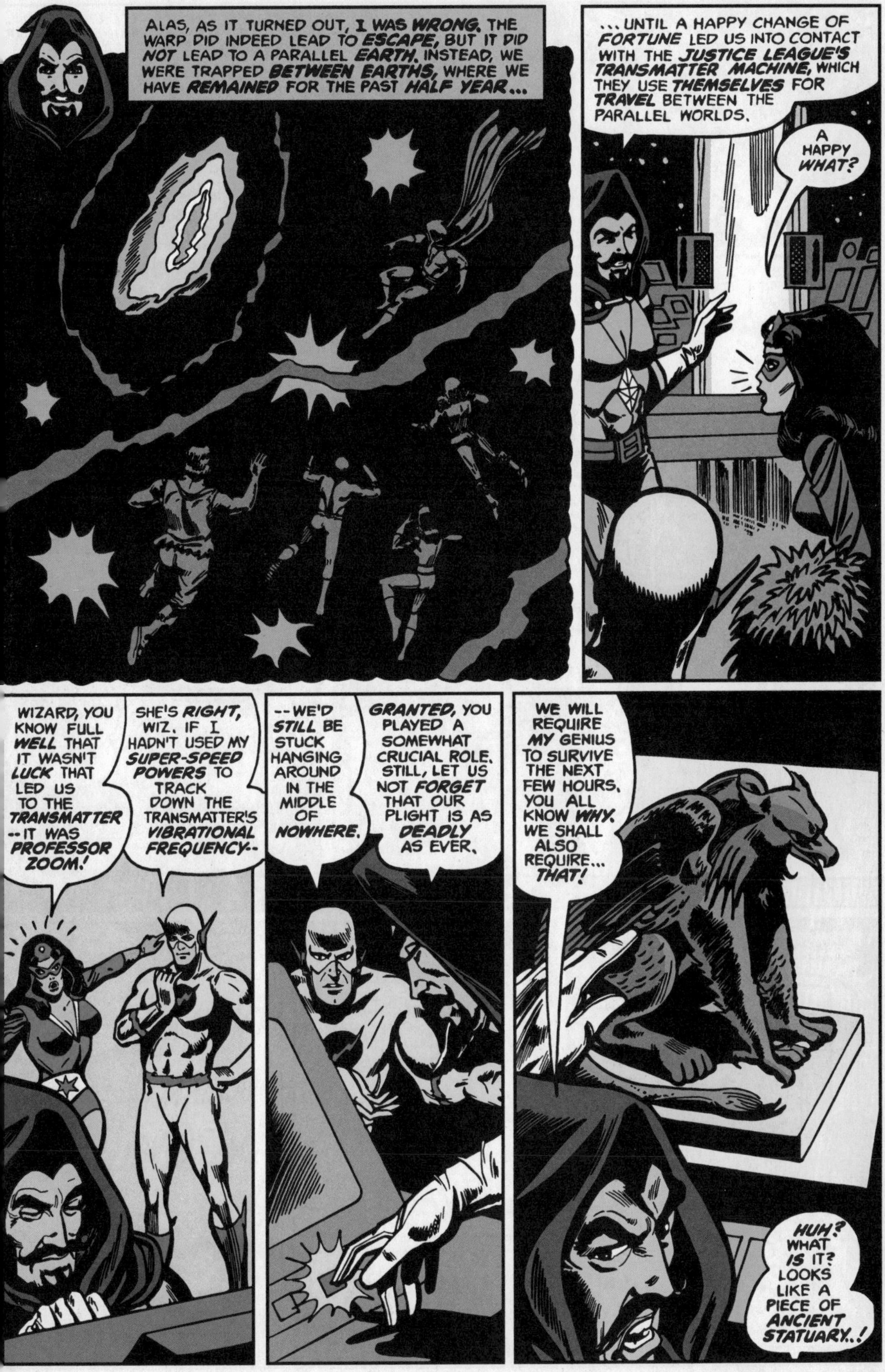

ALAS, AS IT TURNED OUT, I WAS WRONG. THE WARP DID INDEED LEAD TO ESCAPE, BUT IT DID NOT LEAD TO A PARALLEL EARTH. INSTEAD, WE WERE TRAPPED BETWEEN EARTHS, WHERE WE HAVE REMAINED FOR THE PAST HALF YEAR...
...UNTIL A HAPPY CHANGE OF FORTUNE LED US INTO CONTACT WITH THE JUSTICE LEAGUE'S TRANSMATTER MACHINE, WHICH THEY USE THEMSELVES FOR TRAVEL BETWEEN THE PARALLEL WORLDS.
A HAPPY WHAT?
WIZARD, YOU KNOW FULL WELL THAT IT WASN'T LUCK THAT LED US TO THE TRANSMATTER --IT WAS PROFESSOR ZOOM!
SHE'S RIGHT, WIZ. IF I HADN'T USED MY SUPER-SPEED POWERS TO TRACK DOWN THE TRANSMATTER'S VIBRATIONAL FREQUENCY--
--WE'D STILL BE STUCK HANGING AROUND IN THE MIDDLE OF NOWHERE.
GRANTED, YOU PLAYED A SOMEWHAT CRUCIAL ROLE. STILL, LET US NOT FORGET THAT OUR PLIGHT IS AS DEADLY AS EVER.
WE WILL REQUIRE MY GENIUS TO SURVIVE THE NEXT FEW HOURS. YOU ALL KNOW WHY. WE SHALL ALSO REQUIRE... THAT!
HUH? WHAT IS IT? LOOKS LIKE A PIECE OF ANCIENT STATUARY..!

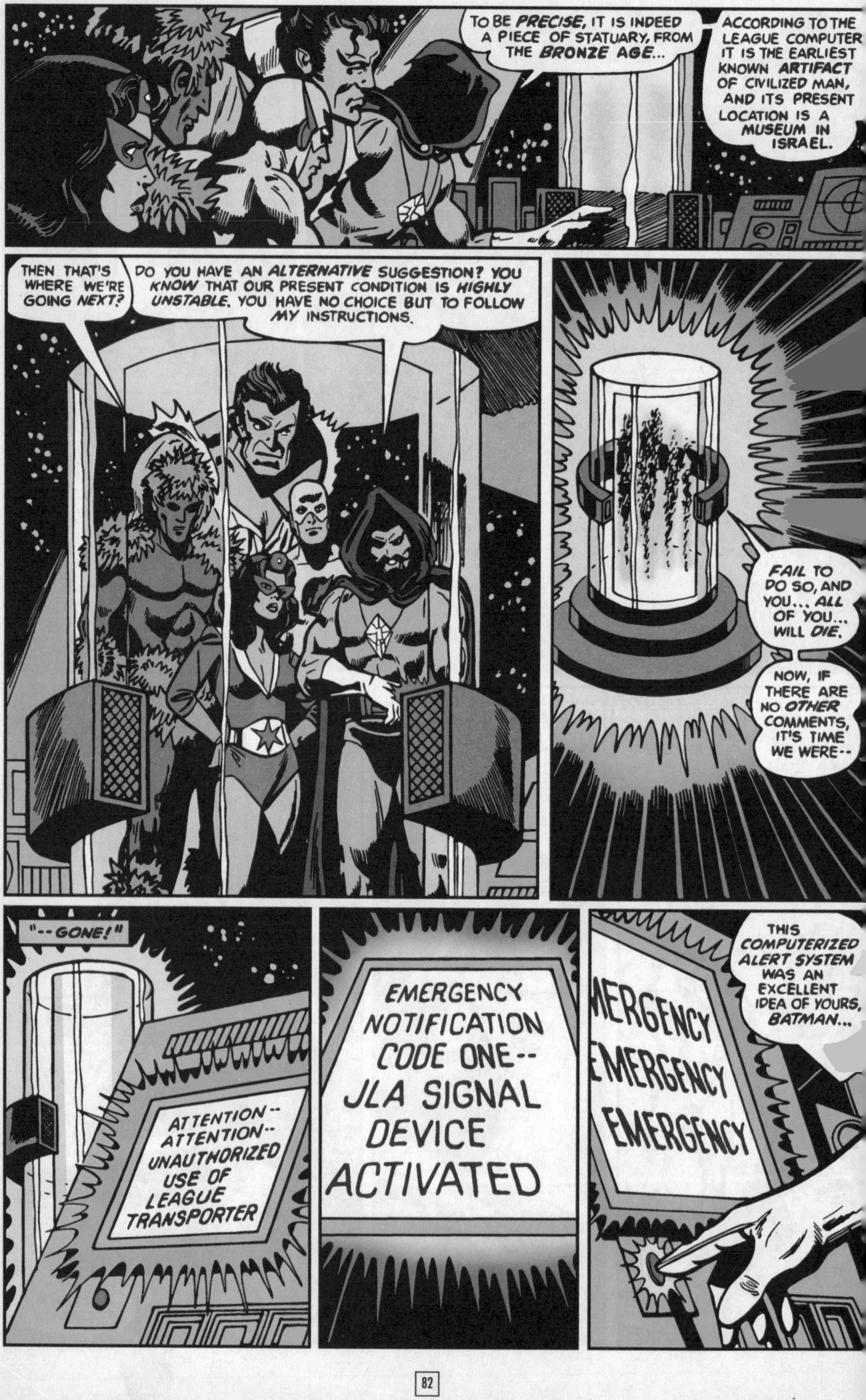

TO BE PRECISE, IT IS INDEED A PIECE OF STATUARY, FROM THE BRONZE AGE...
ACCORDING TO THE LEAGUE COMPUTER IT IS THE EARLIEST KNOWN ARTIFACT OF CIVILIZED MAN, AND ITS PRESENT LOCATION IS A MUSEUM IN ISRAEL.
THEN THAT'S WHERE WE'RE GOING NEXT?
DO YOU HAVE AN ALTERNATIVE SUGGESTION? YOU KNOW THAT OUR PRESENT CONDITION IS HIGHLY UNSTABLE. YOU HAVE NO CHOICE BUT TO FOLLOW MY INSTRUCTIONS.
FAIL TO DO SO, AND YOU... ALL OF YOU... WILL DIE.
NOW, IF THERE ARE NO OTHER COMMENTS, IT'S TIME WE WERE--
"--GONE!"
ATTENTION-- ATTENTION-- UNAUTHORIZED USE OF LEAGUE TRANSPORTER
EMERGENCY NOTIFICATION CODE ONE-- JLA SIGNAL DEVICE ACTIVATED
MERGENCY
EMERGENCY
EMERGENCY
THIS COMPUTERIZED ALERT SYSTEM WAS AN EXCELLENT IDEA OF YOURS, BATMAN...

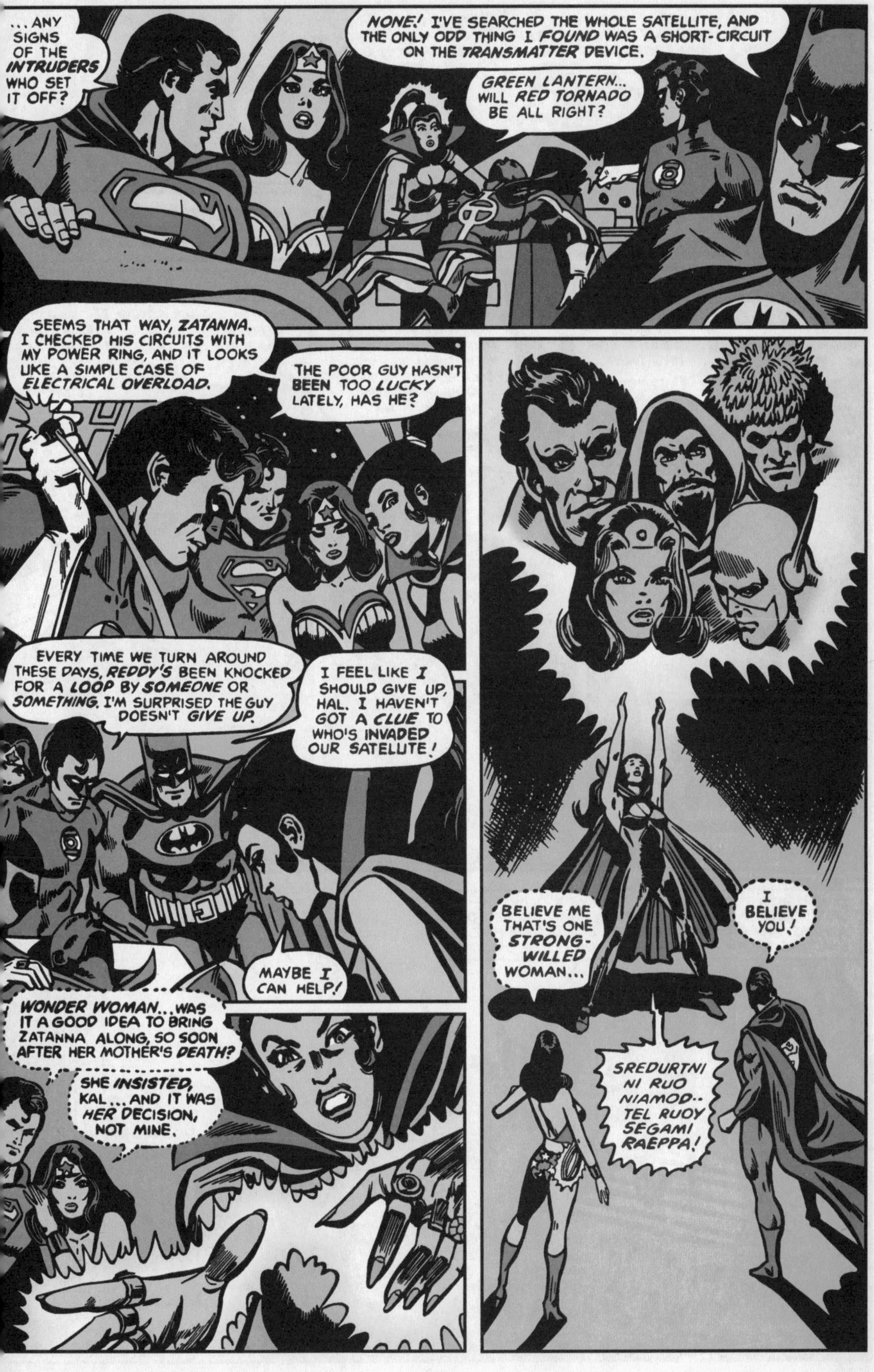

...ANY SIGNS OF THE INTRUDERS WHO SET IT OFF?
NONE! I'VE SEARCHED THE WHOLE SATELLITE, AND THE ONLY ODD THING I FOUND WAS A SHORT-CIRCUIT ON THE TRANSMATTER DEVICE.
GREEN LANTERN... WILL RED TORNADO BE ALL RIGHT?
SEEMS THAT WAY, ZATANNA. I CHECKED HIS CIRCUITS WITH MY POWER RING, AND IT LOOKS LIKE A SIMPLE CASE OF ELECTRICAL OVERLOAD.
THE POOR GUY HASN'T BEEN TOO LUCKY LATELY, HAS HE?
EVERY TIME WE TURN AROUND THESE DAYS, REDDY'S BEEN KNOCKED FOR A LOOP BY SOMEONE OR SOMETHING. I'M SURPRISED THE GUY DOESN'T GIVE UP.
I FEEL LIKE I SHOULD GIVE UP, HAL. I HAVEN'T GOT A CLUE TO WHO'S INVADED OUR SATELLITE!
MAYBE I CAN HELP!
WONDER WOMAN...WAS IT A GOOD IDEA TO BRING ZATANNA ALONG, SO SOON AFTER HER MOTHER'S DEATH?
SHE INSISTED, KAL... AND IT WAS HER DECISION, NOT MINE.
BELIEVE ME THAT'S ONE STRONG-WILLED WOMAN...
I BELIEVE YOU!
SREDURTNI NI RUO NIAMOD.. TEL RUOY SEGAMI RAEPPA!

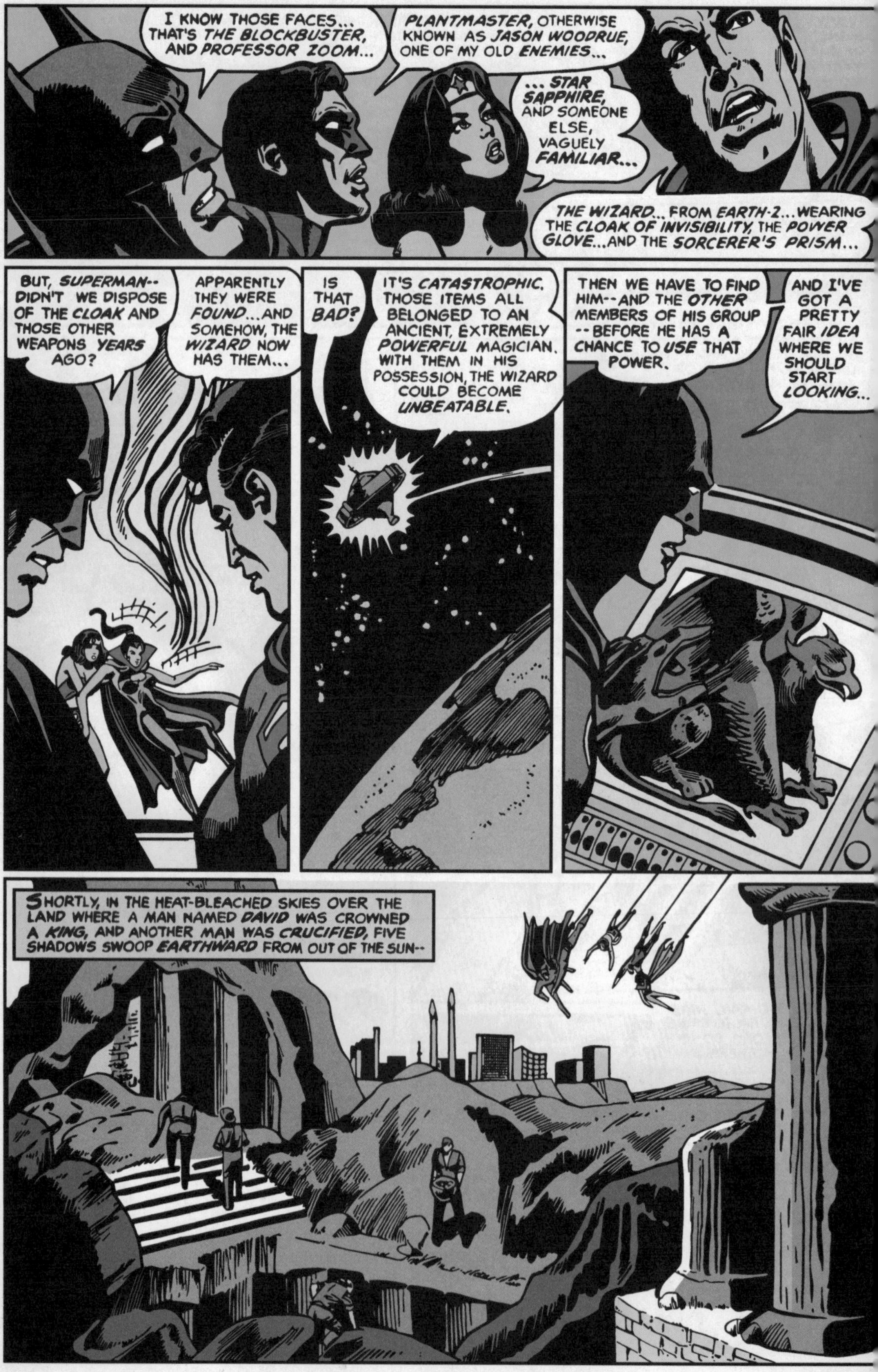
I KNOW THOSE FACES... THAT'S THE BLOCKBUSTER, AND PROFESSOR ZOOM...
PLANTMASTER, OTHERWISE KNOWN AS JASON WOODRUE, ONE OF MY OLD ENEMIES...
... STAR SAPPHIRE, AND SOMEONE ELSE, VAGUELY FAMILIAR...
THE WIZARD... FROM EARTH-2... WEARING THE CLOAK OF INVISIBILITY, THE POWER GLOVE... AND THE SORCERER'S PRISM...
BUT, SUPERMAN-- DIDN'T WE DISPOSE OF THE CLOAK AND THOSE OTHER WEAPONS YEARS AGO?
APPARENTLY THEY WERE FOUND... AND SOMEHOW, THE WIZARD NOW HAS THEM...
IS THAT BAD?
IT'S CATASTROPHIC. THOSE ITEMS ALL BELONGED TO AN ANCIENT, EXTREMELY POWERFUL MAGICIAN. WITH THEM IN HIS POSSESSION, THE WIZARD COULD BECOME UNBEATABLE.
THEN WE HAVE TO FIND HIM-- AND THE OTHER MEMBERS OF HIS GROUP -- BEFORE HE HAS A CHANCE TO USE THAT POWER.
AND I'VE GOT A PRETTY FAIR IDEA WHERE WE SHOULD START LOOKING...
SHORTLY, IN THE HEAT-BLEACHED SKIES OVER THE LAND WHERE A MAN NAMED DAVID WAS CROWNED A KING, AND ANOTHER MAN WAS CRUCIFIED, FIVE SHADOWS SWOOP EARTHWARD FROM OUT OF THE SUN--

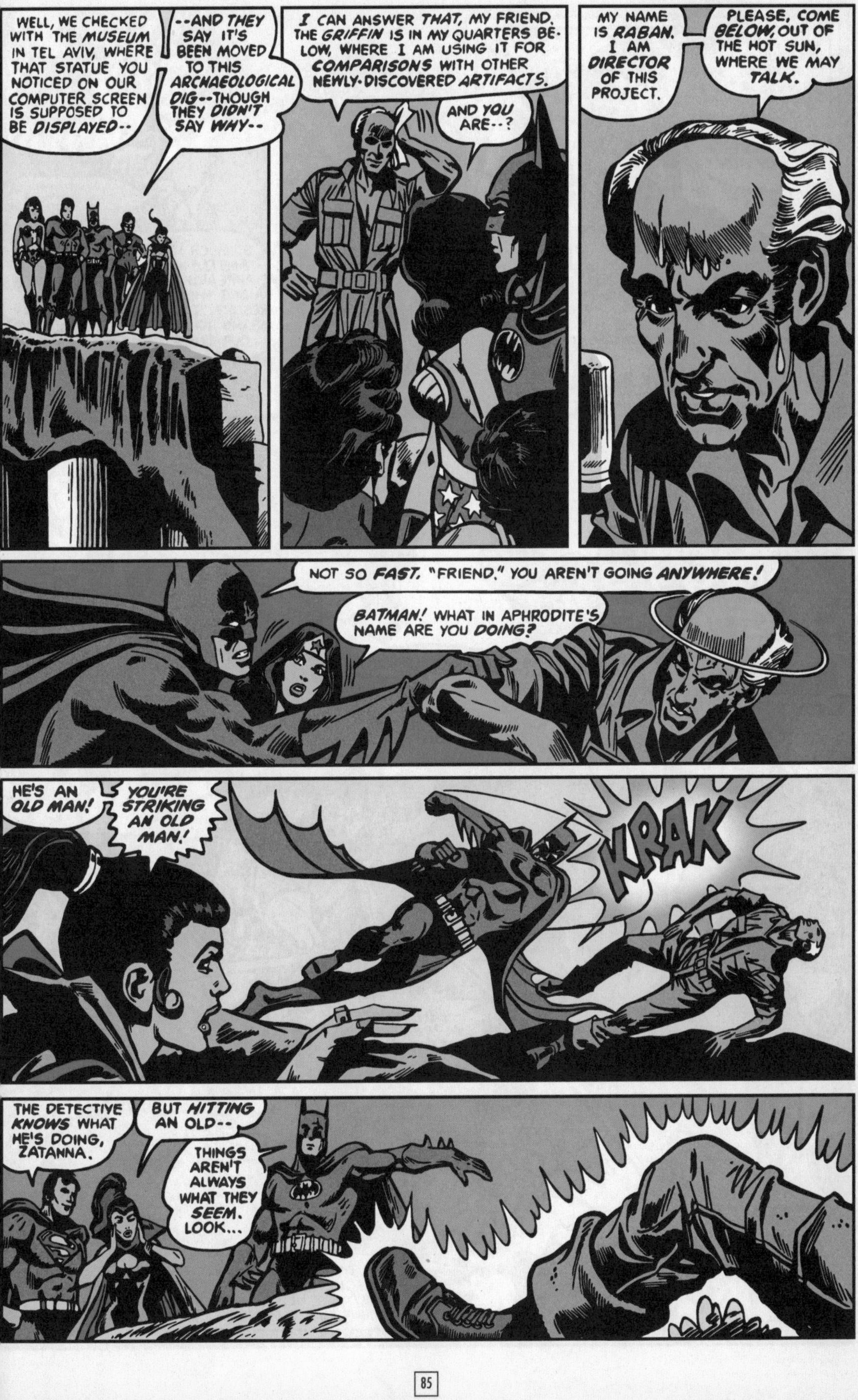
WELL, WE CHECKED WITH THE MUSEUM IN TEL AVIV, WHERE THAT STATUE YOU NOTICED ON OUR COMPUTER SCREEN IS SUPPOSED TO BE DISPLAYED--
--AND THEY SAY IT'S BEEN MOVED TO THIS ARCHAEOLOGICAL DIG--THOUGH THEY DIDN'T SAY WHY--
I CAN ANSWER THAT, MY FRIEND. THE GRIFFIN IS IN MY QUARTERS BELOW, WHERE I AM USING IT FOR COMPARISONS WITH OTHER NEWLY-DISCOVERED ARTIFACTS.
AND YOU ARE--?
MY NAME IS RABAN. I AM DIRECTOR OF THIS PROJECT.
PLEASE, COME BELOW, OUT OF THE HOT SUN, WHERE WE MAY TALK.
NOT SO FAST, "FRIEND." YOU AREN'T GOING ANYWHERE!
BATMAN! WHAT IN APHRODITE'S NAME ARE YOU DOING?
HE'S AN OLD MAN!
YOU'RE STRIKING AN OLD MAN!
KRAK
THE DETECTIVE KNOWS WHAT HE'S DOING, ZATANNA.
BUT HITTING AN OLD--
THINGS AREN'T ALWAYS WHAT THEY SEEM. LOOK...

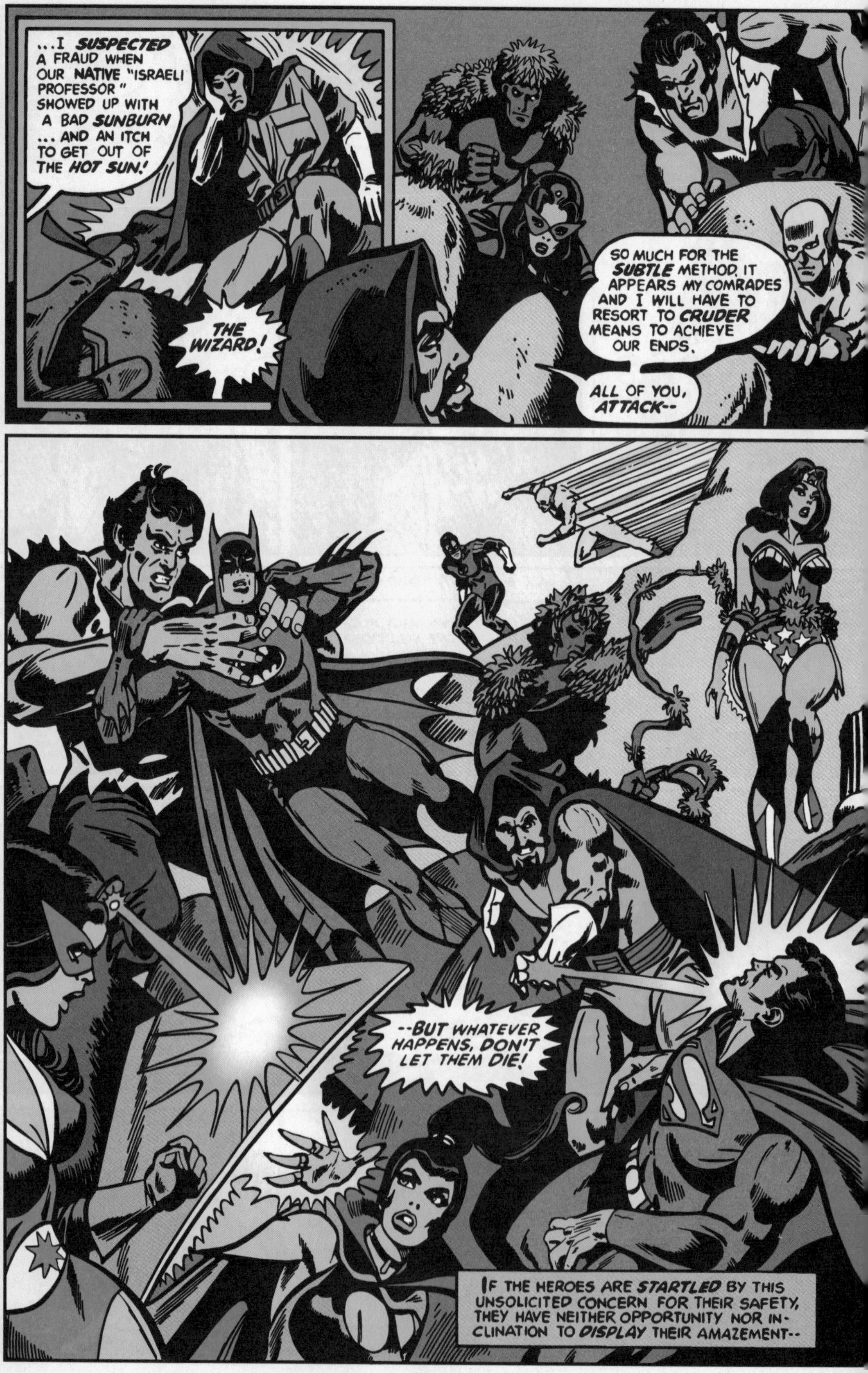
...I SUSPECTED A FRAUD WHEN OUR NATIVE "ISRAELI PROFESSOR" SHOWED UP WITH A BAD SUNBURN ... AND AN ITCH TO GET OUT OF THE HOT SUN!
THE WIZARD!
SO MUCH FOR THE SUBTLE METHOD, IT APPEARS MY COMRADES AND I WILL HAVE TO RESORT TO CRUDER MEANS TO ACHIEVE OUR ENDS.
ALL OF YOU, ATTACK--
--BUT WHATEVER HAPPENS, DON'T LET THEM DIE!
IF THE HEROES ARE STARTLED BY THIS UNSOLICITED CONCERN FOR THEIR SAFETY, THEY HAVE NEITHER OPPORTUNITY NOR IN-CLINATION TO DISPLAY THEIR AMAZEMENT--

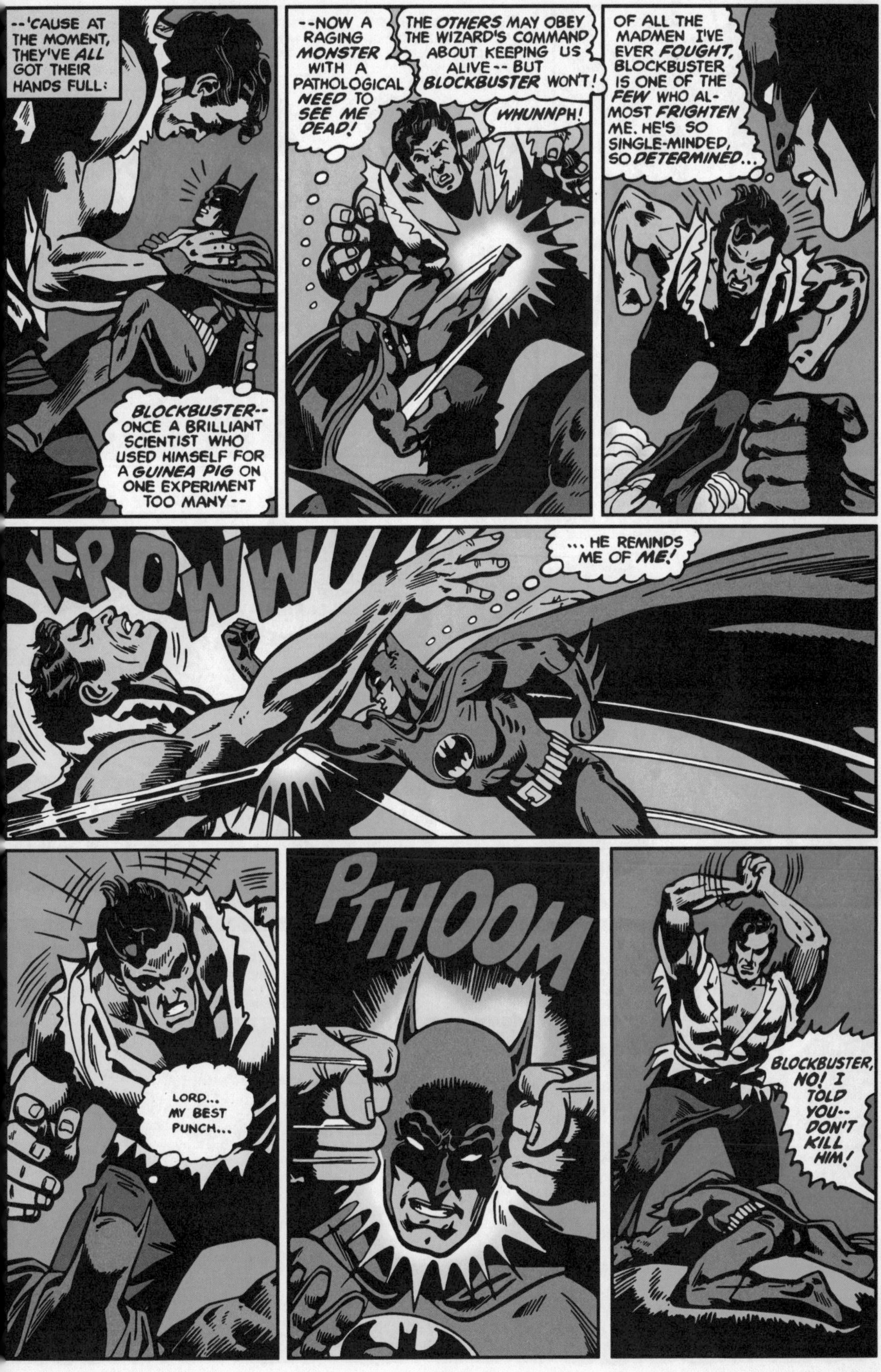
--'CAUSE AT THE MOMENT, THEY'VE ALL GOT THEIR HANDS FULL:
BLOCKBUSTER-- ONCE A BRILLIANT SCIENTIST WHO USED HIMSELF FOR A GUINEA PIG ON ONE EXPERIMENT TOO MANY--
--NOW A RAGING MONSTER WITH A PATHOLOGICAL NEED TO SEE ME DEAD!
THE OTHERS MAY OBEY THE WIZARD'S COMMAND ABOUT KEEPING US ALIVE-- BUT BLOCKBUSTER WON'T!
WHUNNPH!
OF ALL THE MADMEN I'VE EVER FOUGHT, BLOCKBUSTER IS ONE OF THE FEW WHO ALMOST FRIGHTEN ME. HE'S SO SINGLE-MINDED, SO DETERMINED...
KPOWW
...HE REMINDS ME OF ME!
LORD... MY BEST PUNCH...
PTHOOM
BLOCKBUSTER, NO! I TOLD YOU-- DON'T KILL HIM!

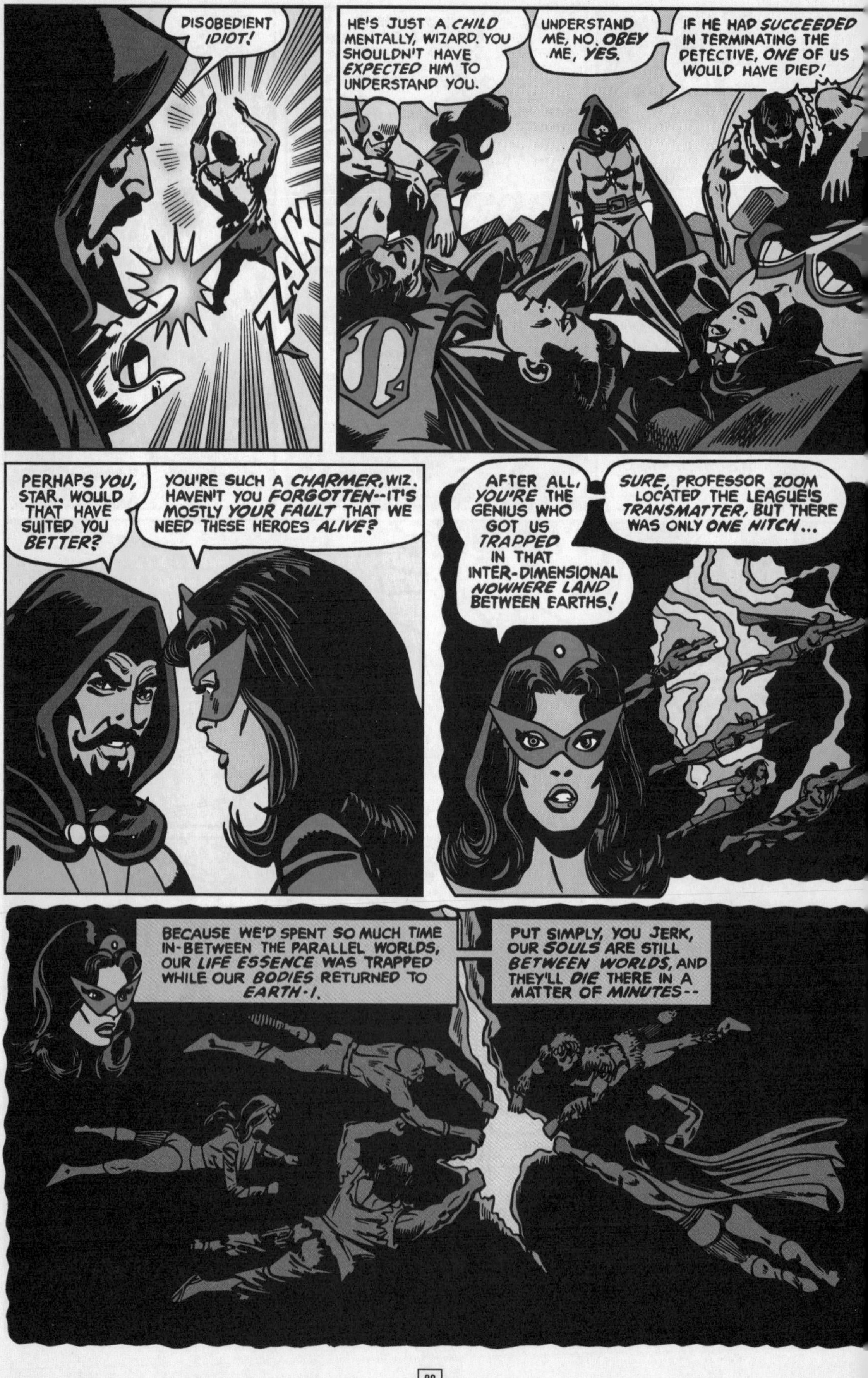
DISOBEDIENT IDIOT!
ZAK
HE'S JUST A CHILD MENTALLY, WIZARD. YOU SHOULDN'T HAVE EXPECTED HIM TO UNDERSTAND YOU.
UNDERSTAND ME, NO. OBEY ME, YES.
IF HE HAD SUCCEEDED IN TERMINATING THE DETECTIVE, ONE OF US WOULD HAVE DIED!
PERHAPS YOU, STAR. WOULD THAT HAVE SUITED YOU BETTER?
YOU'RE SUCH A CHARMER, WIZ. HAVEN'T YOU FORGOTTEN--IT'S MOSTLY YOUR FAULT THAT WE NEED THESE HEROES ALIVE?
AFTER ALL, YOU'RE THE GENIUS WHO GOT US TRAPPED IN THAT INTER-DIMENSIONAL NOWHERE LAND BETWEEN EARTHS!
SURE, PROFESSOR ZOOM LOCATED THE LEAGUE'S TRANSMATTER, BUT THERE WAS ONLY ONE HITCH...
BECAUSE WE'D SPENT SO MUCH TIME IN-BETWEEN THE PARALLEL WORLDS, OUR LIFE ESSENCE WAS TRAPPED WHILE OUR BODIES RETURNED TO EARTH-1.
PUT SIMPLY, YOU JERK, OUR SOULS ARE STILL BETWEEN WORLDS, AND THEY'LL DIE THERE IN A MATTER OF MINUTES--

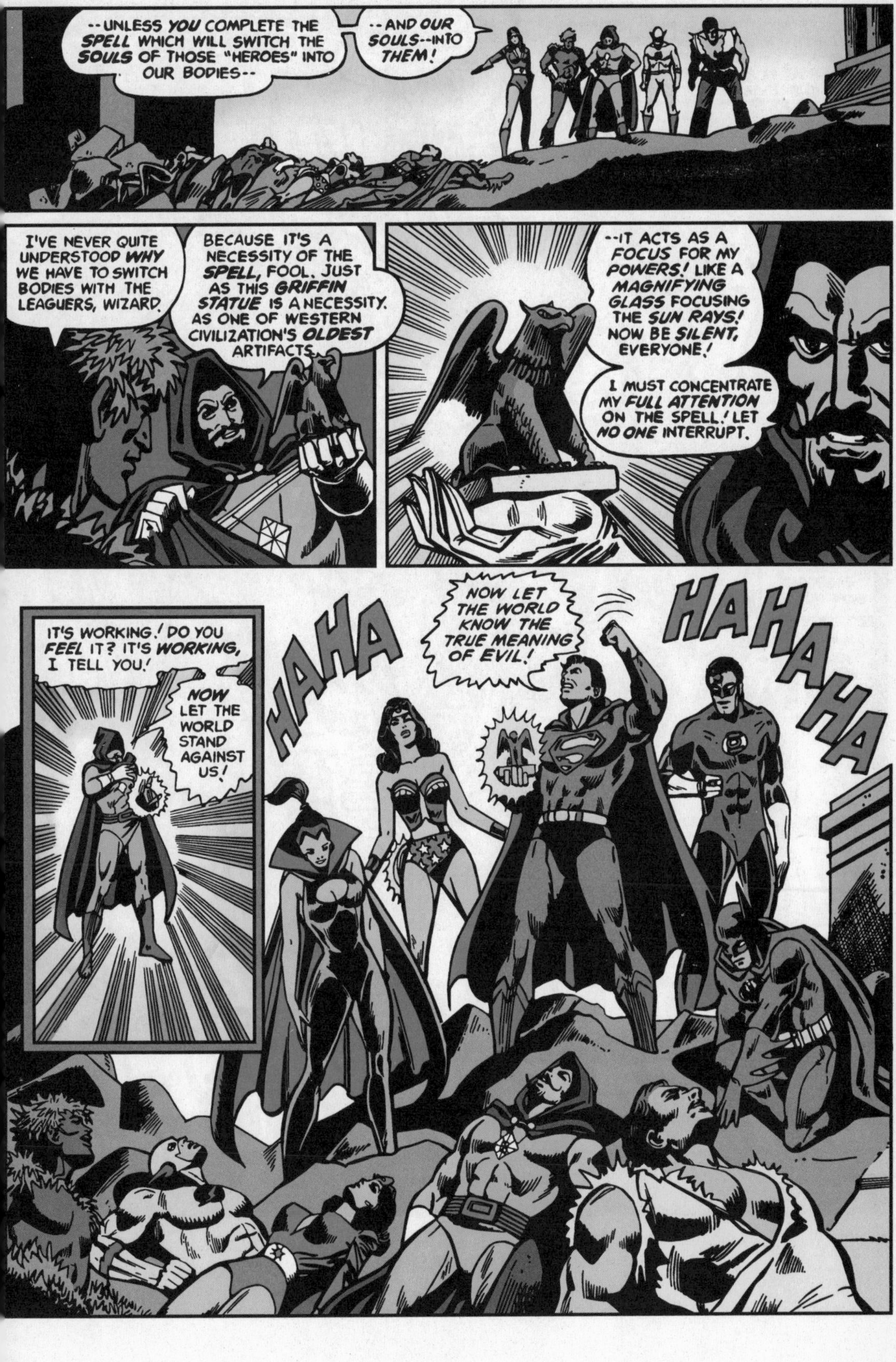
--UNLESS YOU COMPLETE THE SPELL WHICH WILL SWITCH THE SOULS OF THOSE "HEROES" INTO OUR BODIES--
--AND OUR SOULS--INTO THEM!
I'VE NEVER QUITE UNDERSTOOD WHY WE HAVE TO SWITCH BODIES WITH THE LEAGUERS, WIZARD.
BECAUSE IT'S A NECESSITY OF THE SPELL, FOOL. JUST AS THIS GRIFFIN STATUE IS A NECESSITY. AS ONE OF WESTERN CIVILIZATION'S OLDEST ARTIFACTS,
--IT ACTS AS A FOCUS FOR MY POWERS! LIKE A MAGNIFYING GLASS FOCUSING THE SUN RAYS! NOW BE SILENT, EVERYONE!
I MUST CONCENTRATE MY FULL ATTENTION ON THE SPELL! LET NO ONE INTERRUPT.
IT'S WORKING! DO YOU FEEL IT? IT'S WORKING, I TELL YOU!
NOW LET THE WORLD STAND AGAINST US!
HAHA
NOW LET THE WORLD KNOW THE TRUE MEANING OF EVIL!
HAHAHAHA

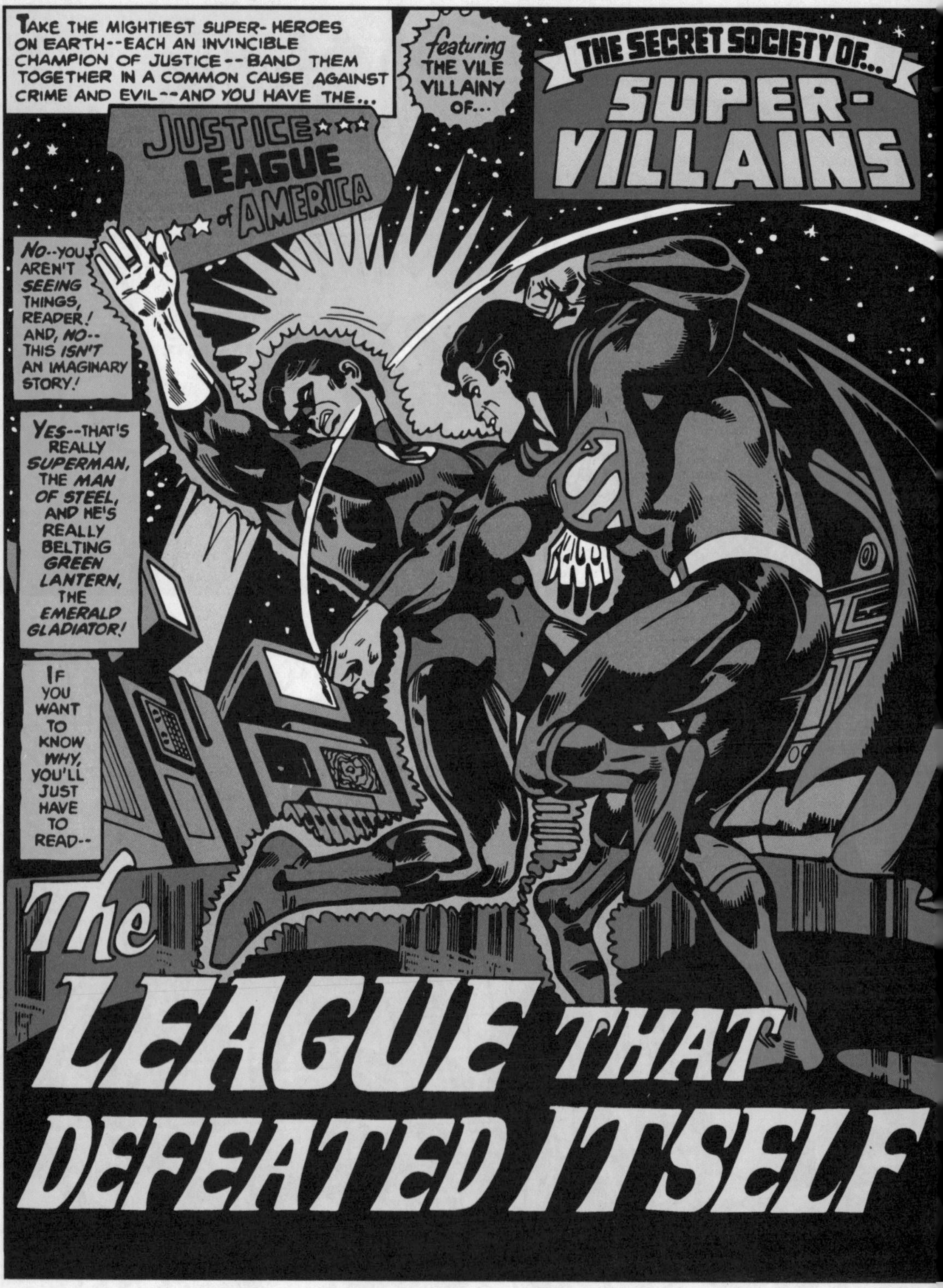

TAKE THE MIGHTIEST SUPER-HEROES ON EARTH--EACH AN INVINCIBLE CHAMPION OF JUSTICE--BAND THEM TOGETHER IN A COMMON CAUSE AGAINST CRIME AND EVIL--AND YOU HAVE THE...
JUSTICE LEAGUE of AMERICA
featuring THE VILE VILLAINY OF...
THE SECRET SOCIETY OF... SUPER-VILLAINS
NO--YOU AREN'T SEEING THINGS, READER! AND, NO--THIS ISN'T AN IMAGINARY STORY!
YES--THAT'S REALLY SUPERMAN, THE MAN OF STEEL, AND HE'S REALLY BELTING GREEN LANTERN, THE EMERALD GLADIATOR!
IF YOU WANT TO KNOW WHY, YOU'LL JUST HAVE TO READ--
The LEAGUE THAT DEFEATED ITSELF

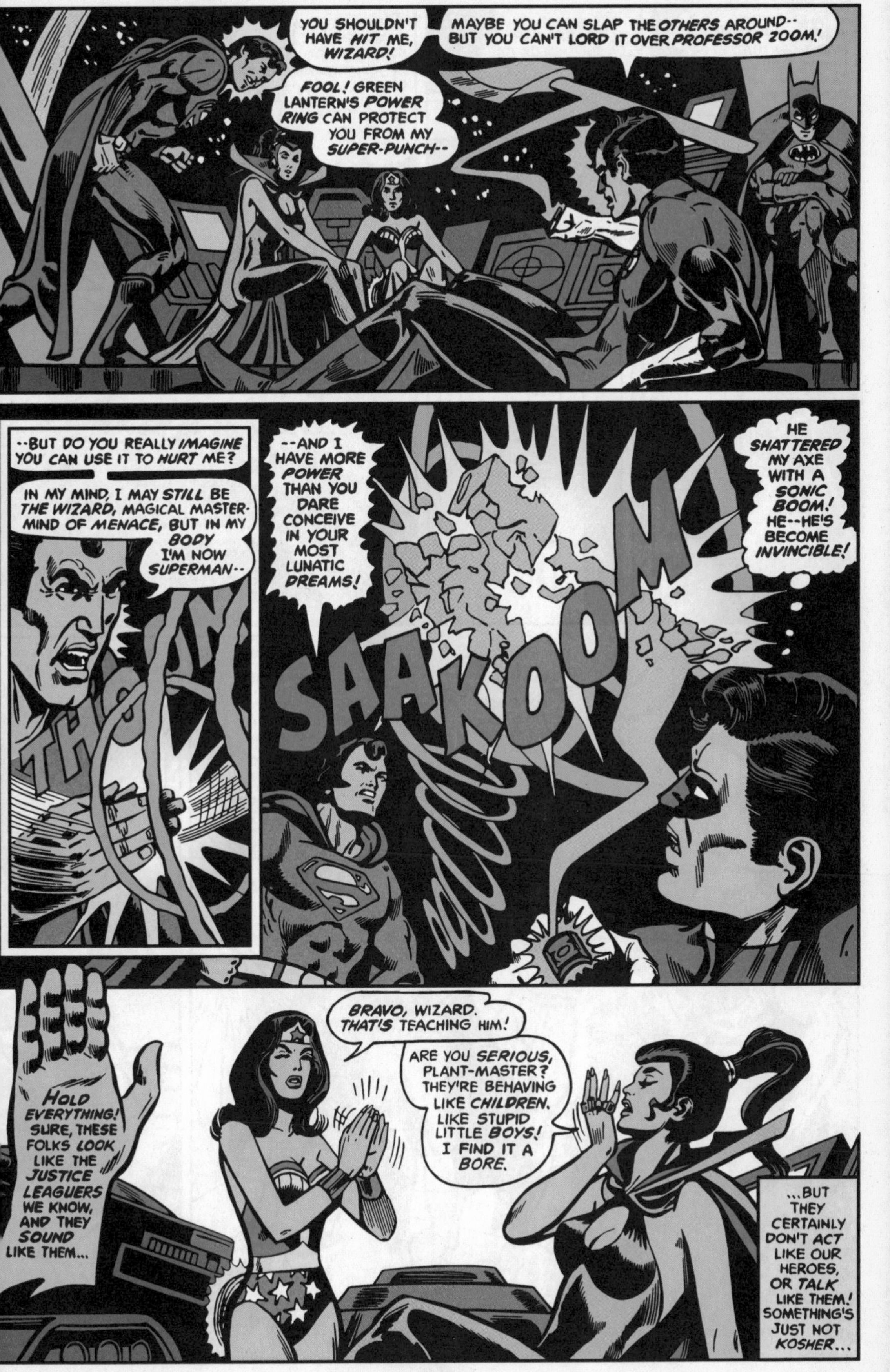

YOU SHOULDN'T HAVE HIT ME, WIZARD!
MAYBE YOU CAN SLAP THE OTHERS AROUND-- BUT YOU CAN'T LORD IT OVER PROFESSOR ZOOM!
FOOL! GREEN LANTERN'S POWER RING CAN PROTECT YOU FROM MY SUPER-PUNCH--
--BUT DO YOU REALLY IMAGINE YOU CAN USE IT TO HURT ME?
IN MY MIND, I MAY STILL BE THE WIZARD, MAGICAL MASTER-MIND OF MENACE, BUT IN MY BODY I'M NOW SUPERMAN--
--AND I HAVE MORE POWER THAN YOU DARE CONCEIVE IN YOUR MOST LUNATIC DREAMS!
SAAKOOM
HE SHATTERED MY AXE WITH A SONIC BOOM! HE--HE'S BECOME INVINCIBLE!
HOLD EVERYTHING! SURE, THESE FOLKS LOOK LIKE THE JUSTICE LEAGUERS WE KNOW, AND THEY SOUND LIKE THEM...
BRAVO, WIZARD. THAT'S TEACHING HIM!
ARE YOU SERIOUS, PLANT-MASTER? THEY'RE BEHAVING LIKE CHILDREN. LIKE STUPID LITTLE BOYS! I FIND IT A BORE.
...BUT THEY CERTAINLY DON'T ACT LIKE OUR HEROES, OR TALK LIKE THEM! SOMETHING'S JUST NOT KOSHER...

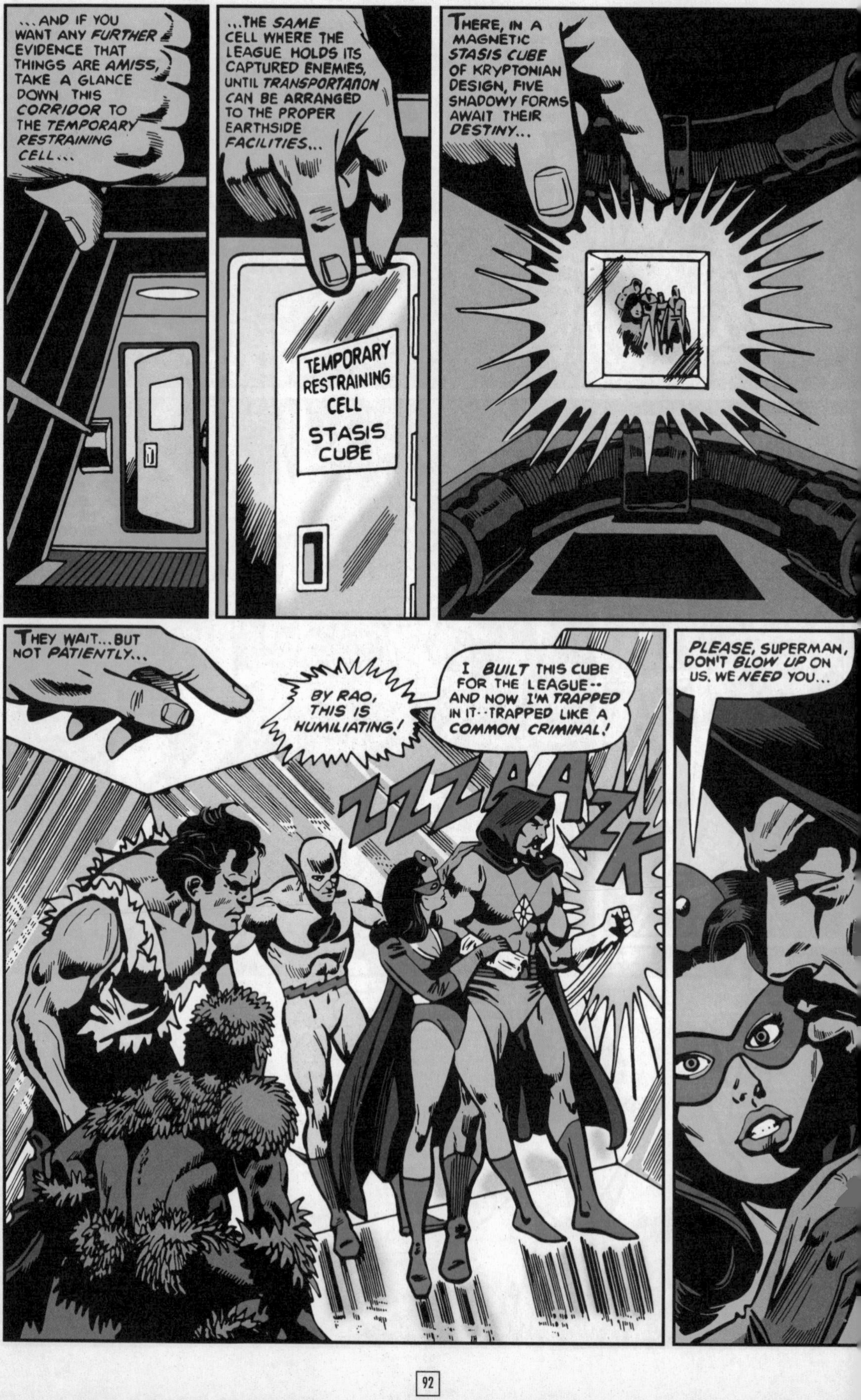
...AND IF YOU WANT ANY FURTHER EVIDENCE THAT THINGS ARE AMISS, TAKE A GLANCE DOWN THIS CORRIDOR TO THE TEMPORARY RESTRAINING CELL...
...THE SAME CELL WHERE THE LEAGUE HOLDS ITS CAPTURED ENEMIES, UNTIL TRANSPORTATION CAN BE ARRANGED TO THE PROPER EARTHSIDE FACILITIES...
TEMPORARY RESTRAINING CELL
STASIS CUBE
THERE, IN A MAGNETIC STASIS CUBE OF KRYPTONIAN DESIGN, FIVE SHADOWY FORMS AWAIT THEIR DESTINY...
THEY WAIT...BUT NOT PATIENTLY...
BY RAO, THIS IS HUMILIATING!
I BUILT THIS CUBE FOR THE LEAGUE-- AND NOW I'M TRAPPED IN IT--TRAPPED LIKE A COMMON CRIMINAL!
ZZZAAAZK
PLEASE, SUPERMAN, DON'T BLOW UP ON US. WE NEED YOU...

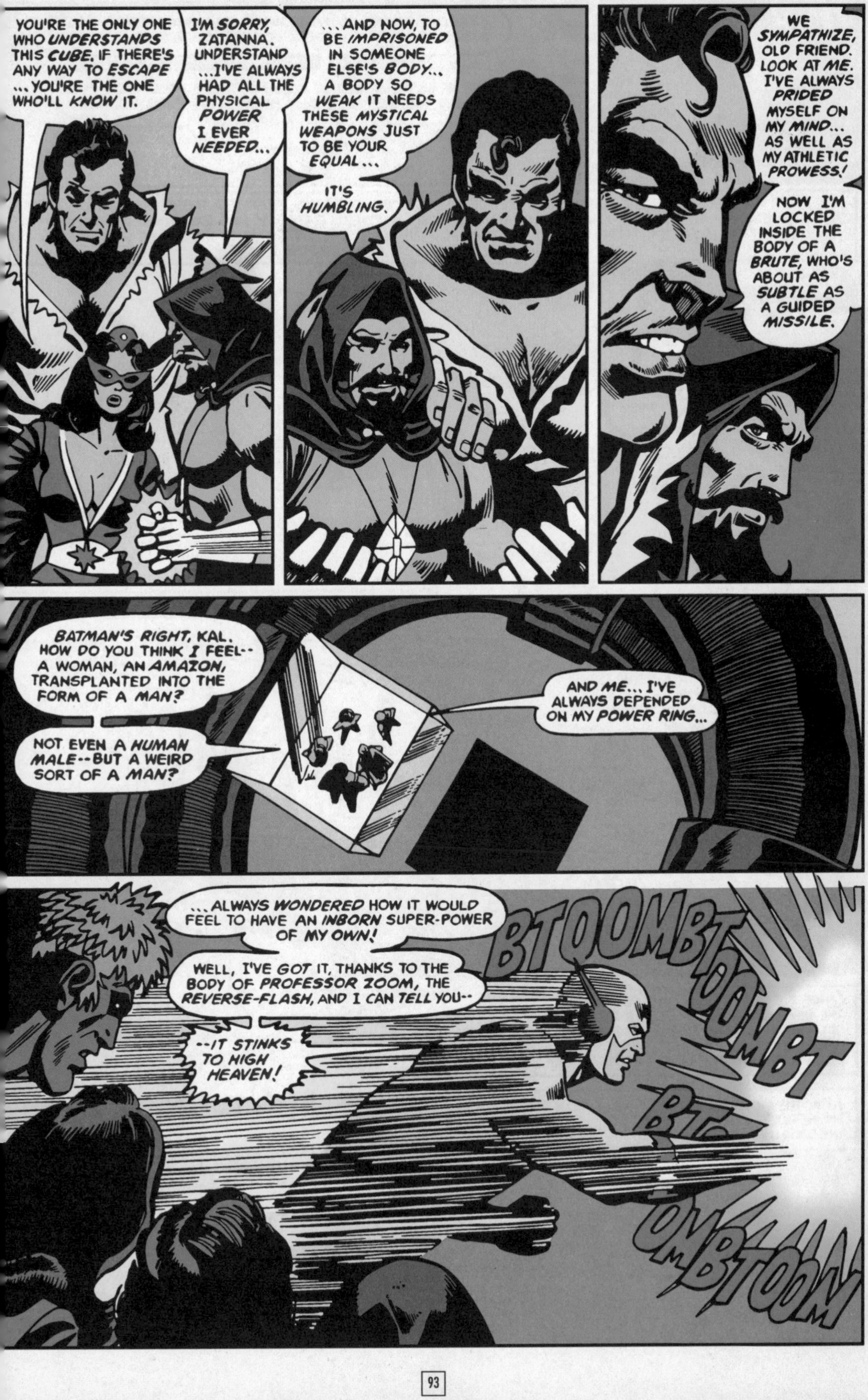
YOU'RE THE ONLY ONE WHO UNDERSTANDS THIS CUBE. IF THERE'S ANY WAY TO ESCAPE ...YOU'RE THE ONE WHO'LL KNOW IT.
I'M SORRY, ZATANNA. UNDERSTAND ...I'VE ALWAYS HAD ALL THE PHYSICAL POWER I EVER NEEDED...
...AND NOW, TO BE IMPRISONED IN SOMEONE ELSE'S BODY... A BODY SO WEAK IT NEEDS THESE MYSTICAL WEAPONS JUST TO BE YOUR EQUAL...
IT'S HUMBLING.
WE SYMPATHIZE, OLD FRIEND. LOOK AT ME. I'VE ALWAYS PRIDED MYSELF ON MY MIND... AS WELL AS MY ATHLETIC PROWESS!
NOW I'M LOCKED INSIDE THE BODY OF A BRUTE, WHO'S ABOUT AS SUBTLE AS A GUIDED MISSILE.
BATMAN'S RIGHT, KAL. HOW DO YOU THINK I FEEL-- A WOMAN, AN AMAZON, TRANSPLANTED INTO THE FORM OF A MAN?
NOT EVEN A HUMAN MALE--BUT A WEIRD SORT OF A MAN?
AND ME... I'VE ALWAYS DEPENDED ON MY POWER RING...
...ALWAYS WONDERED HOW IT WOULD FEEL TO HAVE AN INBORN SUPER-POWER OF MY OWN!
WELL, I'VE GOT IT, THANKS TO THE BODY OF PROFESSOR ZOOM, THE REVERSE-FLASH, AND I CAN TELL YOU--
--IT STINKS TO HIGH HEAVEN!
BTOOMBTOOMBT
BT
OOMBTOOM

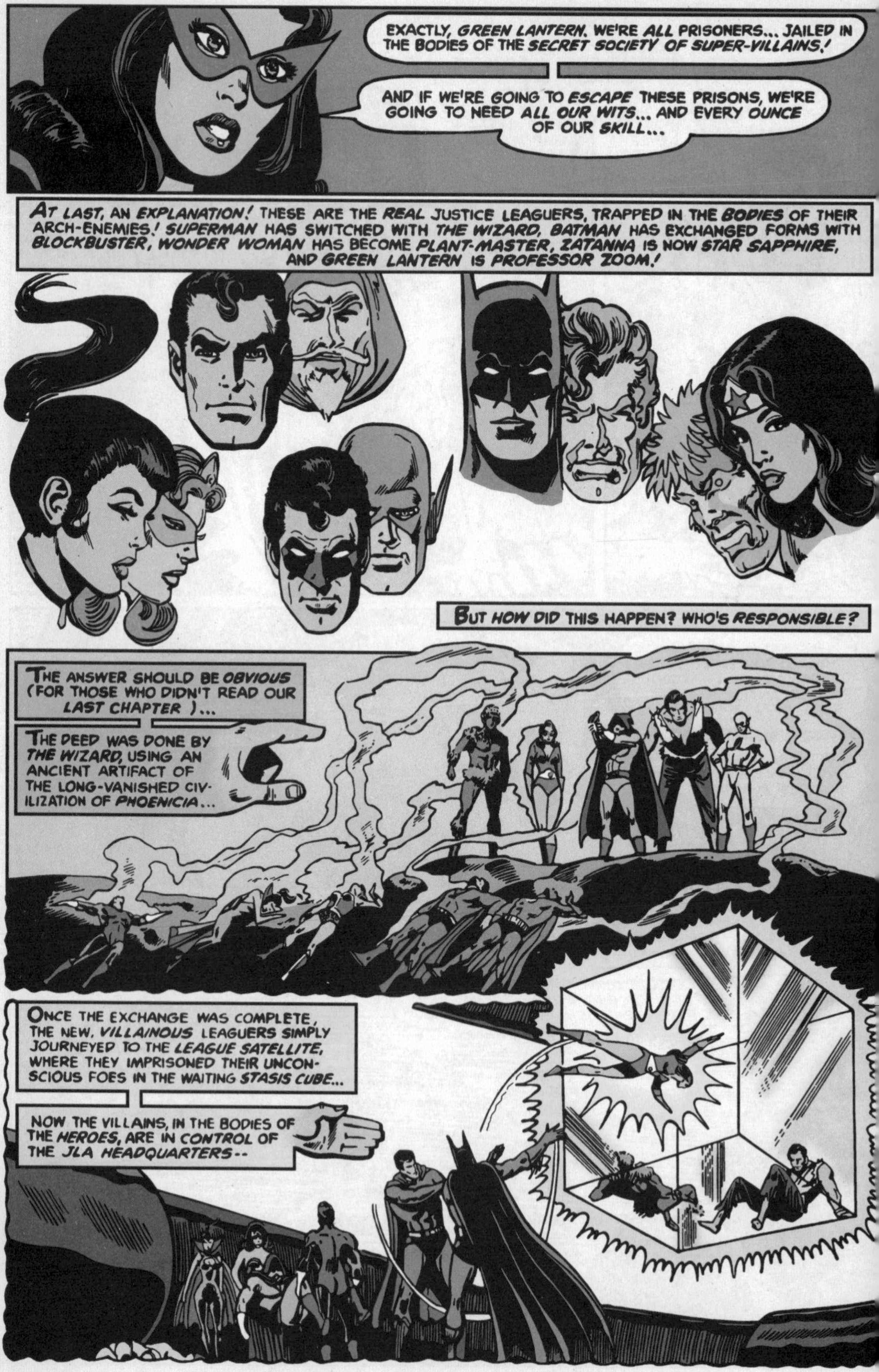
EXACTLY, GREEN LANTERN. WE'RE ALL PRISONERS... JAILED IN THE BODIES OF THE SECRET SOCIETY OF SUPER-VILLAINS!
AND IF WE'RE GOING TO ESCAPE THESE PRISONS, WE'RE GOING TO NEED ALL OUR WITS... AND EVERY OUNCE OF OUR SKILL...
AT LAST, AN EXPLANATION! THESE ARE THE REAL JUSTICE LEAGUERS, TRAPPED IN THE BODIES OF THEIR ARCH-ENEMIES! SUPERMAN HAS SWITCHED WITH THE WIZARD, BATMAN HAS EXCHANGED FORMS WITH BLOCKBUSTER, WONDER WOMAN HAS BECOME PLANT-MASTER, ZATANNA IS NOW STAR SAPPHIRE, AND GREEN LANTERN IS PROFESSOR ZOOM!
BUT HOW DID THIS HAPPEN? WHO'S RESPONSIBLE?
THE ANSWER SHOULD BE OBVIOUS (FOR THOSE WHO DIDN'T READ OUR LAST CHAPTER)...
THE DEED WAS DONE BY THE WIZARD, USING AN ANCIENT ARTIFACT OF THE LONG-VANISHED CIVILIZATION OF PHOENICIA...
ONCE THE EXCHANGE WAS COMPLETE, THE NEW, VILLAINOUS LEAGUERS SIMPLY JOURNEYED TO THE LEAGUE SATELLITE, WHERE THEY IMPRISONED THEIR UNCONSCIOUS FOES IN THE WAITING STASIS CUBE...
NOW THE VILLAINS, IN THE BODIES OF THE HEROES, ARE IN CONTROL OF THE JLA HEADQUARTERS--

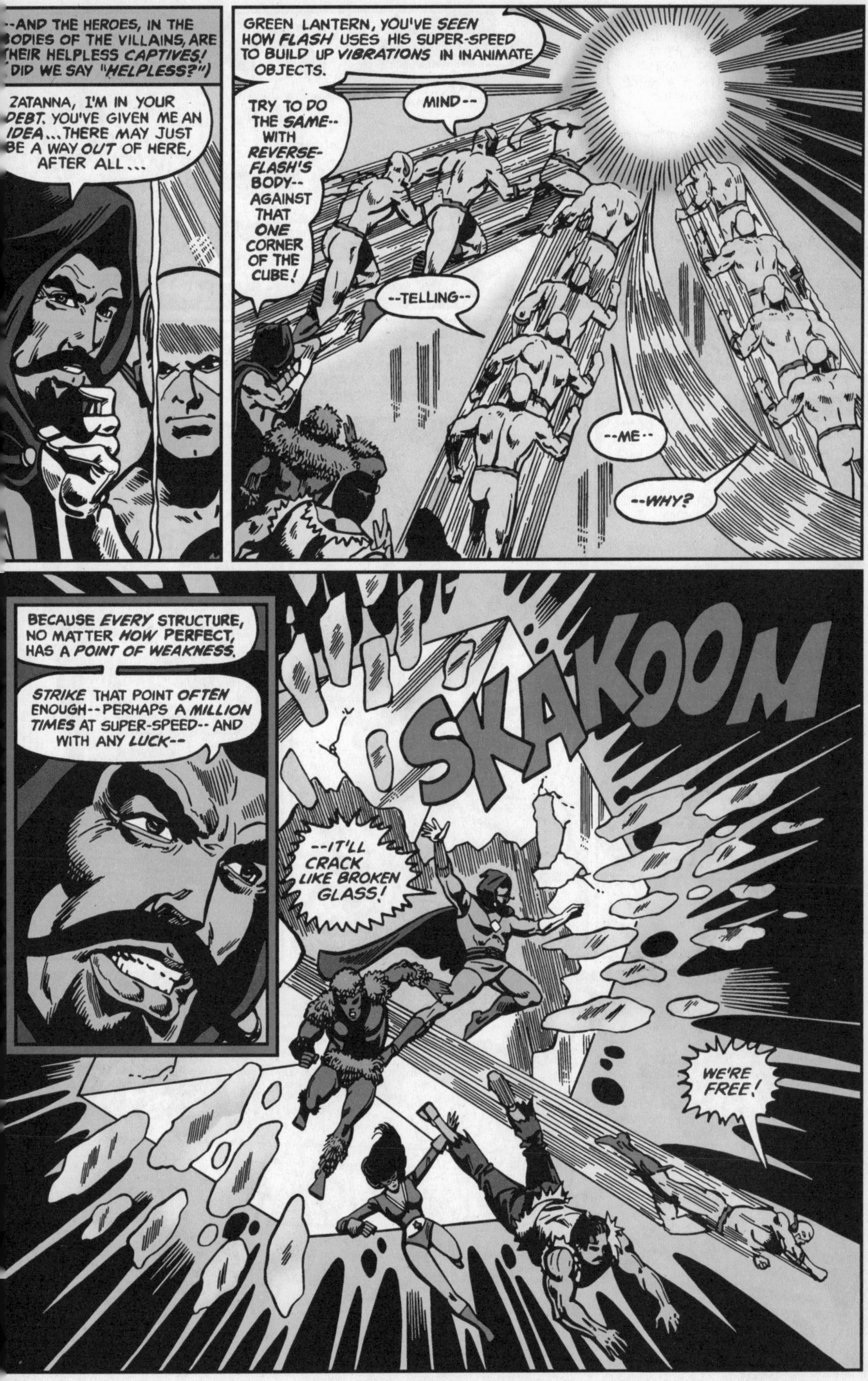
--AND THE HEROES, IN THE BODIES OF THE VILLAINS, ARE THEIR HELPLESS CAPTIVES! (DID WE SAY "HELPLESS?")
ZATANNA, I'M IN YOUR DEBT. YOU'VE GIVEN ME AN IDEA... THERE MAY JUST BE A WAY OUT OF HERE, AFTER ALL...
GREEN LANTERN, YOU'VE SEEN HOW FLASH USES HIS SUPER-SPEED TO BUILD UP VIBRATIONS IN INANIMATE OBJECTS.
TRY TO DO THE SAME--WITH REVERSE-FLASH'S BODY--AGAINST THAT ONE CORNER OF THE CUBE!
MIND--
--TELLING--
--ME--
--WHY?
BECAUSE EVERY STRUCTURE, NO MATTER HOW PERFECT, HAS A POINT OF WEAKNESS.
STRIKE THAT POINT OFTEN ENOUGH--PERHAPS A MILLION TIMES AT SUPER-SPEED--AND WITH ANY LUCK--
SKAKOOM
--IT'LL CRACK LIKE BROKEN GLASS!
WE'RE FREE!

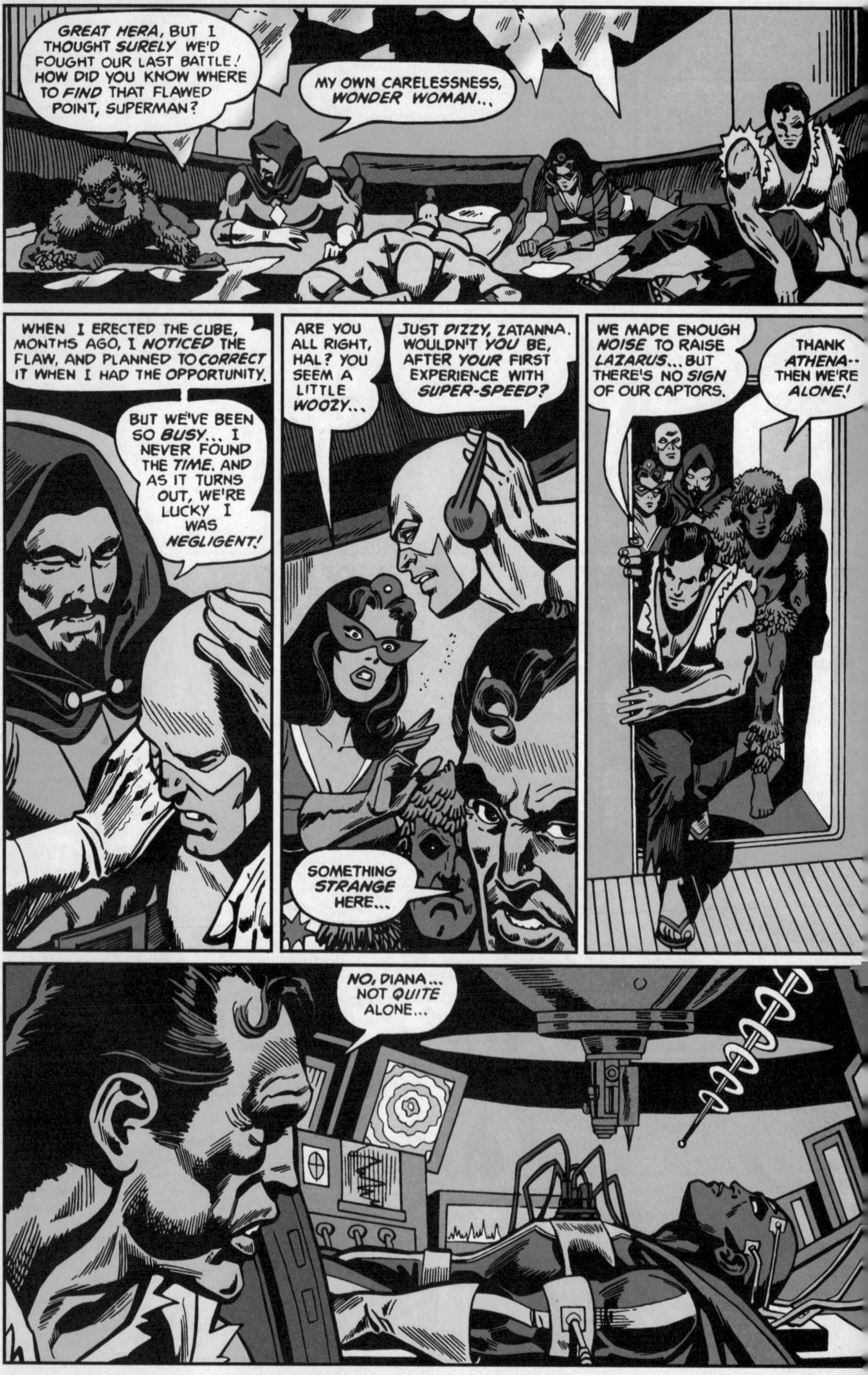
GREAT HERA, BUT I THOUGHT SURELY WE'D FOUGHT OUR LAST BATTLE! HOW DID YOU KNOW WHERE TO FIND THAT FLAWED POINT, SUPERMAN?
MY OWN CARELESSNESS, WONDER WOMAN...
WHEN I ERECTED THE CUBE, MONTHS AGO, I NOTICED THE FLAW, AND PLANNED TO CORRECT IT WHEN I HAD THE OPPORTUNITY.
BUT WE'VE BEEN SO BUSY... I NEVER FOUND THE TIME. AND AS IT TURNS OUT, WE'RE LUCKY I WAS NEGLIGENT!
ARE YOU ALL RIGHT, HAL? YOU SEEM A LITTLE WOOZY...
JUST DIZZY, ZATANNA. WOULDN'T YOU BE, AFTER YOUR FIRST EXPERIENCE WITH SUPER-SPEED?
SOMETHING STRANGE HERE...
WE MADE ENOUGH NOISE TO RAISE LAZARUS... BUT THERE'S NO SIGN OF OUR CAPTORS.
THANK ATHENA-- THEN WE'RE ALONE!
NO, DIANA... NOT QUITE ALONE...

THE HEROES DO A SEARCH OF THE *JUSTICE LEAGUE SATELLITE*, ORBITING 22,300 MILES OVER THE *SAPPHIRE WORLD* WE CALL *EARTH*...

IT'S *CONFIRMED*, KAL. OUR FOES HAVE *VANISHED*.

APPARENTLY, THEY'VE *LEFT* THE SATELLITE FOR SOME DESTINATION ON *EARTH*, BUT *WHERE*, WE DON'T *KNOW*.

HOW'S THE *RED TORNADO* DOING, ZATANNA?

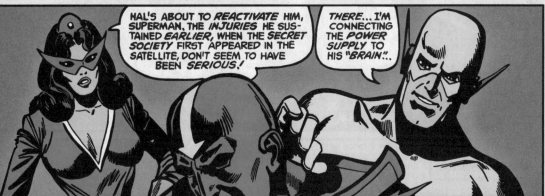

HAL'S ABOUT TO *REACTIVATE* HIM, SUPERMAN. THE *INJURIES* HE SUSTAINED *EARLIER*, WHEN THE *SECRET SOCIETY* FIRST APPEARED IN THE SATELLITE, DON'T SEEM TO HAVE BEEN *SERIOUS*!

THERE... I'M CONNECTING THE *POWER SUPPLY* TO HIS "*BRAIN*"...

...HE SHOULD BE *COMING AROUND* IN A *FEW SECONDS*.

IT'S A *NATURAL* MISTAKE FOR THESE HEROES TO MAKE...

AFTER ALL, *THEY* STILL SEE THEMSELVES AS THEY *TRULY ARE*, LOOKING PAST THE *SURFACE APPEARANCE* TO THE HEROES BENEATH!

BUT THEY'VE *FORGOTTEN* THAT OTHERS MAY NOT *SHARE* THEIR AWARENESS OF THE *TRUE* NATURE OF THINGS...

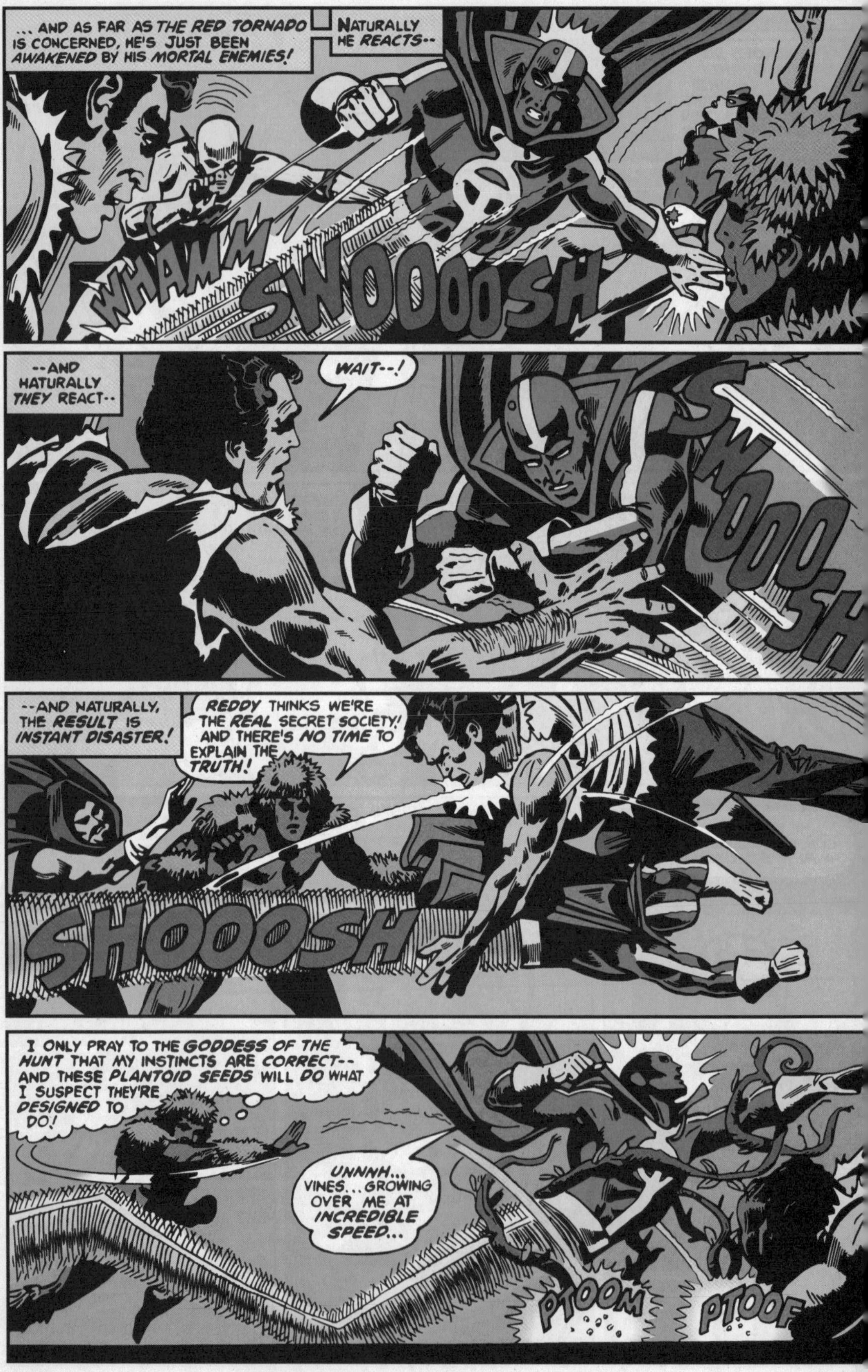

... AND AS FAR AS THE RED TORNADO IS CONCERNED, HE'S JUST BEEN AWAKENED BY HIS MORTAL ENEMIES!
NATURALLY HE REACTS--
WHAMM
SWOOOOSH
--AND NATURALLY THEY REACT--
WAIT--!
SWOOOOSH
--AND NATURALLY, THE RESULT IS INSTANT DISASTER!
REDDY THINKS WE'RE THE REAL SECRET SOCIETY! AND THERE'S NO TIME TO EXPLAIN THE TRUTH!
SHOOOSH
I ONLY PRAY TO THE GODDESS OF THE HUNT THAT MY INSTINCTS ARE CORRECT-- AND THESE PLANTOID SEEDS WILL DO WHAT I SUSPECT THEY'RE DESIGNED TO DO!
UNNNH... VINES... GROWING OVER ME AT INCREDIBLE SPEED...
PTOOM
PTOOF

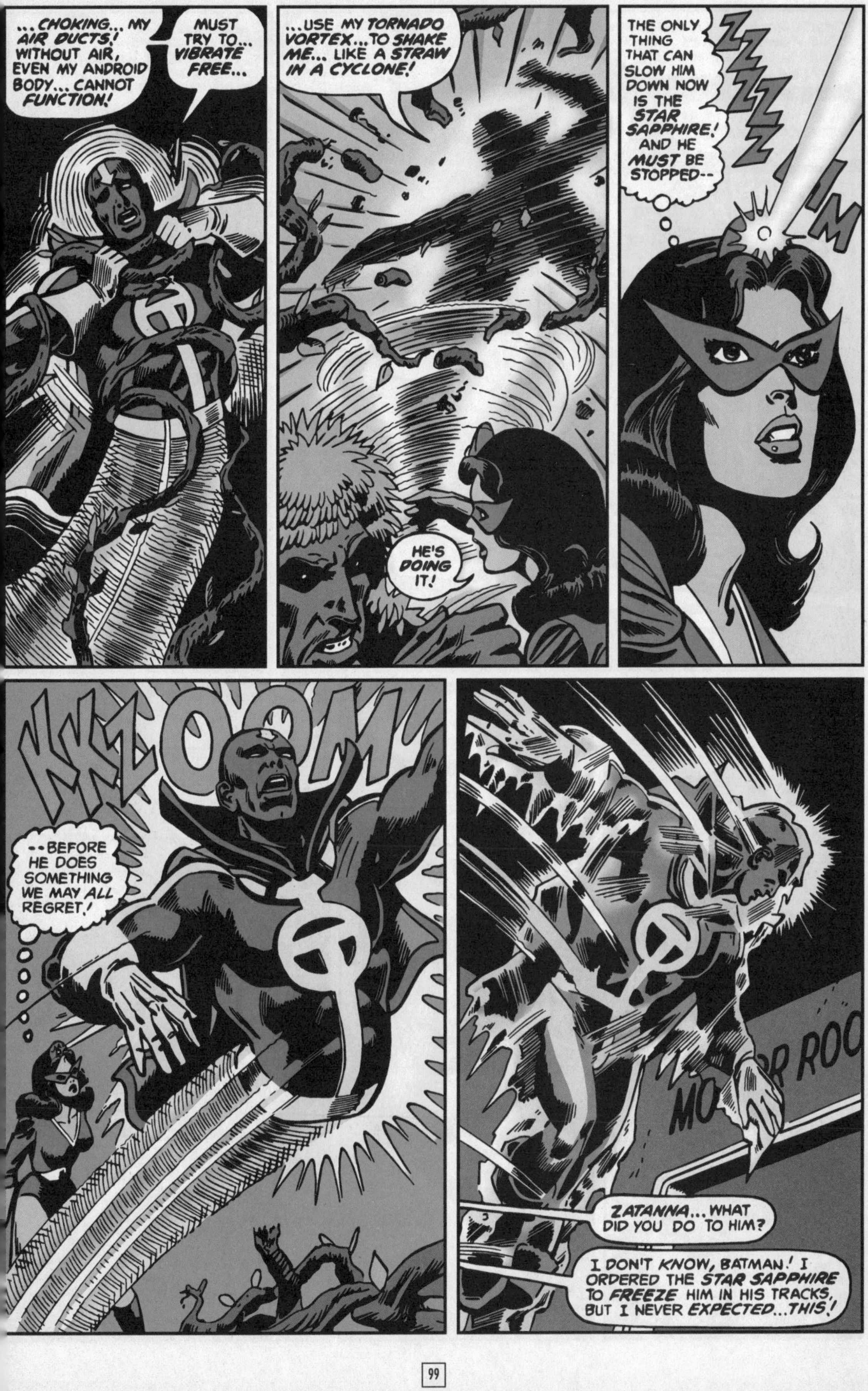
...CHOKING... MY AIR DUCTS! WITHOUT AIR, EVEN MY ANDROID BODY... CANNOT FUNCTION!
MUST TRY TO... VIBRATE FREE...
...USE MY TORNADO VORTEX...TO SHAKE ME... LIKE A STRAW IN A CYCLONE!
HE'S DOING IT!
THE ONLY THING THAT CAN SLOW HIM DOWN NOW IS THE STAR SAPPHIRE! AND HE MUST BE STOPPED--
ZZZZZIM
KKZOOM
--BEFORE HE DOES SOMETHING WE MAY ALL REGRET!
ZATANNA... WHAT DID YOU DO TO HIM?
I DON'T KNOW, BATMAN! I ORDERED THE STAR SAPPHIRE TO FREEZE HIM IN HIS TRACKS, BUT I NEVER EXPECTED...THIS!

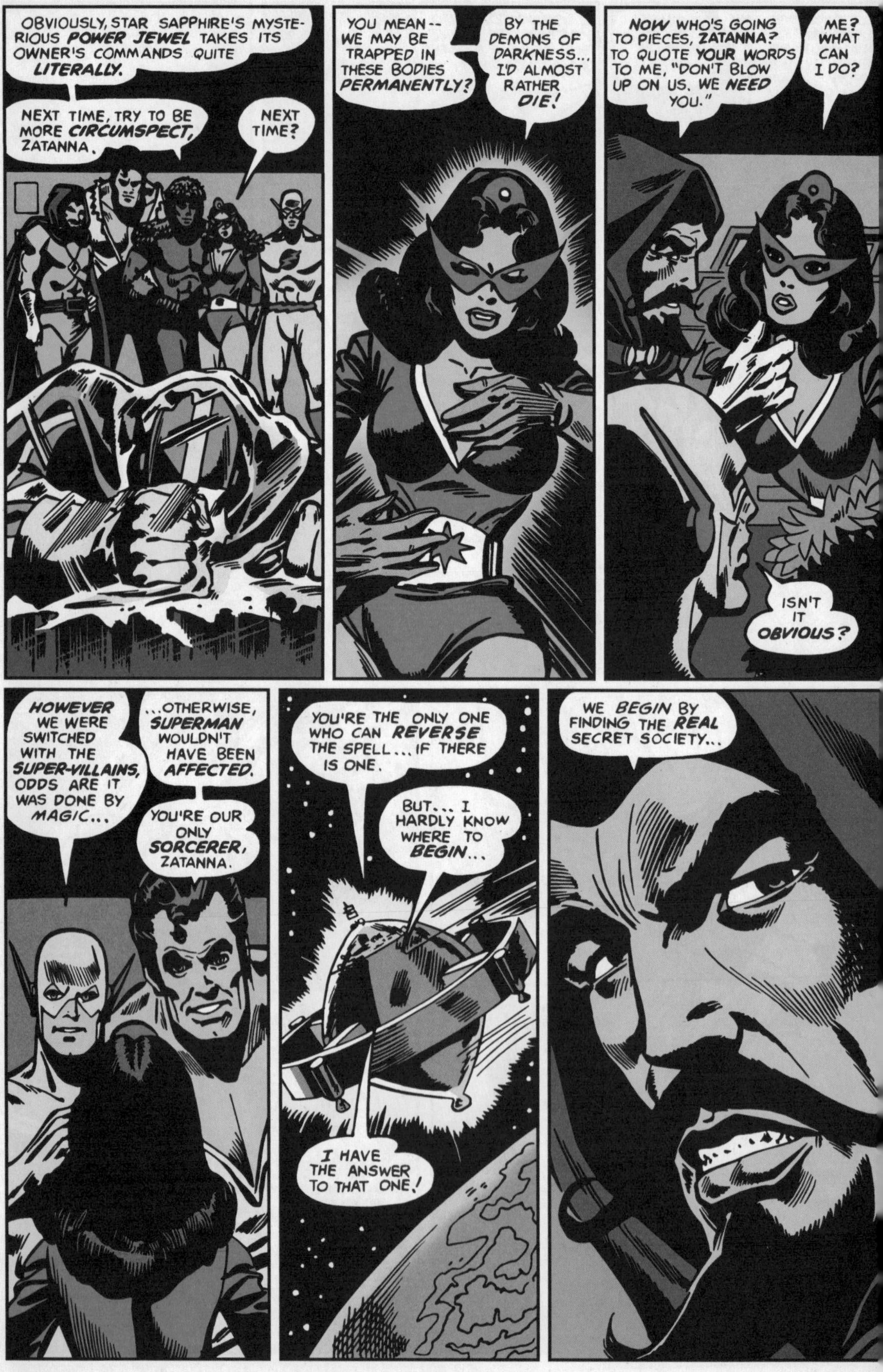
OBVIOUSLY, STAR SAPPHIRE'S MYSTERIOUS POWER JEWEL TAKES ITS OWNER'S COMMANDS QUITE LITERALLY.
NEXT TIME, TRY TO BE MORE CIRCUMSPECT, ZATANNA.
NEXT TIME?
YOU MEAN-- WE MAY BE TRAPPED IN THESE BODIES PERMANENTLY?
BY THE DEMONS OF DARKNESS... I'D ALMOST RATHER DIE!
NOW WHO'S GOING TO PIECES, ZATANNA? TO QUOTE YOUR WORDS TO ME, "DON'T BLOW UP ON US. WE NEED YOU."
ME? WHAT CAN I DO?
ISN'T IT OBVIOUS?
HOWEVER WE WERE SWITCHED WITH THE SUPER-VILLAINS, ODDS ARE IT WAS DONE BY MAGIC...
...OTHERWISE, SUPERMAN WOULDN'T HAVE BEEN AFFECTED.
YOU'RE OUR ONLY SORCERER, ZATANNA.
YOU'RE THE ONLY ONE WHO CAN REVERSE THE SPELL... IF THERE IS ONE.
BUT... I HARDLY KNOW WHERE TO BEGIN...
I HAVE THE ANSWER TO THAT ONE!
WE BEGIN BY FINDING THE REAL SECRET SOCIETY...

THE *MIST* IS THICK HERE ON THE *SAN FRANCISCO BAY*. A FEW MILES WEST OF THE *GOLDEN GATE BRIDGE*...

AT THE *BAY FEDERAL PRISON* ON *GOLDEN GATE ISLAND*, THE SEARCHLIGHTS HAVE TO *STRAIN* TO PIERCE THE FOG...

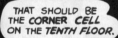
THUS, BECAUSE OF THE FOG, A CERTAIN STAR SAPPHIRE-POWERED *MOTORBOAT* APPROACHES THE ISLAND SILENT AND *UNSEEN*, WHERE...

IF I REMEMBER THE POLICE *BULLETIN* CORRECTLY, HE'S BEING HELD ON LEVEL *TEN*, CELL *TWENTY-FOUR*.

THAT SHOULD BE THE *CORNER CELL* ON THE *TENTH FLOOR*.

IT'S A GOOD THING YOUR MEMORY FOR *DETAIL* WASN'T ALTERED WHEN YOU EXCHANGED BODIES WITH BLOCKBUSTER, *BATMAN*.

I ONLY WISH I HAD MY *X-RAY VISION* -- SO WE COULD BE *CERTAIN*!

THE ONLY *REAL WAY* TO BE *CERTAIN* IS TO *CHECK IT OUT*, KAL.

AND IF I CAN JUST KEEP MY *BALANCE* THE WAY THE *FLASH* DOES--

--THAT'S *EXACTLY* WHAT I PLAN TO *DO*!

WELL, HOW DO YOU LIKE THAT? IT *WORKS*!

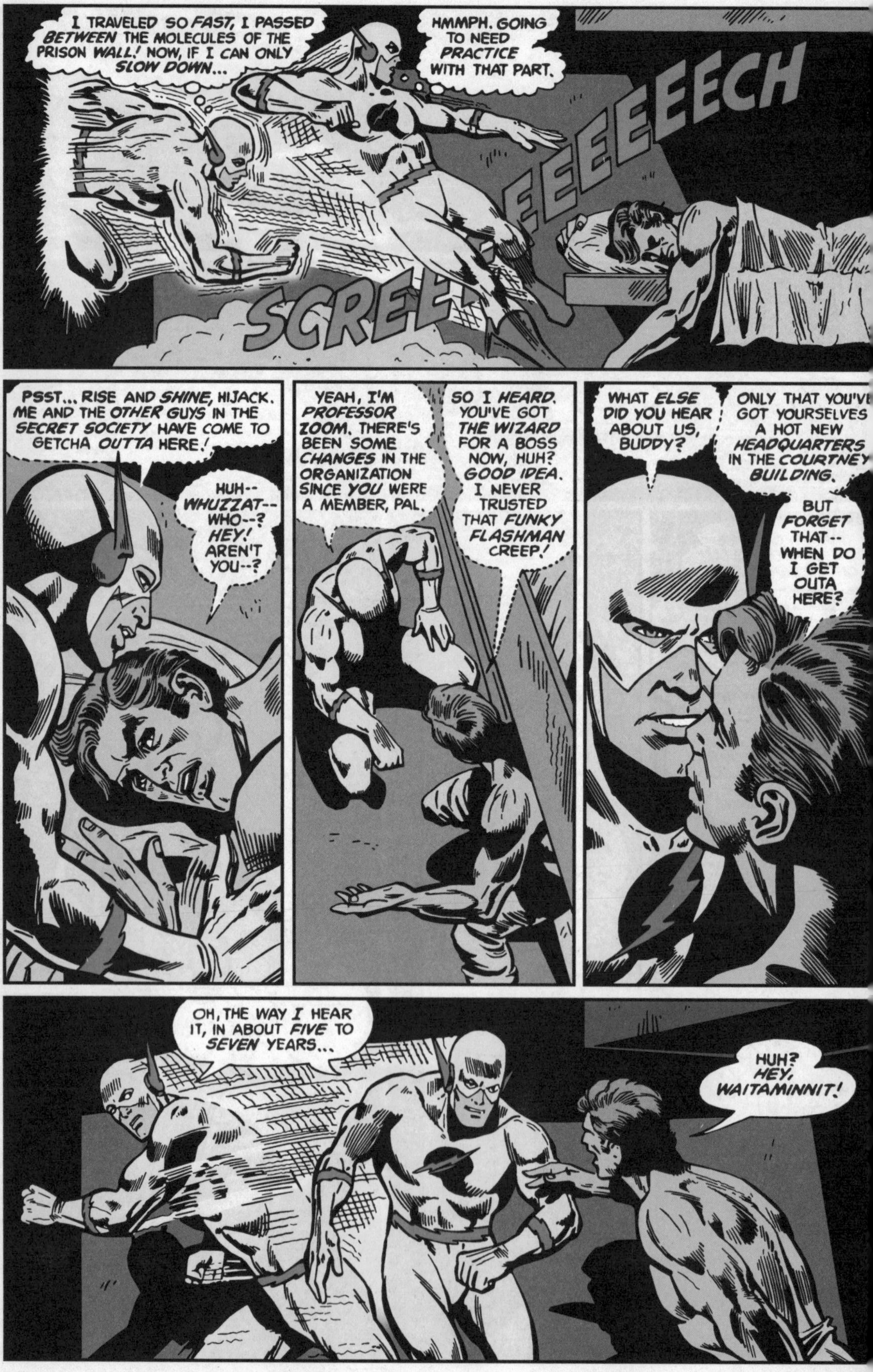
I TRAVELED SO FAST, I PASSED BETWEEN THE MOLECULES OF THE PRISON WALL! NOW, IF I CAN ONLY SLOW DOWN...
HMMPH. GOING TO NEED PRACTICE WITH THAT PART.
SCREEEEEEECH
PSST... RISE AND SHINE, HIJACK. ME AND THE OTHER GUYS IN THE SECRET SOCIETY HAVE COME TO GETCHA OUTTA HERE!
HUH-- WHUZZAT-- WHO--? HEY! AREN'T YOU--?
YEAH, I'M PROFESSOR ZOOM. THERE'S BEEN SOME CHANGES IN THE ORGANIZATION SINCE YOU WERE A MEMBER, PAL.
SO I HEARD. YOU'VE GOT THE WIZARD FOR A BOSS NOW, HUH? GOOD IDEA. I NEVER TRUSTED THAT FUNKY FLASHMAN CREEP!
WHAT ELSE DID YOU HEAR ABOUT US, BUDDY?
ONLY THAT YOU'VE GOT YOURSELVES A HOT NEW HEADQUARTERS IN THE COURTNEY BUILDING.
BUT FORGET THAT-- WHEN DO I GET OUTA HERE?
OH, THE WAY I HEAR IT, IN ABOUT FIVE TO SEVEN YEARS...
HUH? HEY, WAITAMINNIT!

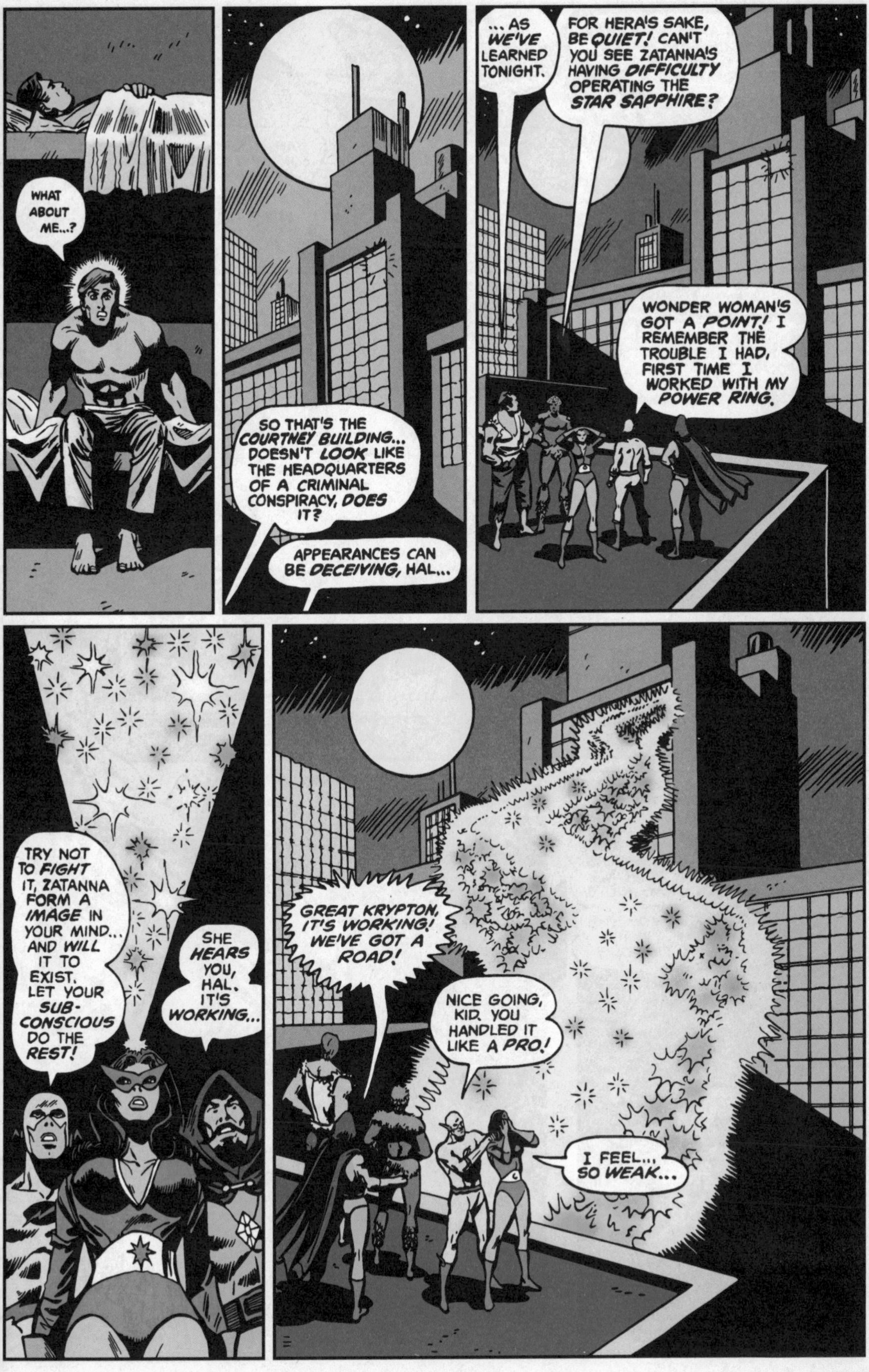

WHAT ABOUT ME...?
SO THAT'S THE COURTNEY BUILDING... DOESN'T LOOK LIKE THE HEADQUARTERS OF A CRIMINAL CONSPIRACY, DOES IT?
APPEARANCES CAN BE DECEIVING, HAL...
... AS WE'VE LEARNED TONIGHT.
FOR HERA'S SAKE, BE QUIET! CAN'T YOU SEE ZATANNA'S HAVING DIFFICULTY OPERATING THE STAR SAPPHIRE?
WONDER WOMAN'S GOT A POINT! I REMEMBER THE TROUBLE I HAD, FIRST TIME I WORKED WITH MY POWER RING.
TRY NOT TO FIGHT IT, ZATANNA FORM A IMAGE IN YOUR MIND... AND WILL IT TO EXIST. LET YOUR SUB-CONSCIOUS DO THE REST!
SHE HEARS YOU, HAL. IT'S WORKING...
GREAT KRYPTON, IT'S WORKING! WE'VE GOT A ROAD!
NICE GOING, KID. YOU HANDLED IT LIKE A PRO!
I FEEL... SO WEAK...

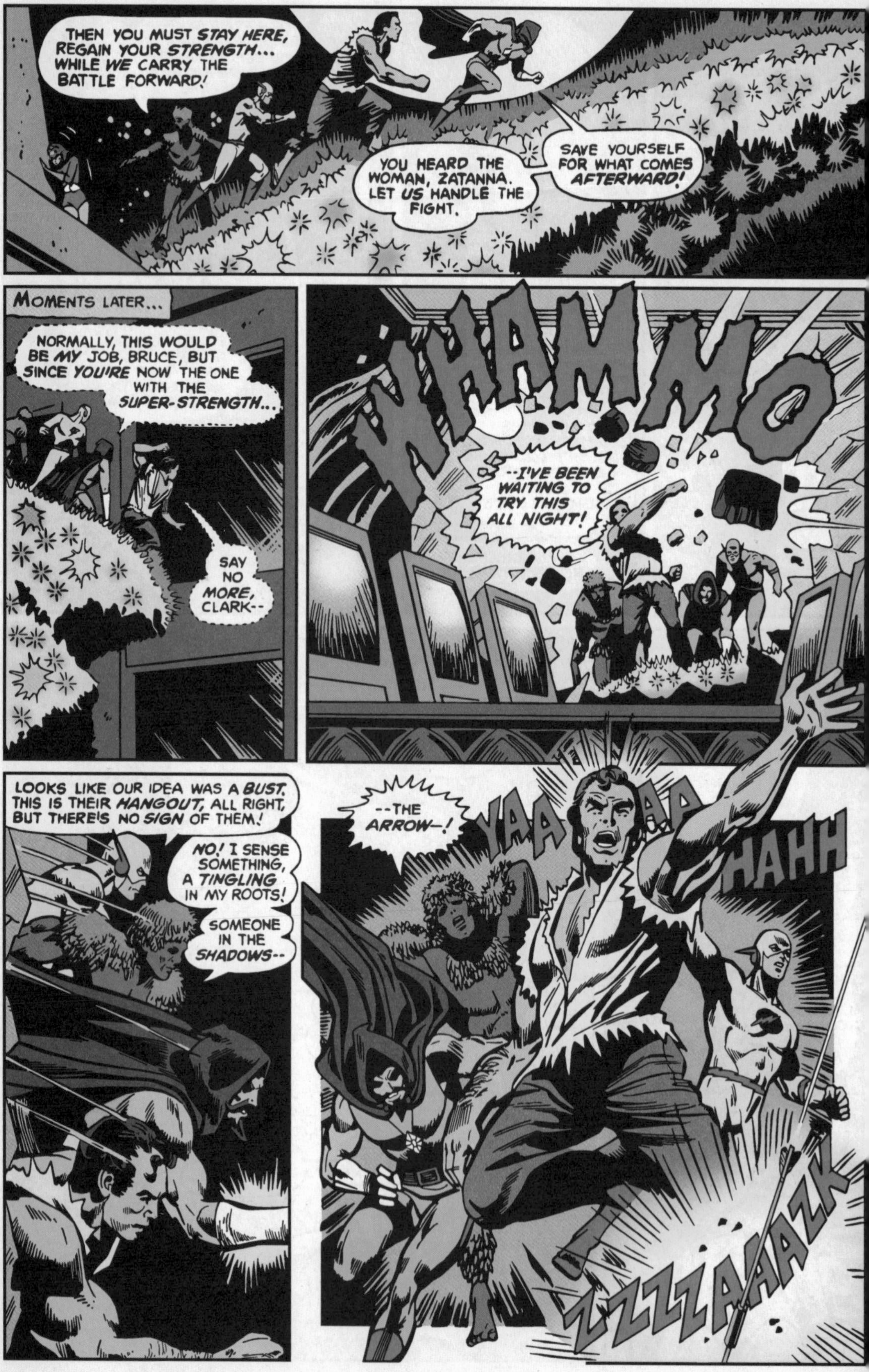
THEN YOU MUST STAY HERE, REGAIN YOUR STRENGTH... WHILE WE CARRY THE BATTLE FORWARD!
YOU HEARD THE WOMAN, ZATANNA. LET US HANDLE THE FIGHT.
SAVE YOURSELF FOR WHAT COMES AFTERWARD!
MOMENTS LATER...
NORMALLY, THIS WOULD BE MY JOB, BRUCE, BUT SINCE YOU'RE NOW THE ONE WITH THE SUPER-STRENGTH...
SAY NO MORE, CLARK--
KHAMMO
--I'VE BEEN WAITING TO TRY THIS ALL NIGHT!
LOOKS LIKE OUR IDEA WAS A BUST. THIS IS THEIR HANGOUT, ALL RIGHT, BUT THERE'S NO SIGN OF THEM!
NO! I SENSE SOMETHING, A TINGLING IN MY ROOTS!
SOMEONE IN THE SHADOWS--
--THE ARROW--!
YAAAAHAHH
ZZZZAAAZK

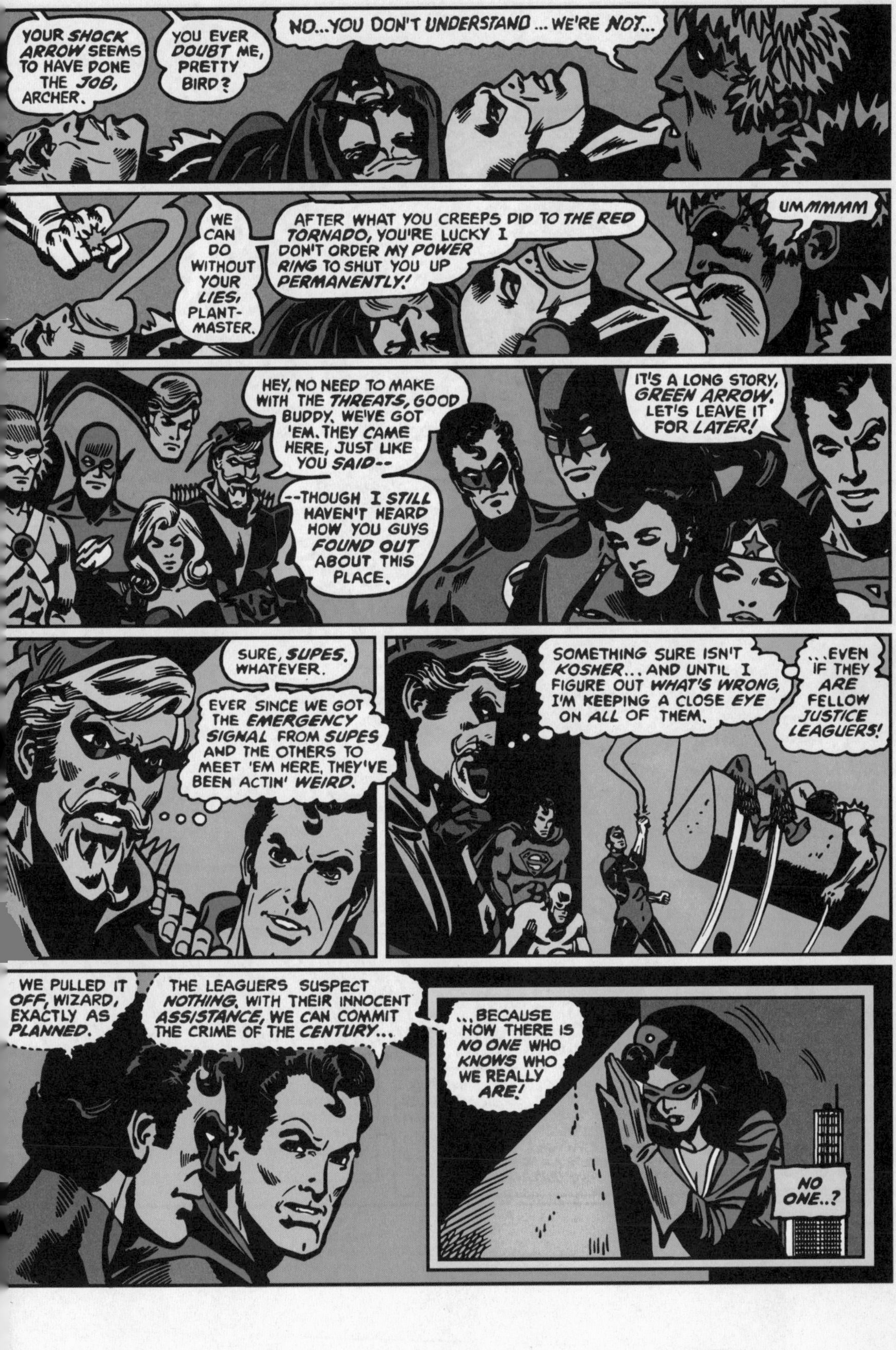
YOUR SHOCK ARROW SEEMS TO HAVE DONE THE JOB, ARCHER.
YOU EVER DOUBT ME, PRETTY BIRD?
NO...YOU DON'T UNDERSTAND ... WE'RE NOT...
WE CAN DO WITHOUT YOUR LIES, PLANT-MASTER.
AFTER WHAT YOU CREEPS DID TO THE RED TORNADO, YOU'RE LUCKY I DON'T ORDER MY POWER RING TO SHUT YOU UP PERMANENTLY!
UMMMMMM
HEY, NO NEED TO MAKE WITH THE THREATS, GOOD BUDDY. WE'VE GOT 'EM. THEY CAME HERE, JUST LIKE YOU SAID--
--THOUGH I STILL HAVEN'T HEARD HOW YOU GUYS FOUND OUT ABOUT THIS PLACE.
IT'S A LONG STORY, GREEN ARROW. LET'S LEAVE IT FOR LATER!
SURE, SUPES. WHATEVER.
EVER SINCE WE GOT THE EMERGENCY SIGNAL FROM SUPES AND THE OTHERS TO MEET 'EM HERE, THEY'VE BEEN ACTIN' WEIRD.
SOMETHING SURE ISN'T KOSHER... AND UNTIL I FIGURE OUT WHAT'S WRONG, I'M KEEPING A CLOSE EYE ON ALL OF THEM.
...EVEN IF THEY ARE FELLOW JUSTICE LEAGUERS!
WE PULLED IT OFF, WIZARD, EXACTLY AS PLANNED.
THE LEAGUERS SUSPECT NOTHING. WITH THEIR INNOCENT ASSISTANCE, WE CAN COMMIT THE CRIME OF THE CENTURY...
...BECAUSE NOW THERE IS NO ONE WHO KNOWS WHO WE REALLY ARE!
NO ONE..?

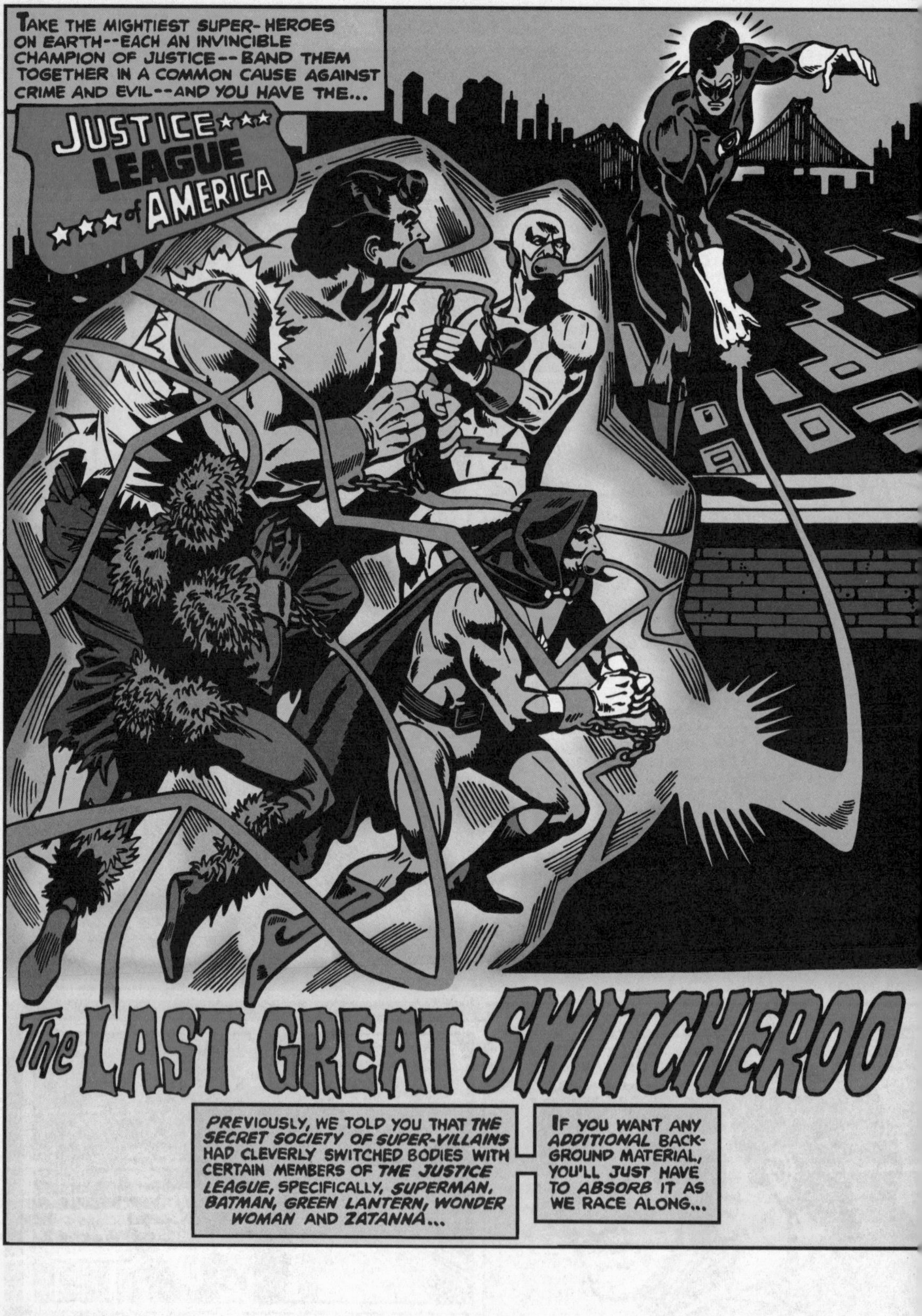

TAKE THE MIGHTIEST SUPER-HEROES ON EARTH--EACH AN INVINCIBLE CHAMPION OF JUSTICE--BAND THEM TOGETHER IN A COMMON CAUSE AGAINST CRIME AND EVIL--AND YOU HAVE THE...
JUSTICE LEAGUE of AMERICA
The LAST GREAT SWITCHEROO
PREVIOUSLY, WE TOLD YOU THAT THE SECRET SOCIETY OF SUPER-VILLAINS HAD CLEVERLY SWITCHED BODIES WITH CERTAIN MEMBERS OF THE JUSTICE LEAGUE, SPECIFICALLY, SUPERMAN, BATMAN, GREEN LANTERN, WONDER WOMAN AND ZATANNA...
IF YOU WANT ANY ADDITIONAL BACK-GROUND MATERIAL, YOU'LL JUST HAVE TO ABSORB IT AS WE RACE ALONG...

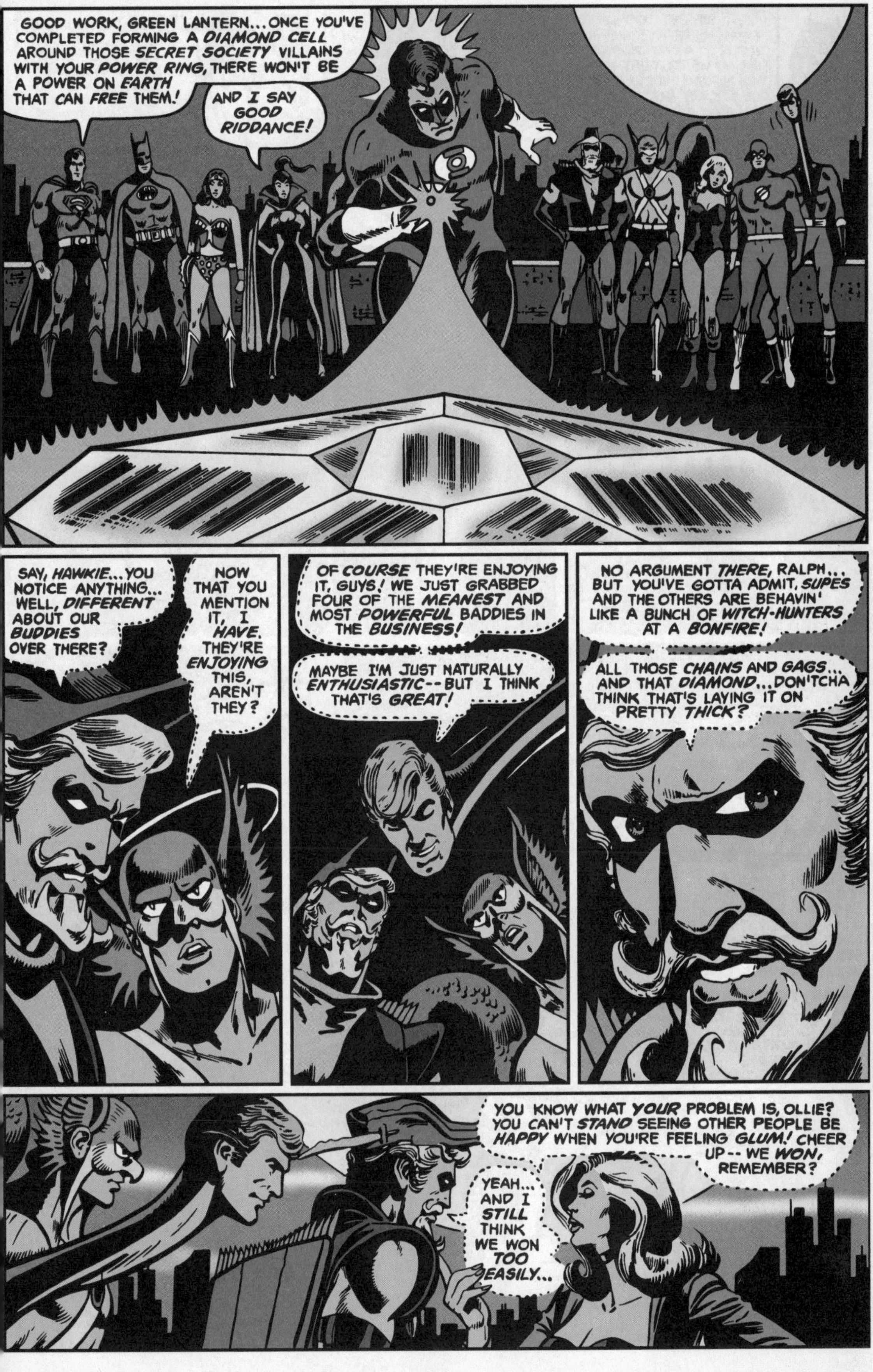
GOOD WORK, GREEN LANTERN...ONCE YOU'VE COMPLETED FORMING A DIAMOND CELL AROUND THOSE SECRET SOCIETY VILLAINS WITH YOUR POWER RING, THERE WON'T BE A POWER ON EARTH THAT CAN FREE THEM!
AND I SAY GOOD RIDDANCE!
SAY, HAWKIE...YOU NOTICE ANYTHING... WELL, DIFFERENT ABOUT OUR BUDDIES OVER THERE?
NOW THAT YOU MENTION IT, I HAVE. THEY'RE ENJOYING THIS, AREN'T THEY?
OF COURSE THEY'RE ENJOYING IT, GUYS! WE JUST GRABBED FOUR OF THE MEANEST AND MOST POWERFUL BADDIES IN THE BUSINESS!
MAYBE I'M JUST NATURALLY ENTHUSIASTIC-- BUT I THINK THAT'S GREAT!
NO ARGUMENT THERE, RALPH... BUT YOU'VE GOTTA ADMIT, SUPES AND THE OTHERS ARE BEHAVIN' LIKE A BUNCH OF WITCH-HUNTERS AT A BONFIRE!
ALL THOSE CHAINS AND GAGS... AND THAT DIAMOND...DON'TCHA THINK THAT'S LAYING IT ON PRETTY THICK?
YOU KNOW WHAT YOUR PROBLEM IS, OLLIE? YOU CAN'T STAND SEEING OTHER PEOPLE BE HAPPY WHEN YOU'RE FEELING GLUM! CHEER UP -- WE WON, REMEMBER?
YEAH... AND I STILL THINK WE WON TOO EASILY...

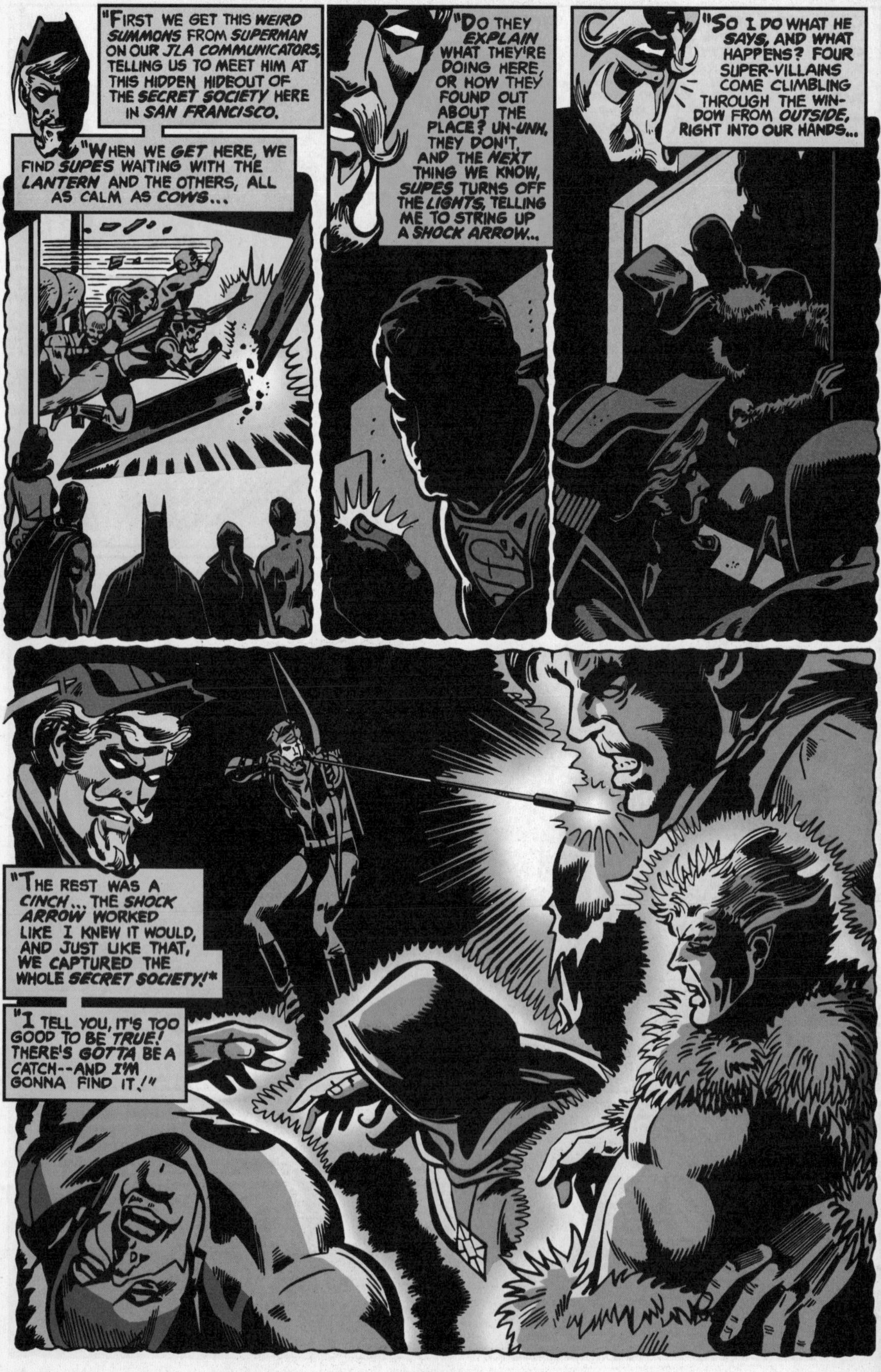
"FIRST WE GET THIS WEIRD SUMMONS FROM SUPERMAN ON OUR JLA COMMUNICATORS, TELLING US TO MEET HIM AT THIS HIDDEN HIDEOUT OF THE SECRET SOCIETY HERE IN SAN FRANCISCO.
"WHEN WE GET HERE, WE FIND SUPES WAITING WITH THE LANTERN AND THE OTHERS, ALL AS CALM AS COWS...
"DO THEY EXPLAIN WHAT THEY'RE DOING HERE, OR HOW THEY FOUND OUT ABOUT THE PLACE? UN-UNH. THEY DON'T, AND THE NEXT THING WE KNOW, SUPES TURNS OFF THE LIGHTS, TELLING ME TO STRING UP A SHOCK ARROW...
"SO I DO WHAT HE SAYS, AND WHAT HAPPENS? FOUR SUPER-VILLAINS COME CLIMBLING THROUGH THE WIN-DOW FROM OUTSIDE, RIGHT INTO OUR HANDS...
"THE REST WAS A CINCH... THE SHOCK ARROW WORKED LIKE I KNEW IT WOULD, AND JUST LIKE THAT, WE CAPTURED THE WHOLE SECRET SOCIETY!*
"I TELL YOU, IT'S TOO GOOD TO BE TRUE! THERE'S GOTTA BE A CATCH--AND I'M GONNA FIND IT!"

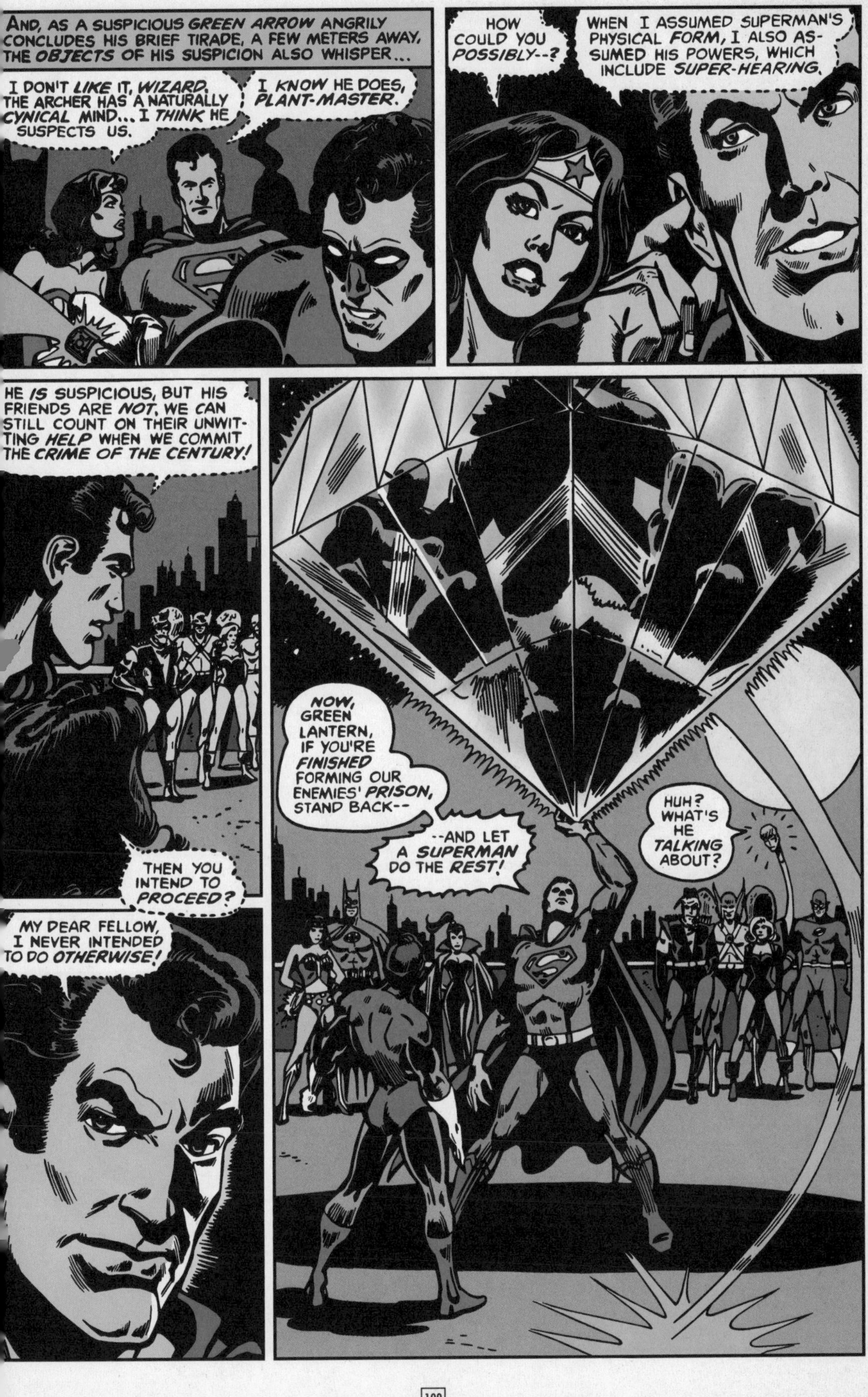
AND, AS A SUSPICIOUS GREEN ARROW ANGRILY CONCLUDES HIS BRIEF TIRADE, A FEW METERS AWAY, THE OBJECTS OF HIS SUSPICION ALSO WHISPER...
I DON'T LIKE IT, WIZARD. THE ARCHER HAS A NATURALLY CYNICAL MIND... I THINK HE SUSPECTS US.
I KNOW HE DOES, PLANT-MASTER.
HOW COULD YOU POSSIBLY--?
WHEN I ASSUMED SUPERMAN'S PHYSICAL FORM, I ALSO ASSUMED HIS POWERS, WHICH INCLUDE SUPER-HEARING.
HE IS SUSPICIOUS, BUT HIS FRIENDS ARE NOT. WE CAN STILL COUNT ON THEIR UNWITTING HELP WHEN WE COMMIT THE CRIME OF THE CENTURY!
THEN YOU INTEND TO PROCEED?
MY DEAR FELLOW, I NEVER INTENDED TO DO OTHERWISE!
NOW, GREEN LANTERN, IF YOU'RE FINISHED FORMING OUR ENEMIES' PRISON, STAND BACK--
--AND LET A SUPERMAN DO THE REST!
HUH? WHAT'S HE TALKING ABOUT?

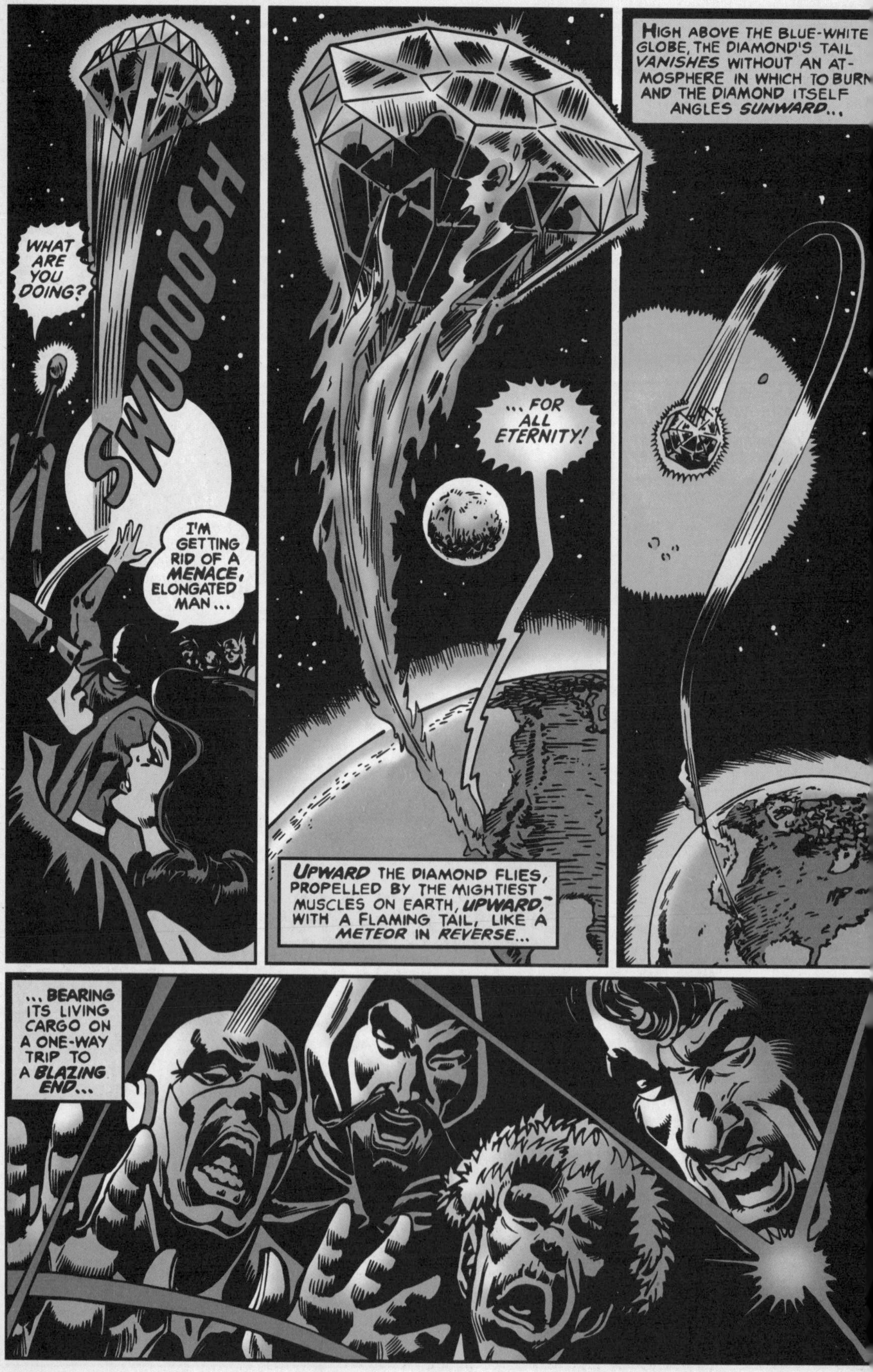

WHAT ARE YOU DOING?
SWOOOSH
I'M GETTING RID OF A MENACE, ELONGATED MAN...
...FOR ALL ETERNITY!
UPWARD THE DIAMOND FLIES, PROPELLED BY THE MIGHTIEST MUSCLES ON EARTH, UPWARD, WITH A FLAMING TAIL, LIKE A METEOR IN REVERSE...
HIGH ABOVE THE BLUE-WHITE GLOBE, THE DIAMOND'S TAIL VANISHES WITHOUT AN ATMOSPHERE IN WHICH TO BURN AND THE DIAMOND ITSELF ANGLES SUNWARD...
...BEARING ITS LIVING CARGO ON A ONE-WAY TRIP TO A BLAZING END...

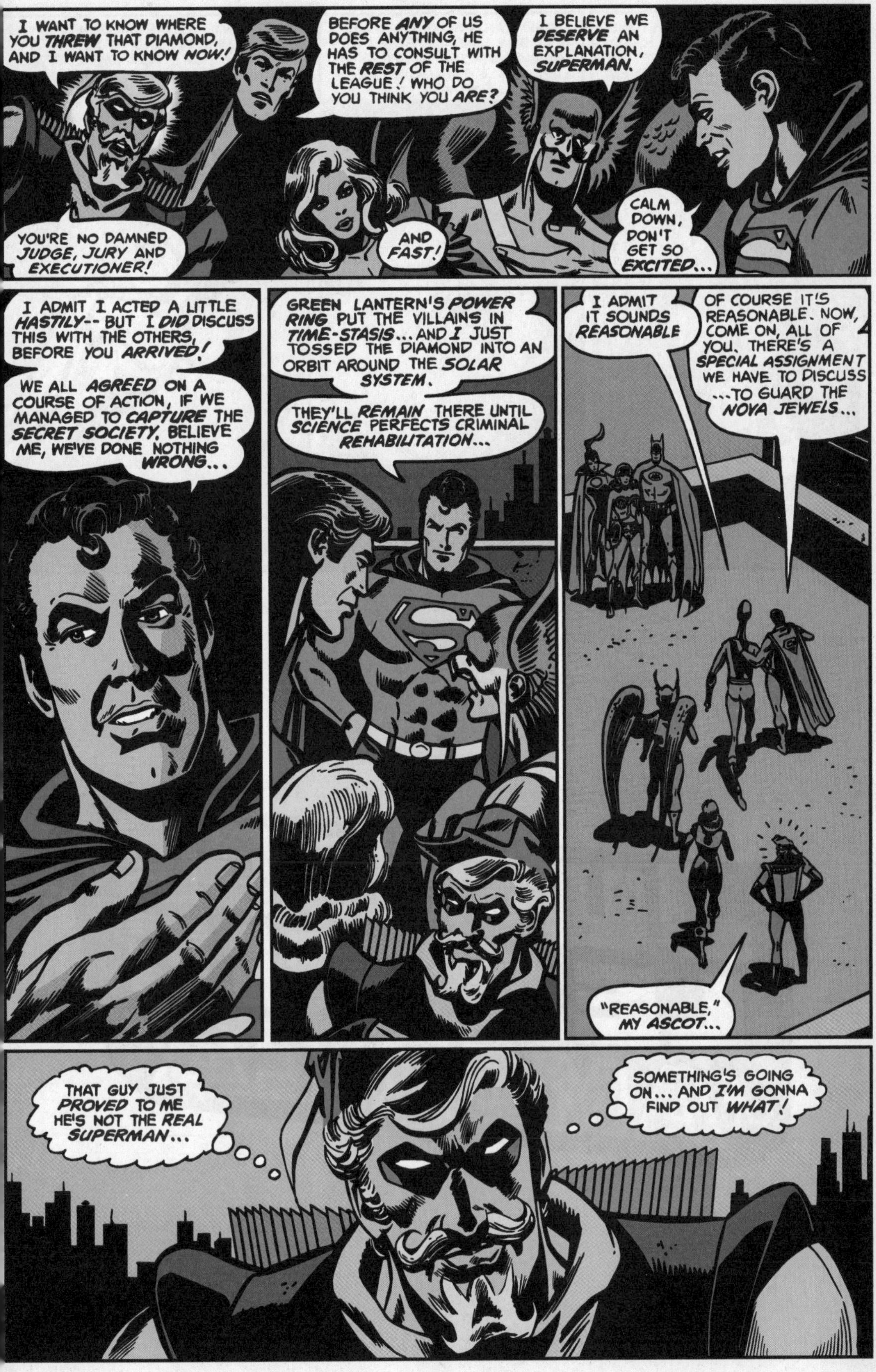
I WANT TO KNOW WHERE YOU THREW THAT DIAMOND, AND I WANT TO KNOW NOW!
YOU'RE NO DAMNED JUDGE, JURY AND EXECUTIONER!
BEFORE ANY OF US DOES ANYTHING, HE HAS TO CONSULT WITH THE REST OF THE LEAGUE! WHO DO YOU THINK YOU ARE?
AND FAST!
I BELIEVE WE DESERVE AN EXPLANATION, SUPERMAN.
CALM DOWN, DON'T GET SO EXCITED...
I ADMIT I ACTED A LITTLE HASTILY-- BUT I DID DISCUSS THIS WITH THE OTHERS, BEFORE YOU ARRIVED!
WE ALL AGREED ON A COURSE OF ACTION, IF WE MANAGED TO CAPTURE THE SECRET SOCIETY. BELIEVE ME, WE'VE DONE NOTHING WRONG...
GREEN LANTERN'S POWER RING PUT THE VILLAINS IN TIME-STASIS... AND I JUST TOSSED THE DIAMOND INTO AN ORBIT AROUND THE SOLAR SYSTEM.
THEY'LL REMAIN THERE UNTIL SCIENCE PERFECTS CRIMINAL REHABILITATION...
I ADMIT IT SOUNDS REASONABLE
OF COURSE IT'S REASONABLE. NOW, COME ON, ALL OF YOU. THERE'S A SPECIAL ASSIGNMENT WE HAVE TO DISCUSS ...TO GUARD THE NOVA JEWELS...
"REASONABLE," MY ASCOT...
THAT GUY JUST PROVED TO ME HE'S NOT THE REAL SUPERMAN...
SOMETHING'S GOING ON... AND I'M GONNA FIND OUT WHAT!

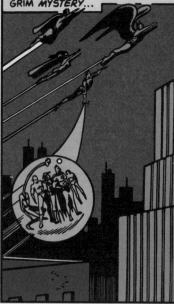

SECONDS LATER, THE COSTUMED BAND SHOOTS SKYWARD, HEADING SOUTH FROM THE CITY ON THE BAY, BEARING AMONG THEM ONE MAN BROODING OVER A GRIM MYSTERY...
...ONE MAN, WHO IS UNAWARE THAT SOMEONE CAPABLE OF UNRAVELING THE MYSTERY LIES NOT A THOUSAND FEET DISTANT...
HER NAME, AT THE MOMENT, IS STAR SAPPHIRE, AND IN HER RESTS THE ONLY HOPE FOR THE JUSTICE LEAGUE...

JUSTICE LEAGUE of AMERICA

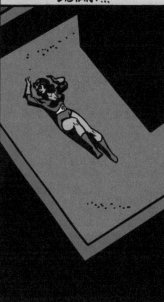

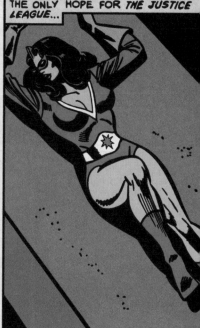

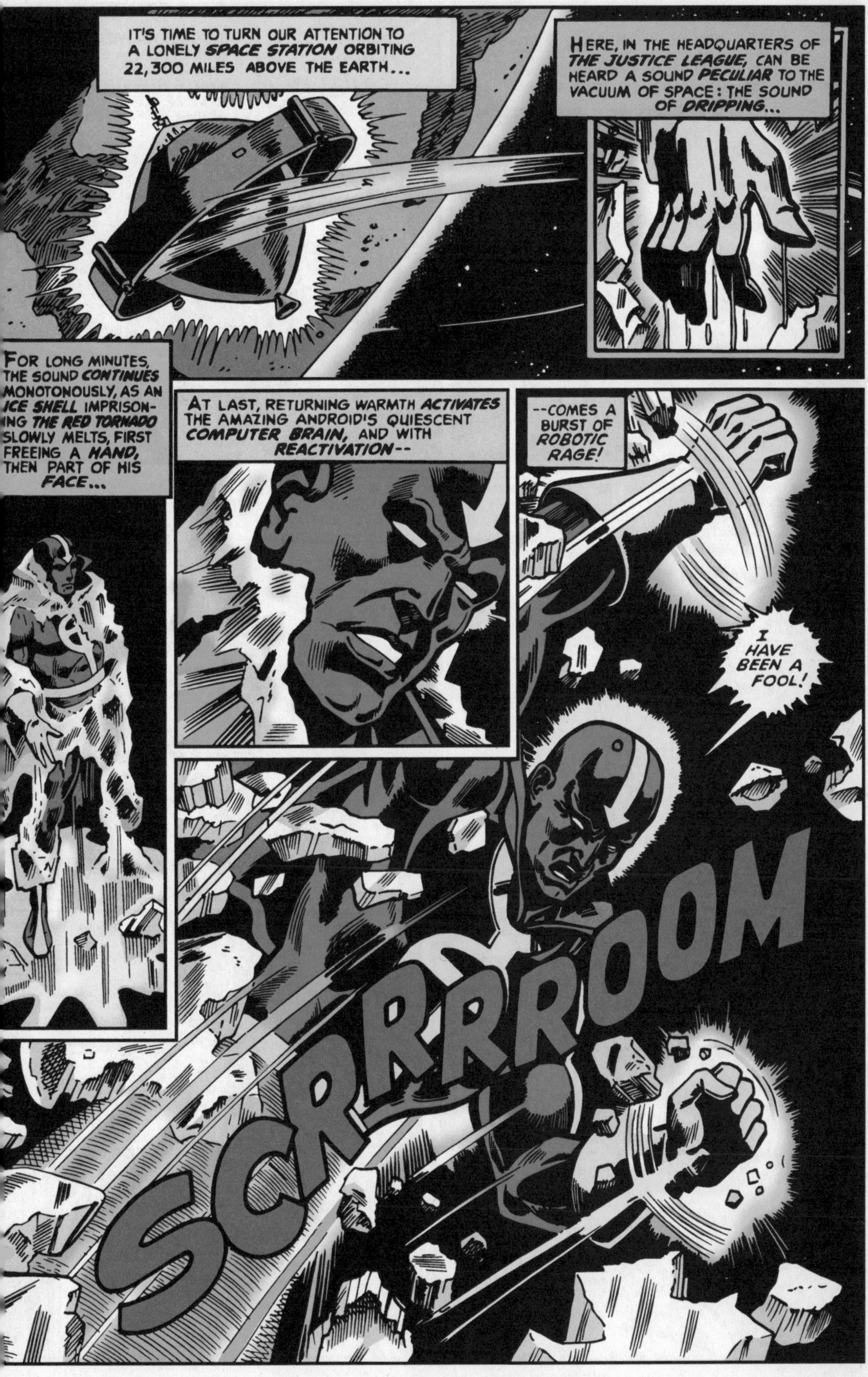
IT'S TIME TO TURN OUR ATTENTION TO A LONELY SPACE STATION ORBITING 22,300 MILES ABOVE THE EARTH...
HERE, IN THE HEADQUARTERS OF THE JUSTICE LEAGUE, CAN BE HEARD A SOUND PECULIAR TO THE VACUUM OF SPACE: THE SOUND OF DRIPPING...
FOR LONG MINUTES, THE SOUND CONTINUES MONOTONOUSLY, AS AN ICE SHELL IMPRISONING THE RED TORNADO SLOWLY MELTS, FIRST FREEING A HAND, THEN PART OF HIS FACE...
AT LAST, RETURNING WARMTH ACTIVATES THE AMAZING ANDROID'S QUIESCENT COMPUTER BRAIN, AND WITH REACTIVATION--
--COMES A BURST OF ROBOTIC RAGE!
I HAVE BEEN A FOOL!
SCRRRROOM

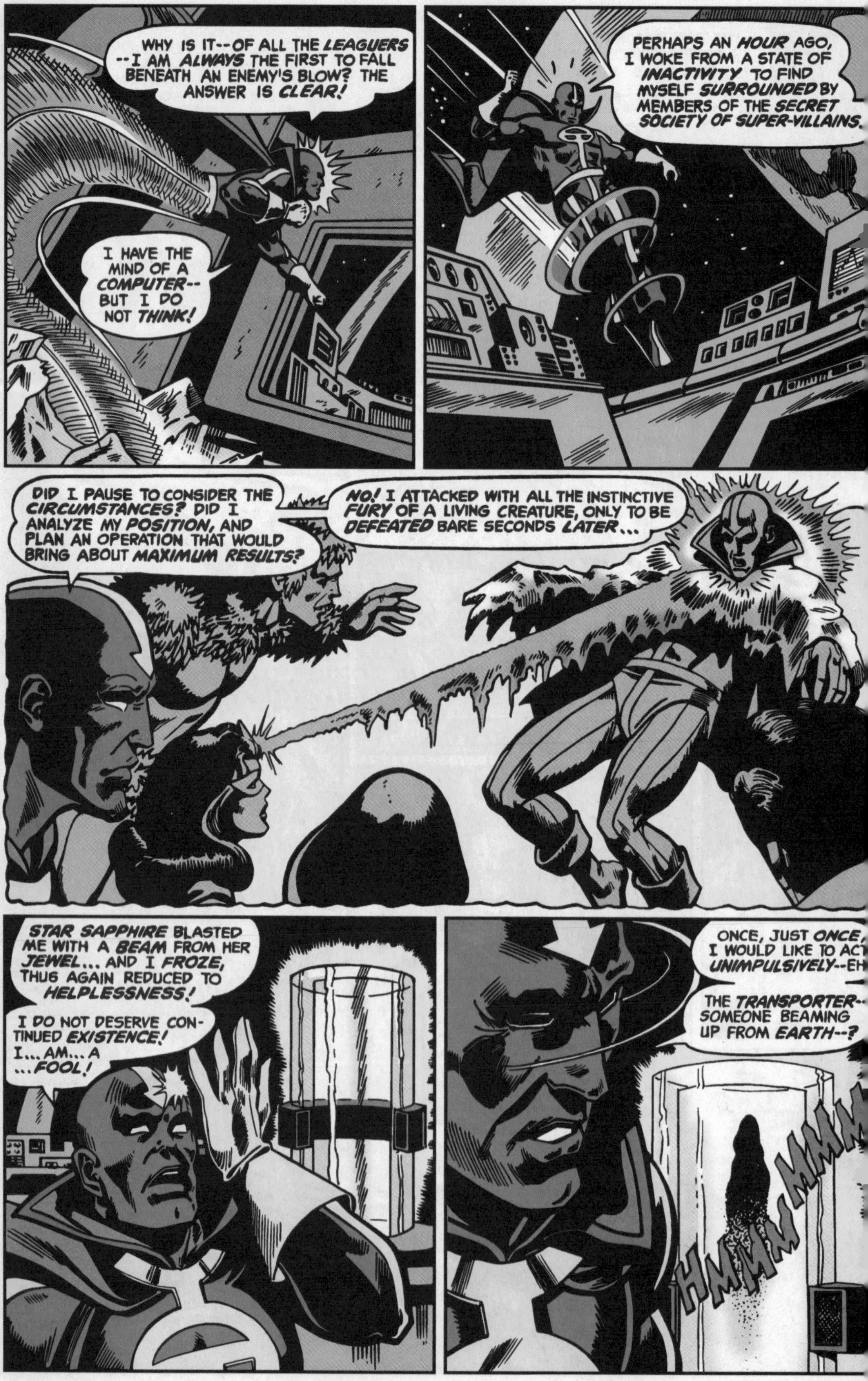
WHY IS IT--OF ALL THE LEAGUERS --I AM ALWAYS THE FIRST TO FALL BENEATH AN ENEMY'S BLOW? THE ANSWER IS CLEAR!
I HAVE THE MIND OF A COMPUTER--BUT I DO NOT THINK!
PERHAPS AN HOUR AGO, I WOKE FROM A STATE OF INACTIVITY TO FIND MYSELF SURROUNDED BY MEMBERS OF THE SECRET SOCIETY OF SUPER-VILLAINS.
DID I PAUSE TO CONSIDER THE CIRCUMSTANCES? DID I ANALYZE MY POSITION, AND PLAN AN OPERATION THAT WOULD BRING ABOUT MAXIMUM RESULTS?
NO! I ATTACKED WITH ALL THE INSTINCTIVE FURY OF A LIVING CREATURE, ONLY TO BE DEFEATED BARE SECONDS LATER...
STAR SAPPHIRE BLASTED ME WITH A BEAM FROM HER JEWEL... AND I FROZE, THUS AGAIN REDUCED TO HELPLESSNESS!
I DO NOT DESERVE CONTINUED EXISTENCE! I... AM... A ...FOOL!
ONCE, JUST ONCE, I WOULD LIKE TO ACT UNIMPULSIVELY--EH
THE TRANSPORTER--SOMEONE BEAMING UP FROM EARTH--?
HMMMMMMM

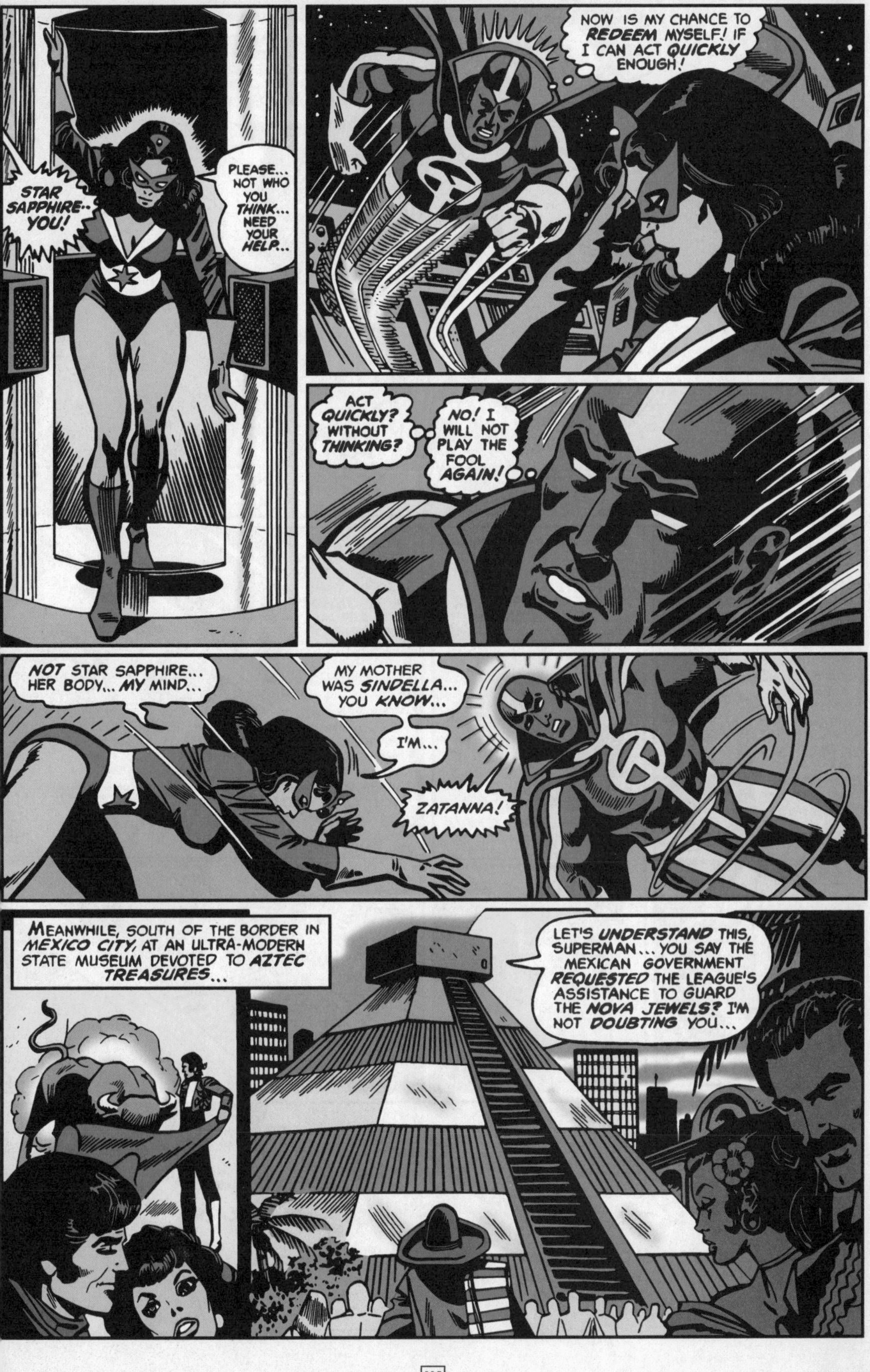
STAR SAPPHIRE.. YOU!
PLEASE... NOT WHO YOU THINK... NEED YOUR HELP...
NOW IS MY CHANCE TO REDEEM MYSELF! IF I CAN ACT QUICKLY ENOUGH!
ACT QUICKLY? WITHOUT THINKING?
NO! I WILL NOT PLAY THE FOOL AGAIN!
NOT STAR SAPPHIRE... HER BODY... MY MIND...
MY MOTHER WAS SINDELLA... YOU KNOW...
I'M...
ZATANNA!
MEANWHILE, SOUTH OF THE BORDER IN MEXICO CITY, AT AN ULTRA-MODERN STATE MUSEUM DEVOTED TO AZTEC TREASURES...
LET'S UNDERSTAND THIS, SUPERMAN... YOU SAY THE MEXICAN GOVERNMENT REQUESTED THE LEAGUE'S ASSISTANCE TO GUARD THE NOVA JEWELS? I'M NOT DOUBTING YOU...

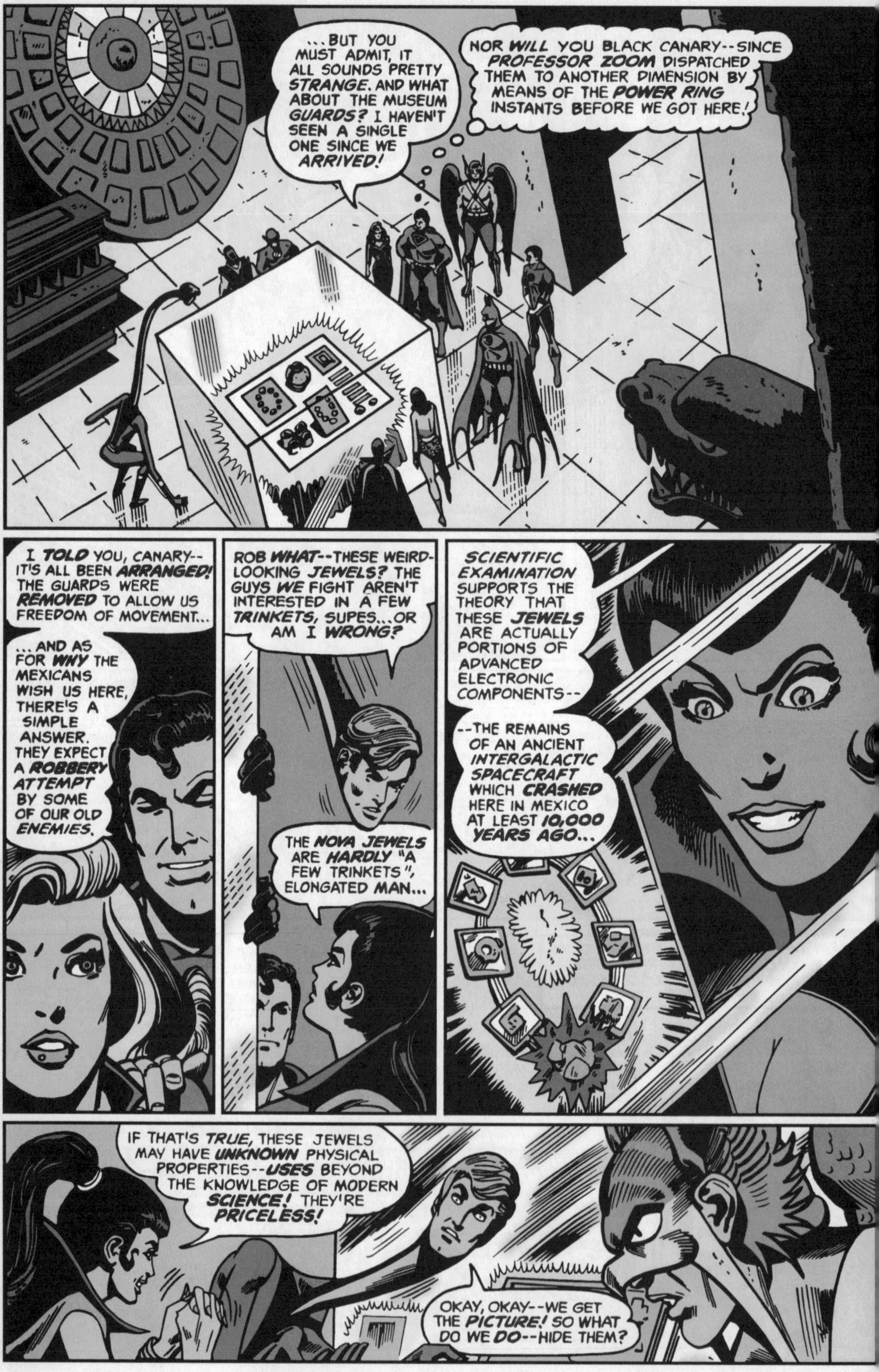
...BUT YOU MUST ADMIT, IT ALL SOUNDS PRETTY STRANGE. AND WHAT ABOUT THE MUSEUM GUARDS? I HAVEN'T SEEN A SINGLE ONE SINCE WE ARRIVED!
NOR WILL YOU BLACK CANARY--SINCE PROFESSOR ZOOM DISPATCHED THEM TO ANOTHER DIMENSION BY MEANS OF THE POWER RING INSTANTS BEFORE WE GOT HERE!
I TOLD YOU, CANARY--IT'S ALL BEEN ARRANGED! THE GUARDS WERE REMOVED TO ALLOW US FREEDOM OF MOVEMENT...
...AND AS FOR WHY THE MEXICANS WISH US HERE, THERE'S A SIMPLE ANSWER. THEY EXPECT A ROBBERY ATTEMPT BY SOME OF OUR OLD ENEMIES.
ROB WHAT--THESE WEIRD-LOOKING JEWELS? THE GUYS WE FIGHT AREN'T INTERESTED IN A FEW TRINKETS, SUPES...OR AM I WRONG?
THE NOVA JEWELS ARE HARDLY "A FEW TRINKETS", ELONGATED MAN...
SCIENTIFIC EXAMINATION SUPPORTS THE THEORY THAT THESE JEWELS ARE ACTUALLY PORTIONS OF ADVANCED ELECTRONIC COMPONENTS--
--THE REMAINS OF AN ANCIENT INTERGALACTIC SPACECRAFT WHICH CRASHED HERE IN MEXICO AT LEAST 10,000 YEARS AGO...
IF THAT'S TRUE, THESE JEWELS MAY HAVE UNKNOWN PHYSICAL PROPERTIES--USES BEYOND THE KNOWLEDGE OF MODERN SCIENCE! THEY'RE PRICELESS!
OKAY, OKAY--WE GET THE PICTURE! SO WHAT DO WE DO--HIDE THEM?

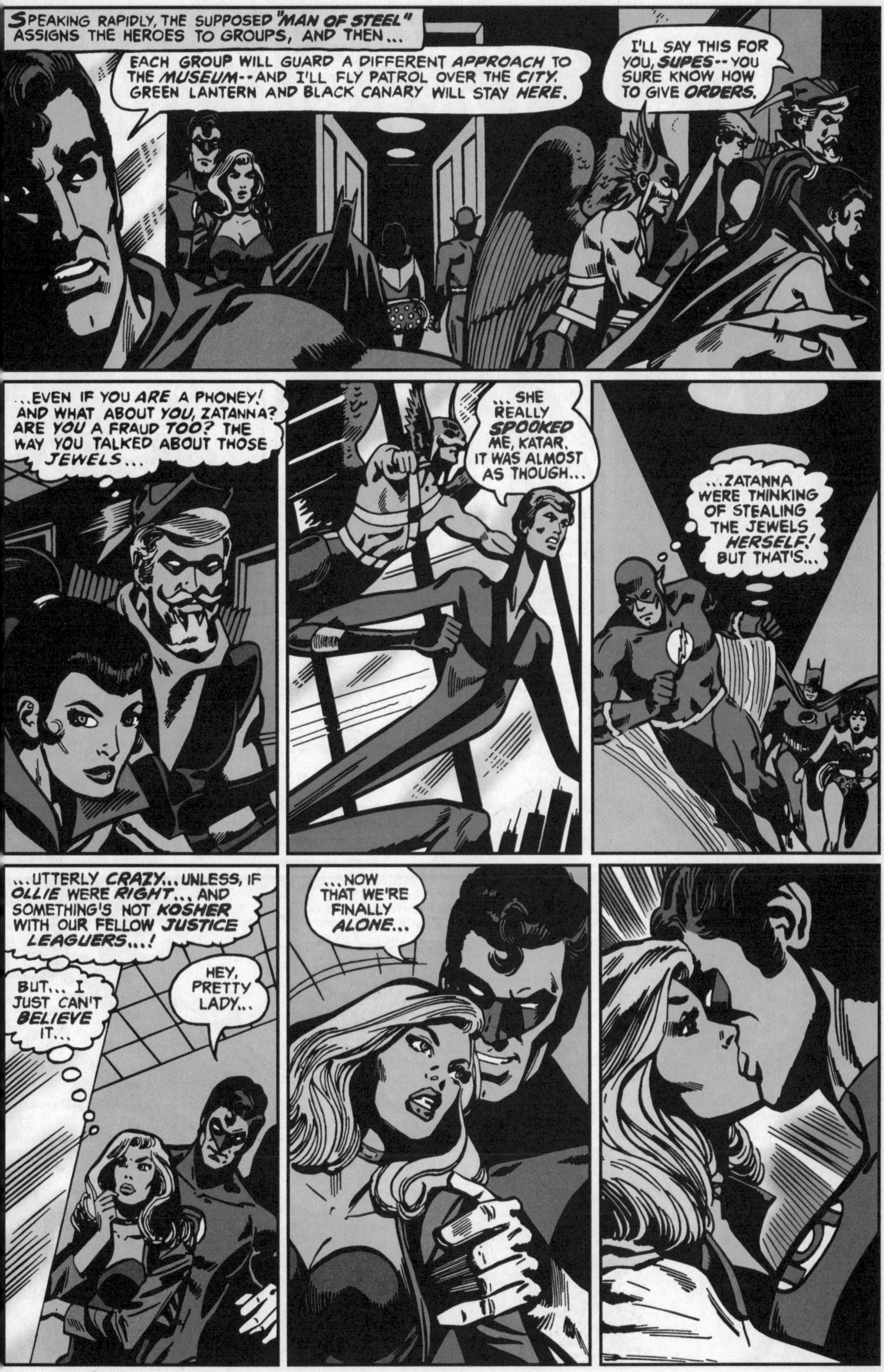
SPEAKING RAPIDLY, THE SUPPOSED "MAN OF STEEL" ASSIGNS THE HEROES TO GROUPS, AND THEN...
EACH GROUP WILL GUARD A DIFFERENT APPROACH TO THE MUSEUM--AND I'LL FLY PATROL OVER THE CITY. GREEN LANTERN AND BLACK CANARY WILL STAY HERE.
I'LL SAY THIS FOR YOU, SUPES--YOU SURE KNOW HOW TO GIVE ORDERS.
...EVEN IF YOU ARE A PHONEY! AND WHAT ABOUT YOU, ZATANNA? ARE YOU A FRAUD TOO? THE WAY YOU TALKED ABOUT THOSE JEWELS...
...SHE REALLY SPOOKED ME, KATAR. IT WAS ALMOST AS THOUGH...
...ZATANNA WERE THINKING OF STEALING THE JEWELS HERSELF! BUT THAT'S...
...UTTERLY CRAZY...UNLESS, IF OLLIE WERE RIGHT..., AND SOMETHING'S NOT KOSHER WITH OUR FELLOW JUSTICE LEAGUERS...!
BUT,... I JUST CAN'T BELIEVE IT...
HEY, PRETTY LADY...
...NOW THAT WE'RE FINALLY ALONE...

YOU **KNOW** SOMETHING? SUDDENLY--

UNNNHH

THLNK

-- I **BELIEVE** IT!

GREEN ARROW-- HEADS UP!

CHAWHAMMO

THEY'RE IMPOSTERS

THAT'S **CANARY!** THEN I WAS **RIGHT!** YOU'RE ALL **FAKES!**

FAKES WE MAY **BE**, ARCHER, BUT WE ARE NOT WITHOUT **POWER**-- THE SAME POWERS POSSESSED BY YOUR **FRIENDS**, WHOSE **BODIES** WE WEAR! OBSERVE-- AND DIE!

STRRRRK

GNINTHGIL EK'IRTS-- LLIK YM EOF!

SORRY, LADY--BUT I'VE BEEN **READY** FOR THIS FOR THE PAST COUPLE'A **HOURS!** YOU MAY HAVE **ZATANNA'S** BACKWARDS-MAGIC POWERS--

--BUT THEY DON'T DO YOU MUCH **GOOD** IF YOU CAN'T MOVE YOUR **MOUTH** TO CAST THE **SPELLS!**

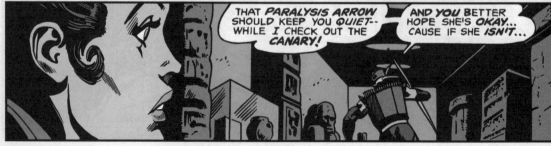

THAT **PARALYSIS** ARROW SHOULD KEEP YOU **QUIET**-- WHILE I CHECK OUT THE **CANARY!**

AND **YOU** BETTER HOPE SHE'S **OKAY**... CAUSE IF SHE **ISN'T**...

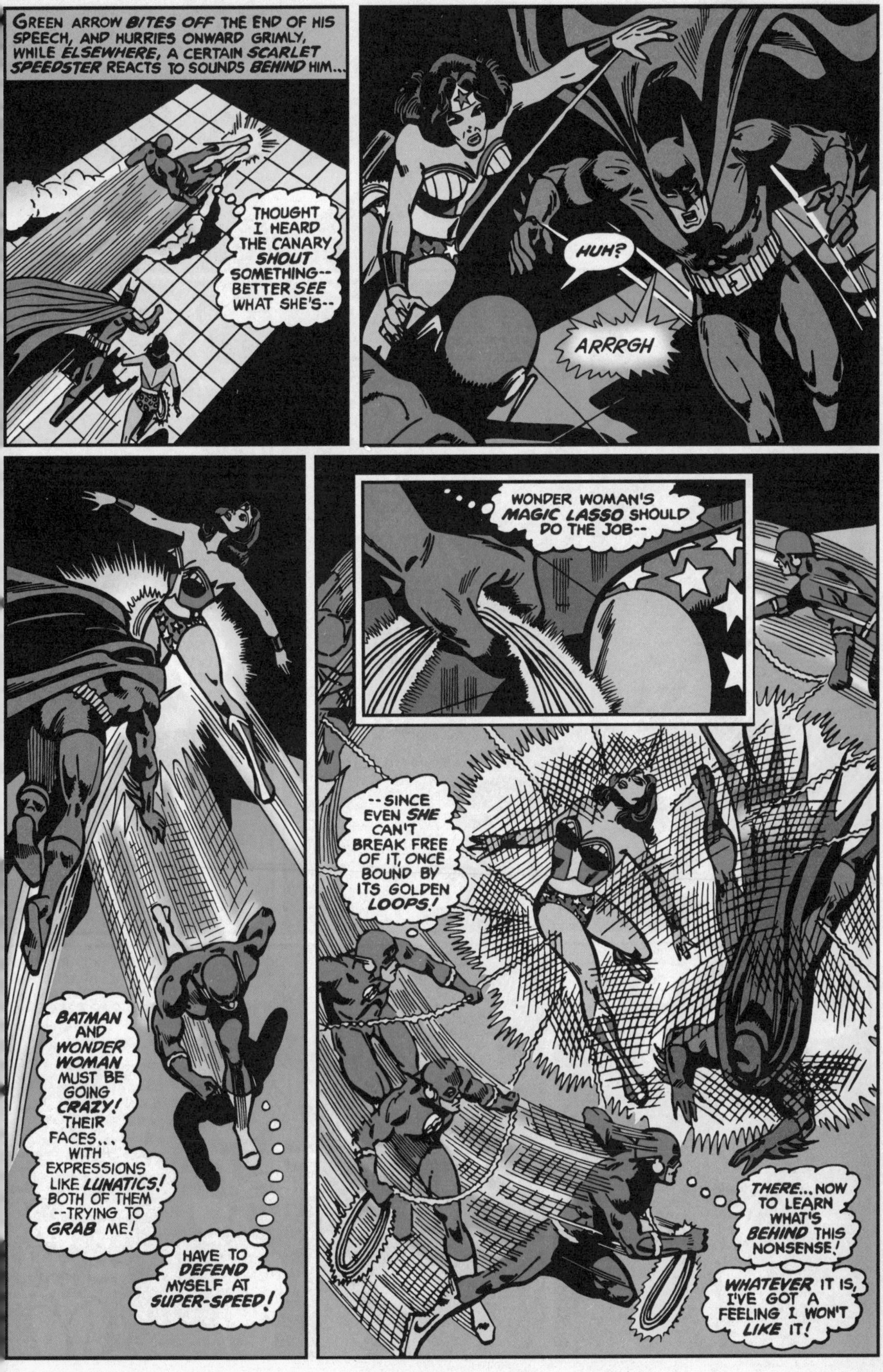
GREEN ARROW BITES OFF THE END OF HIS SPEECH, AND HURRIES ONWARD GRIMLY, WHILE ELSEWHERE, A CERTAIN SCARLET SPEEDSTER REACTS TO SOUNDS BEHIND HIM...
THOUGHT I HEARD THE CANARY SHOUT SOMETHING-- BETTER SEE WHAT SHE'S--
HUH?
ARRRGH
BATMAN AND WONDER WOMAN MUST BE GOING CRAZY! THEIR FACES... WITH EXPRESSIONS LIKE LUNATICS! BOTH OF THEM --TRYING TO GRAB ME!
HAVE TO DEFEND MYSELF AT SUPER-SPEED!
WONDER WOMAN'S MAGIC LASSO SHOULD DO THE JOB--
--SINCE EVEN SHE CAN'T BREAK FREE OF IT, ONCE BOUND BY ITS GOLDEN LOOPS!
THERE... NOW TO LEARN WHAT'S BEHIND THIS NONSENSE!
WHATEVER IT IS, I'VE GOT A FEELING I WON'T LIKE IT!

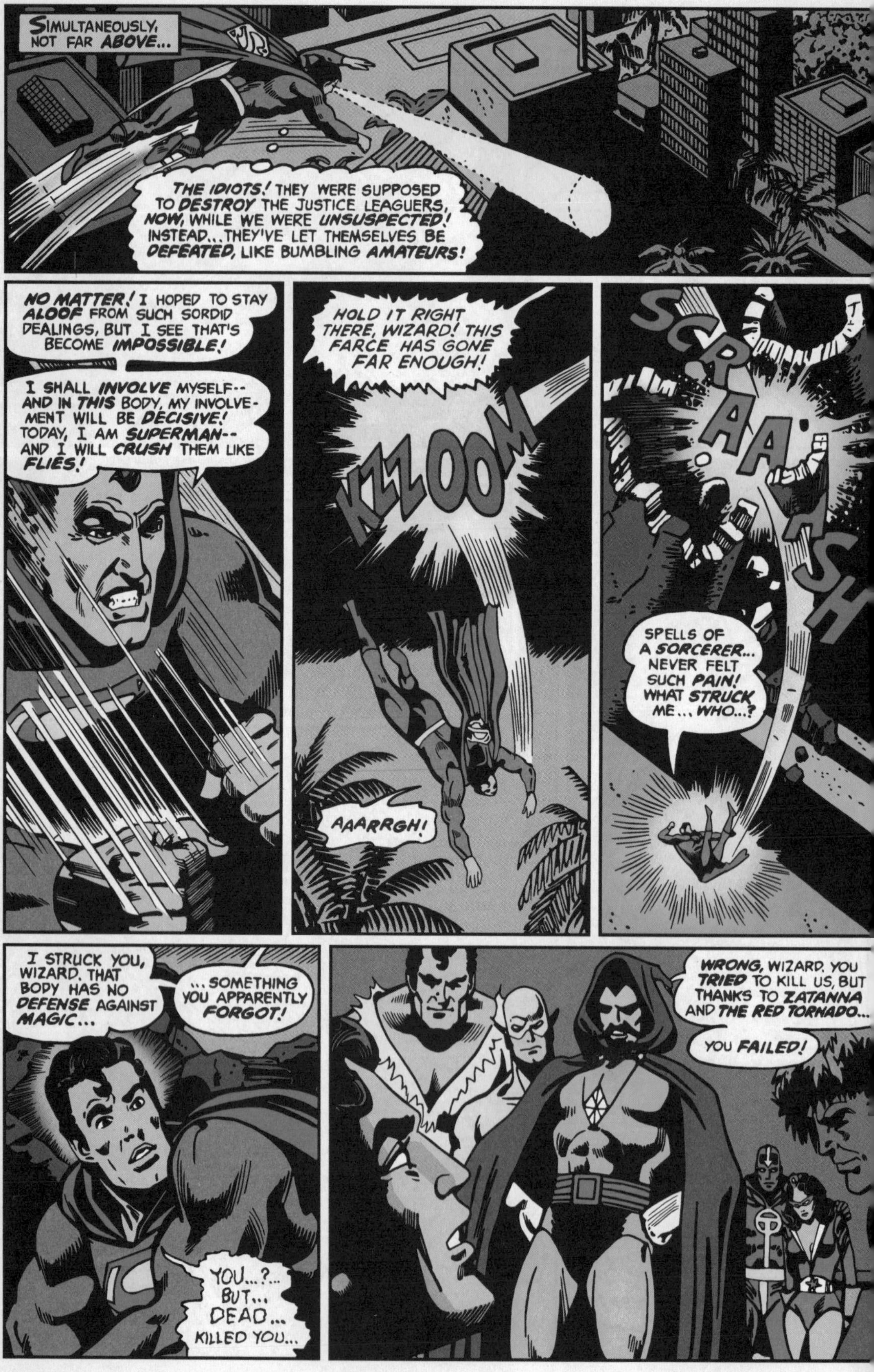
SIMULTANEOUSLY, NOT FAR ABOVE...
THE IDIOTS! THEY WERE SUPPOSED TO DESTROY THE JUSTICE LEAGUERS, NOW, WHILE WE WERE UNSUSPECTED! INSTEAD...THEY'VE LET THEMSELVES BE DEFEATED, LIKE BUMBLING AMATEURS!
NO MATTER! I HOPED TO STAY ALOOF FROM SUCH SORDID DEALINGS, BUT I SEE THAT'S BECOME IMPOSSIBLE!
I SHALL INVOLVE MYSELF-- AND IN THIS BODY, MY INVOLVEMENT WILL BE DECISIVE! TODAY, I AM SUPERMAN-- AND I WILL CRUSH THEM LIKE FLIES!
HOLD IT RIGHT THERE, WIZARD! THIS FARCE HAS GONE FAR ENOUGH!
KZZOOM
AAARRGH!
SCRAAASH
SPELLS OF A SORCERER... NEVER FELT SUCH PAIN! WHAT STRUCK ME... WHO...?
I STRUCK YOU, WIZARD. THAT BODY HAS NO DEFENSE AGAINST MAGIC...
...SOMETHING YOU APPARENTLY FORGOT!
YOU...?... BUT... DEAD... KILLED YOU...
WRONG, WIZARD. YOU TRIED TO KILL US, BUT THANKS TO ZATANNA AND THE RED TORNADO...
YOU FAILED!

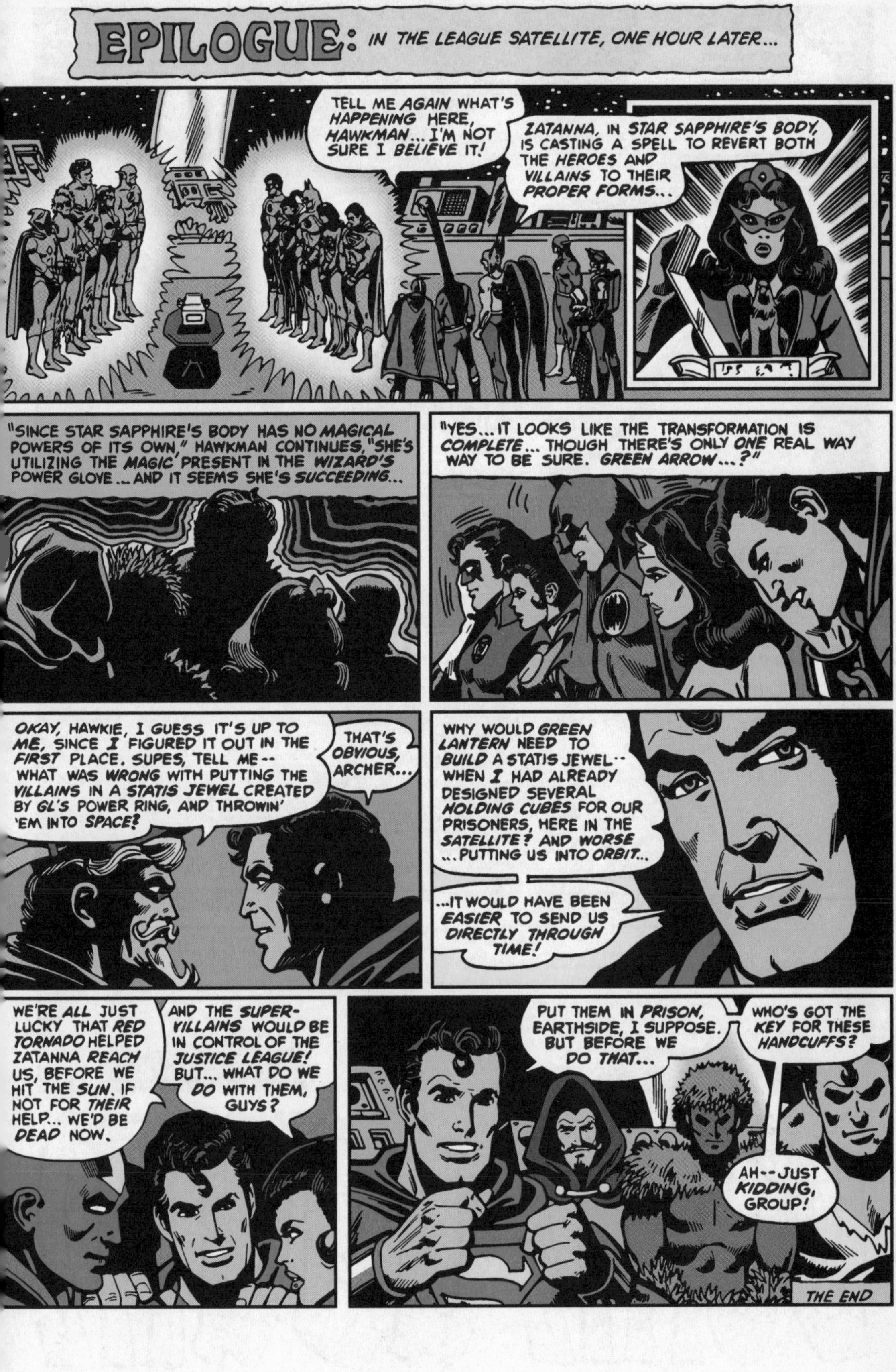
EPILOGUE: IN THE LEAGUE SATELLITE, ONE HOUR LATER...
TELL ME AGAIN WHAT'S HAPPENING HERE, HAWKMAN... I'M NOT SURE I BELIEVE IT!
ZATANNA, IN STAR SAPPHIRE'S BODY, IS CASTING A SPELL TO REVERT BOTH THE HEROES AND VILLAINS TO THEIR PROPER FORMS...
"SINCE STAR SAPPHIRE'S BODY HAS NO MAGICAL POWERS OF ITS OWN," HAWKMAN CONTINUES, "SHE'S UTILIZING THE MAGIC PRESENT IN THE WIZARD'S POWER GLOVE... AND IT SEEMS SHE'S SUCCEEDING...
"YES... IT LOOKS LIKE THE TRANSFORMATION IS COMPLETE... THOUGH THERE'S ONLY ONE REAL WAY WAY TO BE SURE. GREEN ARROW...?"
OKAY, HAWKIE, I GUESS IT'S UP TO ME, SINCE I FIGURED IT OUT IN THE FIRST PLACE. SUPES, TELL ME-- WHAT WAS WRONG WITH PUTTING THE VILLAINS IN A STATIS JEWEL CREATED BY GL'S POWER RING, AND THROWIN' 'EM INTO SPACE?
THAT'S OBVIOUS, ARCHER...
WHY WOULD GREEN LANTERN NEED TO BUILD A STATIS JEWEL-- WHEN I HAD ALREADY DESIGNED SEVERAL HOLDING CUBES FOR OUR PRISONERS, HERE IN THE SATELLITE? AND WORSE ...PUTTING US INTO ORBIT...
...IT WOULD HAVE BEEN EASIER TO SEND US DIRECTLY THROUGH TIME!
WE'RE ALL JUST LUCKY THAT RED TORNADO HELPED ZATANNA REACH US, BEFORE WE HIT THE SUN. IF NOT FOR THEIR HELP... WE'D BE DEAD NOW.
AND THE SUPER-VILLAINS WOULD BE IN CONTROL OF THE JUSTICE LEAGUE! BUT... WHAT DO WE DO WITH THEM, GUYS?
PUT THEM IN PRISON, EARTHSIDE, I SUPPOSE. BUT BEFORE WE DO THAT...
WHO'S GOT THE KEY FOR THESE HANDCUFFS?
AH--JUST KIDDING, GROUP!
THE END

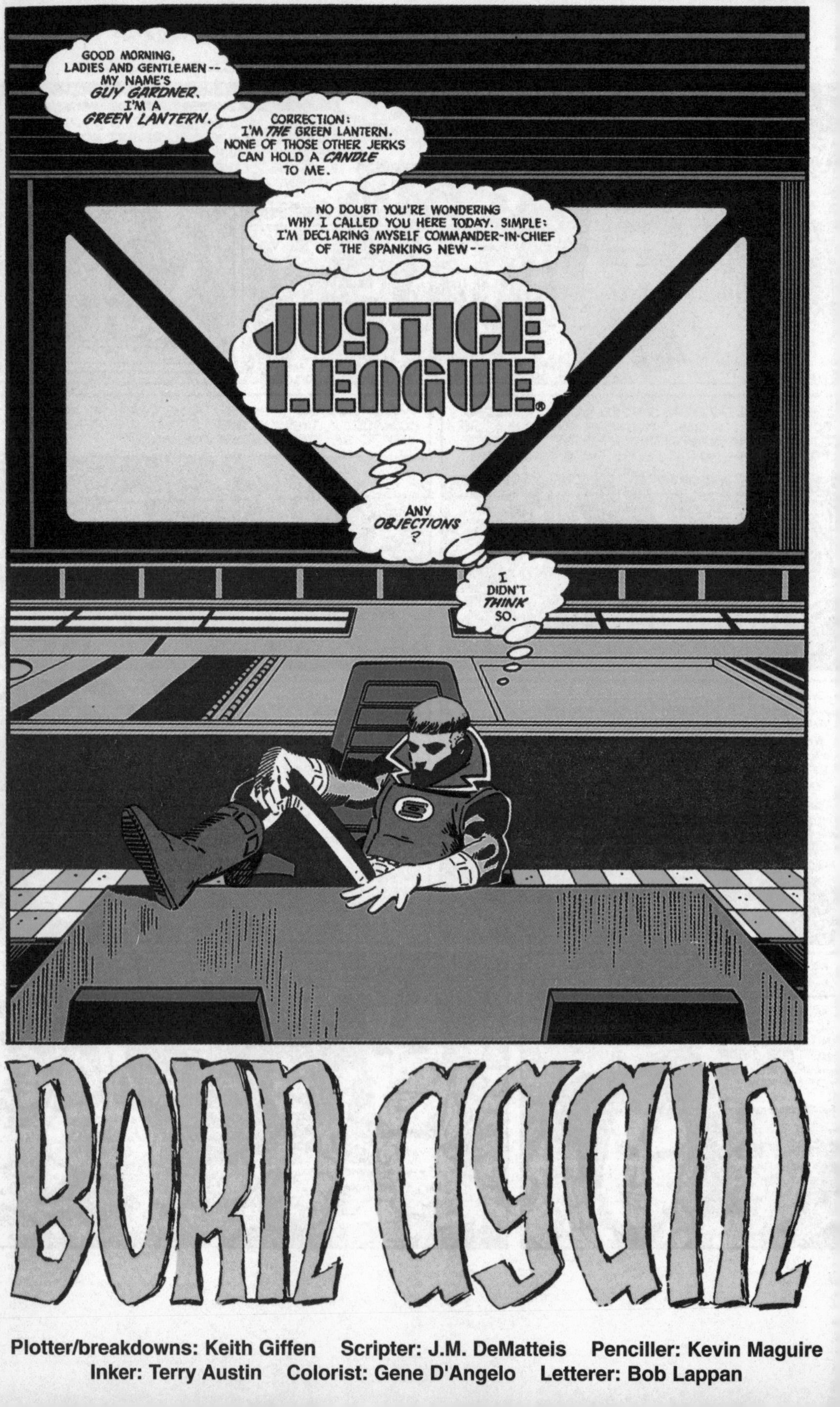
GOOD MORNING, LADIES AND GENTLEMEN-- MY NAME'S GUY GARDNER. I'M A GREEN LANTERN.
CORRECTION: I'M THE GREEN LANTERN. NONE OF THOSE OTHER JERKS CAN HOLD A CANDLE TO ME.
NO DOUBT YOU'RE WONDERING WHY I CALLED YOU HERE TODAY. SIMPLE: I'M DECLARING MYSELF COMMANDER-IN-CHIEF OF THE SPANKING NEW--
JUSTICE LEAGUE®
ANY OBJECTIONS?
I DIDN'T THINK SO.

BORN AGAIN

Plotter/breakdowns: Keith Giffen Scripter: J.M. DeMatteis Penciller: Kevin Maguire
Inker: Terry Austin Colorist: Gene D'Angelo Letterer: Bob Lappan

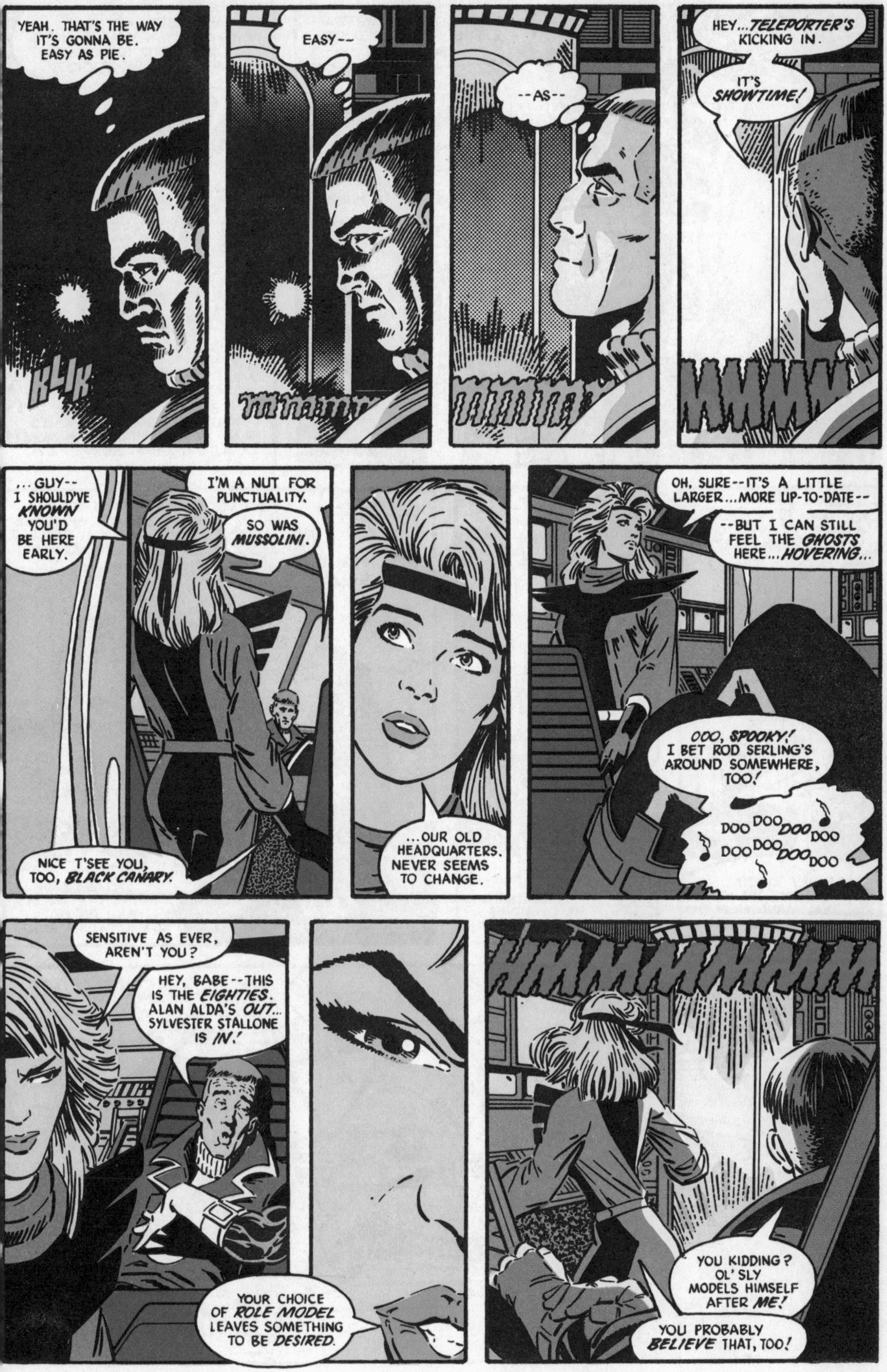

YEAH. THAT'S THE WAY IT'S GONNA BE. EASY AS PIE.
KLIK
EASY--
--AS--
HEY...TELEPORTER'S KICKING IN.
IT'S SHOWTIME!
MMMMM
...GUY-- I SHOULD'VE KNOWN YOU'D BE HERE EARLY.
I'M A NUT FOR PUNCTUALITY.
SO WAS MUSSOLINI.
NICE T'SEE YOU, TOO, BLACK CANARY.
...OUR OLD HEADQUARTERS. NEVER SEEMS TO CHANGE.
OH, SURE--IT'S A LITTLE LARGER...MORE UP-TO-DATE--
--BUT I CAN STILL FEEL THE GHOSTS HERE...HOVERING...
OOO, SPOOKY! I BET ROD SERLING'S AROUND SOMEWHERE, TOO!
DOO DOO DOO DOO DOO DOO DOO DOO
SENSITIVE AS EVER, AREN'T YOU?
HEY, BABE--THIS IS THE EIGHTIES. ALAN ALDA'S OUT... SYLVESTER STALLONE IS IN!
YOUR CHOICE OF ROLE MODEL LEAVES SOMETHING TO BE DESIRED.
HMMMMMMMM
YOU KIDDING? OL' SLY MODELS HIMSELF AFTER ME!
YOU PROBABLY BELIEVE THAT, TOO!

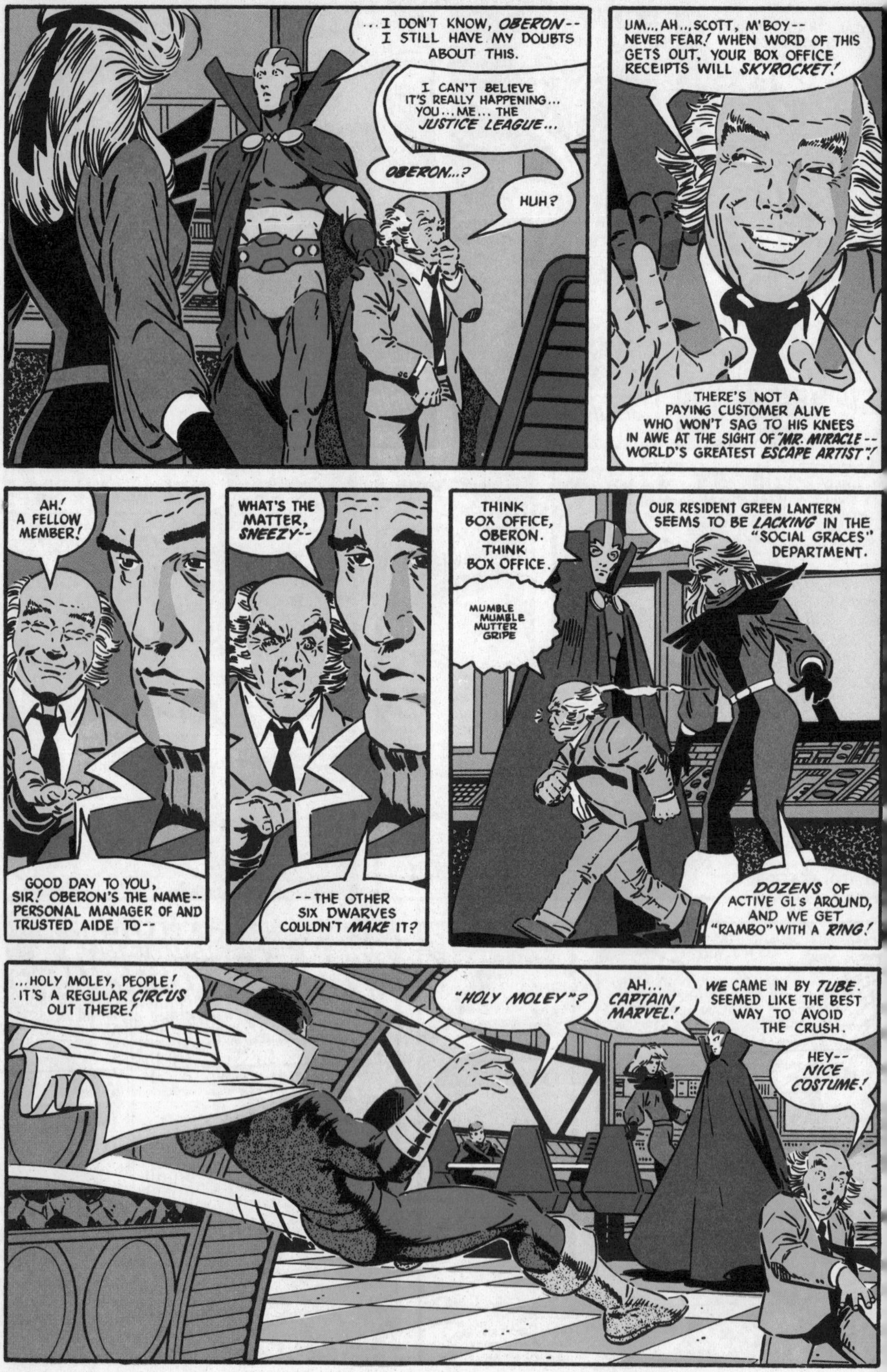

...I DON'T KNOW, OBERON-- I STILL HAVE MY DOUBTS ABOUT THIS.
I CAN'T BELIEVE IT'S REALLY HAPPENING... YOU... ME... THE JUSTICE LEAGUE...
OBERON...?
HUH?
UM... AH.., SCOTT, M'BOY-- NEVER FEAR! WHEN WORD OF THIS GETS OUT, YOUR BOX OFFICE RECEIPTS WILL SKYROCKET!
THERE'S NOT A PAYING CUSTOMER ALIVE WHO WON'T SAG TO HIS KNEES IN AWE AT THE SIGHT OF "MR. MIRACLE -- WORLD'S GREATEST ESCAPE ARTIST"!
AH! A FELLOW MEMBER!
GOOD DAY TO YOU, SIR! OBERON'S THE NAME-- PERSONAL MANAGER OF AND TRUSTED AIDE TO--
WHAT'S THE MATTER, SNEEZY--
--THE OTHER SIX DWARVES COULDN'T MAKE IT?
THINK BOX OFFICE, OBERON. THINK BOX OFFICE.
MUMBLE MUMBLE MUTTER GRIPE
OUR RESIDENT GREEN LANTERN SEEMS TO BE LACKING IN THE "SOCIAL GRACES" DEPARTMENT.
DOZENS OF ACTIVE GLs AROUND, AND WE GET "RAMBO" WITH A RING!
...HOLY MOLEY, PEOPLE! IT'S A REGULAR CIRCUS OUT THERE!
"HOLY MOLEY"?
AH... CAPTAIN MARVEL!
WE CAME IN BY TUBE. SEEMED LIKE THE BEST WAY TO AVOID THE CRUSH.
HEY-- NICE COSTUME!

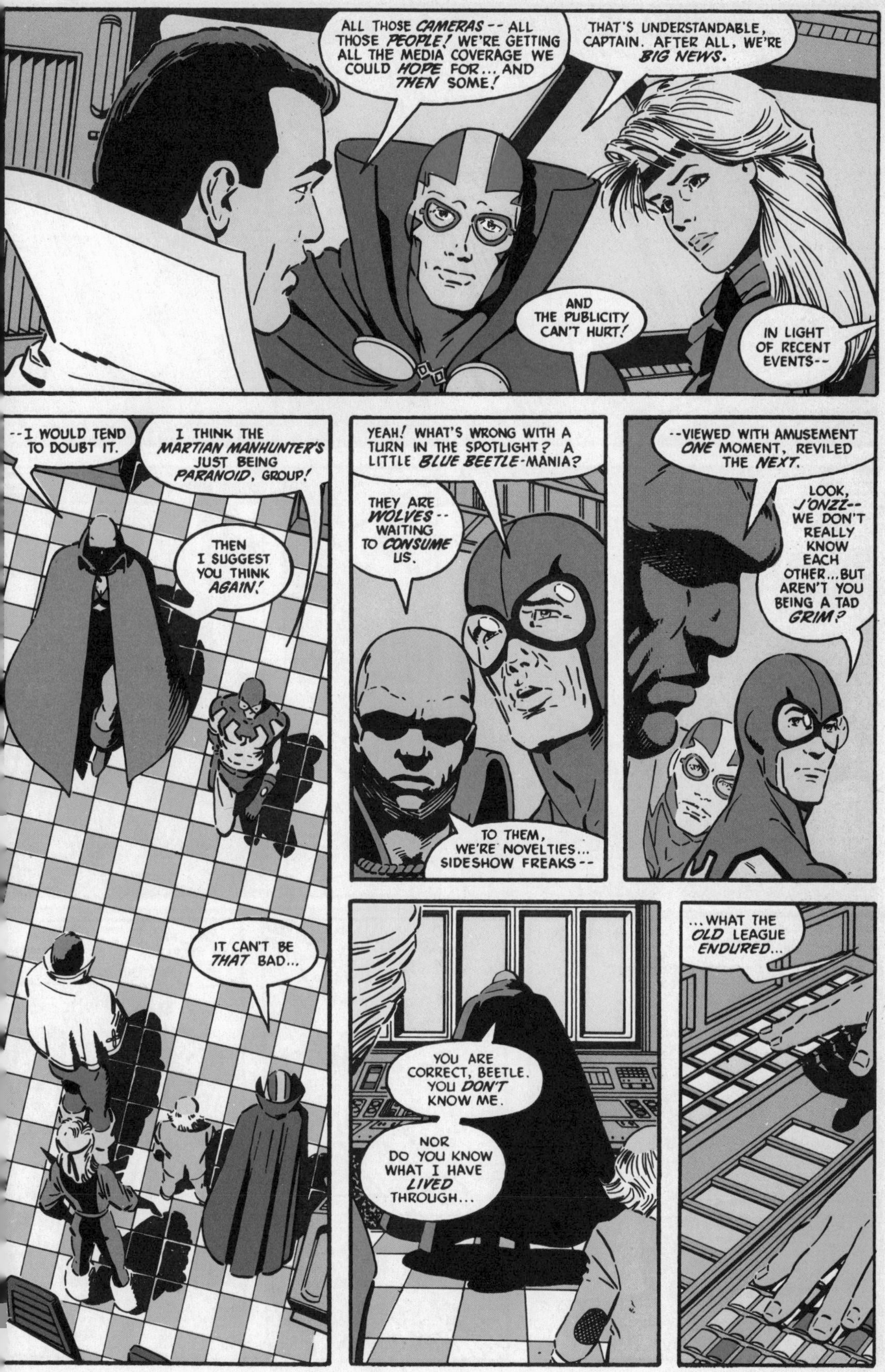
ALL THOSE CAMERAS -- ALL THOSE PEOPLE! WE'RE GETTING ALL THE MEDIA COVERAGE WE COULD HOPE FOR... AND THEN SOME!
THAT'S UNDERSTANDABLE, CAPTAIN. AFTER ALL, WE'RE BIG NEWS.
AND THE PUBLICITY CAN'T HURT!
IN LIGHT OF RECENT EVENTS--
--I WOULD TEND TO DOUBT IT.
I THINK THE MARTIAN MANHUNTER'S JUST BEING PARANOID, GROUP!
THEN I SUGGEST YOU THINK AGAIN!
YEAH! WHAT'S WRONG WITH A TURN IN THE SPOTLIGHT? A LITTLE BLUE BEETLE-MANIA?
THEY ARE WOLVES-- WAITING TO CONSUME US.
TO THEM, WE'RE NOVELTIES... SIDESHOW FREAKS--
--VIEWED WITH AMUSEMENT ONE MOMENT, REVILED THE NEXT.
LOOK, J'ONZZ-- WE DON'T REALLY KNOW EACH OTHER... BUT AREN'T YOU BEING A TAD GRIM?
IT CAN'T BE THAT BAD...
YOU ARE CORRECT, BEETLE. YOU DON'T KNOW ME.
NOR DO YOU KNOW WHAT I HAVE LIVED THROUGH...
...WHAT THE OLD LEAGUE ENDURED...

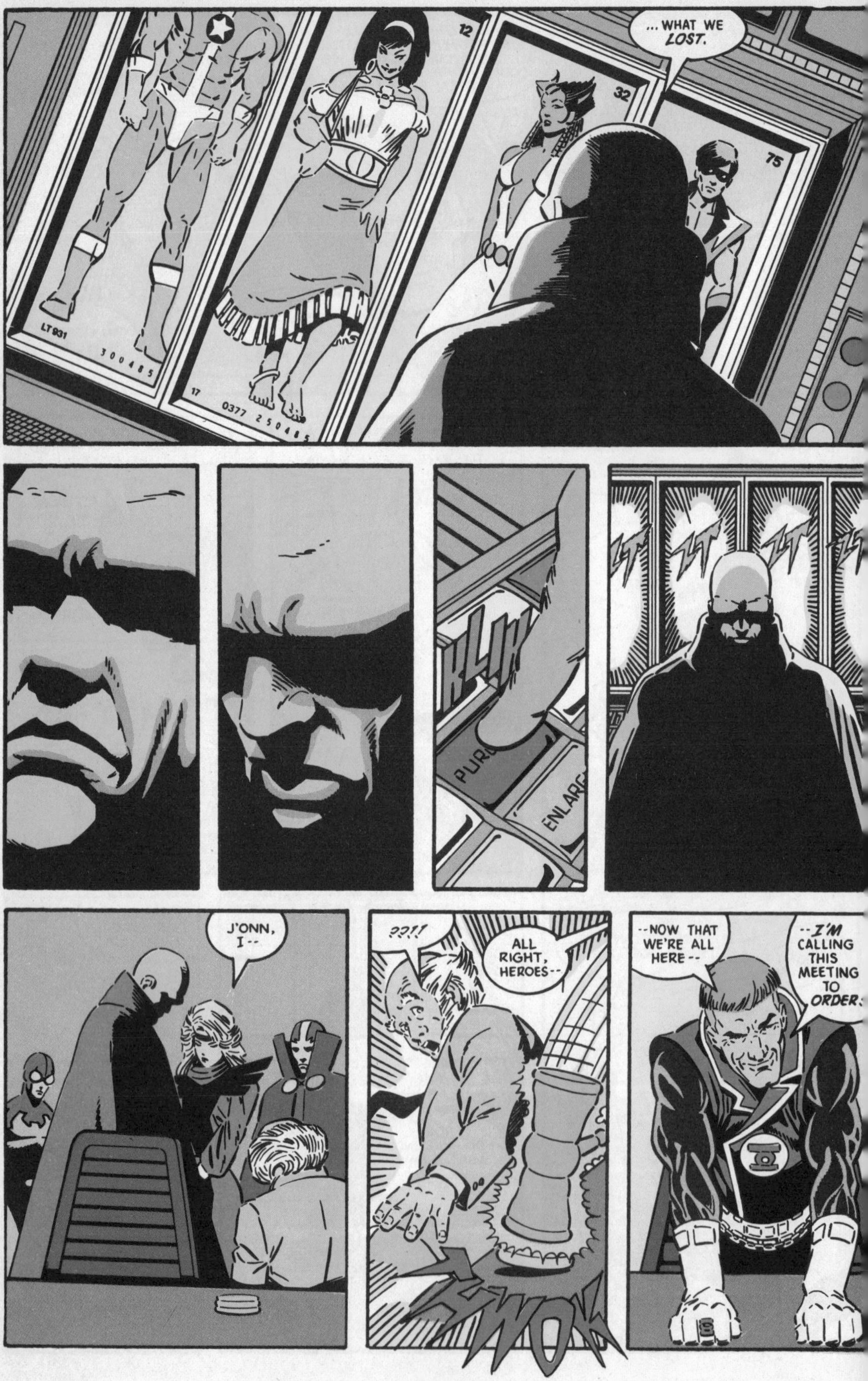

... WHAT WE LOST.
KLIK
J'ONN, I--
??!!
ALL RIGHT, HEROES--
--NOW THAT WE'RE ALL HERE--
--I'M CALLING THIS MEETING TO ORDER!

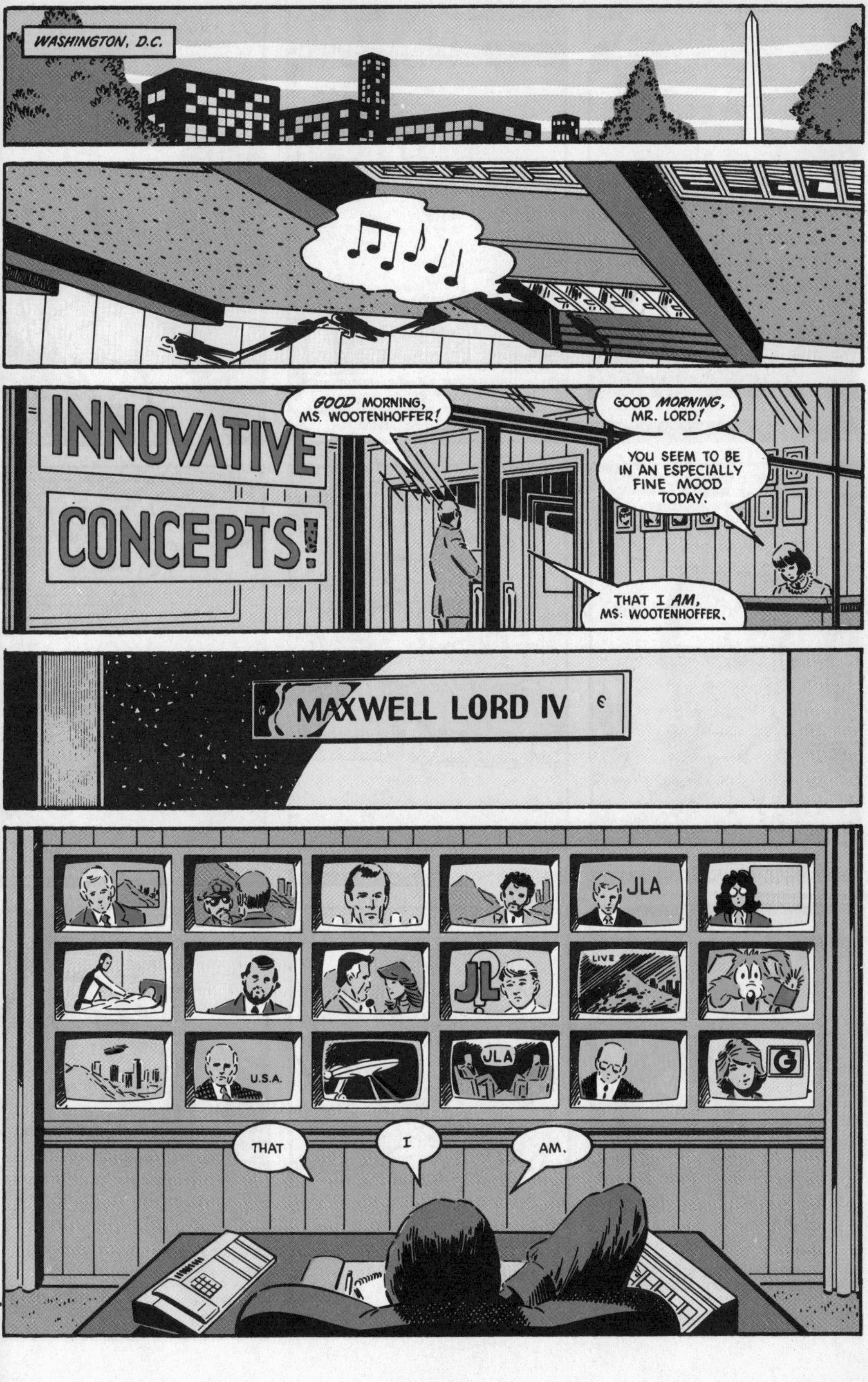
WASHINGTON, D.C.
GOOD MORNING, MS. WOOTENHOFFER!
GOOD MORNING, MR. LORD!
YOU SEEM TO BE IN AN ESPECIALLY FINE MOOD TODAY.
THAT I AM, MS. WOOTENHOFFER.
INNOVATIVE CONCEPTS!
MAXWELL LORD IV
JLA
LIVE
U.S.A.
JLA
THAT
I
AM.

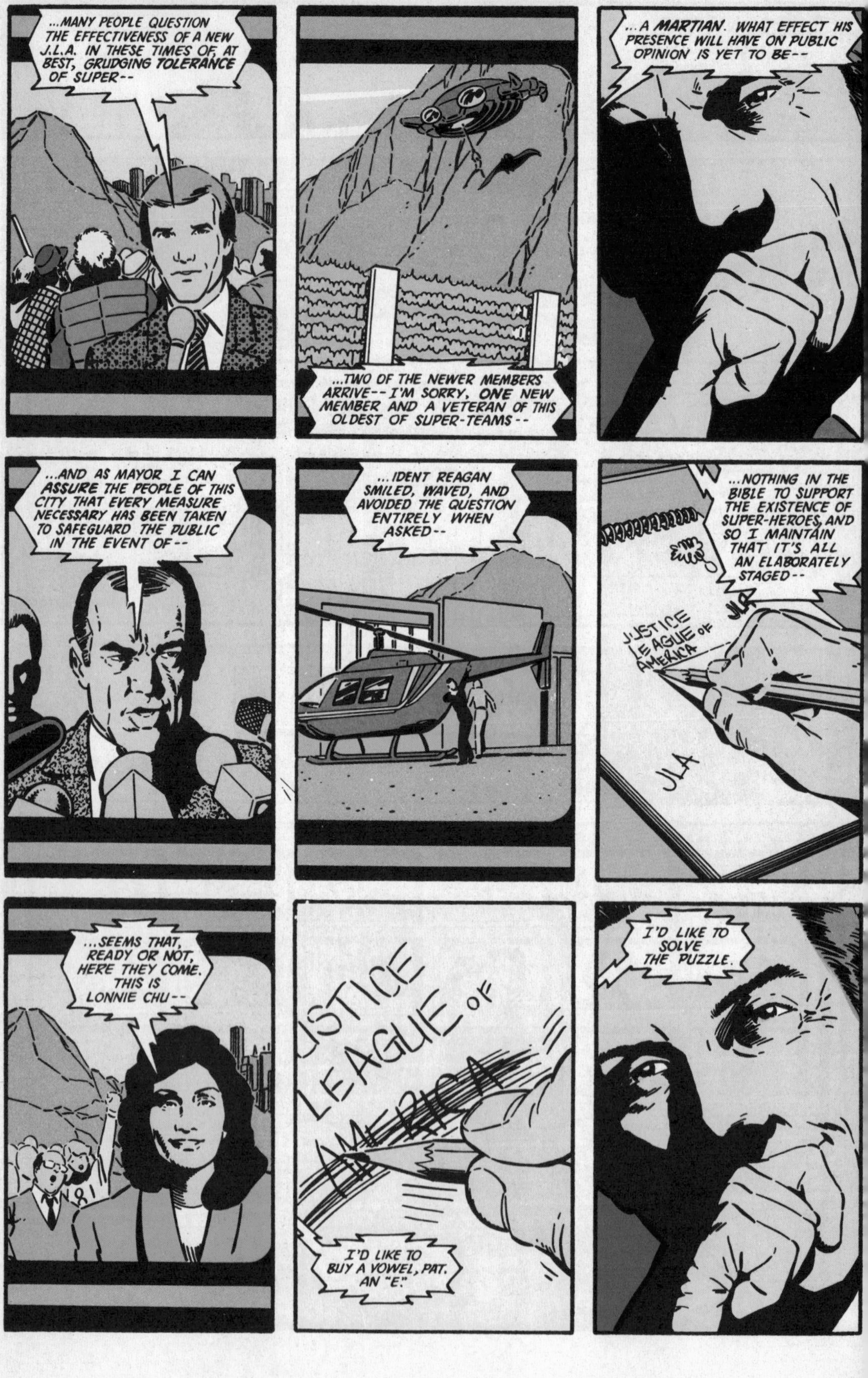
...MANY PEOPLE QUESTION THE EFFECTIVENESS OF A NEW J.L.A. IN THESE TIMES OF, AT BEST, GRUDGING TOLERANCE OF SUPER--
...TWO OF THE NEWER MEMBERS ARRIVE--I'M SORRY, ONE NEW MEMBER AND A VETERAN OF THIS OLDEST OF SUPER-TEAMS--
...A MARTIAN. WHAT EFFECT HIS PRESENCE WILL HAVE ON PUBLIC OPINION IS YET TO BE--
...AND AS MAYOR I CAN ASSURE THE PEOPLE OF THIS CITY THAT EVERY MEASURE NECESSARY HAS BEEN TAKEN TO SAFEGUARD THE PUBLIC IN THE EVENT OF--
...IDENT REAGAN SMILED, WAVED, AND AVOIDED THE QUESTION ENTIRELY WHEN ASKED--
...NOTHING IN THE BIBLE TO SUPPORT THE EXISTENCE OF SUPER-HEROES, AND SO I MAINTAIN THAT IT'S ALL AN ELABORATELY STAGED--
JUSTICE LEAGUE OF AMERICA
JLA
JLA
...SEEMS THAT, READY OR NOT, HERE THEY COME. THIS IS LONNIE CHU--
JUSTICE LEAGUE OF AMERICA
I'D LIKE TO BUY A VOWEL, PAT. AN "E."
I'D LIKE TO SOLVE THE PUZZLE.

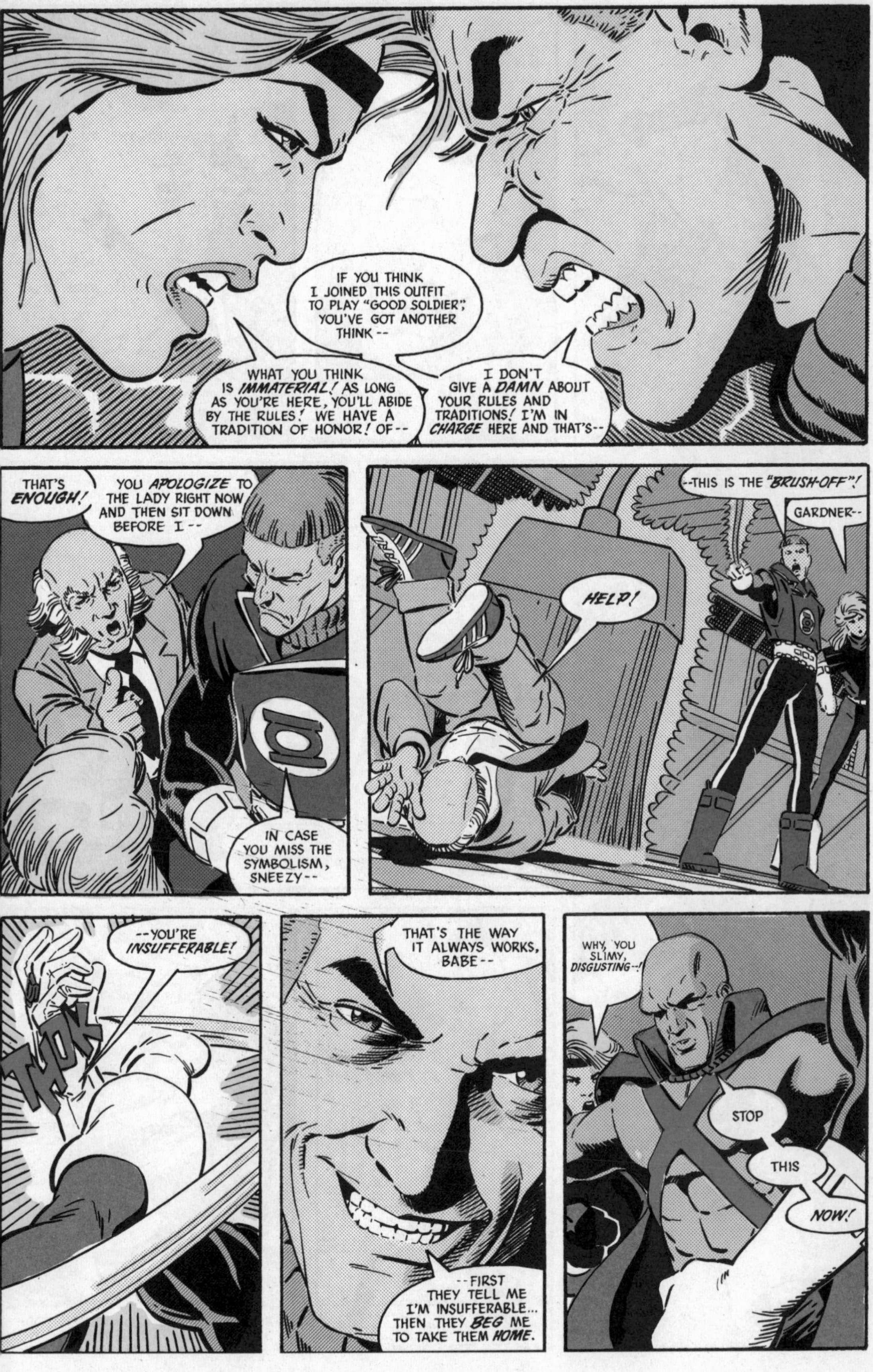
IF YOU THINK I JOINED THIS OUTFIT TO PLAY "GOOD SOLDIER", YOU'VE GOT ANOTHER THINK --
WHAT YOU THINK IS *IMMATERIAL!* AS LONG AS YOU'RE HERE, YOU'LL ABIDE BY THE RULES! WE HAVE A TRADITION OF HONOR! OF--
I DON'T GIVE A *DAMN* ABOUT YOUR RULES AND TRADITIONS! I'M IN *CHARGE* HERE AND THAT'S--
THAT'S *ENOUGH!*
YOU *APOLOGIZE* TO THE LADY RIGHT NOW AND THEN SIT DOWN BEFORE I --
IN CASE YOU MISS THE SYMBOLISM, SNEEZY--
--THIS IS THE *"BRUSH-OFF"!*
HELP!
GARDNER--
--YOU'RE *INSUFFERABLE!*
THOK
THAT'S THE WAY IT ALWAYS WORKS, BABE--
--FIRST THEY TELL ME I'M INSUFFERABLE... THEN THEY *BEG* ME TO TAKE THEM *HOME*.
WHY, YOU SLIMY, *DISGUSTING*--!
STOP
THIS
NOW!

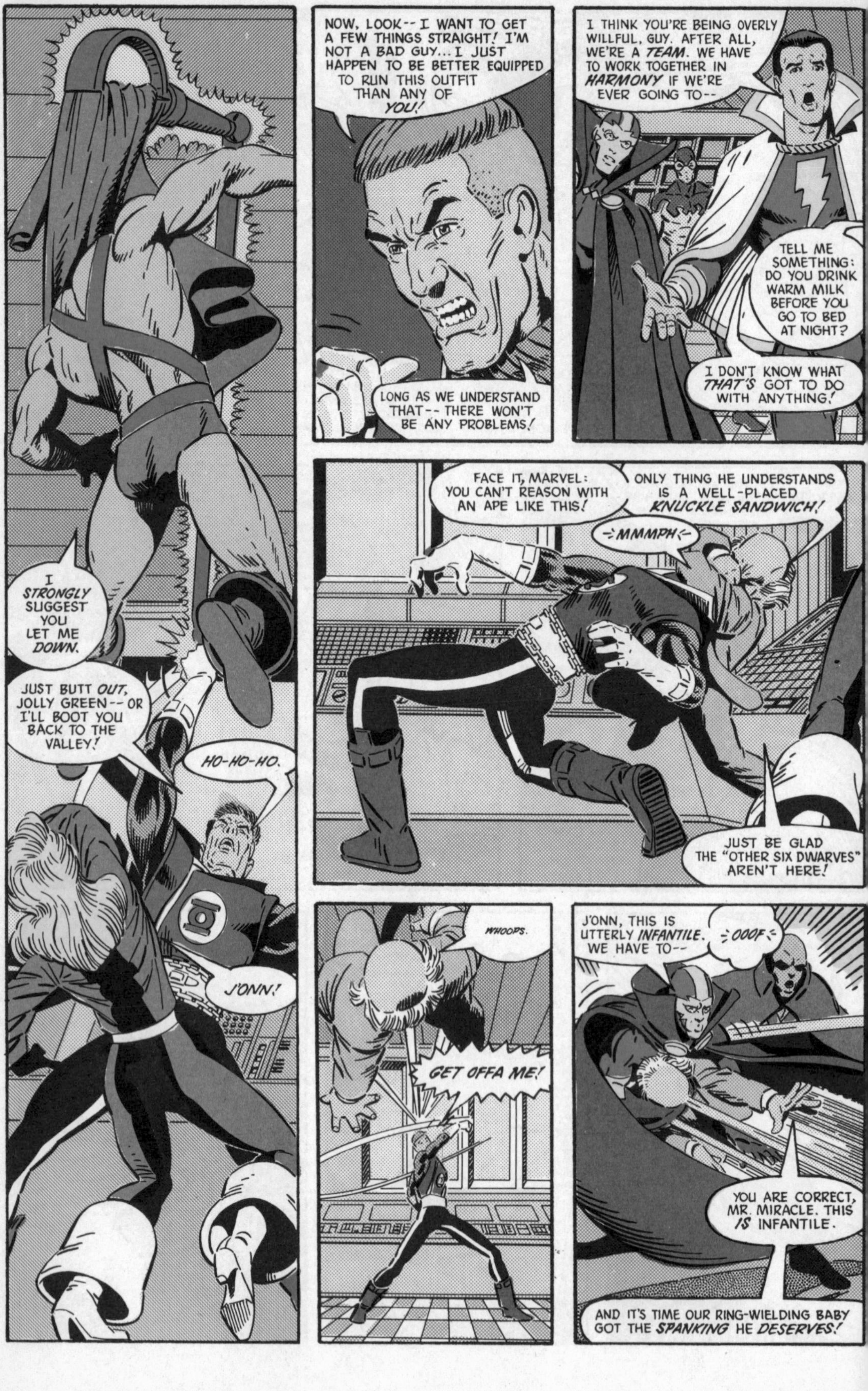
I STRONGLY SUGGEST YOU LET ME DOWN.
JUST BUTT OUT, JOLLY GREEN--OR I'LL BOOT YOU BACK TO THE VALLEY!
HO-HO-HO.
J'ONN!
NOW, LOOK--I WANT TO GET A FEW THINGS STRAIGHT! I'M NOT A BAD GUY... I JUST HAPPEN TO BE BETTER EQUIPPED TO RUN THIS OUTFIT THAN ANY OF YOU!
LONG AS WE UNDERSTAND THAT--THERE WON'T BE ANY PROBLEMS!
I THINK YOU'RE BEING OVERLY WILLFUL, GUY. AFTER ALL, WE'RE A TEAM. WE HAVE TO WORK TOGETHER IN HARMONY IF WE'RE EVER GOING TO--
TELL ME SOMETHING: DO YOU DRINK WARM MILK BEFORE YOU GO TO BED AT NIGHT?
I DON'T KNOW WHAT THAT'S GOT TO DO WITH ANYTHING!
FACE IT, MARVEL: YOU CAN'T REASON WITH AN APE LIKE THIS!
ONLY THING HE UNDERSTANDS IS A WELL-PLACED KNUCKLE SANDWICH!
MMMPH
JUST BE GLAD THE "OTHER SIX DWARVES" AREN'T HERE!
WHOOPS.
GET OFFA ME!
J'ONN, THIS IS UTTERLY INFANTILE. WE HAVE TO--
OOOF
YOU ARE CORRECT, MR. MIRACLE. THIS IS INFANTILE.
AND IT'S TIME OUR RING-WIELDING BABY GOT THE SPANKING HE DESERVES!

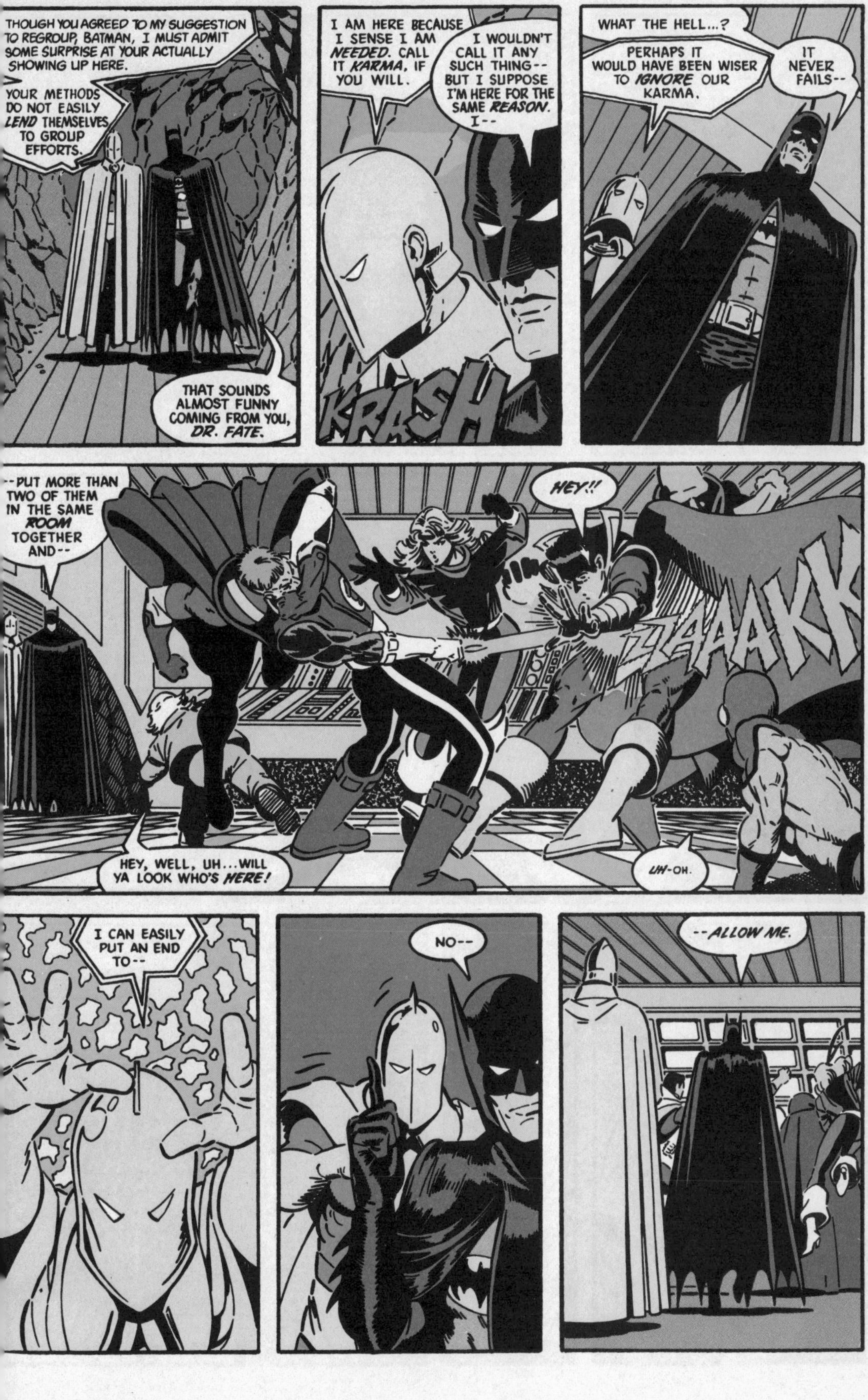
THOUGH YOU AGREED TO MY SUGGESTION TO REGROUP, BATMAN, I MUST ADMIT SOME SURPRISE AT YOUR ACTUALLY SHOWING UP HERE.
YOUR METHODS DO NOT EASILY LEND THEMSELVES TO GROUP EFFORTS.
THAT SOUNDS ALMOST FUNNY COMING FROM YOU, DR. FATE.
I AM HERE BECAUSE I SENSE I AM NEEDED. CALL IT KARMA, IF YOU WILL.
I WOULDN'T CALL IT ANY SUCH THING-- BUT I SUPPOSE I'M HERE FOR THE SAME REASON. I--
KRASH
WHAT THE HELL...?
PERHAPS IT WOULD HAVE BEEN WISER TO IGNORE OUR KARMA.
IT NEVER FAILS--
--PUT MORE THAN TWO OF THEM IN THE SAME ROOM TOGETHER AND--
HEY!!
ZZAAAKK
HEY, WELL, UH...WILL YA LOOK WHO'S HERE!
UH-OH.
I CAN EASILY PUT AN END TO--
NO--
--ALLOW ME.

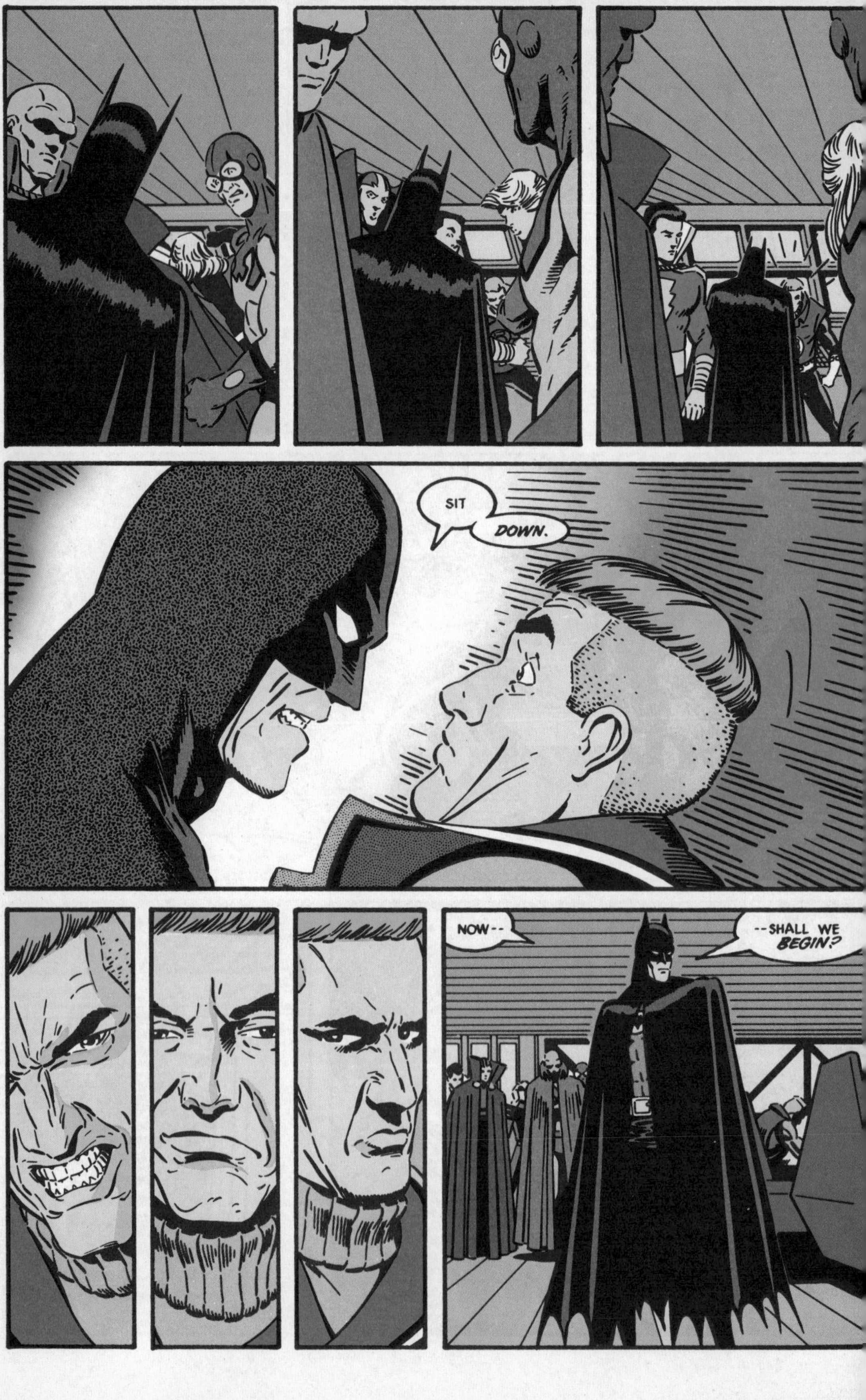
SIT DOWN.
NOW--
--SHALL WE BEGIN?

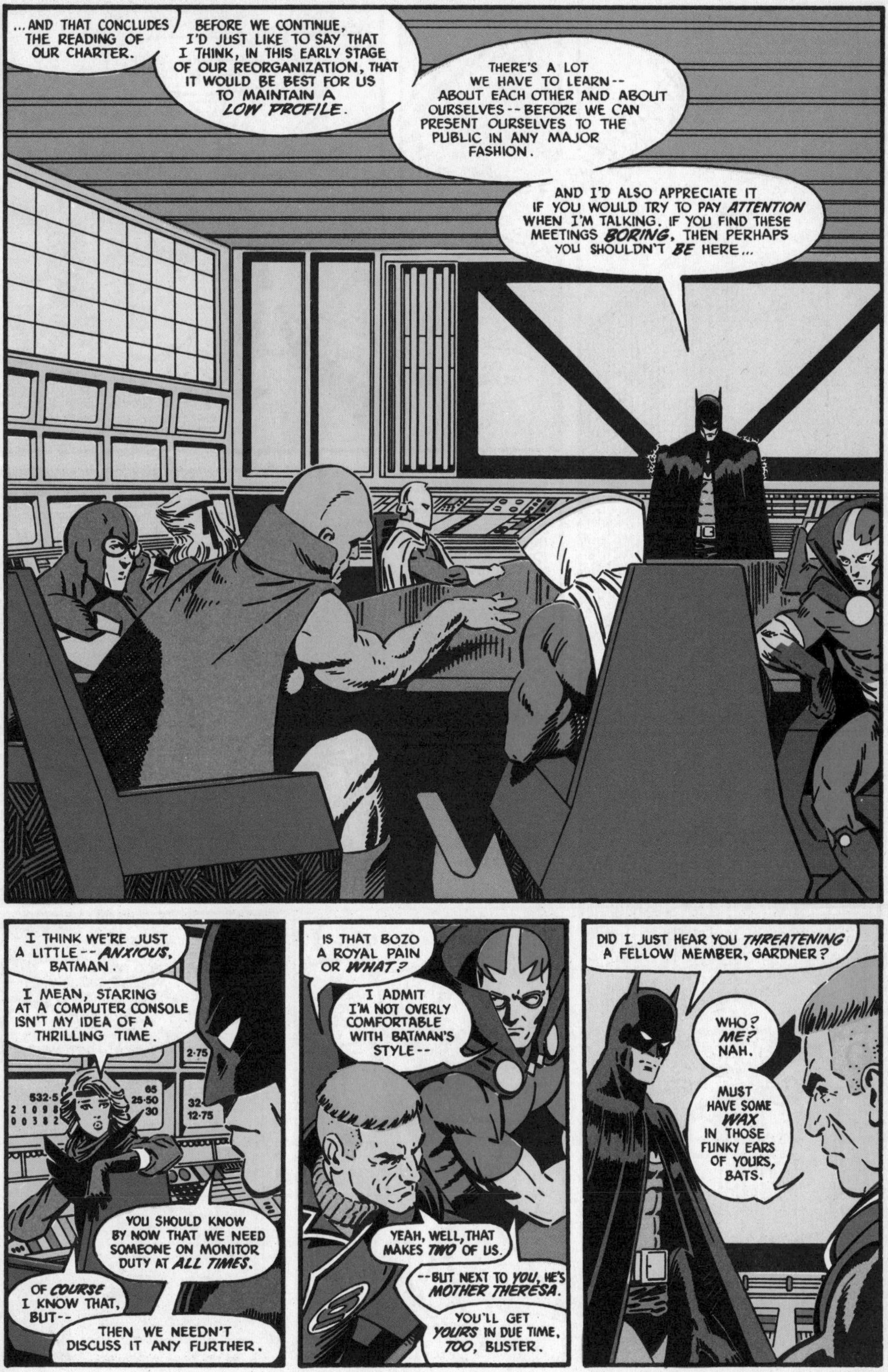
...AND THAT CONCLUDES THE READING OF OUR CHARTER.
BEFORE WE CONTINUE, I'D JUST LIKE TO SAY THAT I THINK, IN THIS EARLY STAGE OF OUR REORGANIZATION, THAT IT WOULD BE BEST FOR US TO MAINTAIN A LOW PROFILE.
THERE'S A LOT WE HAVE TO LEARN-- ABOUT EACH OTHER AND ABOUT OURSELVES--BEFORE WE CAN PRESENT OURSELVES TO THE PUBLIC IN ANY MAJOR FASHION.
AND I'D ALSO APPRECIATE IT IF YOU WOULD TRY TO PAY ATTENTION WHEN I'M TALKING. IF YOU FIND THESE MEETINGS BORING, THEN PERHAPS YOU SHOULDN'T BE HERE...
I THINK WE'RE JUST A LITTLE--ANXIOUS, BATMAN.
I MEAN, STARING AT A COMPUTER CONSOLE ISN'T MY IDEA OF A THRILLING TIME.
YOU SHOULD KNOW BY NOW THAT WE NEED SOMEONE ON MONITOR DUTY AT ALL TIMES.
OF COURSE I KNOW THAT, BUT--
THEN WE NEEDN'T DISCUSS IT ANY FURTHER.
IS THAT BOZO A ROYAL PAIN OR WHAT?
I ADMIT I'M NOT OVERLY COMFORTABLE WITH BATMAN'S STYLE--
YEAH, WELL, THAT MAKES TWO OF US.
--BUT NEXT TO YOU, HE'S MOTHER THERESA.
YOU'LL GET YOURS IN DUE TIME, TOO, BUSTER.
DID I JUST HEAR YOU THREATENING A FELLOW MEMBER, GARDNER?
WHO? ME? NAH.
MUST HAVE SOME WAX IN THOSE FUNKY EARS OF YOURS, BATS.

NEW YORK CITY.

BLRRRRRRRRZZZZ

LADIES

OH... *PLEASE!*

STOPSTOP*STOP!*

NOT ANOTHER "BEEP" *OUT* OF YOU!

I'VE GOT TO ADDRESS THE *GENERAL ASSEMBLY* IN FIVE MINUTES -- AND THEY DECIDE TO CALL A MEETING *NOW?*

BEEP BEEP

WELL, SORRY. NO, THANKS. *FORGET* IT. IF IT'S A CHOICE BETWEEN ZAPPING SUPER-VILLAINS AND FEEDING THE HUNGRY... WELL, THEN, THERE *IS* NO CHOICE!

THE NEW SOLAR STORAGE UNITS I'VE DEVELOPED COULD OPEN UP THE OCEAN FLOOR TO ALL *MANNER* OF AGRICULTURAL DEVELOPMENT, IF I CAN ONLY GET THE *FUNDING...*

BEEP BEEP

SHUT UP.

PLEASE?

PRETTY PLEASE?

QUIET!!

WHACK

BEEP BEEP

BEEP BEEP

I'M *TALKING* TO IT.

I'M TALKING TO *MYSELF.*

I'M *LOSING* MY *MIND!*

WELL, IF I CAN'T SHUT THE STUPID THING OFF, I CAN AT LEAST SHOVE IT INTO MY PURSE AND HOPE IT'S MUFFLED ENOUGH SO NO ONE *ELSE* WILL BE ABLE TO HEAR IT.

HOW DO I GET MYSELF *INTO* THESE THINGS?

LADIES

134

...DR. *KIMIYO HOSHI*...?

YES, BUT-- HOW DID YOU GET INTO MY OFFICE? *WHO*--

WHO I AM AND WHO *SENT* ME DOESN'T REALLY MATTER... AT THE MOMENT. WHAT MATTERS IS *WHY* I'VE BEEN SENT.

VERY MYSTERIOUS.

ARE YOU INTRIGUED?

MILDLY ANNOYED IS MORE LIKE IT.

I THINK THAT WILL PASS, DR. HOSHI -- OR SHOULD I SAY--

--*DOCTOR LIGHT.*

WHA--? I--I DON'T KNOW *WHAT* YOU'RE TALKING AB--

PLEASE, DOCTOR-- LET'S NOT WASTE TIME WITH DENIALS. OR WITH *FEAR*..I'M NOT AN ENEMY... I'M A FRIEND. PERHAPS THE *BEST* FRIEND YOU'LL EVER KNOW.

UH-- HOW DO YOU FIGURE *THAT?*

BECAUSE I'M HERE TO OFFER YOU CHARTER MEMBERSHIP IN THE NEWLY RE-FORMED *JUSTICE LEAGUE.*

JUSTICE LEAGUE?

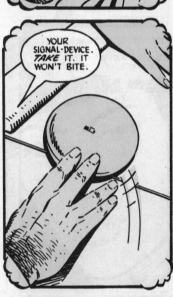

YOUR SIGNAL-DEVICE. *TAKE* IT. IT WON'T BITE.

HMMM...

WE'LL BE IN *TOUCH.*

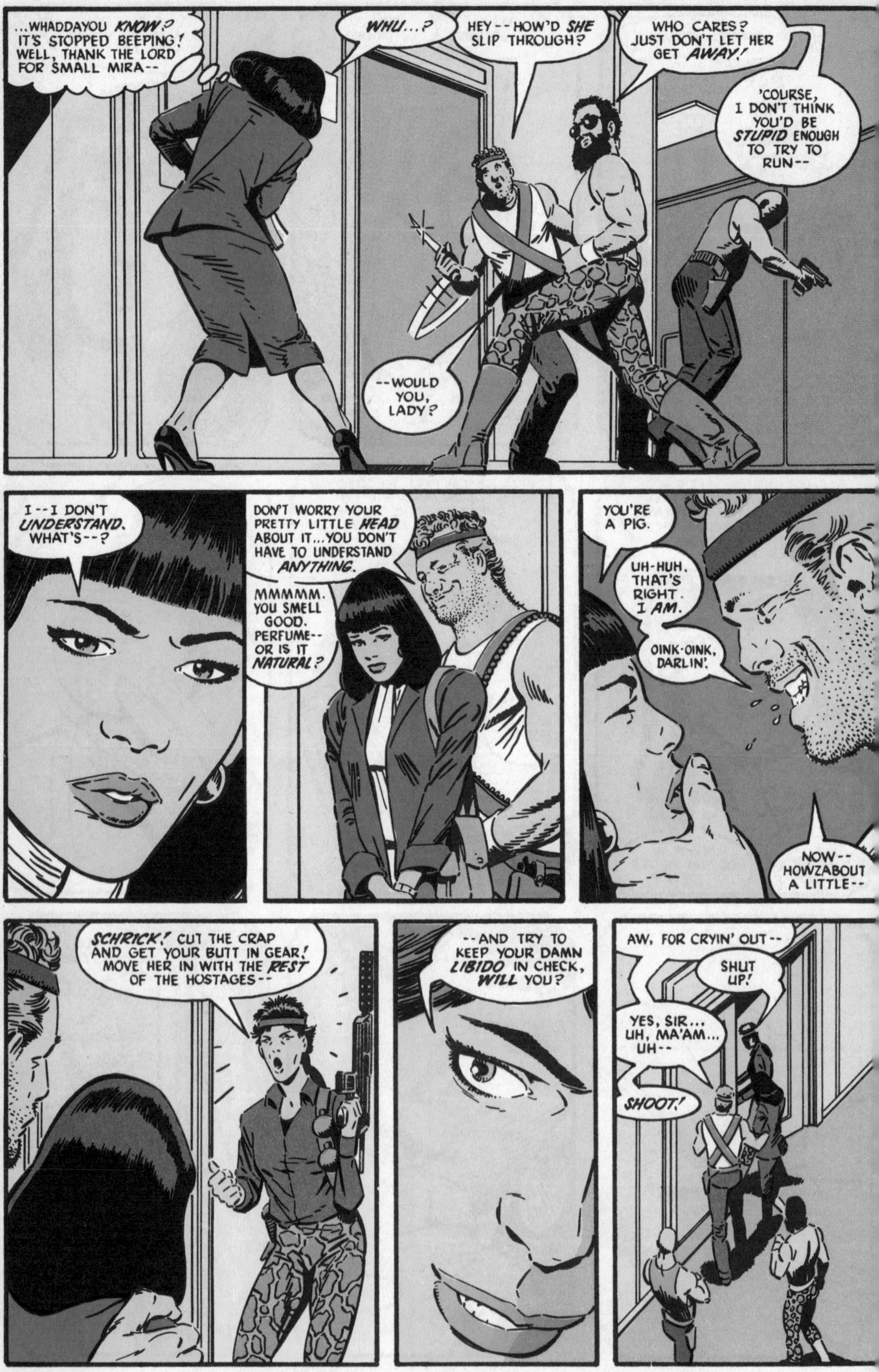
...WHADDAYOU KNOW? IT'S STOPPED BEEPING! WELL, THANK THE LORD FOR SMALL MIRA--
WHU...?
HEY--HOW'D SHE SLIP THROUGH?
WHO CARES? JUST DON'T LET HER GET AWAY!
'COURSE, I DON'T THINK YOU'D BE STUPID ENOUGH TO TRY TO RUN--
--WOULD YOU, LADY?
I--I DON'T UNDERSTAND. WHAT'S--?
DON'T WORRY YOUR PRETTY LITTLE HEAD ABOUT IT...YOU DON'T HAVE TO UNDERSTAND ANYTHING.
MMMMM. YOU SMELL GOOD. PERFUME--OR IS IT NATURAL?
YOU'RE A PIG.
UH-HUH. THAT'S RIGHT. I AM.
OINK-OINK, DARLIN'.
NOW--HOWZABOUT A LITTLE--
SCHRICK! CUT THE CRAP AND GET YOUR BUTT IN GEAR! MOVE HER IN WITH THE REST OF THE HOSTAGES--
--AND TRY TO KEEP YOUR DAMN LIBIDO IN CHECK, WILL YOU?
AW, FOR CRYIN' OUT--
SHUT UP!
YES, SIR... UH, MA'AM... UH--
SHOOT!

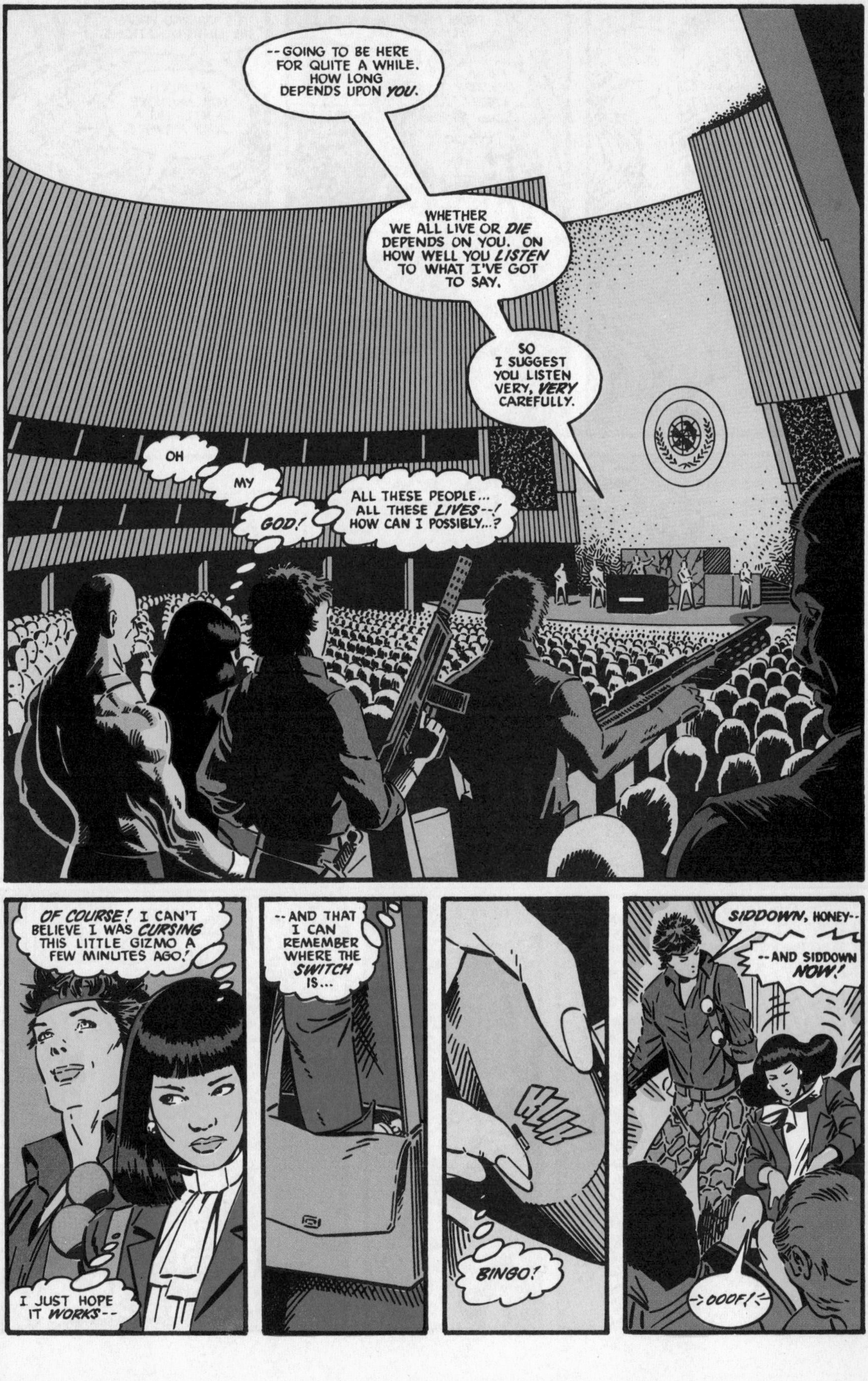
--GOING TO BE HERE FOR QUITE A WHILE. HOW LONG DEPENDS UPON YOU.
WHETHER WE ALL LIVE OR DIE DEPENDS ON YOU. ON HOW WELL YOU LISTEN TO WHAT I'VE GOT TO SAY.
SO I SUGGEST YOU LISTEN VERY, VERY CAREFULLY.
OH
MY
GOD!
ALL THESE PEOPLE... ALL THESE LIVES--! HOW CAN I POSSIBLY...?
OF COURSE! I CAN'T BELIEVE I WAS CURSING THIS LITTLE GIZMO A FEW MINUTES AGO!
I JUST HOPE IT WORKS--
--AND THAT I CAN REMEMBER WHERE THE SWITCH IS...
KLIK
BINGO!
SIDDOWN, HONEY--
--AND SIDDOWN NOW!
OOOF!

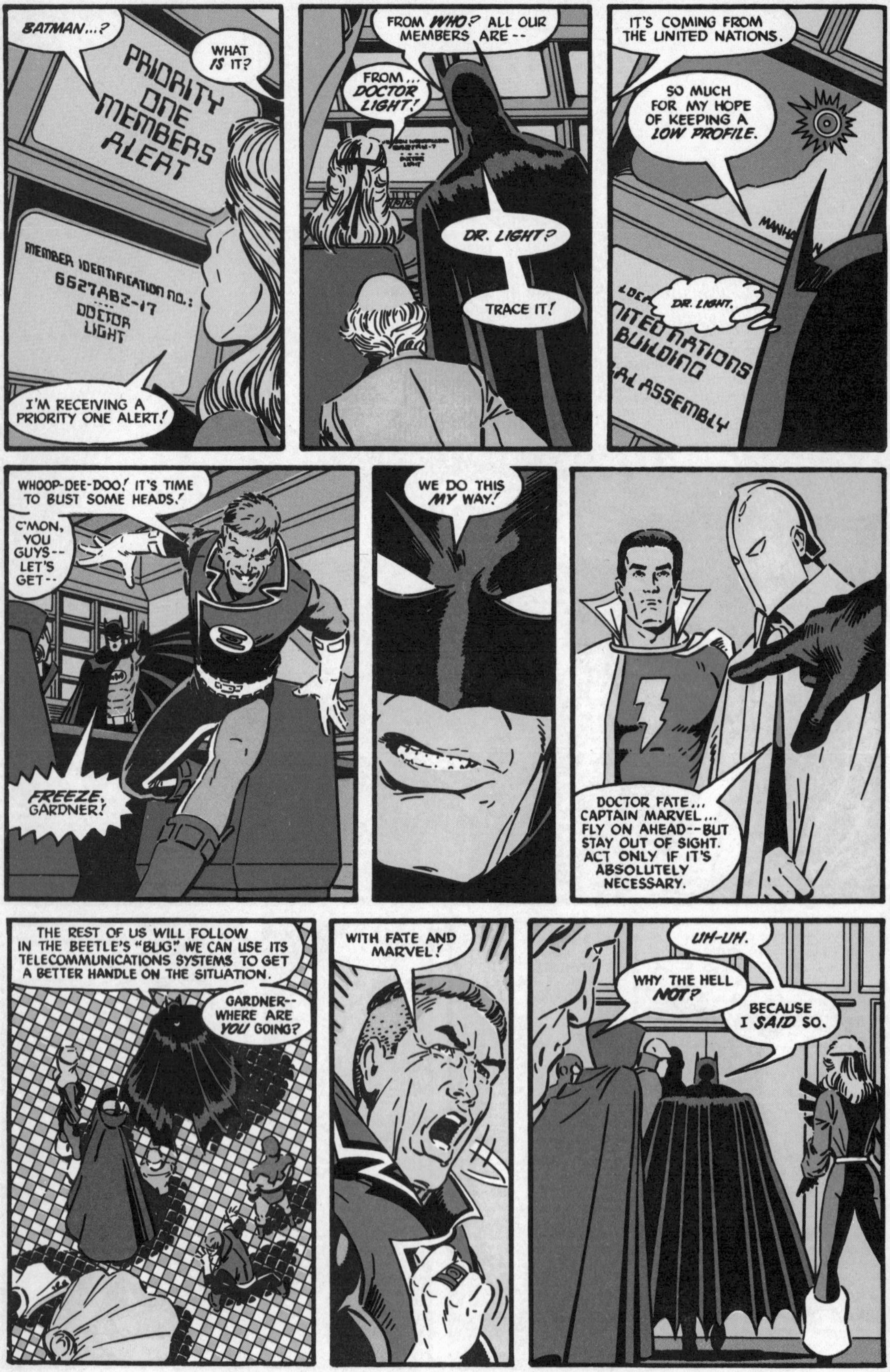
BATMAN...?
WHAT IS IT?
PRIORITY ONE MEMBERS ALERT
MEMBER IDENTIFICATION NO.: 6627ABZ-17 DOCTOR LIGHT
I'M RECEIVING A PRIORITY ONE ALERT!
FROM WHO? ALL OUR MEMBERS ARE--
FROM... DOCTOR LIGHT!
DR. LIGHT?
TRACE IT!
IT'S COMING FROM THE UNITED NATIONS.
SO MUCH FOR MY HOPE OF KEEPING A LOW PROFILE.
DR. LIGHT.
NITED NATIONS BUILDING
AL ASSEMBLY
WHOOP-DEE-DOO! IT'S TIME TO BUST SOME HEADS!
C'MON, YOU GUYS-- LET'S GET--
FREEZE, GARDNER!
WE DO THIS MY WAY!
DOCTOR FATE... CAPTAIN MARVEL... FLY ON AHEAD--BUT STAY OUT OF SIGHT. ACT ONLY IF IT'S ABSOLUTELY NECESSARY.
THE REST OF US WILL FOLLOW IN THE BEETLE'S "BUG." WE CAN USE ITS TELECOMMUNICATIONS SYSTEMS TO GET A BETTER HANDLE ON THE SITUATION.
GARDNER-- WHERE ARE YOU GOING?
WITH FATE AND MARVEL!
UH-UH.
WHY THE HELL NOT?
BECAUSE I SAID SO.

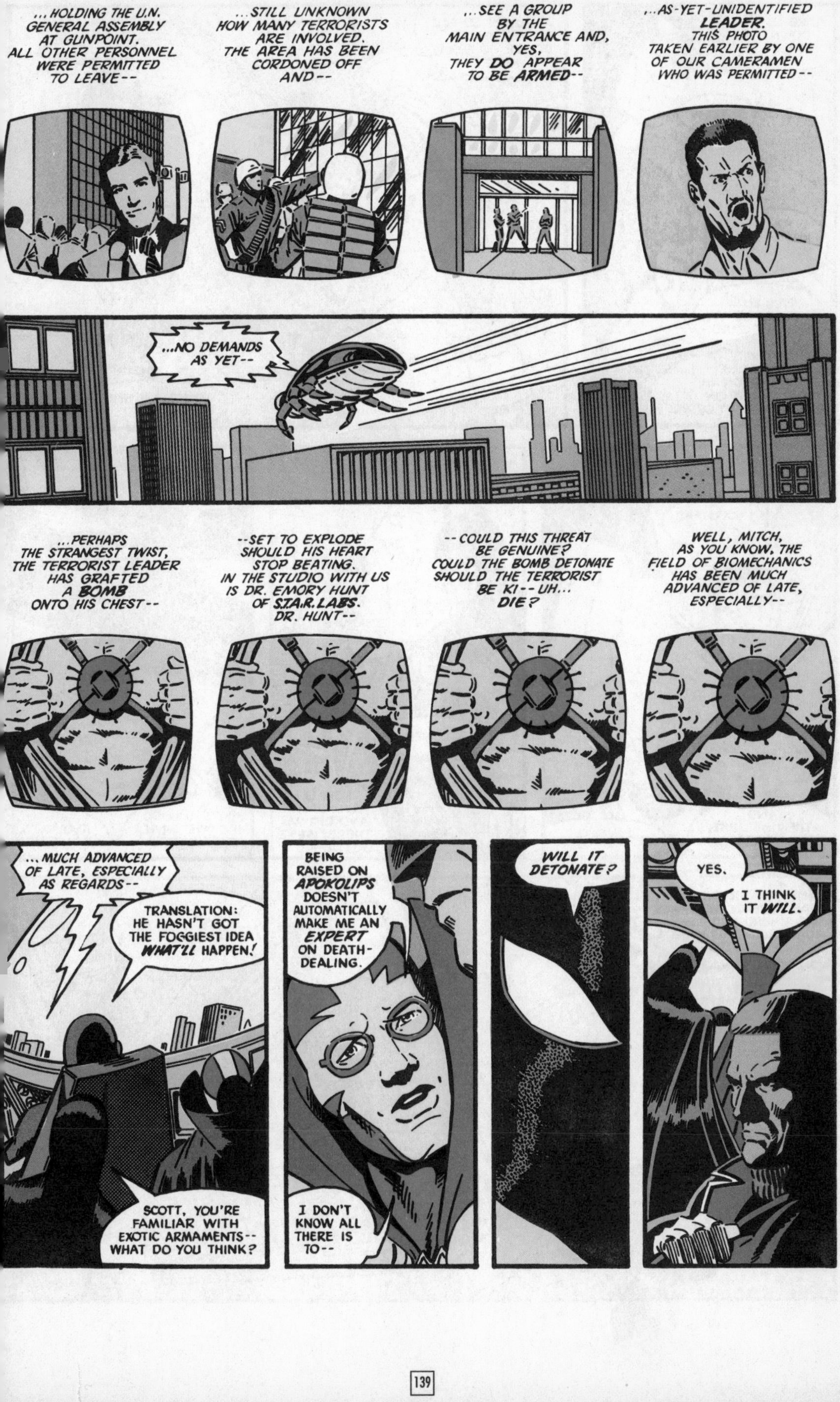

...HOLDING THE U.N. GENERAL ASSEMBLY AT GUNPOINT. ALL OTHER PERSONNEL WERE PERMITTED TO LEAVE--
...STILL UNKNOWN HOW MANY TERRORISTS ARE INVOLVED. THE AREA HAS BEEN CORDONED OFF AND--
...SEE A GROUP BY THE MAIN ENTRANCE AND, YES, THEY DO APPEAR TO BE ARMED--
...AS-YET-UNIDENTIFIED LEADER. THIS PHOTO TAKEN EARLIER BY ONE OF OUR CAMERAMEN WHO WAS PERMITTED--
...NO DEMANDS AS YET--
...PERHAPS THE STRANGEST TWIST, THE TERRORIST LEADER HAS GRAFTED A BOMB ONTO HIS CHEST--
--SET TO EXPLODE SHOULD HIS HEART STOP BEATING. IN THE STUDIO WITH US IS DR. EMORY HUNT OF S.T.A.R. LABS. DR. HUNT--
--COULD THIS THREAT BE GENUINE? COULD THE BOMB DETONATE SHOULD THE TERRORIST BE KI--UH... DIE?
WELL, MITCH, AS YOU KNOW, THE FIELD OF BIOMECHANICS HAS BEEN MUCH ADVANCED OF LATE, ESPECIALLY--
...MUCH ADVANCED OF LATE, ESPECIALLY AS REGARDS--
TRANSLATION: HE HASN'T GOT THE FOGGIEST IDEA WHAT'LL HAPPEN!
SCOTT, YOU'RE FAMILIAR WITH EXOTIC ARMAMENTS--WHAT DO YOU THINK?
BEING RAISED ON APOKOLIPS DOESN'T AUTOMATICALLY MAKE ME AN EXPERT ON DEATH-DEALING.
I DON'T KNOW ALL THERE IS TO--
WILL IT DETONATE?
YES.
I THINK IT WILL.

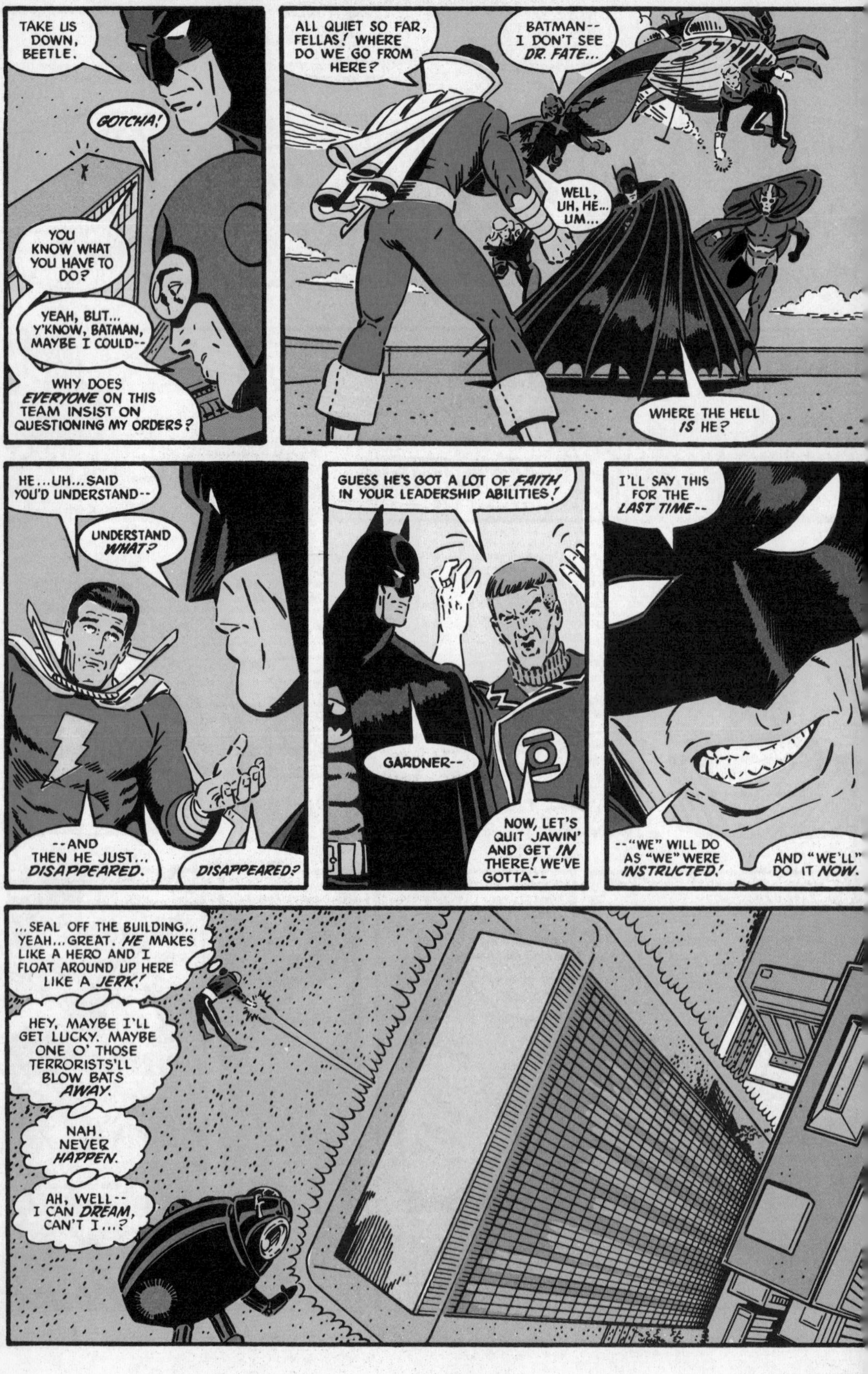
TAKE US DOWN, BEETLE.
GOTCHA!
YOU KNOW WHAT YOU HAVE TO DO?
YEAH, BUT... Y'KNOW, BATMAN, MAYBE I COULD--
WHY DOES EVERYONE ON THIS TEAM INSIST ON QUESTIONING MY ORDERS?
ALL QUIET SO FAR, FELLAS! WHERE DO WE GO FROM HERE?
BATMAN-- I DON'T SEE DR. FATE...
WELL, UH, HE... UM...
WHERE THE HELL IS HE?
HE...UH...SAID YOU'D UNDERSTAND--
UNDERSTAND WHAT?
--AND THEN HE JUST... DISAPPEARED.
DISAPPEARED?
GUESS HE'S GOT A LOT OF FAITH IN YOUR LEADERSHIP ABILITIES!
GARDNER--
NOW, LET'S QUIT JAWIN' AND GET IN THERE! WE'VE GOTTA--
I'LL SAY THIS FOR THE LAST TIME--
--"WE" WILL DO AS "WE" WERE INSTRUCTED!
AND "WE'LL" DO IT NOW.
...SEAL OFF THE BUILDING... YEAH...GREAT. HE MAKES LIKE A HERO AND I FLOAT AROUND UP HERE LIKE A JERK!
HEY, MAYBE I'LL GET LUCKY. MAYBE ONE O' THOSE TERRORISTS'LL BLOW BATS AWAY.
NAH. NEVER HAPPEN.
AH, WELL-- I CAN DREAM, CAN'T I...?

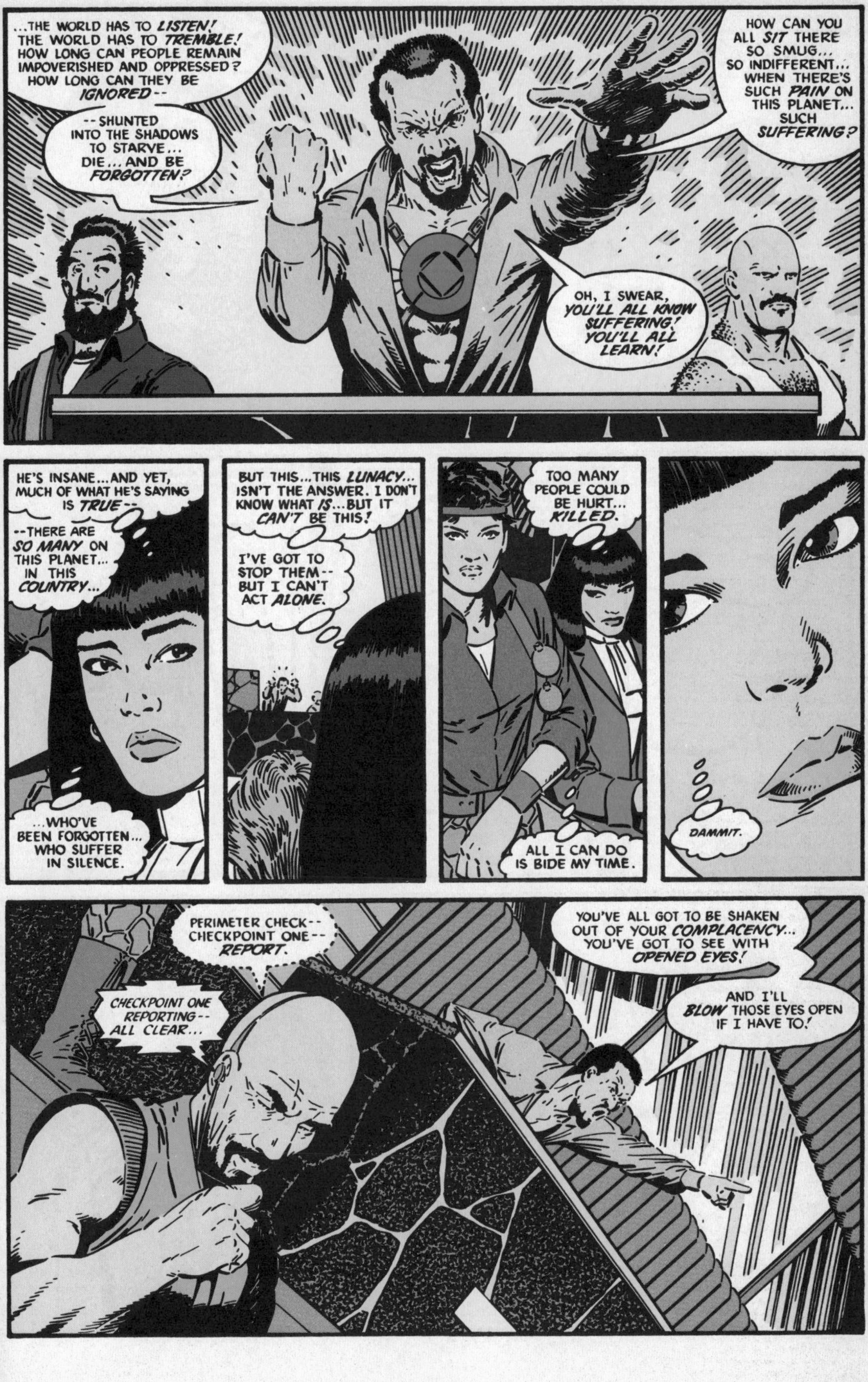

...THE WORLD HAS TO LISTEN! THE WORLD HAS TO TREMBLE! HOW LONG CAN PEOPLE REMAIN IMPOVERISHED AND OPPRESSED? HOW LONG CAN THEY BE IGNORED--
--SHUNTED INTO THE SHADOWS TO STARVE... DIE... AND BE FORGOTTEN?
HOW CAN YOU ALL SIT THERE SO SMUG... SO INDIFFERENT... WHEN THERE'S SUCH PAIN ON THIS PLANET... SUCH SUFFERING?
OH, I SWEAR, YOU'LL ALL KNOW SUFFERING! YOU'LL ALL LEARN!
HE'S INSANE...AND YET, MUCH OF WHAT HE'S SAYING IS TRUE--
--THERE ARE SO MANY ON THIS PLANET... IN THIS COUNTRY...
...WHO'VE BEEN FORGOTTEN... WHO SUFFER IN SILENCE.
BUT THIS...THIS LUNACY... ISN'T THE ANSWER. I DON'T KNOW WHAT IS...BUT IT CAN'T BE THIS!
I'VE GOT TO STOP THEM-- BUT I CAN'T ACT ALONE.
TOO MANY PEOPLE COULD BE HURT... KILLED.
ALL I CAN DO IS BIDE MY TIME.
DAMMIT.
PERIMETER CHECK-- CHECKPOINT ONE-- REPORT.
CHECKPOINT ONE REPORTING-- ALL CLEAR...
YOU'VE ALL GOT TO BE SHAKEN OUT OF YOUR COMPLACENCY... YOU'VE GOT TO SEE WITH OPENED EYES!
AND I'LL BLOW THOSE EYES OPEN IF I HAVE TO!

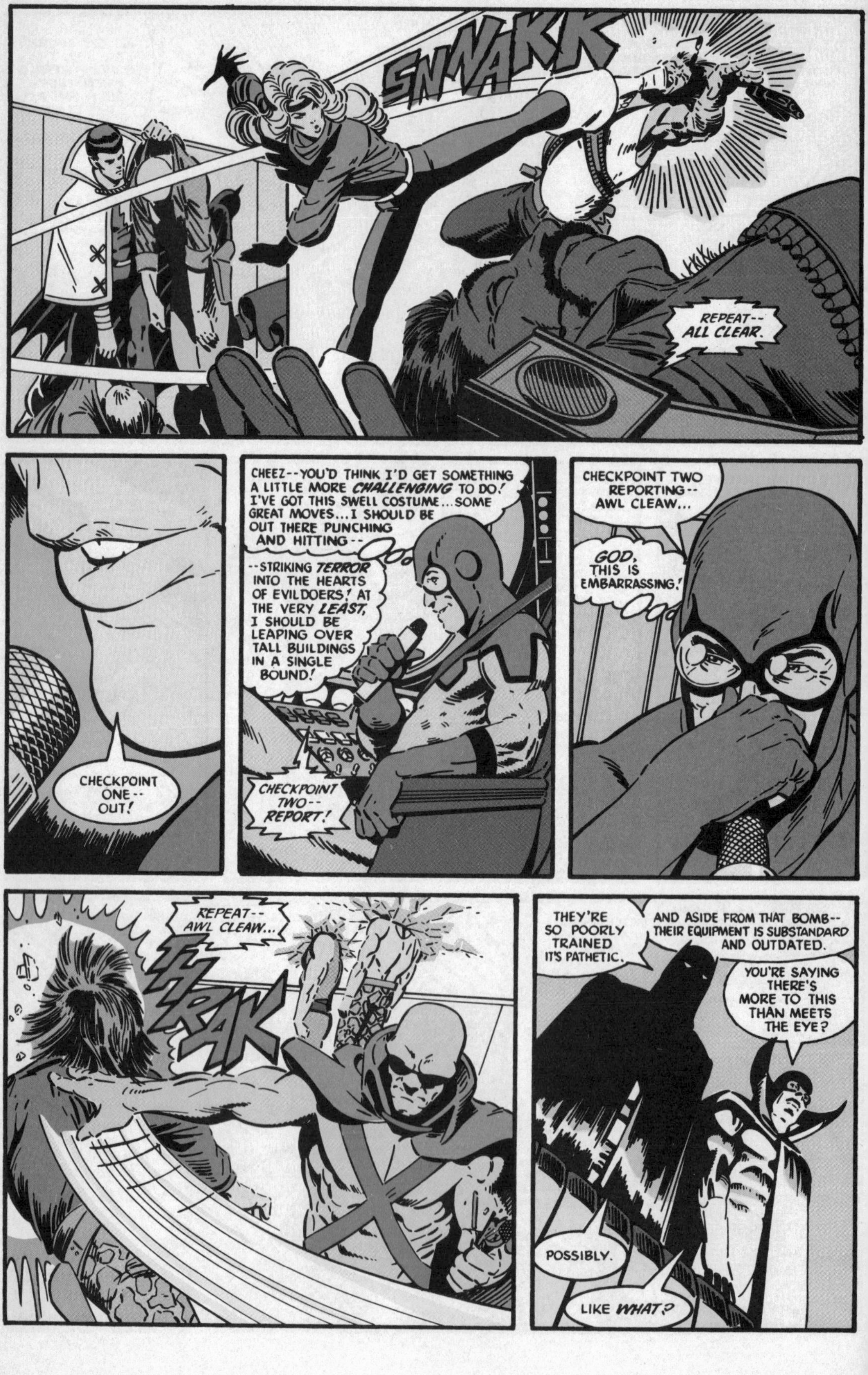
SNNAKK
REPEAT-- ALL CLEAR.
CHECKPOINT ONE-- OUT!
CHEEZ--YOU'D THINK I'D GET SOMETHING A LITTLE MORE CHALLENGING TO DO! I'VE GOT THIS SWELL COSTUME...SOME GREAT MOVES...I SHOULD BE OUT THERE PUNCHING AND HITTING--
--STRIKING TERROR INTO THE HEARTS OF EVILDOERS! AT THE VERY LEAST, I SHOULD BE LEAPING OVER TALL BUILDINGS IN A SINGLE BOUND!
CHECKPOINT TWO-- REPORT!
CHECKPOINT TWO REPORTING-- AWL CLEAW...
GOD, THIS IS EMBARRASSING!
REPEAT-- AWL CLEAW...
THRAK
THEY'RE SO POORLY TRAINED IT'S PATHETIC.
AND ASIDE FROM THAT BOMB-- THEIR EQUIPMENT IS SUBSTANDARD AND OUTDATED.
YOU'RE SAYING THERE'S MORE TO THIS THAN MEETS THE EYE?
POSSIBLY.
LIKE WHAT?

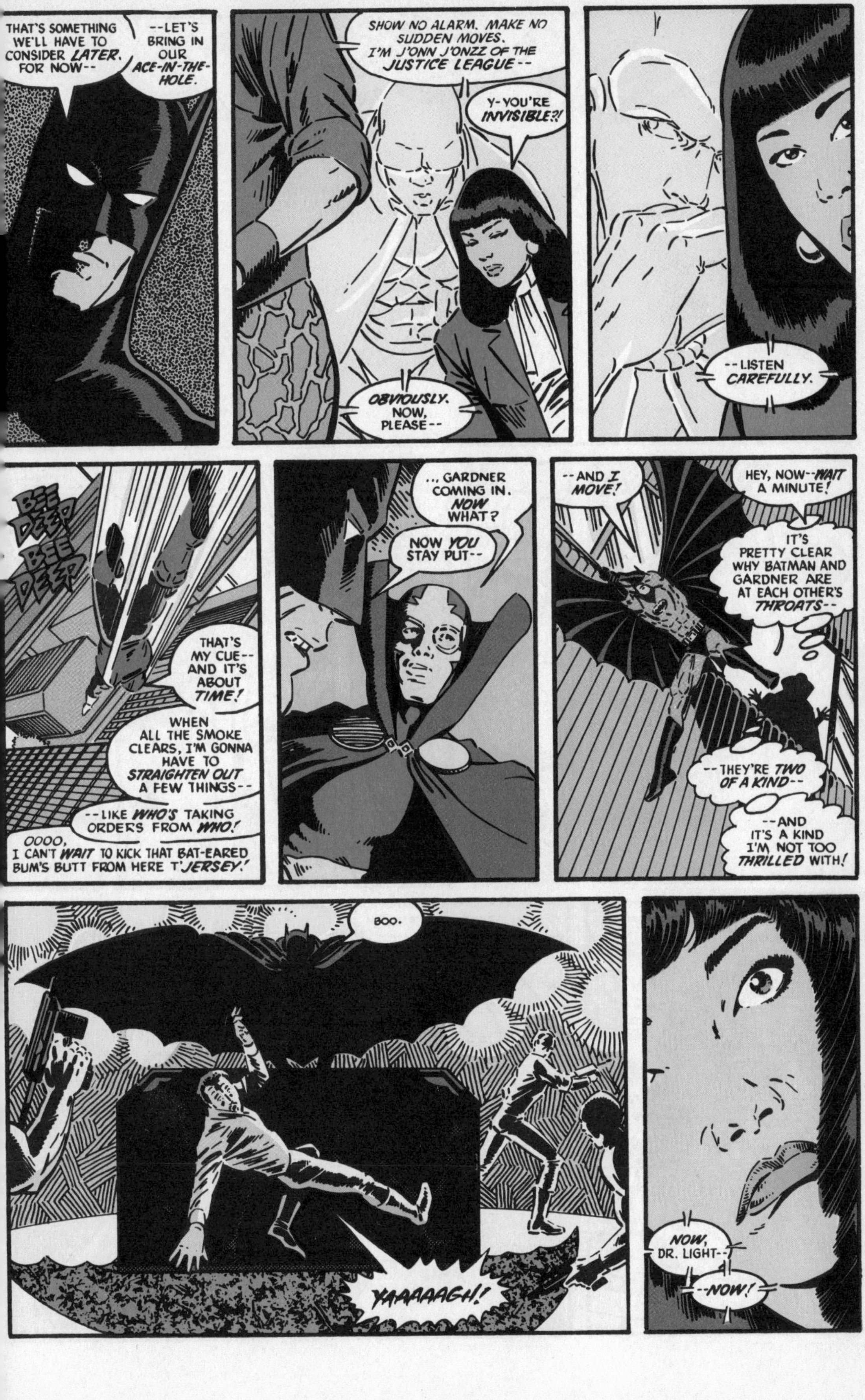
THAT'S SOMETHING WE'LL HAVE TO CONSIDER LATER. FOR NOW--
--LET'S BRING IN OUR ACE-IN-THE-HOLE.
SHOW NO ALARM. MAKE NO SUDDEN MOVES. I'M J'ONN J'ONZZ OF THE JUSTICE LEAGUE--
Y-YOU'RE INVISIBLE?!
OBVIOUSLY. NOW, PLEASE--
--LISTEN CAREFULLY.
BEE DEEP BEE DEEP
THAT'S MY CUE-- AND IT'S ABOUT TIME!
WHEN ALL THE SMOKE CLEARS, I'M GONNA HAVE TO STRAIGHTEN OUT A FEW THINGS--
--LIKE WHO'S TAKING ORDERS FROM WHO!
OOOO, I CAN'T WAIT TO KICK THAT BAT-EARED BUM'S BUTT FROM HERE T'JERSEY!
... GARDNER COMING IN. NOW WHAT?
NOW YOU STAY PUT--
--AND I MOVE!
HEY, NOW--WAIT A MINUTE!
IT'S PRETTY CLEAR WHY BATMAN AND GARDNER ARE AT EACH OTHER'S THROATS--
--THEY'RE TWO OF A KIND--
--AND IT'S A KIND I'M NOT TOO THRILLED WITH!
BOO.
YAAAAAGH!
NOW, DR. LIGHT--
--NOW!

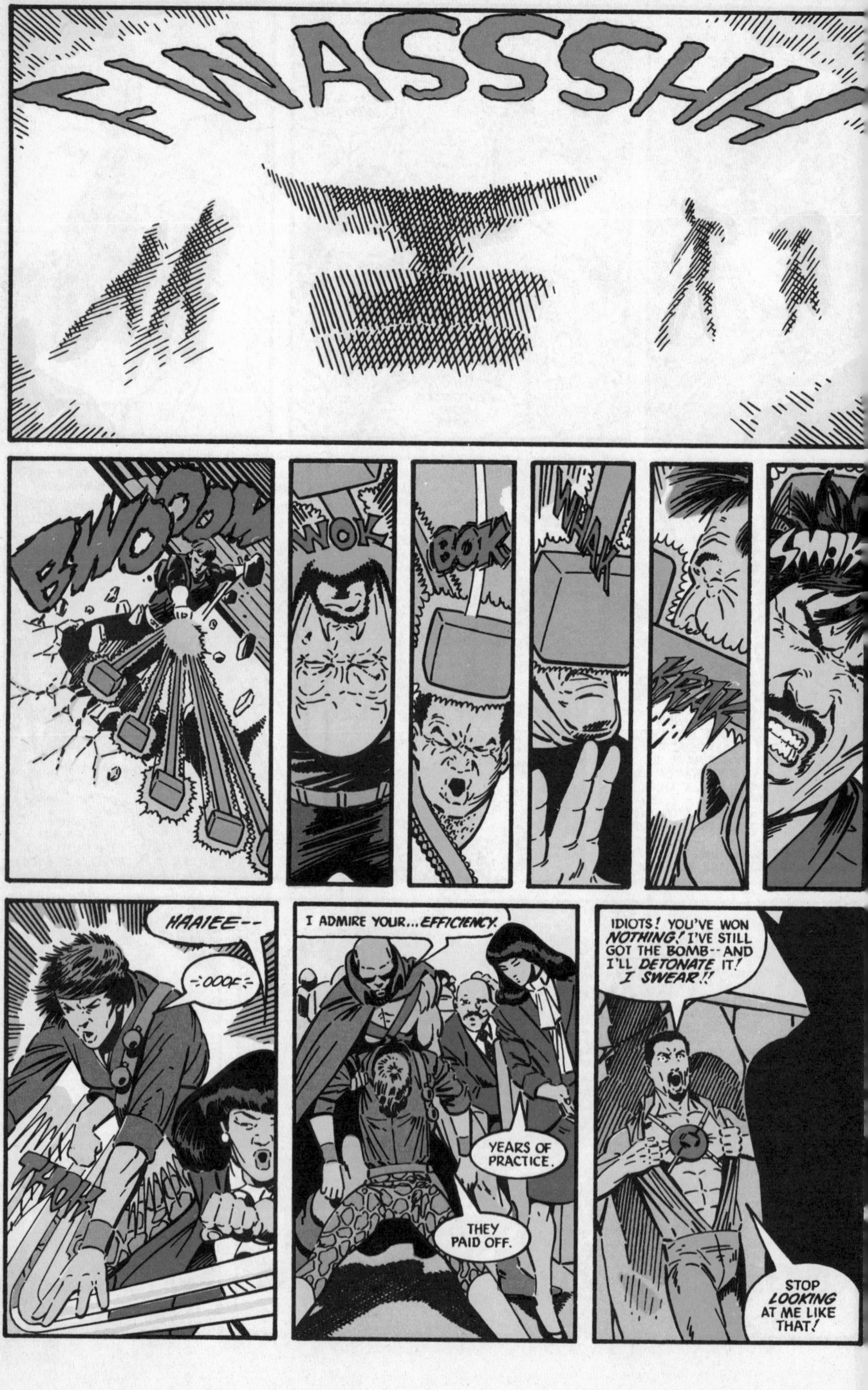
FWASSSHH
BWOOOM
WOK
BOK
WHAK
KRAK
SMAK
HAAIEE--
-:OOOF:-
THOK
I ADMIRE YOUR... EFFICIENCY.
YEARS OF PRACTICE.
THEY PAID OFF.
IDIOTS! YOU'VE WON NOTHING! I'VE STILL GOT THE BOMB-- AND I'LL DETONATE IT! I SWEAR!!
STOP LOOKING AT ME LIKE THAT!

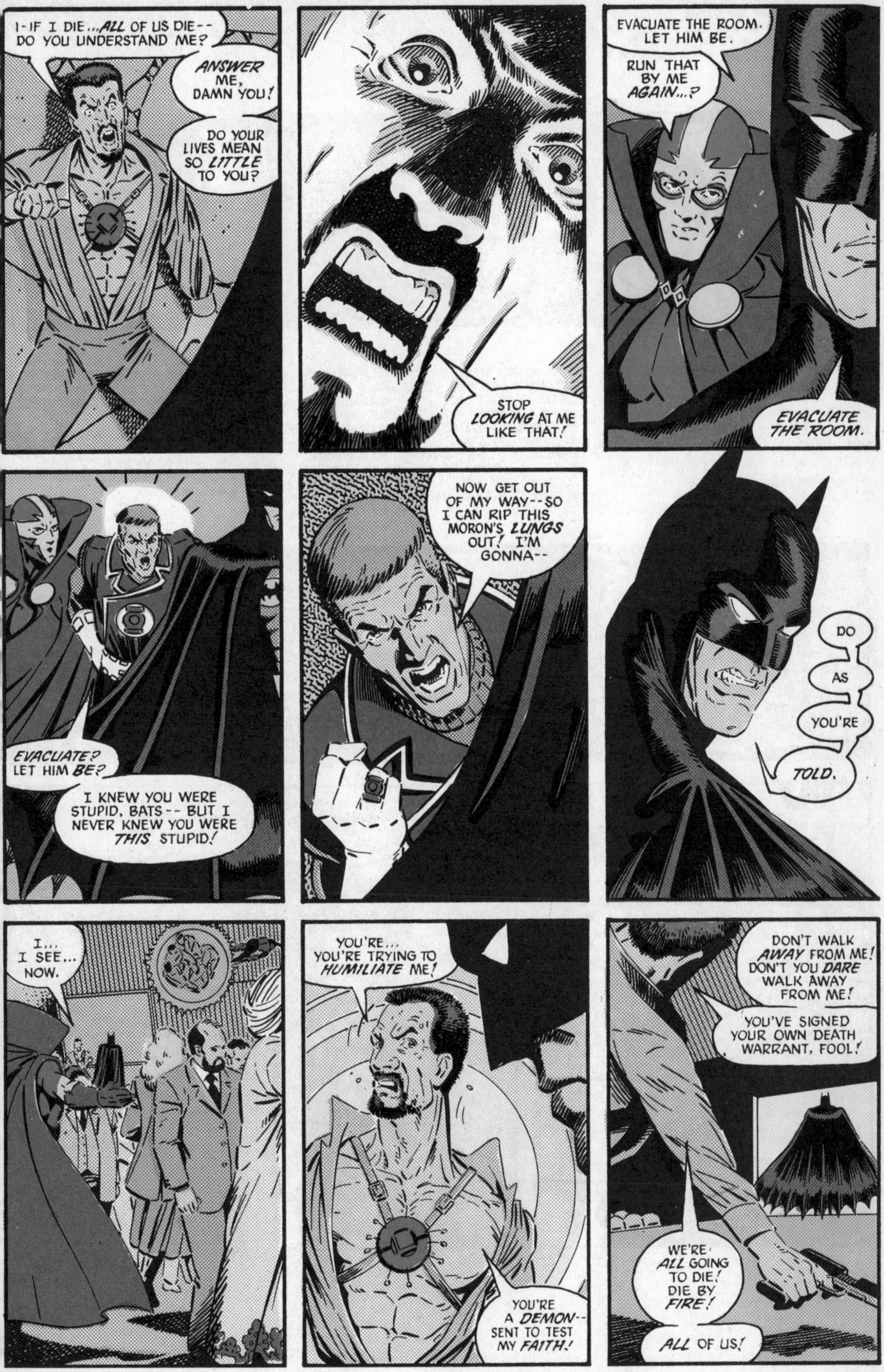
I-IF I DIE...ALL OF US DIE--
DO YOU UNDERSTAND ME?
ANSWER ME, DAMN YOU!
DO YOUR LIVES MEAN SO LITTLE TO YOU?
STOP LOOKING AT ME LIKE THAT!
EVACUATE THE ROOM. LET HIM BE.
RUN THAT BY ME AGAIN...?
EVACUATE THE ROOM.
EVACUATE? LET HIM BE?
I KNEW YOU WERE STUPID, BATS-- BUT I NEVER KNEW YOU WERE THIS STUPID!
NOW GET OUT OF MY WAY--SO I CAN RIP THIS MORON'S LUNGS OUT! I'M GONNA--
DO
AS
YOU'RE
TOLD.
I... I SEE... NOW.
YOU'RE... YOU'RE TRYING TO HUMILIATE ME!
YOU'RE A DEMON-- SENT TO TEST MY FAITH!
DON'T WALK AWAY FROM ME! DON'T YOU DARE WALK AWAY FROM ME!
YOU'VE SIGNED YOUR OWN DEATH WARRANT, FOOL!
WE'RE ALL GOING TO DIE! DIE BY FIRE!
ALL OF US!

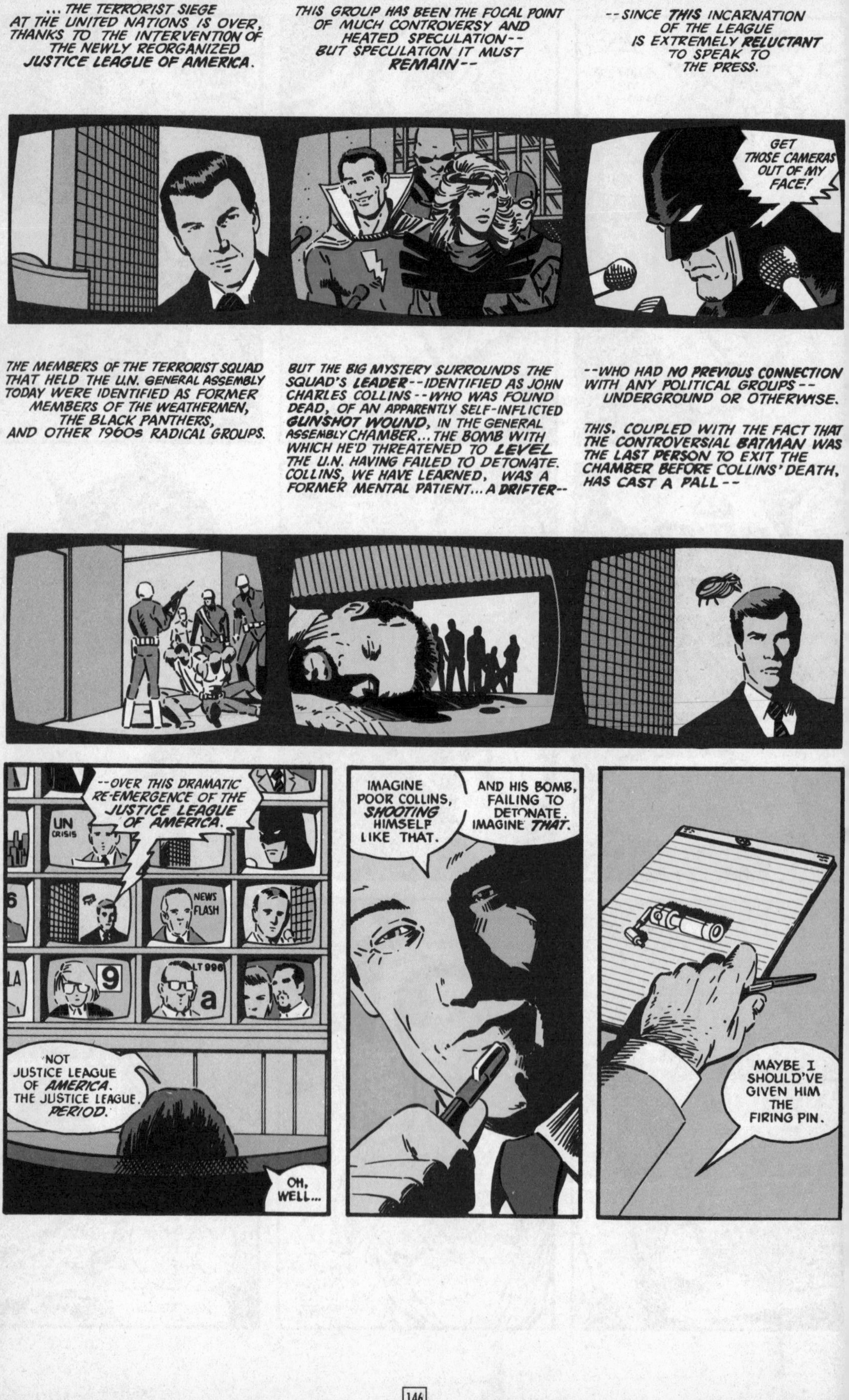
...THE TERRORIST SIEGE AT THE UNITED NATIONS IS OVER, THANKS TO THE INTERVENTION OF THE NEWLY REORGANIZED JUSTICE LEAGUE OF AMERICA.
THIS GROUP HAS BEEN THE FOCAL POINT OF MUCH CONTROVERSY AND HEATED SPECULATION-- BUT SPECULATION IT MUST REMAIN--
--SINCE THIS INCARNATION OF THE LEAGUE IS EXTREMELY RELUCTANT TO SPEAK TO THE PRESS.
GET THOSE CAMERAS OUT OF MY FACE!
THE MEMBERS OF THE TERRORIST SQUAD THAT HELD THE U.N. GENERAL ASSEMBLY TODAY WERE IDENTIFIED AS FORMER MEMBERS OF THE WEATHERMEN, THE BLACK PANTHERS, AND OTHER 1960s RADICAL GROUPS.
BUT THE BIG MYSTERY SURROUNDS THE SQUAD'S LEADER--IDENTIFIED AS JOHN CHARLES COLLINS--WHO WAS FOUND DEAD, OF AN APPARENTLY SELF-INFLICTED GUNSHOT WOUND, IN THE GENERAL ASSEMBLY CHAMBER... THE BOMB WITH WHICH HE'D THREATENED TO LEVEL THE U.N. HAVING FAILED TO DETONATE. COLLINS, WE HAVE LEARNED, WAS A FORMER MENTAL PATIENT... A DRIFTER--
--WHO HAD NO PREVIOUS CONNECTION WITH ANY POLITICAL GROUPS-- UNDERGROUND OR OTHERWISE.
THIS, COUPLED WITH THE FACT THAT THE CONTROVERSIAL BATMAN WAS THE LAST PERSON TO EXIT THE CHAMBER BEFORE COLLINS' DEATH, HAS CAST A PALL--
--OVER THIS DRAMATIC RE-EMERGENCE OF THE JUSTICE LEAGUE OF AMERICA.
UN CRISIS
NEWS FLASH
LT 996
9
a
NOT JUSTICE LEAGUE OF AMERICA. THE JUSTICE LEAGUE. PERIOD.
OH, WELL...
IMAGINE POOR COLLINS, SHOOTING HIMSELF LIKE THAT.
AND HIS BOMB, FAILING TO DETONATE. IMAGINE THAT.
MAYBE I SHOULD'VE GIVEN HIM THE FIRING PIN.

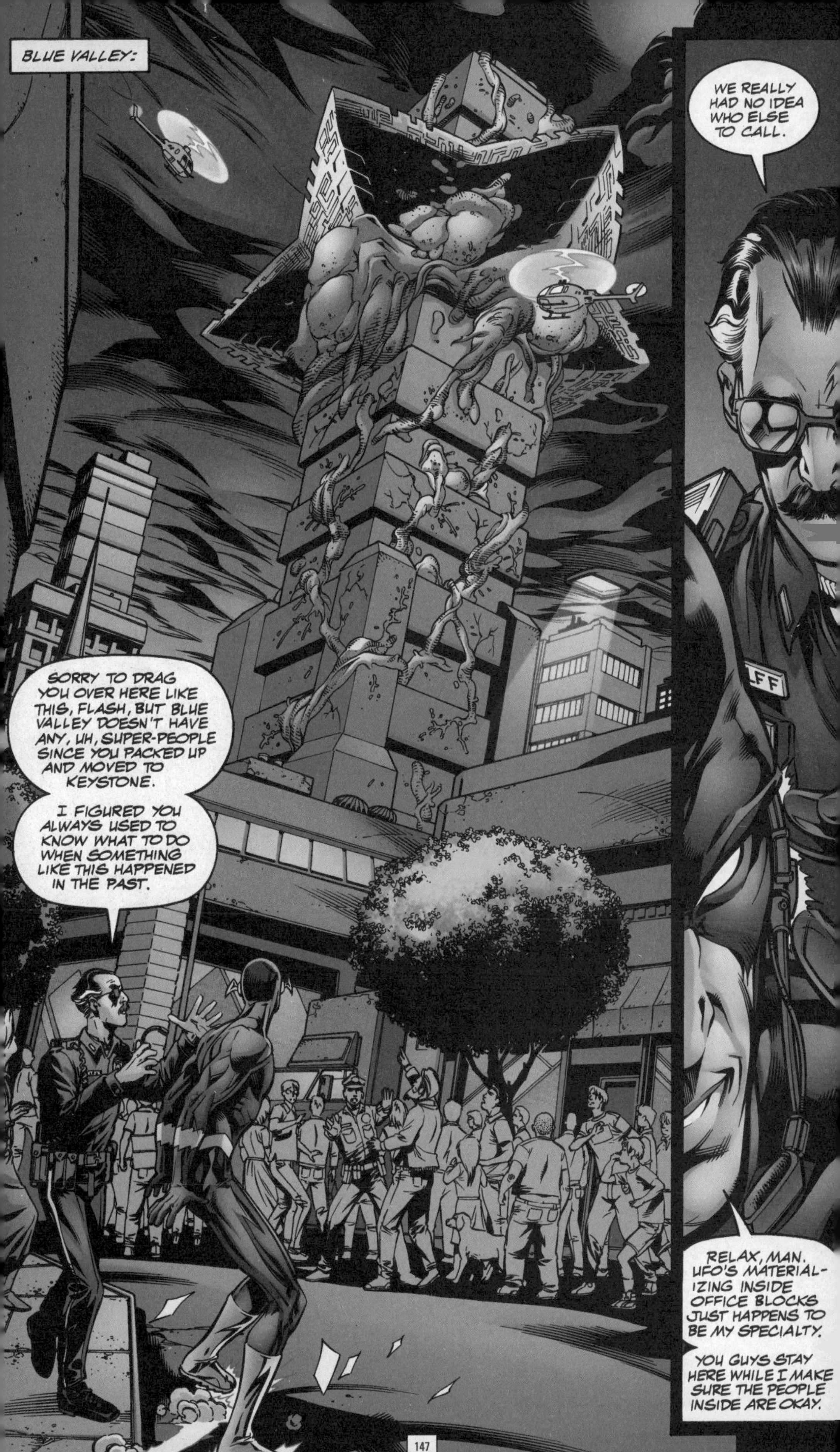
BLUE VALLEY:
WE REALLY HAD NO IDEA WHO ELSE TO CALL.
SORRY TO DRAG YOU OVER HERE LIKE THIS, FLASH, BUT BLUE VALLEY DOESN'T HAVE ANY, UH, SUPER-PEOPLE SINCE YOU PACKED UP AND MOVED TO KEYSTONE.
I FIGURED YOU ALWAYS USED TO KNOW WHAT TO DO WHEN SOMETHING LIKE THIS HAPPENED IN THE PAST.
RELAX, MAN. UFO'S MATERIAL-IZING INSIDE OFFICE BLOCKS JUST HAPPENS TO BE MY SPECIALTY.
YOU GUYS STAY HERE WHILE I MAKE SURE THE PEOPLE INSIDE ARE OKAY.

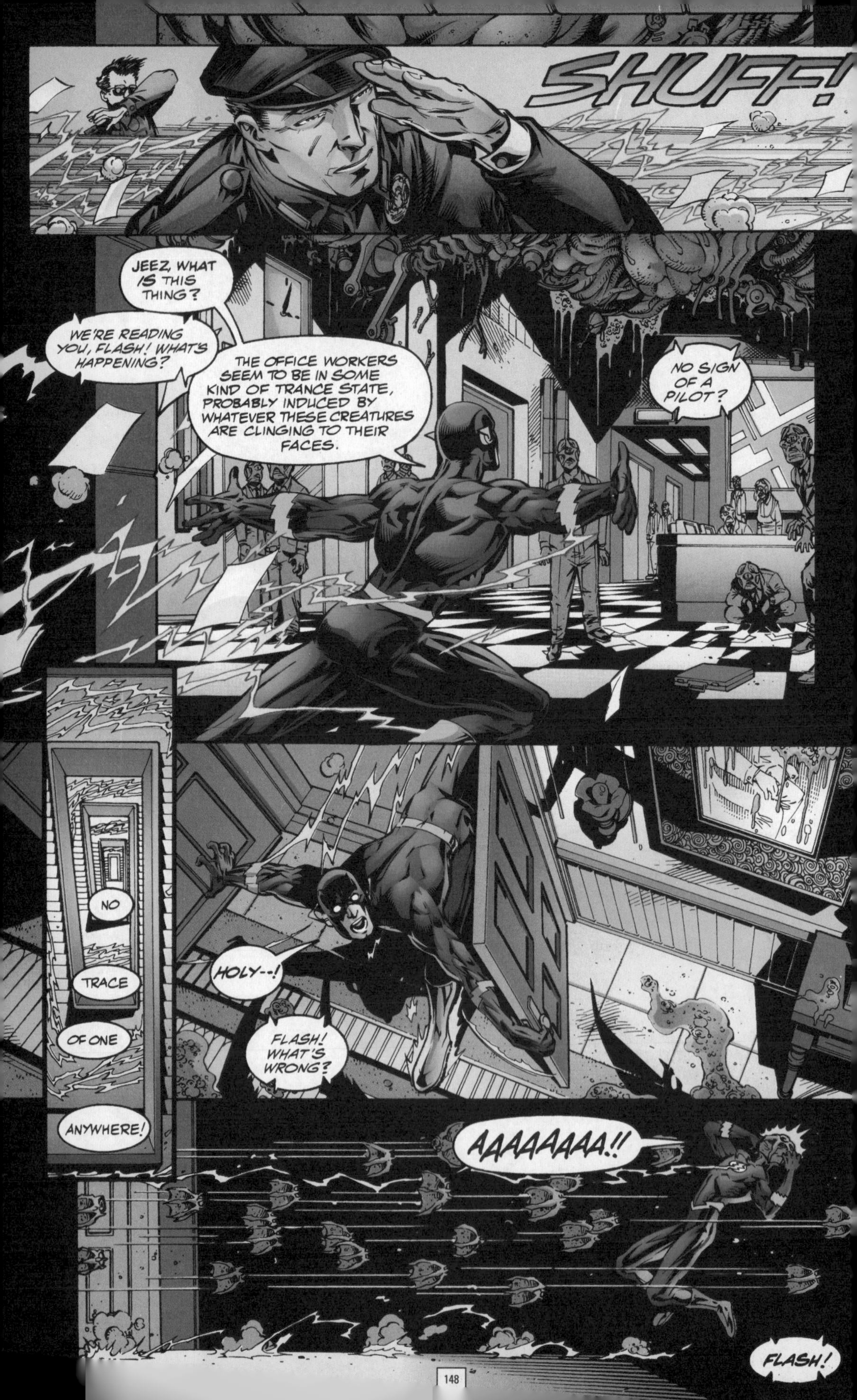
SHUFF!
JEEZ, WHAT IS THIS THING?
WE'RE READING YOU, FLASH! WHAT'S HAPPENING?
THE OFFICE WORKERS SEEM TO BE IN SOME KIND OF TRANCE STATE, PROBABLY INDUCED BY WHATEVER THESE CREATURES ARE CLINGING TO THEIR FACES.
NO SIGN OF A PILOT?
NO
TRACE
OF ONE
ANYWHERE!
HOLY--!
FLASH! WHAT'S WRONG?
AAAAAAAA!!
FLASH!

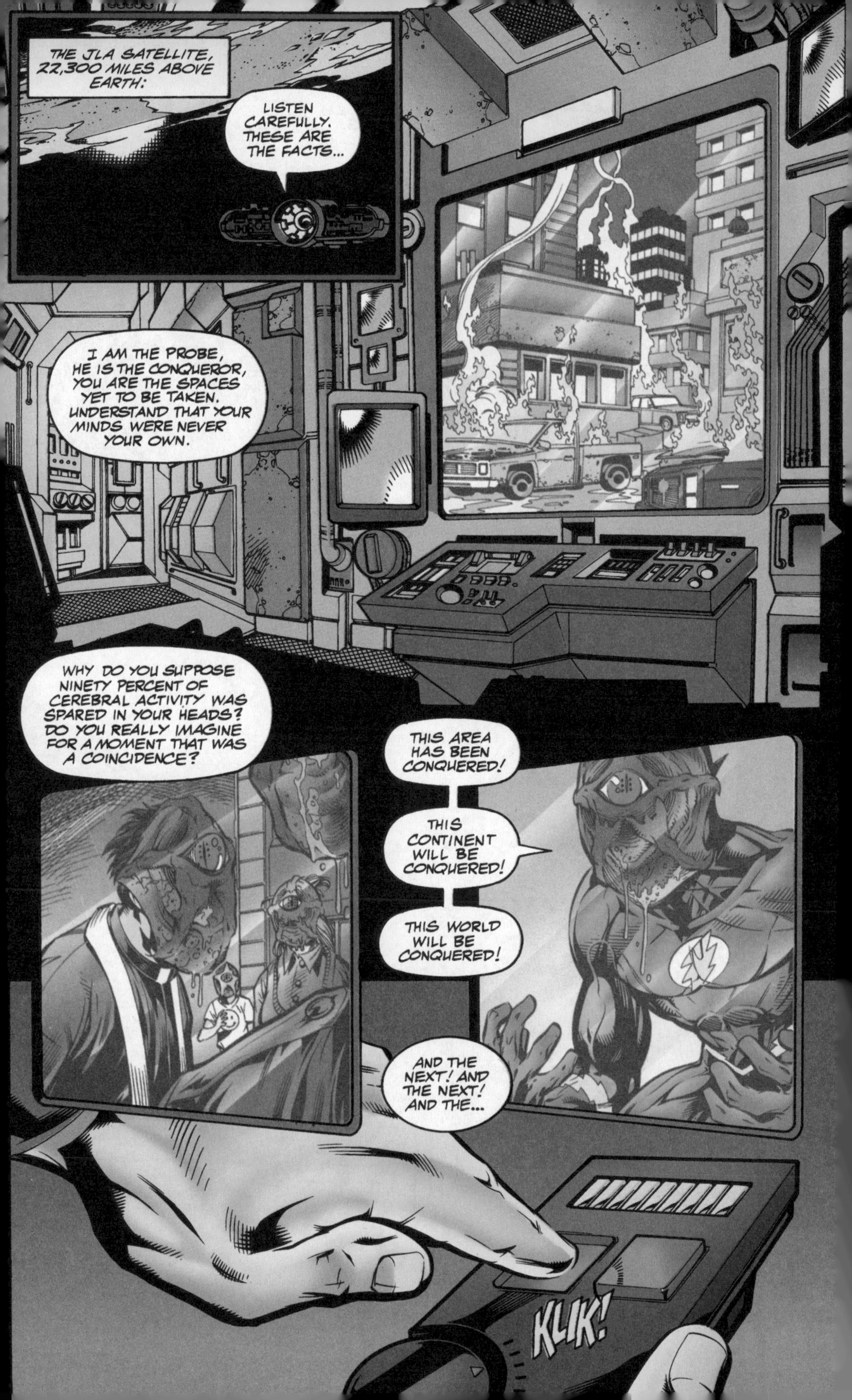
THE JLA SATELLITE, 22,300 MILES ABOVE EARTH:
LISTEN CAREFULLY. THESE ARE THE FACTS...
I AM THE PROBE, HE IS THE CONQUEROR, YOU ARE THE SPACES YET TO BE TAKEN. UNDERSTAND THAT YOUR MINDS WERE NEVER YOUR OWN.
WHY DO YOU SUPPOSE NINETY PERCENT OF CEREBRAL ACTIVITY WAS SPARED IN YOUR HEADS? DO YOU REALLY IMAGINE FOR A MOMENT THAT WAS A COINCIDENCE?
THIS AREA HAS BEEN CONQUERED!
THIS CONTINENT WILL BE CONQUERED!
THIS WORLD WILL BE CONQUERED!
AND THE NEXT! AND THE NEXT! AND THE...
KLIK!

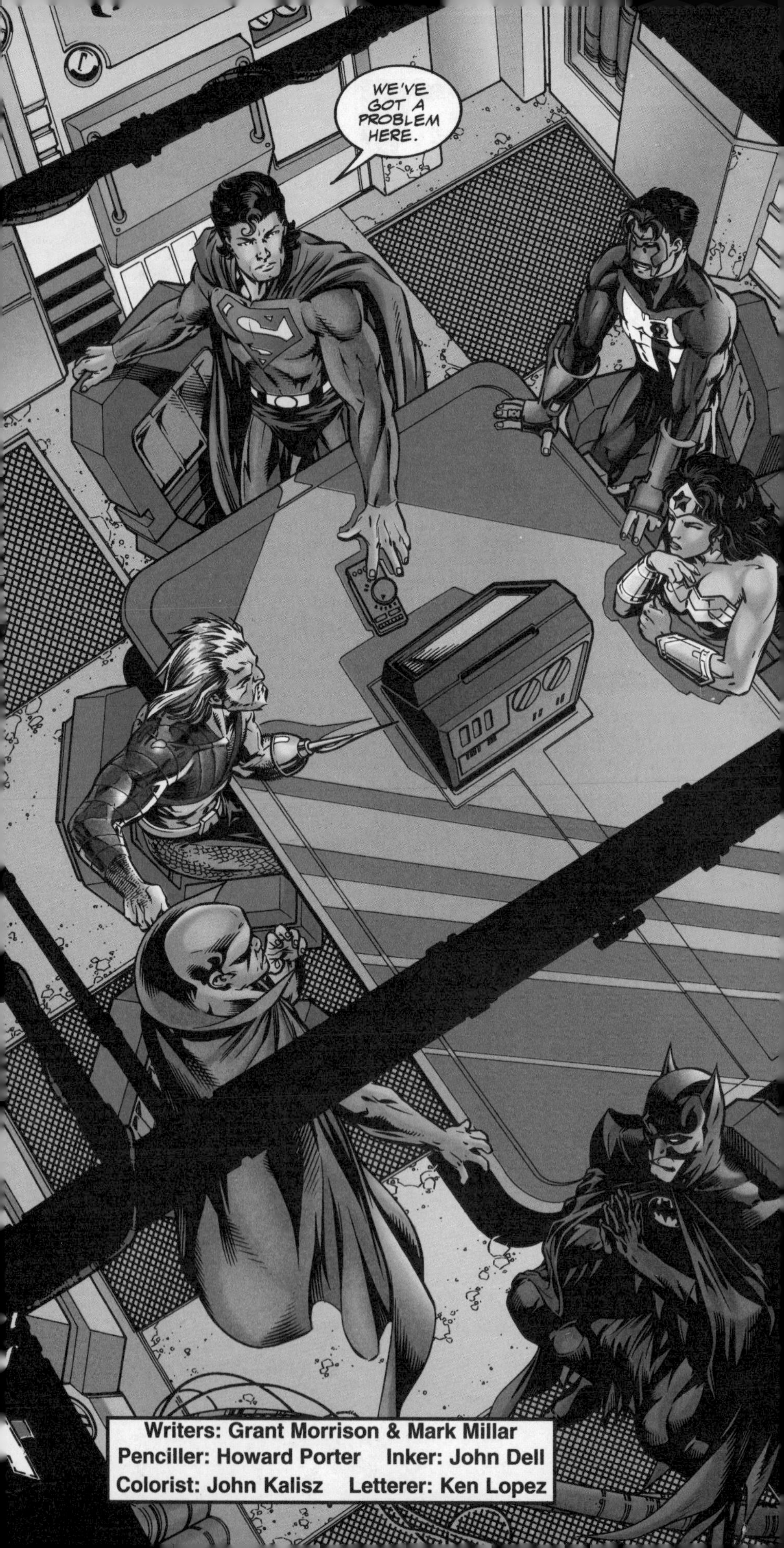
WE'VE GOT A PROBLEM HERE.
Writers: Grant Morrison & Mark Millar
Penciller: Howard Porter Inker: John Dell
Colorist: John Kalisz Letterer: Ken Lopez

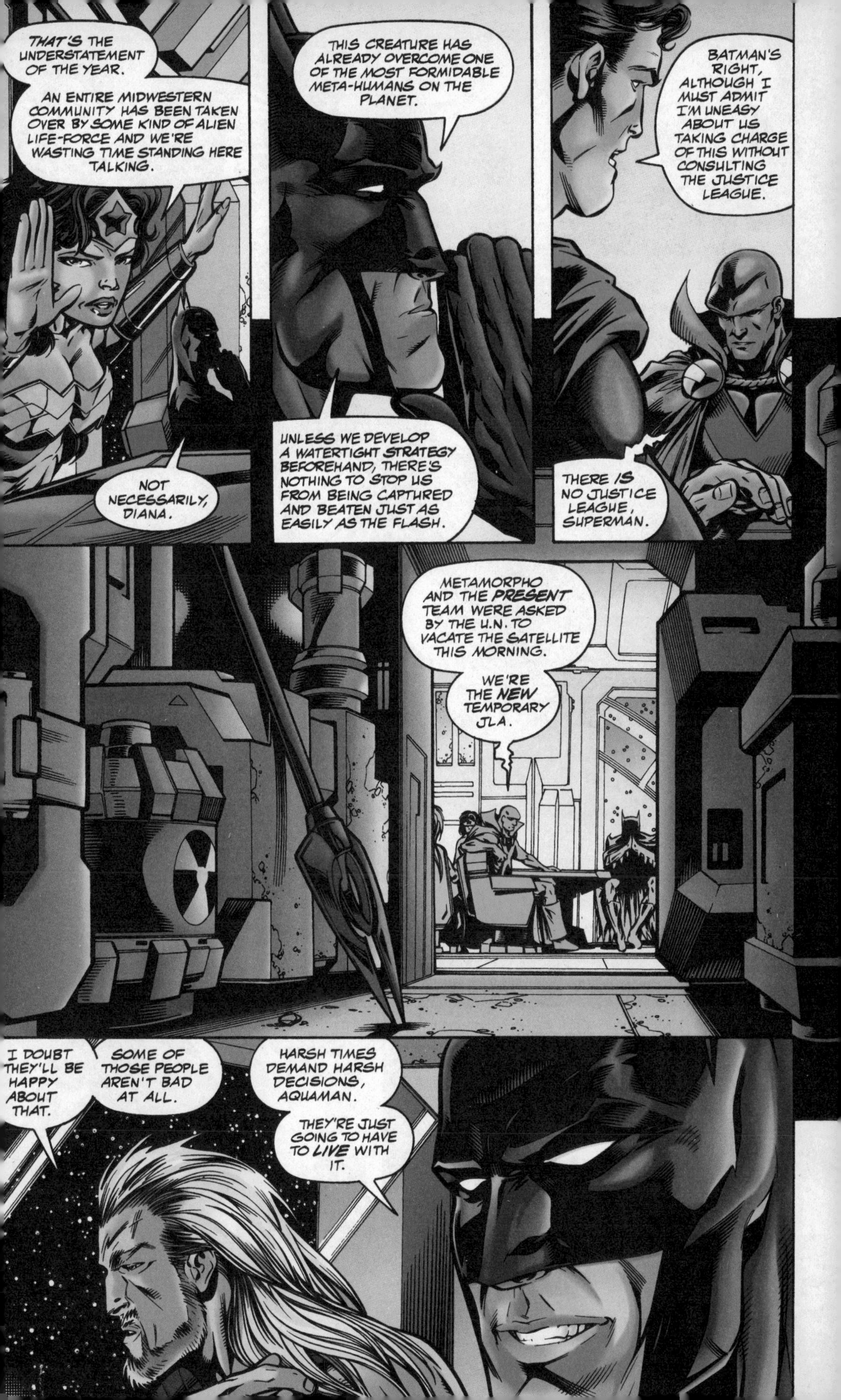
THAT'S THE UNDERSTATEMENT OF THE YEAR.
AN ENTIRE MIDWESTERN COMMUNITY HAS BEEN TAKEN OVER BY SOME KIND OF ALIEN LIFE-FORCE AND WE'RE WASTING TIME STANDING HERE TALKING.
NOT NECESSARILY, DIANA.
THIS CREATURE HAS ALREADY OVERCOME ONE OF THE MOST FORMIDABLE META-HUMANS ON THE PLANET.
UNLESS WE DEVELOP A WATERTIGHT STRATEGY BEFOREHAND, THERE'S NOTHING TO STOP US FROM BEING CAPTURED AND BEATEN JUST AS EASILY AS THE FLASH.
BATMAN'S RIGHT, ALTHOUGH I MUST ADMIT I'M UNEASY ABOUT US TAKING CHARGE OF THIS WITHOUT CONSULTING THE JUSTICE LEAGUE.
THERE IS NO JUSTICE LEAGUE, SUPERMAN.
METAMORPHO AND THE PRESENT TEAM WERE ASKED BY THE U.N. TO VACATE THE SATELLITE THIS MORNING.
WE'RE THE NEW TEMPORARY JLA.
I DOUBT THEY'LL BE HAPPY ABOUT THAT.
SOME OF THOSE PEOPLE AREN'T BAD AT ALL.
HARSH TIMES DEMAND HARSH DECISIONS, AQUAMAN.
THEY'RE JUST GOING TO HAVE TO LIVE WITH IT.

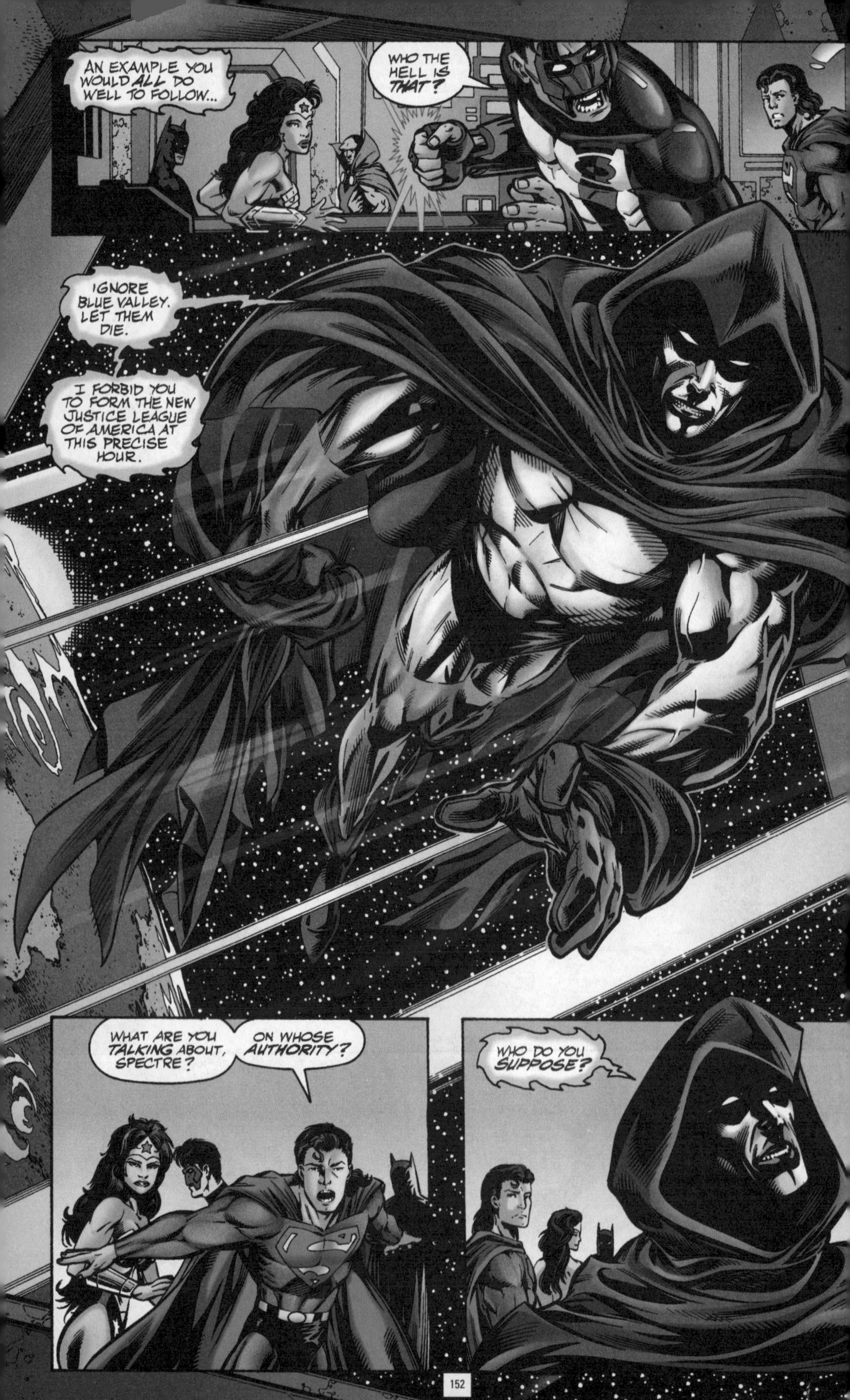

AN EXAMPLE YOU WOULD ALL DO WELL TO FOLLOW...
WHO THE HELL IS THAT?
IGNORE BLUE VALLEY. LET THEM DIE.
I FORBID YOU TO FORM THE NEW JUSTICE LEAGUE OF AMERICA AT THIS PRECISE HOUR.
WHAT ARE YOU TALKING ABOUT, SPECTRE?
ON WHOSE AUTHORITY?
WHO DO YOU SUPPOSE?

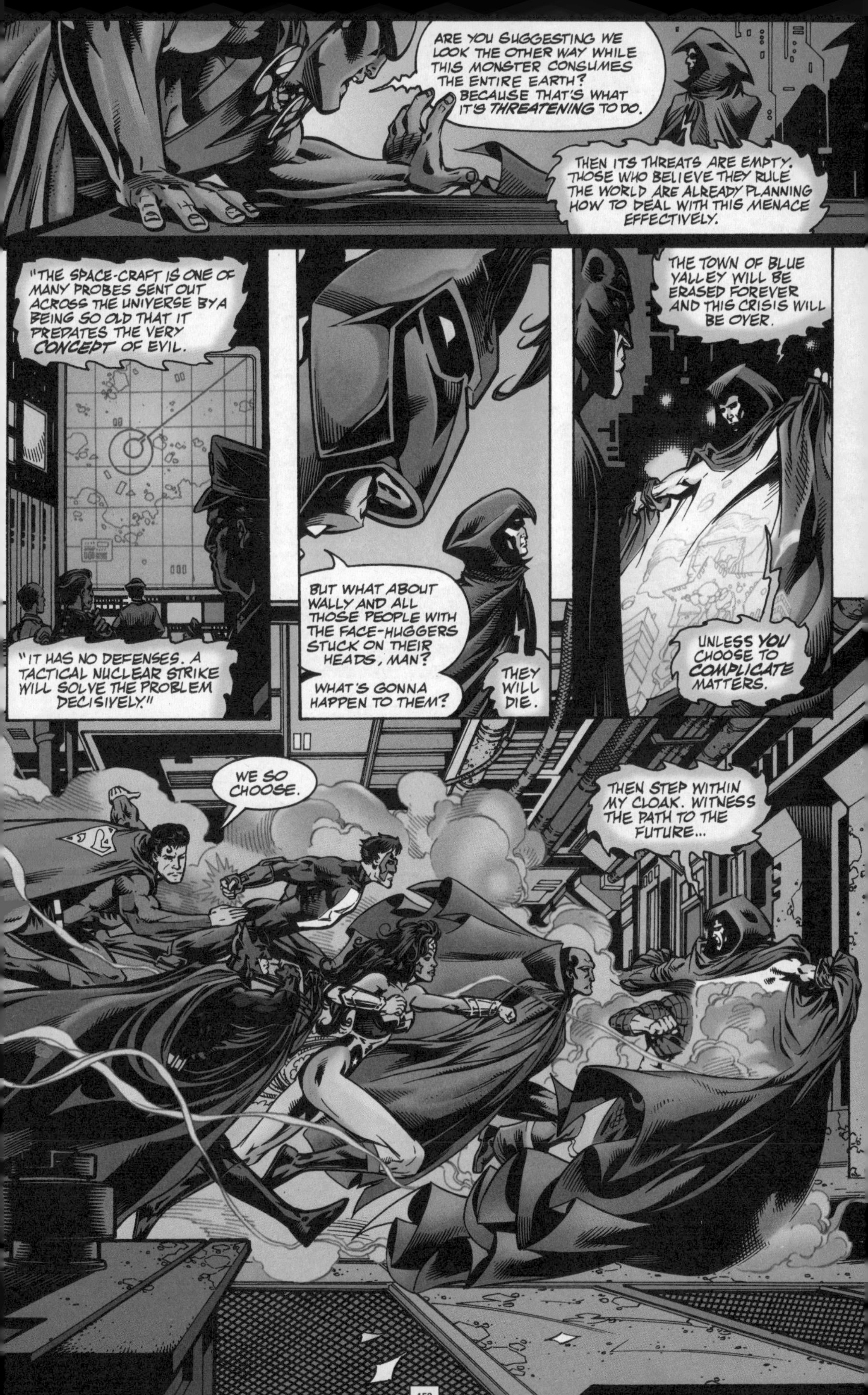

ARE YOU SUGGESTING WE LOOK THE OTHER WAY WHILE THIS MONSTER CONSUMES THE ENTIRE EARTH?
BECAUSE THAT'S WHAT IT'S THREATENING TO DO.
THEN ITS THREATS ARE EMPTY. THOSE WHO BELIEVE THEY RULE THE WORLD ARE ALREADY PLANNING HOW TO DEAL WITH THIS MENACE EFFECTIVELY.
"THE SPACE-CRAFT IS ONE OF MANY PROBES SENT OUT ACROSS THE UNIVERSE BY A BEING SO OLD THAT IT PREDATES THE VERY CONCEPT OF EVIL.
"IT HAS NO DEFENSES. A TACTICAL NUCLEAR STRIKE WILL SOLVE THE PROBLEM DECISIVELY."
BUT WHAT ABOUT WALLY AND ALL THOSE PEOPLE WITH THE FACE-HUGGERS STUCK ON THEIR HEADS, MAN?
WHAT'S GONNA HAPPEN TO THEM?
THEY WILL DIE.
THE TOWN OF BLUE VALLEY WILL BE ERASED FOREVER AND THIS CRISIS WILL BE OVER.
UNLESS YOU CHOOSE TO COMPLICATE MATTERS.
WE SO CHOOSE.
THEN STEP WITHIN MY CLOAK. WITNESS THE PATH TO THE FUTURE...

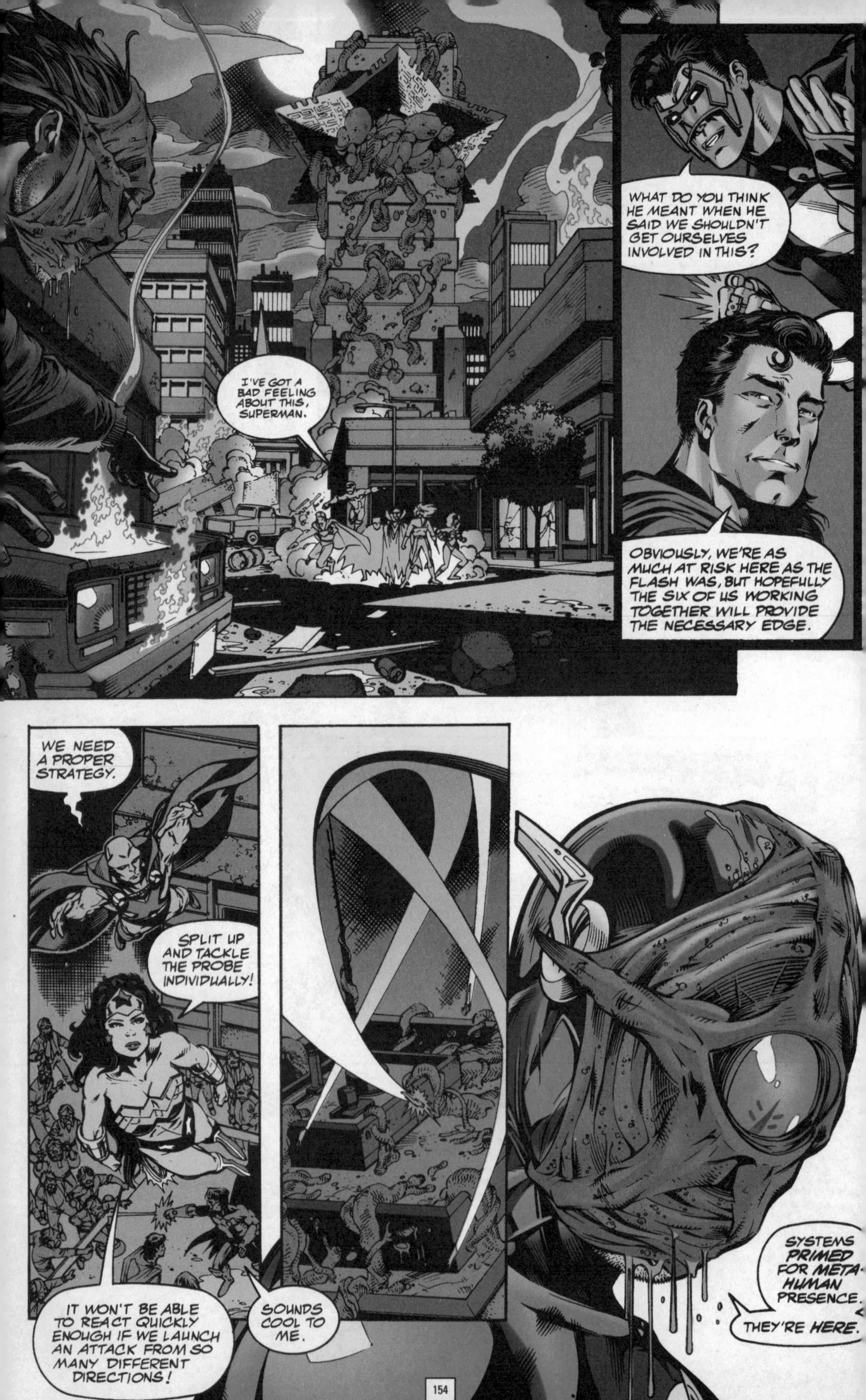
I'VE GOT A BAD FEELING ABOUT THIS, SUPERMAN.
WHAT DO YOU THINK HE MEANT WHEN HE SAID WE SHOULDN'T GET OURSELVES INVOLVED IN THIS?
OBVIOUSLY, WE'RE AS MUCH AT RISK HERE AS THE FLASH WAS, BUT HOPEFULLY THE SIX OF US WORKING TOGETHER WILL PROVIDE THE NECESSARY EDGE.
WE NEED A PROPER STRATEGY.
SPLIT UP AND TACKLE THE PROBE INDIVIDUALLY!
IT WON'T BE ABLE TO REACT QUICKLY ENOUGH IF WE LAUNCH AN ATTACK FROM SO MANY DIFFERENT DIRECTIONS!
SOUNDS COOL TO ME.
SYSTEMS PRIMED FOR META-HUMAN PRESENCE.
THEY'RE HERE.

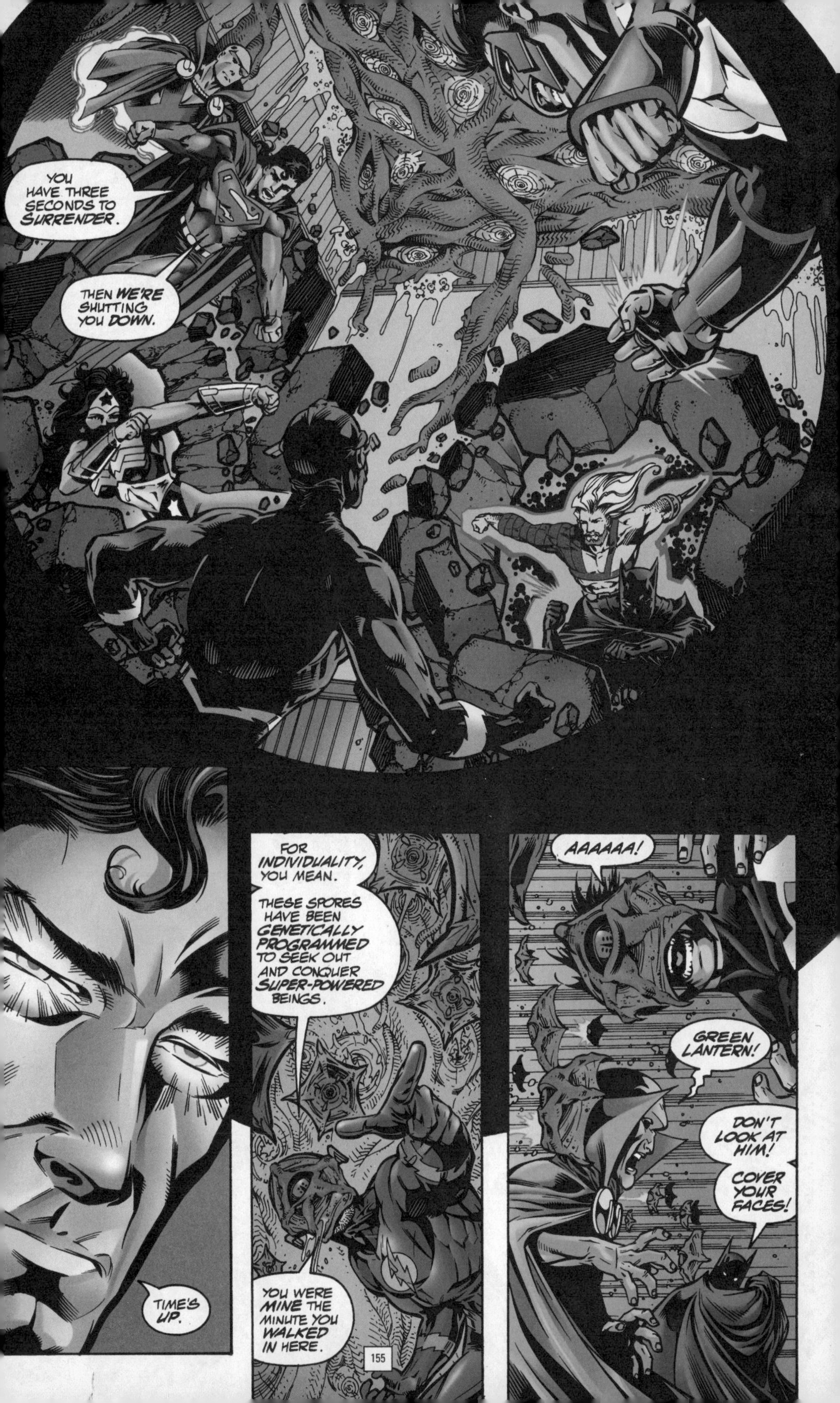

YOU HAVE THREE SECONDS TO SURRENDER.
THEN WE'RE SHUTTING YOU DOWN.
TIME'S UP.
FOR INDIVIDUALITY, YOU MEAN.
THESE SPORES HAVE BEEN GENETICALLY PROGRAMMED TO SEEK OUT AND CONQUER SUPER-POWERED BEINGS.
YOU WERE MINE THE MINUTE YOU WALKED IN HERE.
AAAAAA!
GREEN LANTERN!
DON'T LOOK AT HIM!
COVER YOUR FACES!

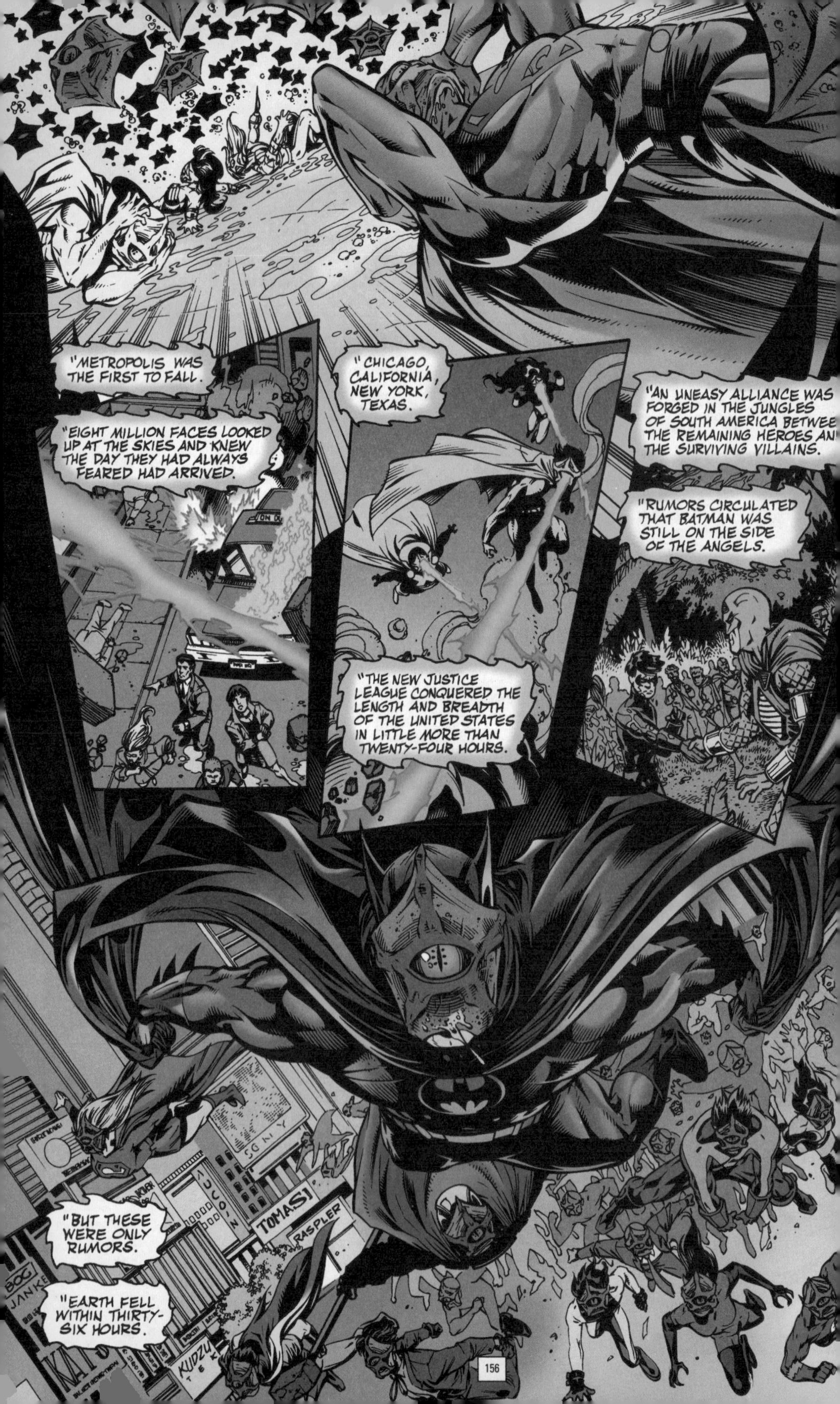
"METROPOLIS WAS THE FIRST TO FALL.
"EIGHT MILLION FACES LOOKED UP AT THE SKIES AND KNEW THE DAY THEY HAD ALWAYS FEARED HAD ARRIVED.
"CHICAGO, CALIFORNIA, NEW YORK, TEXAS.
"THE NEW JUSTICE LEAGUE CONQUERED THE LENGTH AND BREADTH OF THE UNITED STATES IN LITTLE MORE THAN TWENTY-FOUR HOURS.
"AN UNEASY ALLIANCE WAS FORGED IN THE JUNGLES OF SOUTH AMERICA BETWEE THE REMAINING HEROES AN THE SURVIVING VILLAINS.
"RUMORS CIRCULATED THAT BATMAN WAS STILL ON THE SIDE OF THE ANGELS.
"BUT THESE WERE ONLY RUMORS.
"EARTH FELL WITHIN THIRTY-SIX HOURS.
TOMASI
RASPLER
KUDZU
JANKE

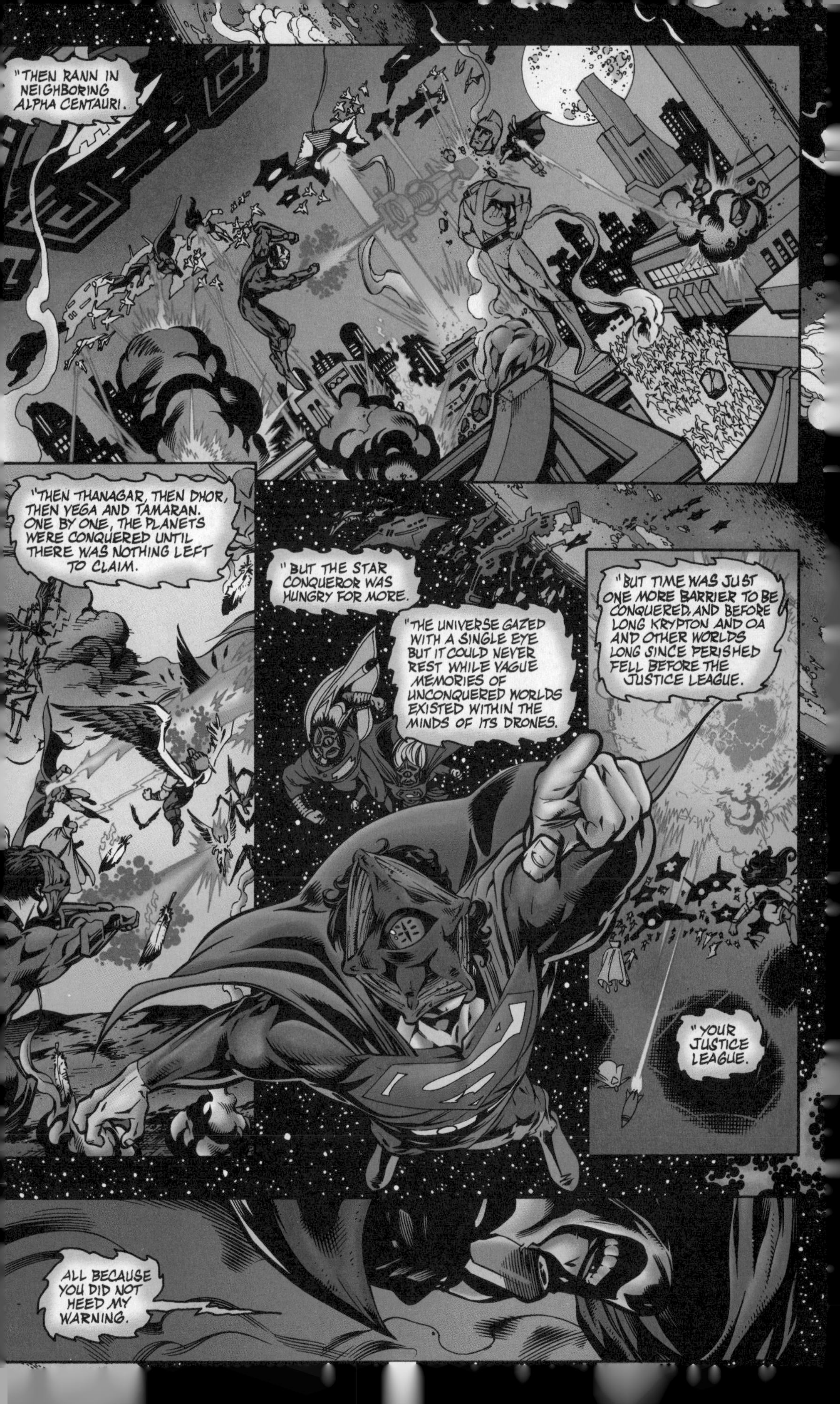
"THEN RANN IN NEIGHBORING ALPHA CENTAURI.
"THEN THANAGAR, THEN DHOR, THEN VEGA AND TAMARAN. ONE BY ONE, THE PLANETS WERE CONQUERED UNTIL THERE WAS NOTHING LEFT TO CLAIM.
"BUT THE STAR CONQUEROR WAS HUNGRY FOR MORE.
"THE UNIVERSE GAZED WITH A SINGLE EYE BUT IT COULD NEVER REST WHILE VAGUE MEMORIES OF UNCONQUERED WORLDS EXISTED WITHIN THE MINDS OF ITS DRONES.
"BUT TIME WAS JUST ONE MORE BARRIER TO BE CONQUERED, AND BEFORE LONG KRYPTON AND OA AND OTHER WORLDS LONG SINCE PERISHED FELL BEFORE THE JUSTICE LEAGUE.
"YOUR JUSTICE LEAGUE.
ALL BECAUSE YOU DID NOT HEED MY WARNING.

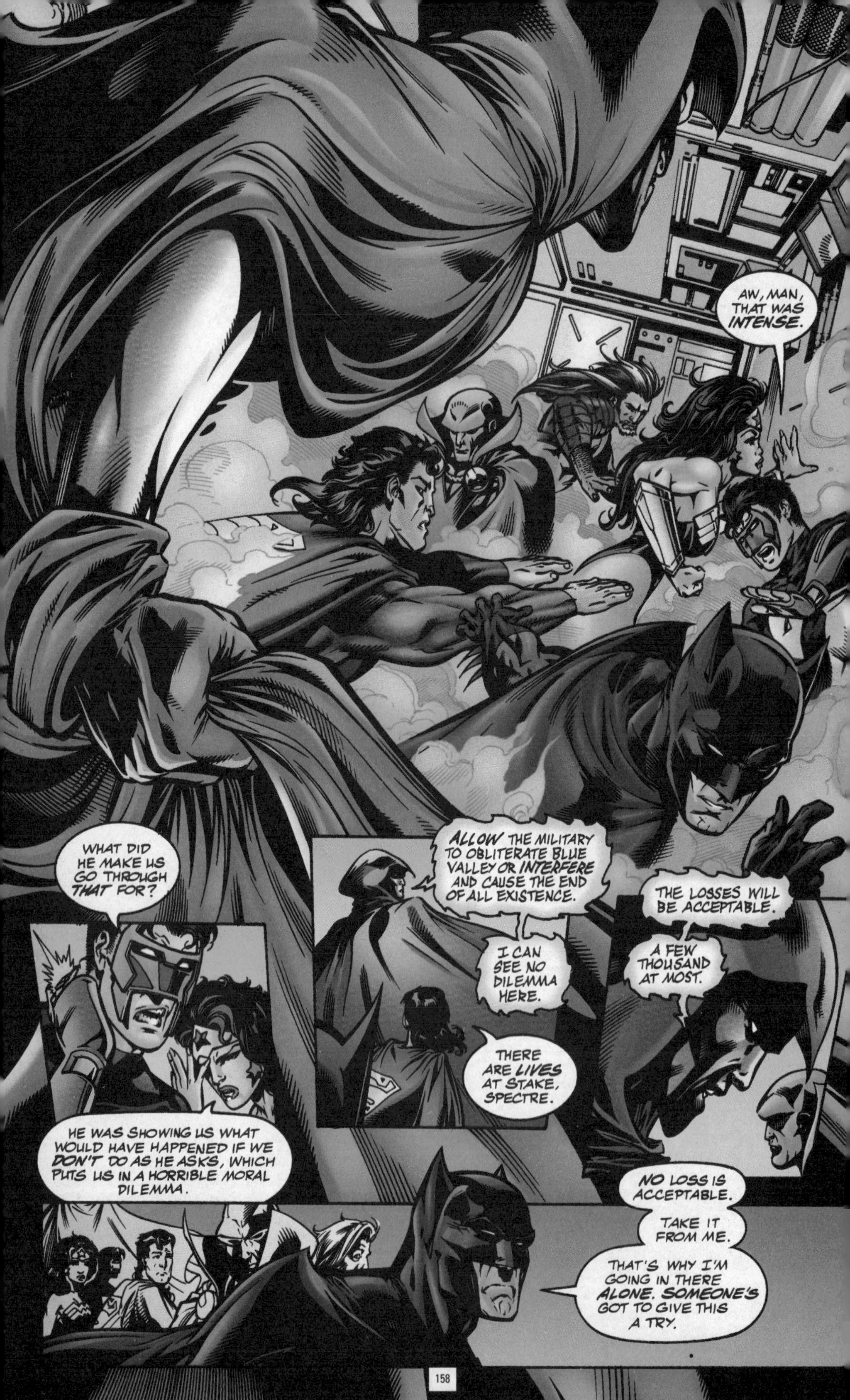
AW, MAN, THAT WAS INTENSE.
WHAT DID HE MAKE US GO THROUGH THAT FOR?
HE WAS SHOWING US WHAT WOULD HAVE HAPPENED IF WE DON'T DO AS HE ASKS, WHICH PUTS US IN A HORRIBLE MORAL DILEMMA.
ALLOW THE MILITARY TO OBLITERATE BLUE VALLEY OR INTERFERE AND CAUSE THE END OF ALL EXISTENCE.
I CAN SEE NO DILEMMA HERE.
THERE ARE LIVES AT STAKE, SPECTRE.
THE LOSSES WILL BE ACCEPTABLE.
A FEW THOUSAND AT MOST.
NO LOSS IS ACCEPTABLE.
TAKE IT FROM ME.
THAT'S WHY I'M GOING IN THERE ALONE. SOMEONE'S GOT TO GIVE THIS A TRY.

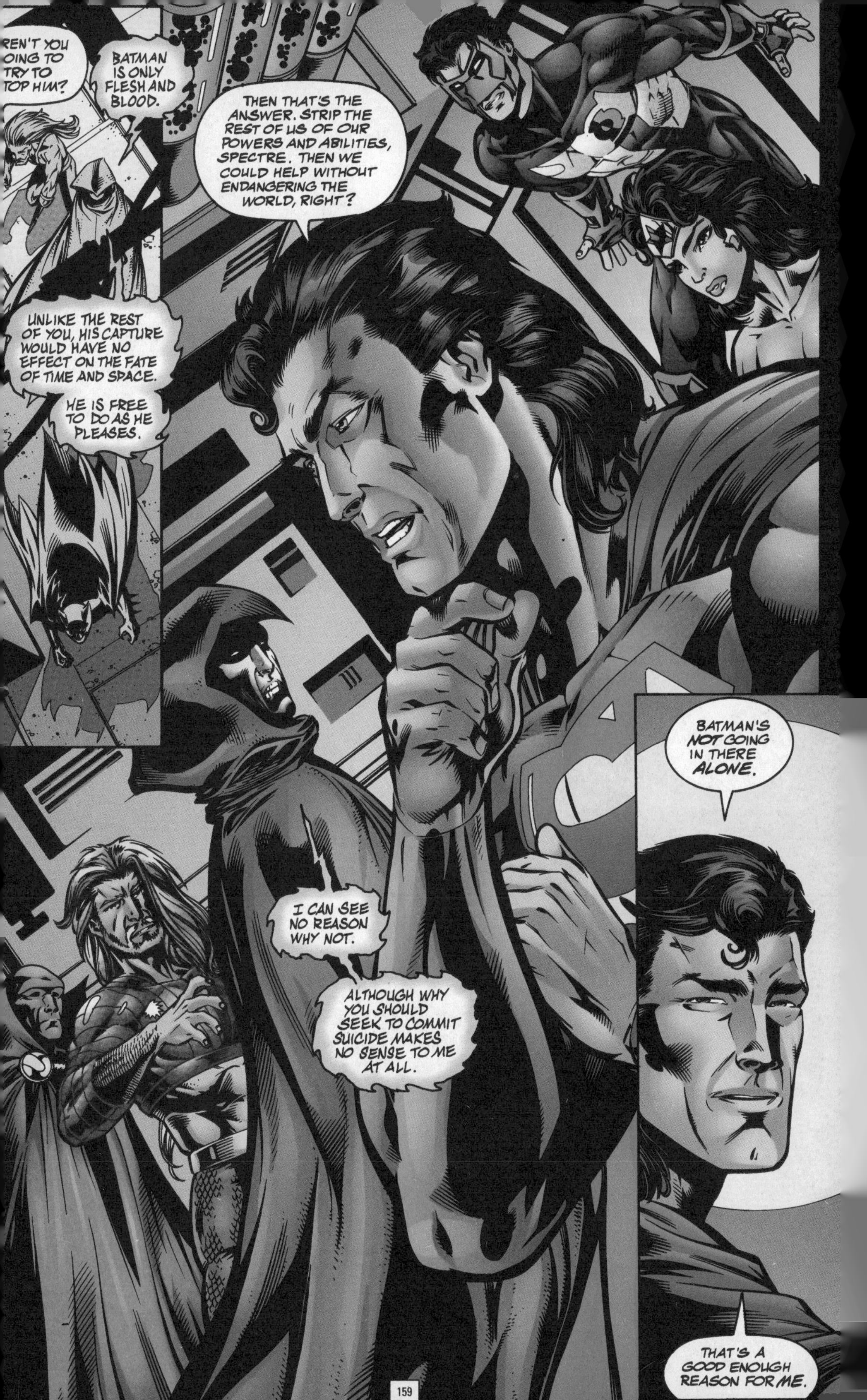

RENT'T YOU OING TO TRY TO TOP HIM?
BATMAN IS ONLY FLESH AND BLOOD.
THEN THAT'S THE ANSWER. STRIP THE REST OF US OF OUR POWERS AND ABILITIES, SPECTRE. THEN WE COULD HELP WITHOUT ENDANGERING THE WORLD, RIGHT?
UNLIKE THE REST OF YOU, HIS CAPTURE WOULD HAVE NO EFFECT ON THE FATE OF TIME AND SPACE.
HE IS FREE TO DO AS HE PLEASES.
I CAN SEE NO REASON WHY NOT.
ALTHOUGH WHY YOU SHOULD SEEK TO COMMIT SUICIDE MAKES NO SENSE TO ME AT ALL.
BATMAN'S NOT GOING IN THERE ALONE.
THAT'S A GOOD ENOUGH REASON FOR ME.

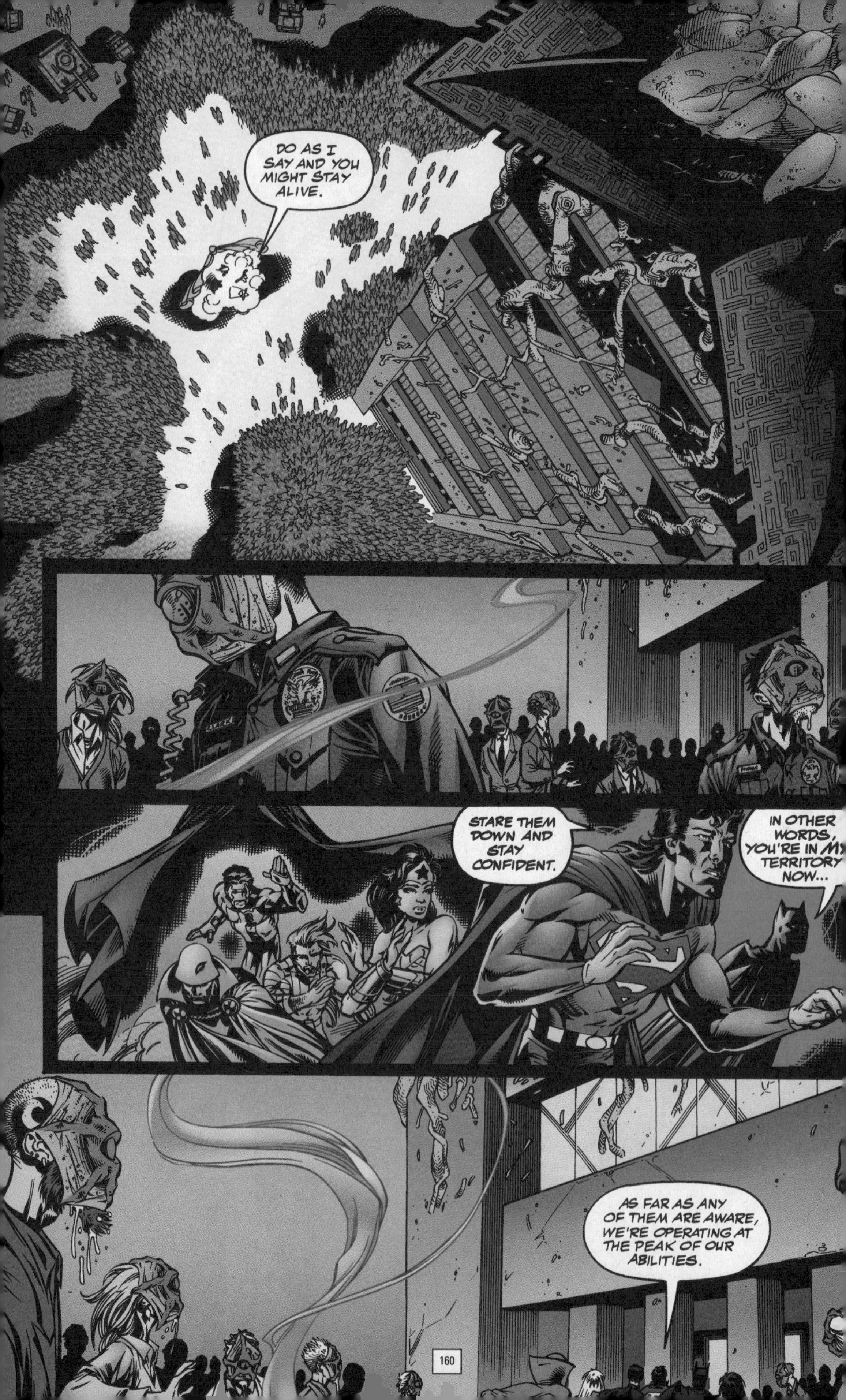
DO AS I SAY AND YOU MIGHT STAY ALIVE.
STARE THEM DOWN AND STAY CONFIDENT.
IN OTHER WORDS, YOU'RE IN MY TERRITORY NOW...
AS FAR AS ANY OF THEM ARE AWARE, WE'RE OPERATING AT THE PEAK OF OUR ABILITIES.

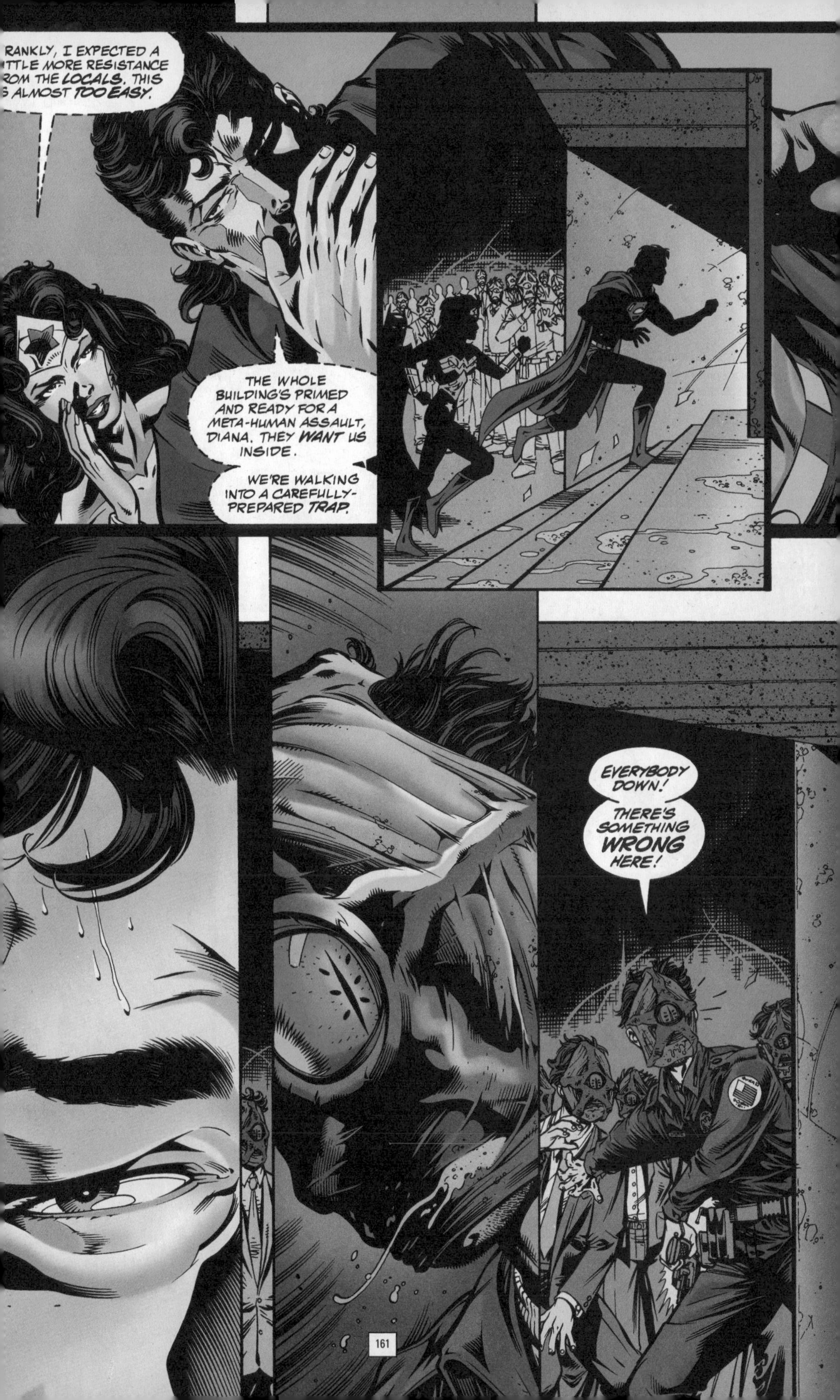
RANKLY, I EXPECTED A
TTLE MORE RESISTANCE
ROM THE LOCALS. THIS
S ALMOST TOO EASY.
THE WHOLE BUILDING'S PRIMED AND READY FOR A META-HUMAN ASSAULT, DIANA. THEY WANT US INSIDE.
WE'RE WALKING INTO A CAREFULLY-PREPARED TRAP.
EVERYBODY DOWN!
THERE'S SOMETHING WRONG HERE!

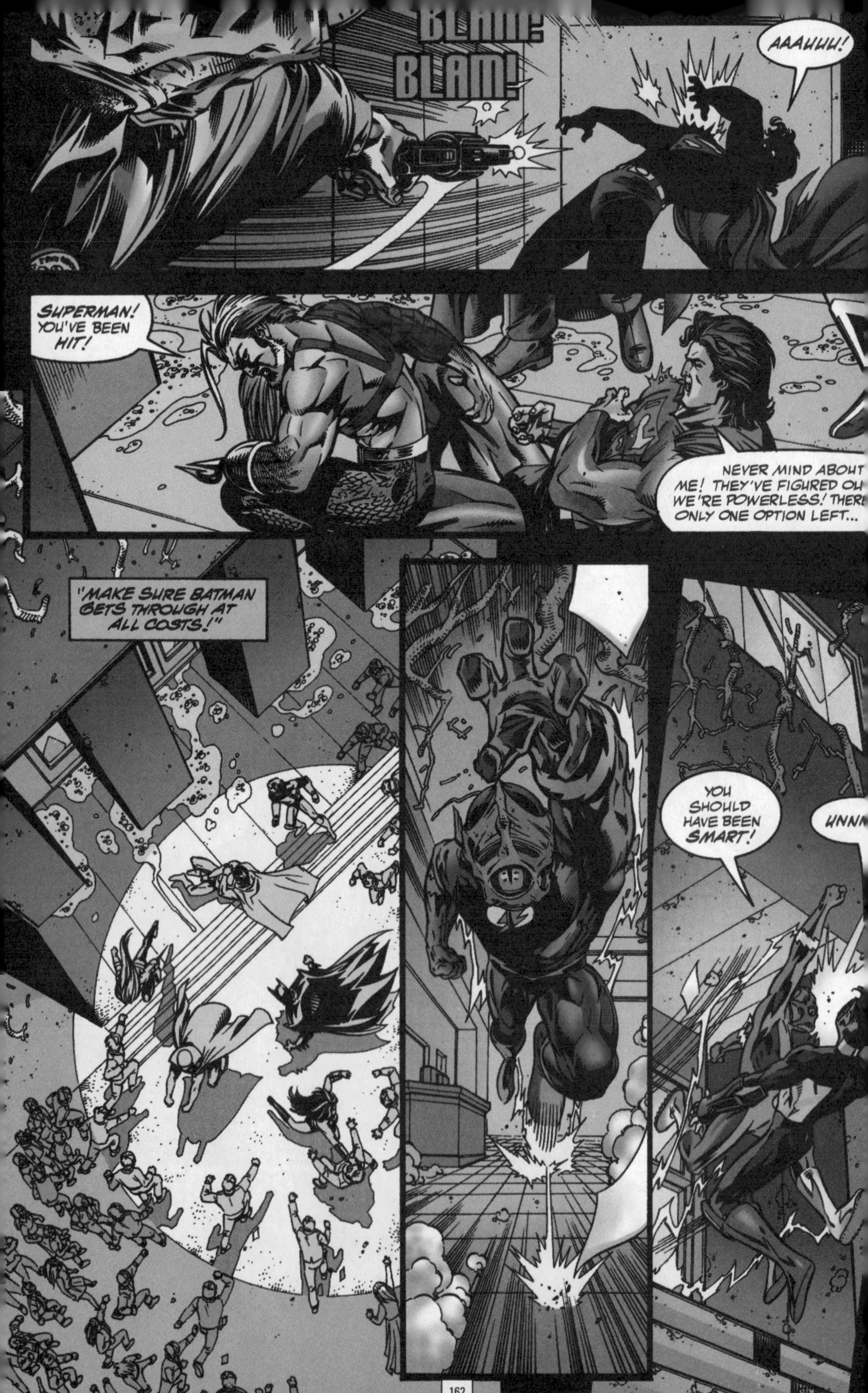
BLAM! BLAM!
AAAUUU!
SUPERMAN! YOU'VE BEEN HIT!
NEVER MIND ABOUT ME! THEY'VE FIGURED OU WE'RE POWERLESS! THERE ONLY ONE OPTION LEFT...
"MAKE SURE BATMAN GETS THROUGH AT ALL COSTS!"
YOU SHOULD HAVE BEEN SMART!
UNNN

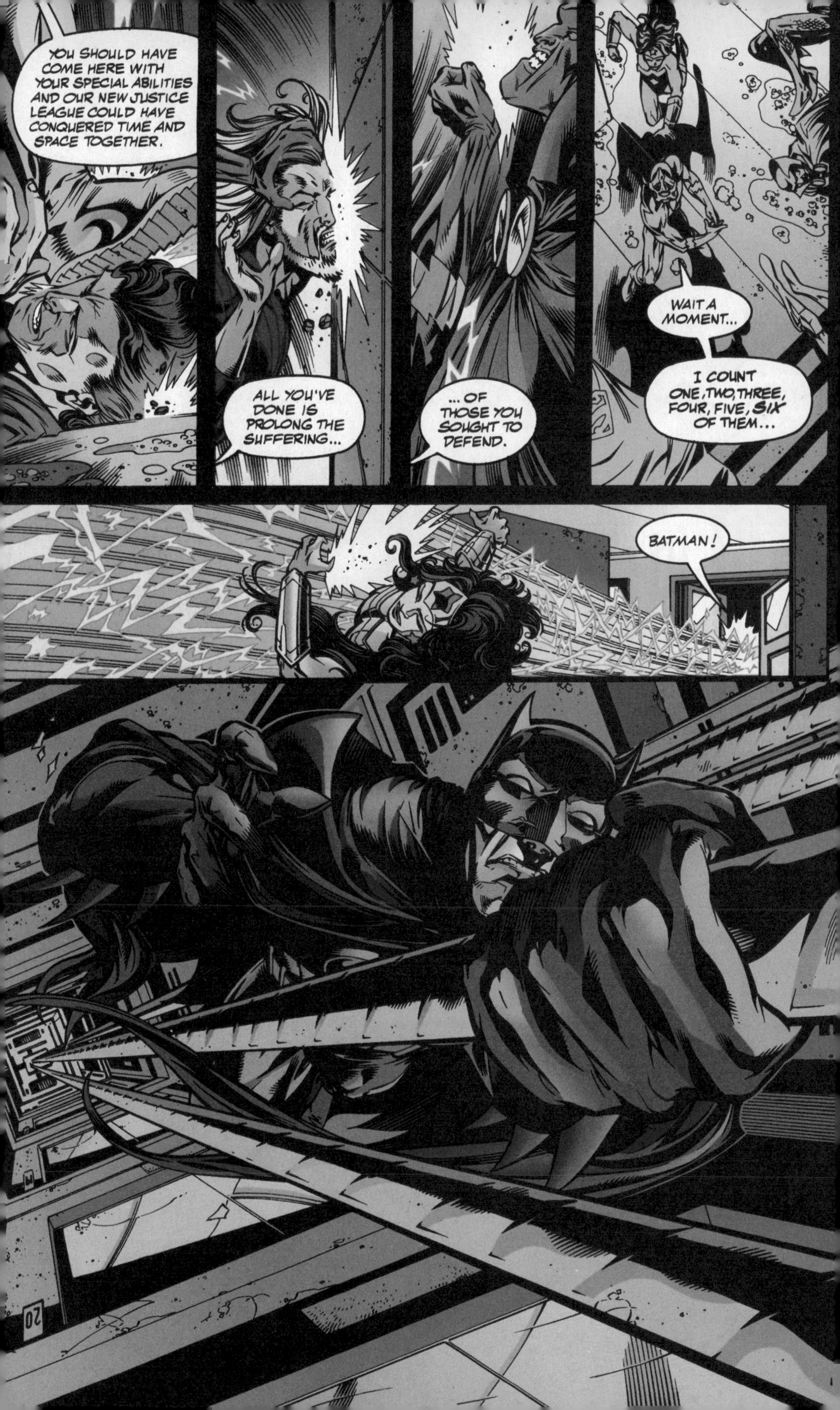
YOU SHOULD HAVE COME HERE WITH YOUR SPECIAL ABILITIES AND OUR NEW JUSTICE LEAGUE COULD HAVE CONQUERED TIME AND SPACE TOGETHER.
ALL YOU'VE DONE IS PROLONG THE SUFFERING...
...OF THOSE YOU SOUGHT TO DEFEND.
WAIT A MOMENT...
I COUNT ONE, TWO, THREE, FOUR, FIVE, SIX OF THEM...
BATMAN!
20

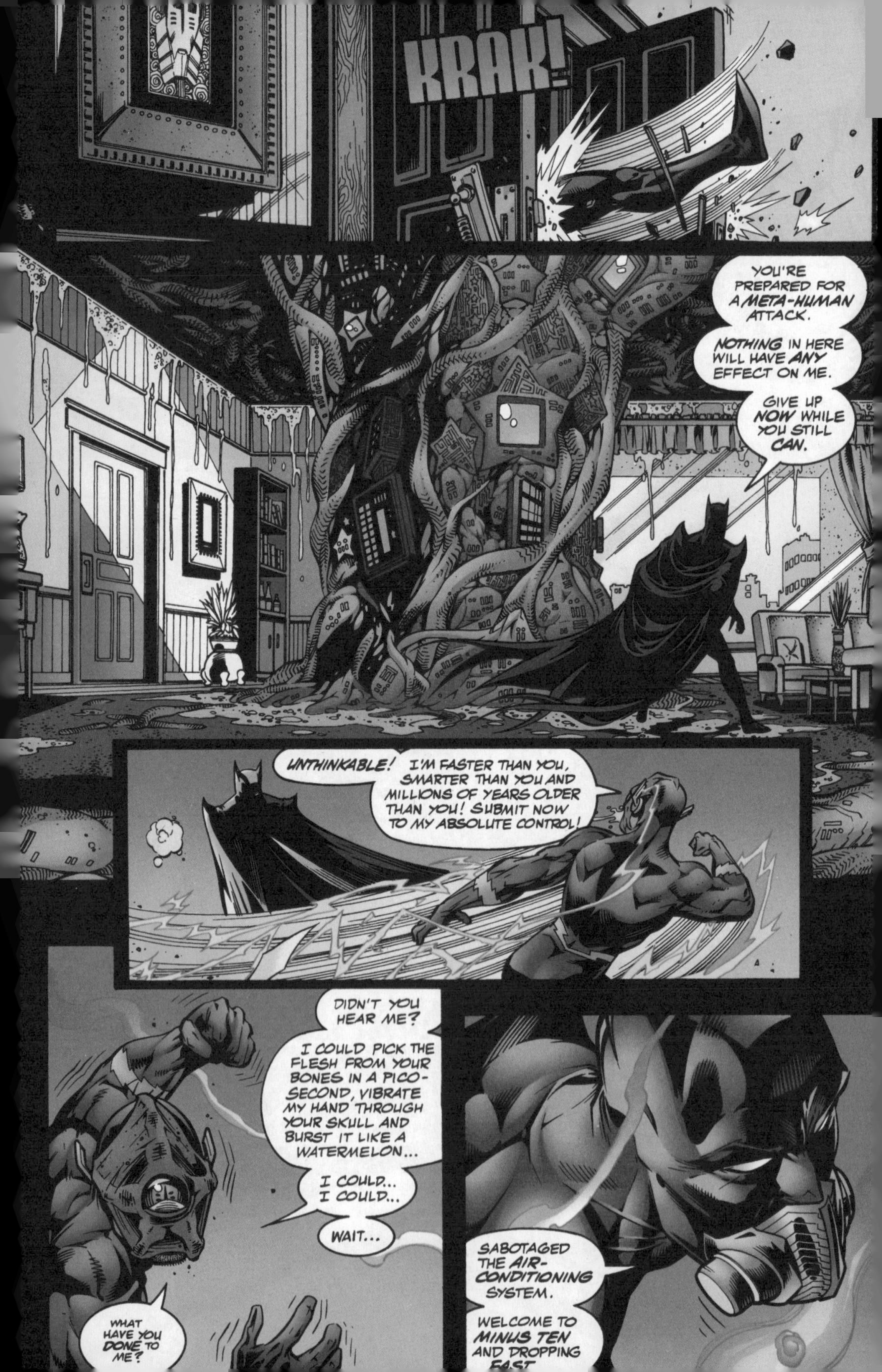
KRAK!
YOU'RE PREPARED FOR A META-HUMAN ATTACK.
NOTHING IN HERE WILL HAVE ANY EFFECT ON ME.
GIVE UP NOW WHILE YOU STILL CAN.
UNTHINKABLE! I'M FASTER THAN YOU, SMARTER THAN YOU AND MILLIONS OF YEARS OLDER THAN YOU! SUBMIT NOW TO MY ABSOLUTE CONTROL!
DIDN'T YOU HEAR ME?
I COULD PICK THE FLESH FROM YOUR BONES IN A PICO-SECOND, VIBRATE MY HAND THROUGH YOUR SKULL AND BURST IT LIKE A WATERMELON...
I COULD... I COULD...
WAIT...
WHAT HAVE YOU DONE TO ME?
SABOTAGED THE AIR-CONDITIONING SYSTEM.
WELCOME TO MINUS TEN AND DROPPING

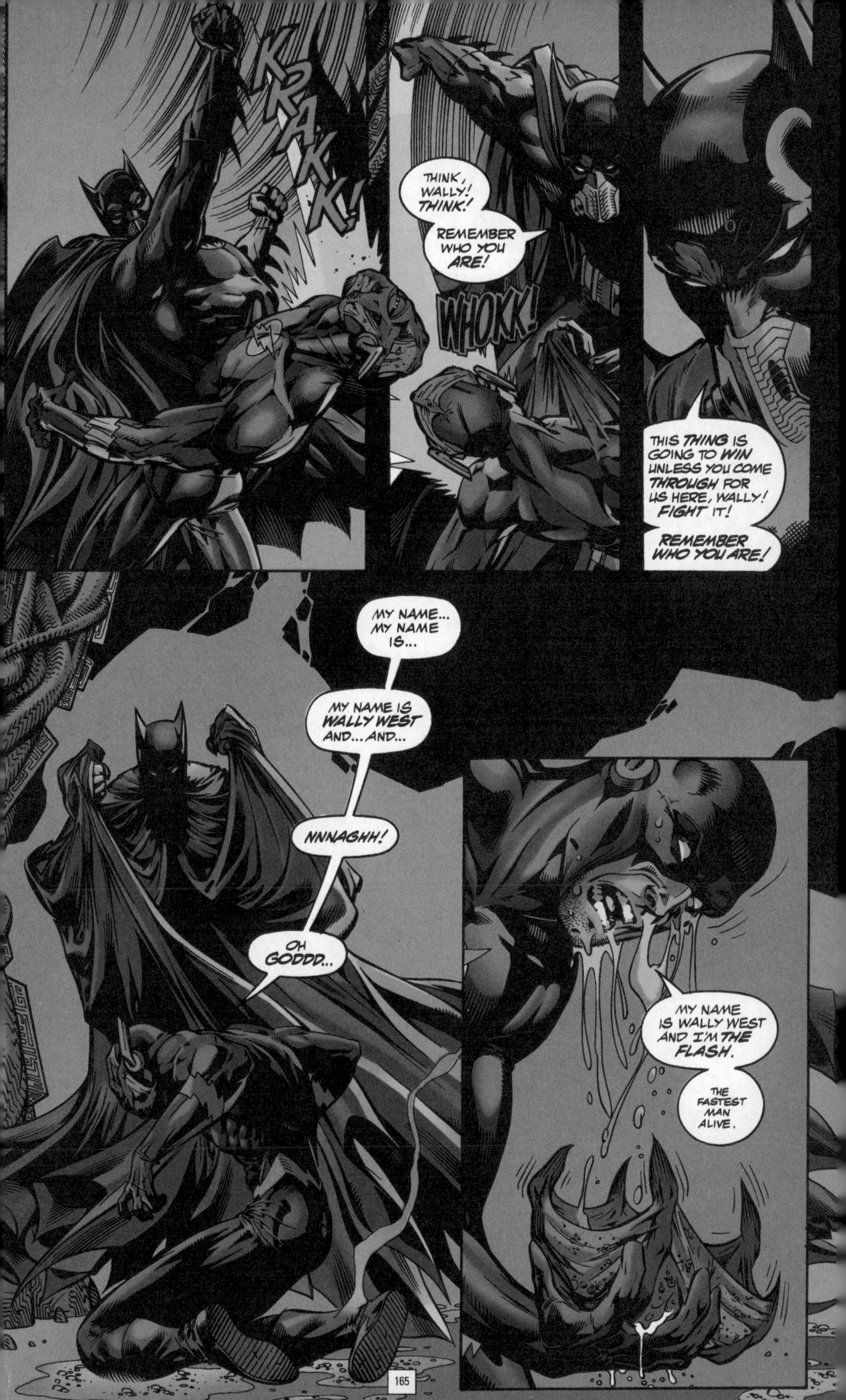
KRAKK!
THINK, WALLY! THINK!
REMEMBER WHO YOU ARE!
WHOKK!
THIS THING IS GOING TO WIN UNLESS YOU COME THROUGH FOR US HERE, WALLY! FIGHT IT!
REMEMBER WHO YOU ARE!
MY NAME... MY NAME IS...
MY NAME IS WALLY WEST AND... AND...
NNNAGHH!
OH GODDD...
MY NAME IS WALLY WEST AND I'M THE FLASH.
THE FASTEST MAN ALIVE.

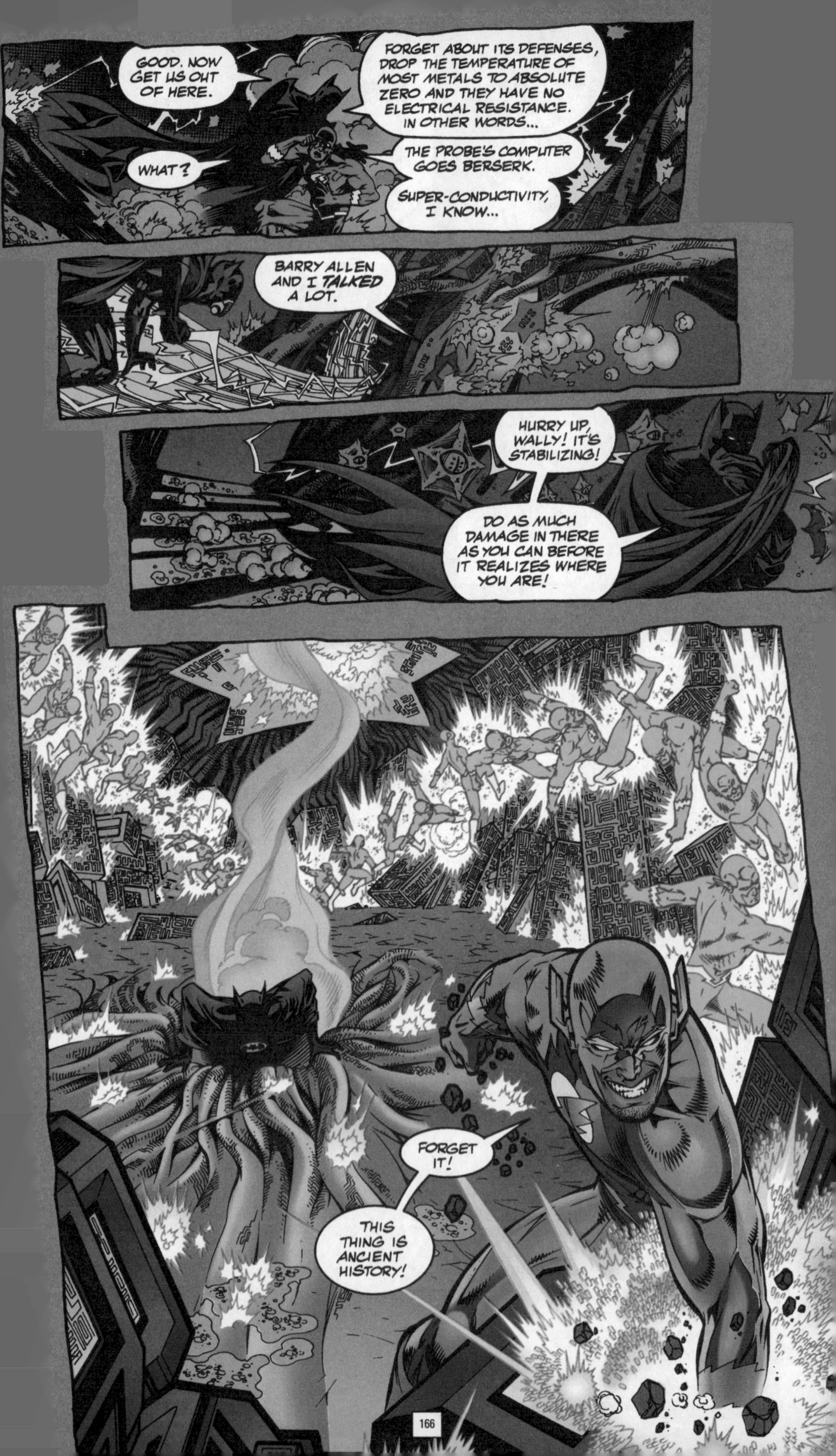
GOOD. NOW GET US OUT OF HERE.
FORGET ABOUT ITS DEFENSES, DROP THE TEMPERATURE OF MOST METALS TO ABSOLUTE ZERO AND THEY HAVE NO ELECTRICAL RESISTANCE. IN OTHER WORDS...
WHAT?
THE PROBE'S COMPUTER GOES BERSERK.
SUPER-CONDUCTIVITY, I KNOW...
BARRY ALLEN AND I TALKED A LOT.
HURRY UP, WALLY! IT'S STABILIZING!
DO AS MUCH DAMAGE IN THERE AS YOU CAN BEFORE IT REALIZES WHERE YOU ARE!
FORGET IT!
THIS THING IS ANCIENT HISTORY!

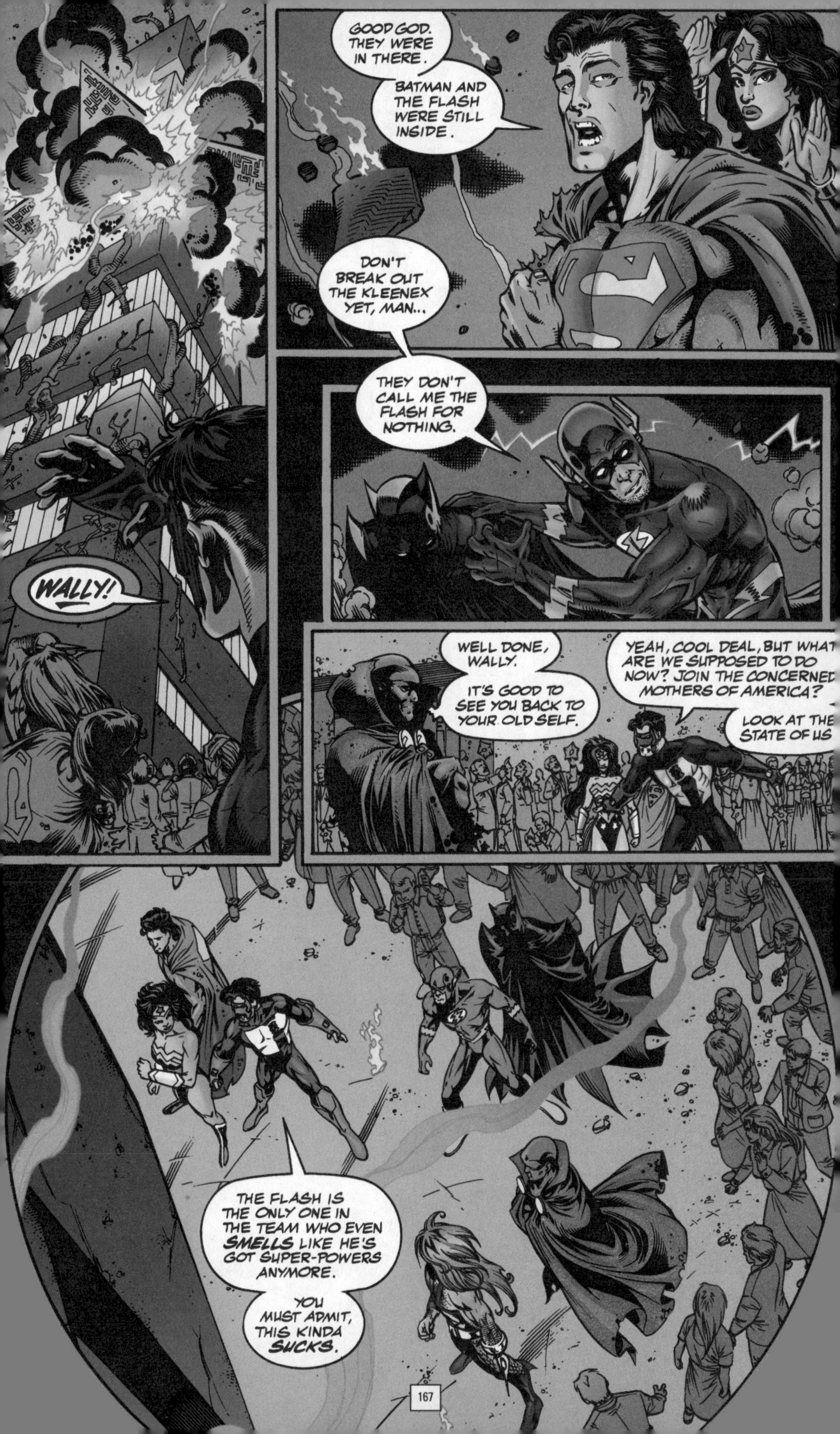
GOOD GOD. THEY WERE IN THERE.
BATMAN AND THE FLASH WERE STILL INSIDE.
WALLY!
DON'T BREAK OUT THE KLEENEX YET, MAN...
THEY DON'T CALL ME THE FLASH FOR NOTHING.
WELL DONE, WALLY.
IT'S GOOD TO SEE YOU BACK TO YOUR OLD SELF.
YEAH, COOL DEAL, BUT WHAT ARE WE SUPPOSED TO DO NOW? JOIN THE CONCERNED MOTHERS OF AMERICA?
LOOK AT THE STATE OF US
THE FLASH IS THE ONLY ONE IN THE TEAM WHO EVEN SMELLS LIKE HE'S GOT SUPER-POWERS ANYMORE.
YOU MUST ADMIT, THIS KINDA SUCKS.

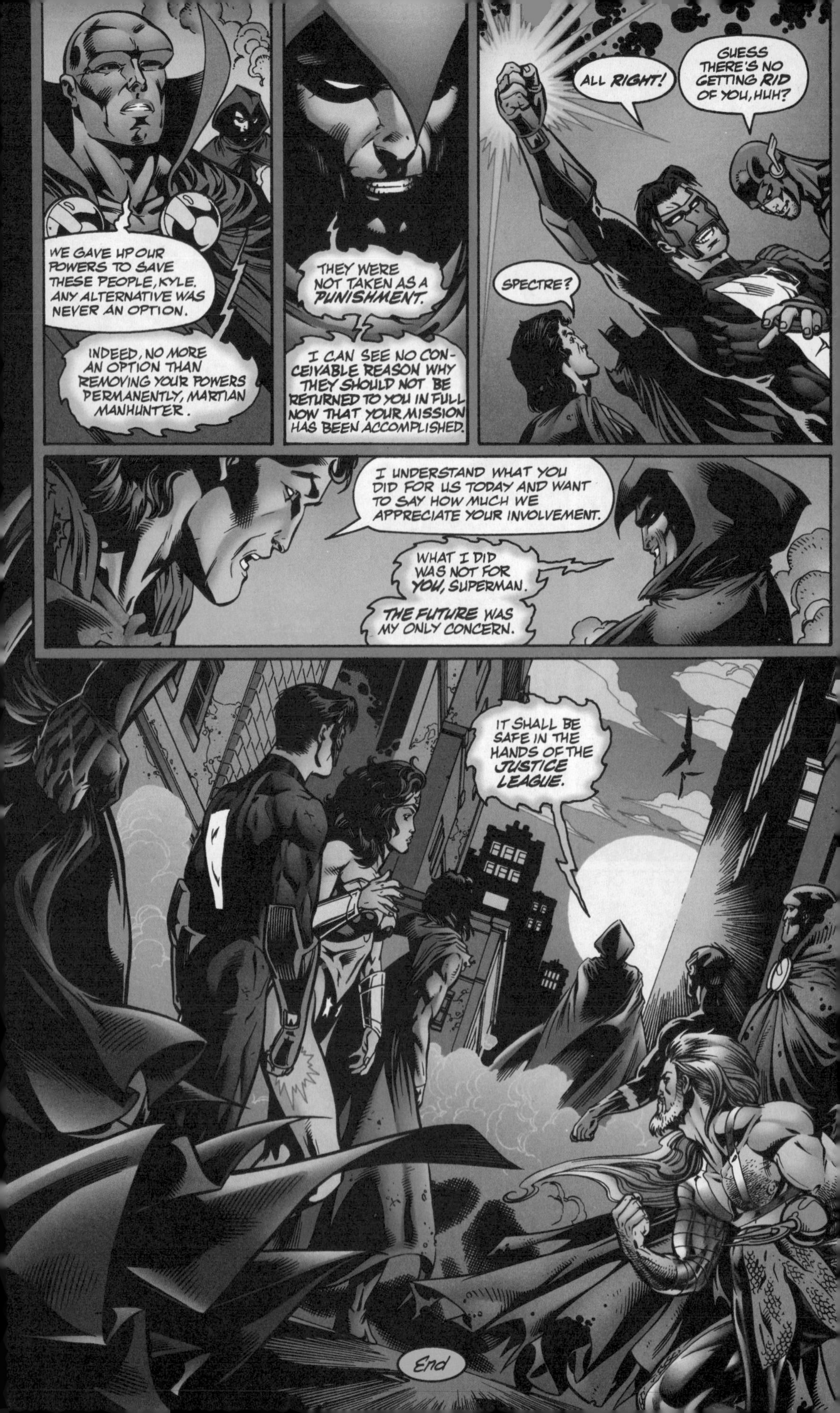
WE GAVE UP OUR POWERS TO SAVE THESE PEOPLE, KYLE. ANY ALTERNATIVE WAS NEVER AN OPTION.
INDEED, NO MORE AN OPTION THAN REMOVING YOUR POWERS PERMANENTLY, MARTIAN MANHUNTER.
THEY WERE NOT TAKEN AS A PUNISHMENT.
I CAN SEE NO CONCEIVABLE REASON WHY THEY SHOULD NOT BE RETURNED TO YOU IN FULL NOW THAT YOUR MISSION HAS BEEN ACCOMPLISHED.
ALL RIGHT!
GUESS THERE'S NO GETTING RID OF YOU, HUH?
SPECTRE?
I UNDERSTAND WHAT YOU DID FOR US TODAY AND WANT TO SAY HOW MUCH WE APPRECIATE YOUR INVOLVEMENT.
WHAT I DID WAS NOT FOR YOU, SUPERMAN.
THE FUTURE WAS MY ONLY CONCERN.
IT SHALL BE SAFE IN THE HANDS OF THE JUSTICE LEAGUE.
End

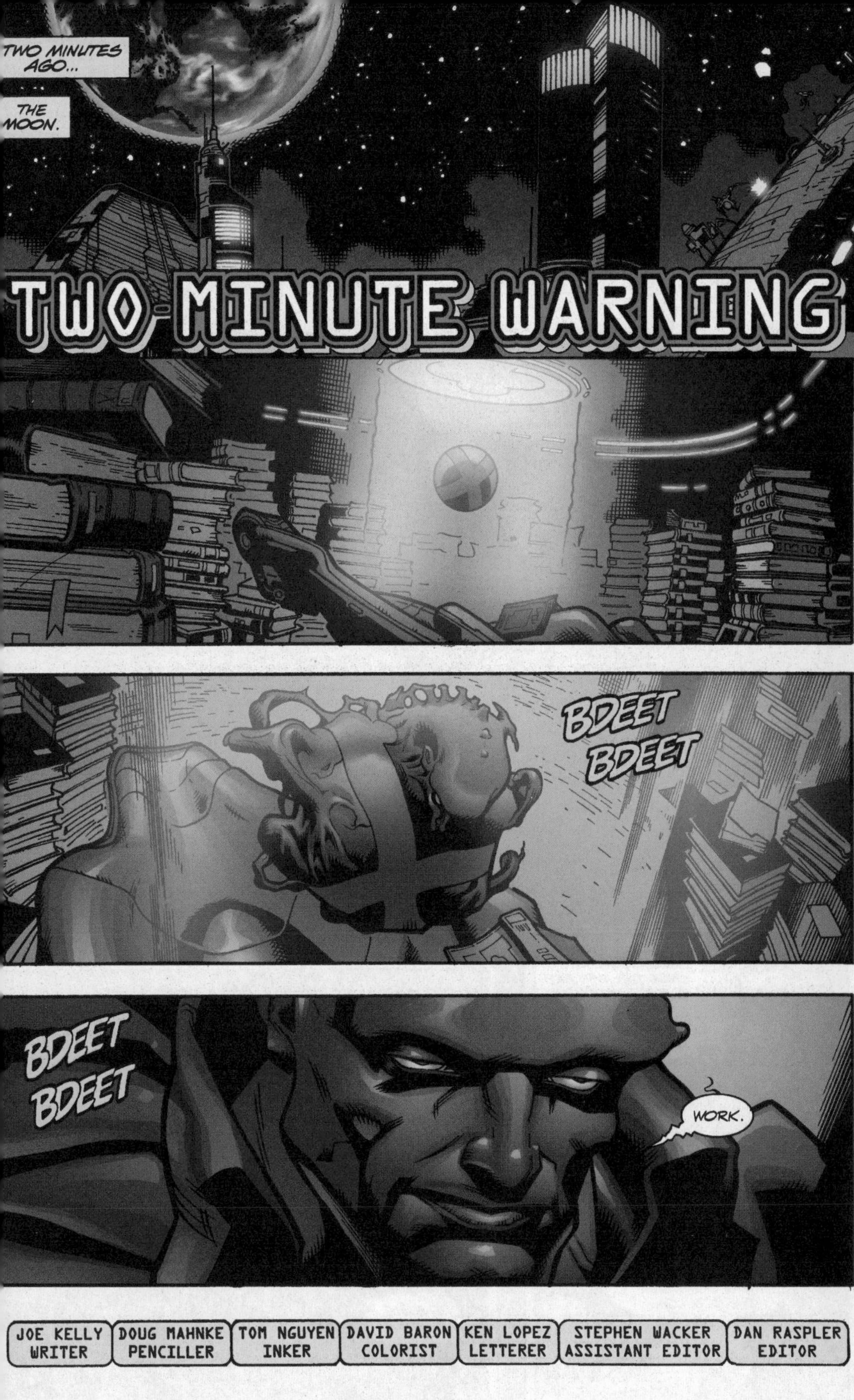
TWO MINUTES AGO...
THE MOON.
TWO MINUTE WARNING
BDEET BDEET
BDEET BDEET
WORK.
JOE KELLY WRITER
DOUG MAHNKE PENCILLER
TOM NGUYEN INKER
DAVID BARON COLORIST
KEN LOPEZ LETTERER
STEPHEN WACKER ASSISTANT EDITOR
DAN RASPLER EDITOR

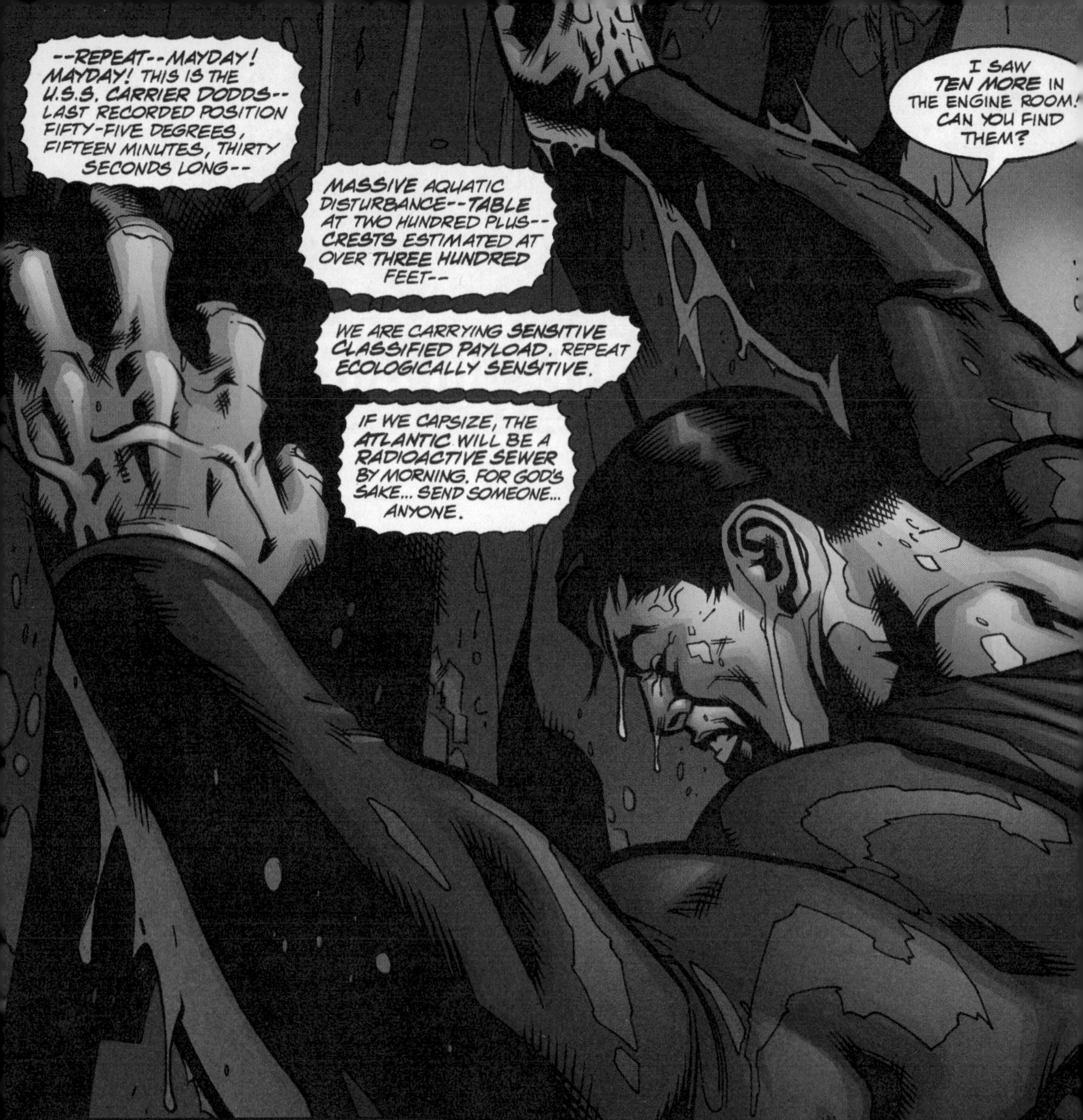
--REPEAT--MAYDAY! MAYDAY! THIS IS THE U.S.S. CARRIER DODDS-- LAST RECORDED POSITION FIFTY-FIVE DEGREES, FIFTEEN MINUTES, THIRTY SECONDS LONG--
I SAW TEN MORE IN THE ENGINE ROOM! CAN YOU FIND THEM?
MASSIVE AQUATIC DISTURBANCE--TABLE AT TWO HUNDRED PLUS--CRESTS ESTIMATED AT OVER THREE HUNDRED FEET--
WE ARE CARRYING SENSITIVE CLASSIFIED PAYLOAD. REPEAT ECOLOGICALLY SENSITIVE.
IF WE CAPSIZE, THE ATLANTIC WILL BE A RADIOACTIVE SEWER BY MORNING. FOR GOD'S SAKE... SEND SOMEONE... ANYONE.

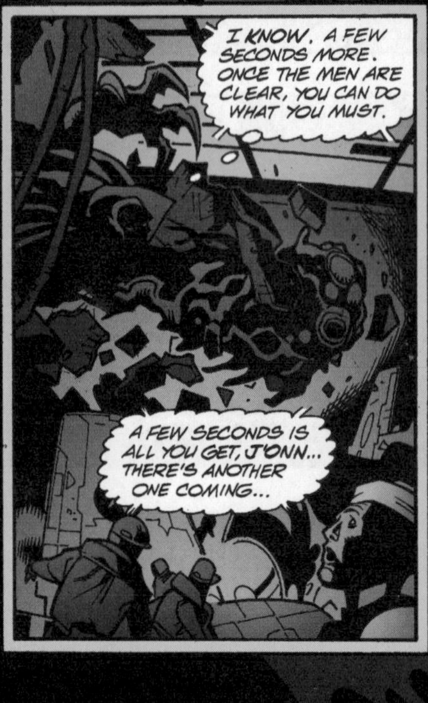
I KNOW. A FEW SECONDS MORE. ONCE THE MEN ARE CLEAR, YOU CAN DO WHAT YOU MUST.
A FEW SECONDS IS ALL YOU GET, J'ONN... THERE'S ANOTHER ONE COMING...

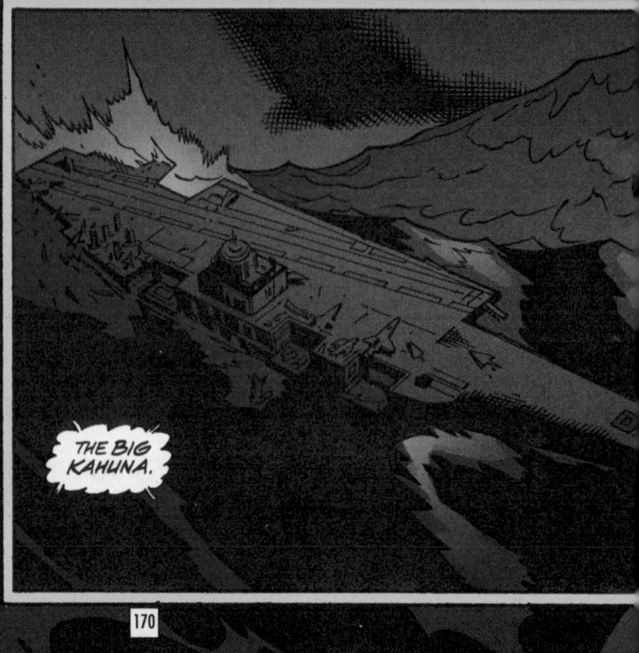
THE BIG KAHUNA.

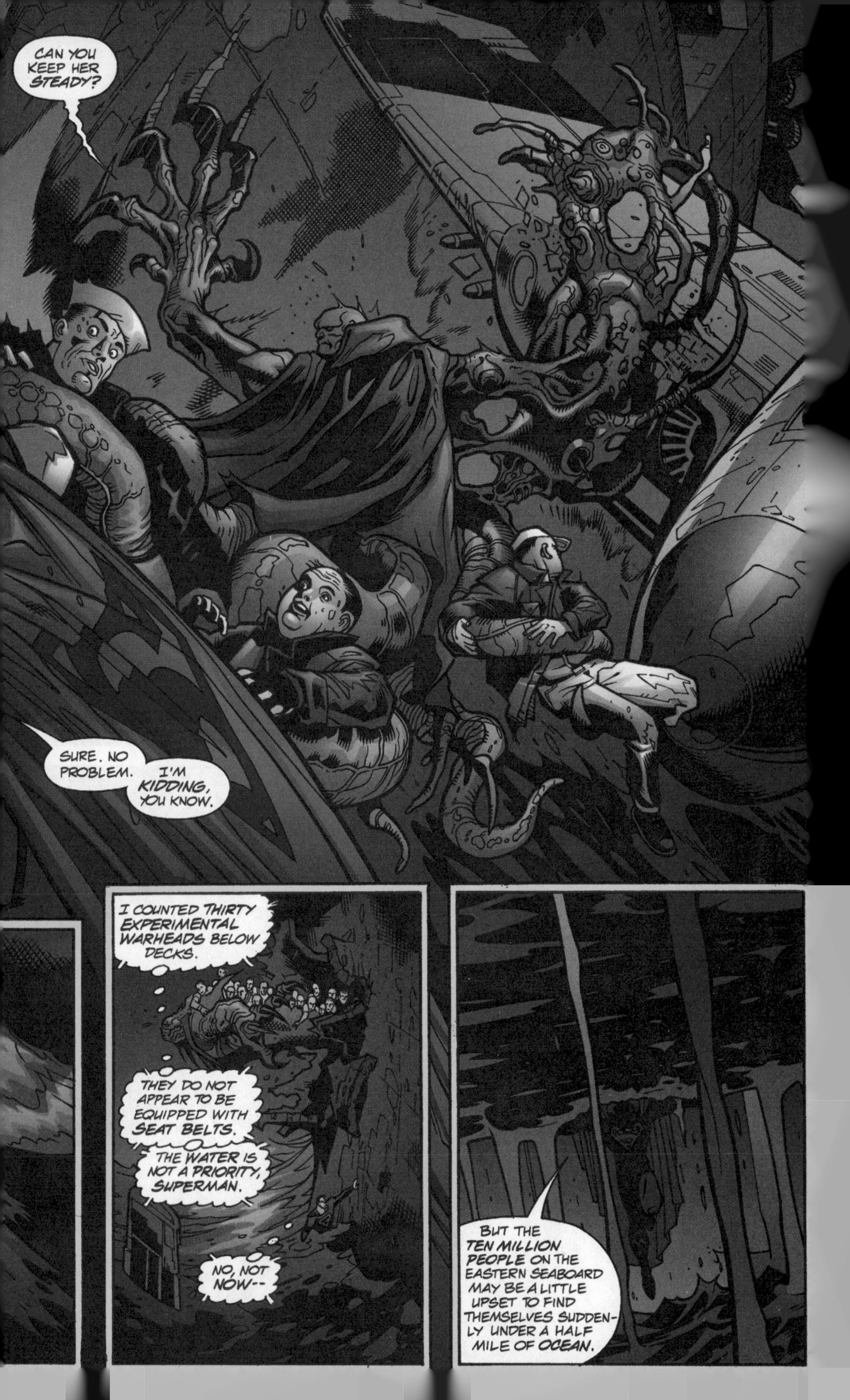
CAN YOU KEEP HER STEADY?
SURE. NO PROBLEM.
I'M KIDDING, YOU KNOW.
I COUNTED THIRTY EXPERIMENTAL WARHEADS BELOW DECKS.
THEY DO NOT APPEAR TO BE EQUIPPED WITH SEAT BELTS.
THE WATER IS NOT A PRIORITY, SUPERMAN.
NO, NOT NOW--
BUT THE TEN MILLION PEOPLE ON THE EASTERN SEABOARD MAY BE A LITTLE UPSET TO FIND THEMSELVES SUDDEN-LY UNDER A HALF MILE OF OCEAN.

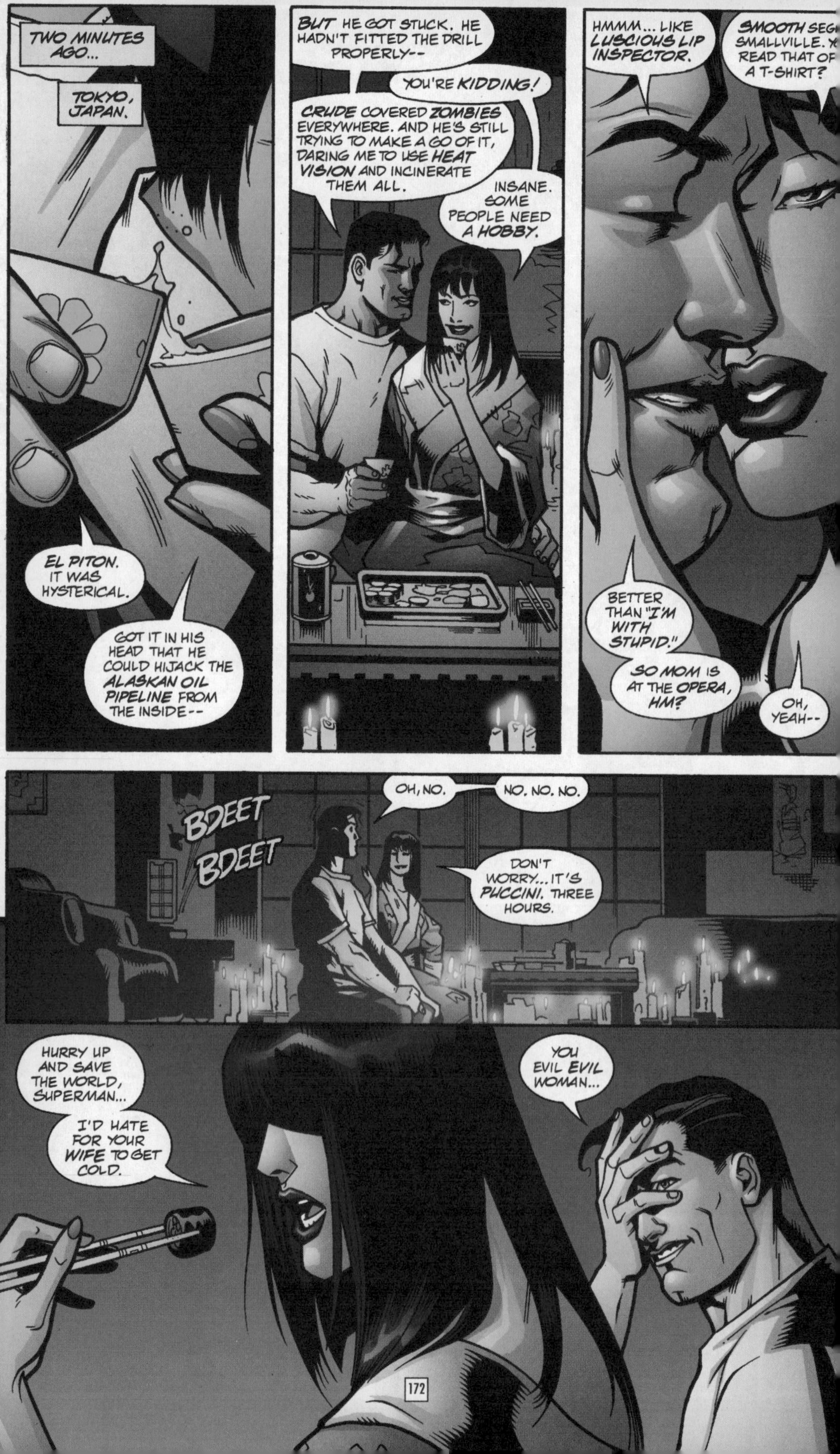

TWO MINUTES AGO...
TOKYO, JAPAN.
EL PITON. IT WAS HYSTERICAL.
GOT IT IN HIS HEAD THAT HE COULD HIJACK THE ALASKAN OIL PIPELINE FROM THE INSIDE--
BUT HE GOT STUCK. HE HADN'T FITTED THE DRILL PROPERLY--
YOU'RE KIDDING!
CRUDE COVERED ZOMBIES EVERYWHERE. AND HE'S STILL TRYING TO MAKE A GO OF IT, DARING ME TO USE HEAT VISION AND INCINERATE THEM ALL.
INSANE. SOME PEOPLE NEED A HOBBY.
HMMM... LIKE LUSCIOUS LIP INSPECTOR.
BETTER THAN "I'M WITH STUPID."
SO MOM IS AT THE OPERA, HM?
OH, YEAH--
BDEET
BDEET
OH, NO.
NO. NO. NO.
DON'T WORRY... IT'S PUCCINI. THREE HOURS.
HURRY UP AND SAVE THE WORLD, SUPERMAN...
I'D HATE FOR YOUR WIFE TO GET COLD.
YOU EVIL EVIL WOMAN...

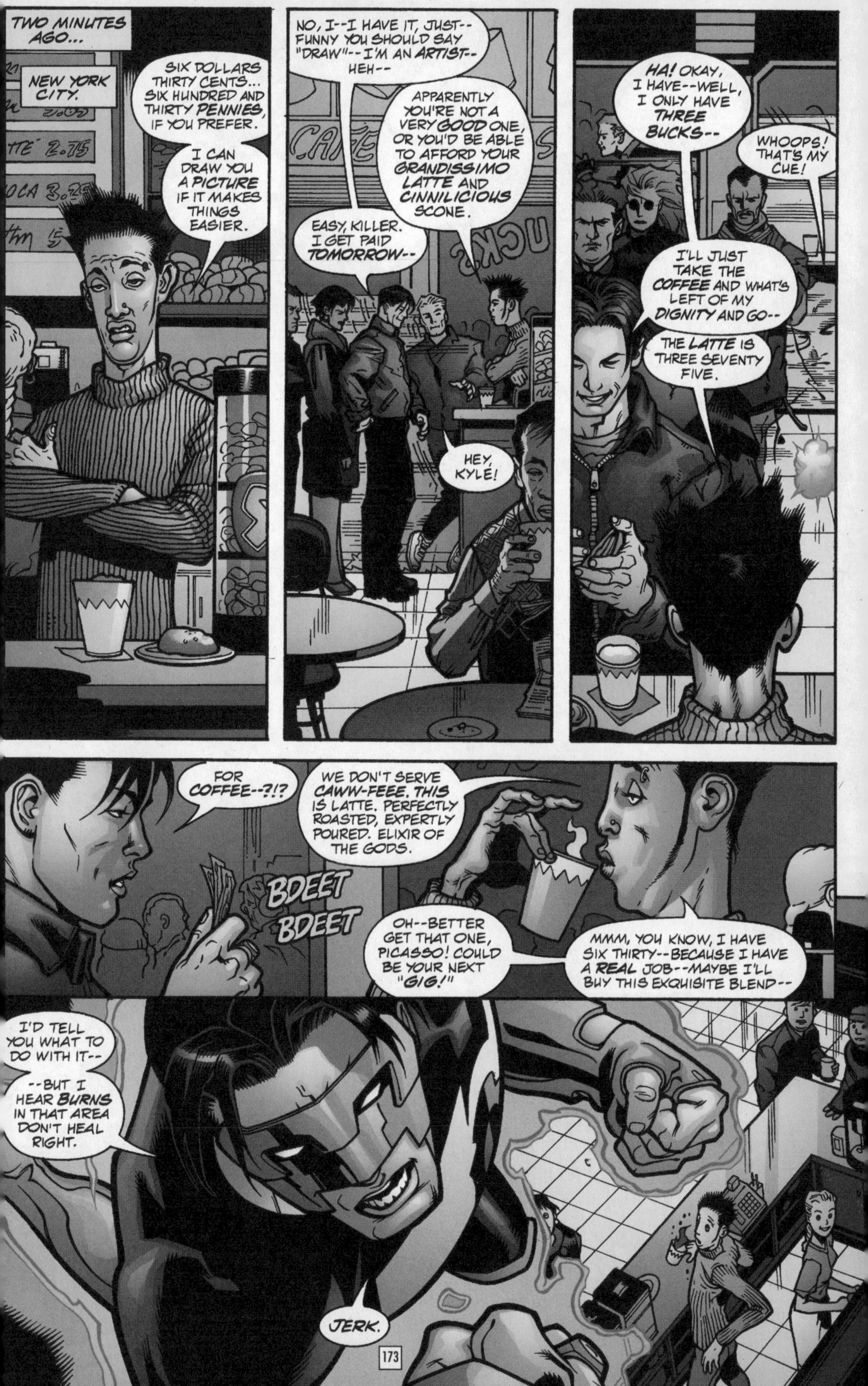
TWO MINUTES AGO...
NEW YORK CITY.
SIX DOLLARS THIRTY CENTS... SIX HUNDRED AND THIRTY PENNIES, IF YOU PREFER.
I CAN DRAW YOU A PICTURE IF IT MAKES THINGS EASIER.
NO, I--I HAVE IT, JUST-- FUNNY YOU SHOULD SAY "DRAW"--I'M AN ARTIST-- HEH--
APPARENTLY YOU'RE NOT A VERY GOOD ONE, OR YOU'D BE ABLE TO AFFORD YOUR GRANDISSIMO LATTE AND CINNILICIOUS SCONE.
EASY, KILLER. I GET PAID TOMORROW--
HEY, KYLE!
HA! OKAY, I HAVE--WELL, I ONLY HAVE THREE BUCKS--
WHOOPS! THAT'S MY CUE!
I'LL JUST TAKE THE COFFEE AND WHAT'S LEFT OF MY DIGNITY AND GO--
THE LATTE IS THREE SEVENTY FIVE.
FOR COFFEE--?!?
WE DON'T SERVE CAWW-FEEE. THIS IS LATTE. PERFECTLY ROASTED, EXPERTLY POURED. ELIXIR OF THE GODS.
BDEET
BDEET
OH--BETTER GET THAT ONE, PICASSO! COULD BE YOUR NEXT "GIG!"
MMM, YOU KNOW, I HAVE SIX THIRTY--BECAUSE I HAVE A REAL JOB--MAYBE I'LL BUY THIS EXQUISITE BLEND--
I'D TELL YOU WHAT TO DO WITH IT--
--BUT I HEAR BURNS IN THAT AREA DON'T HEAL RIGHT.
JERK.

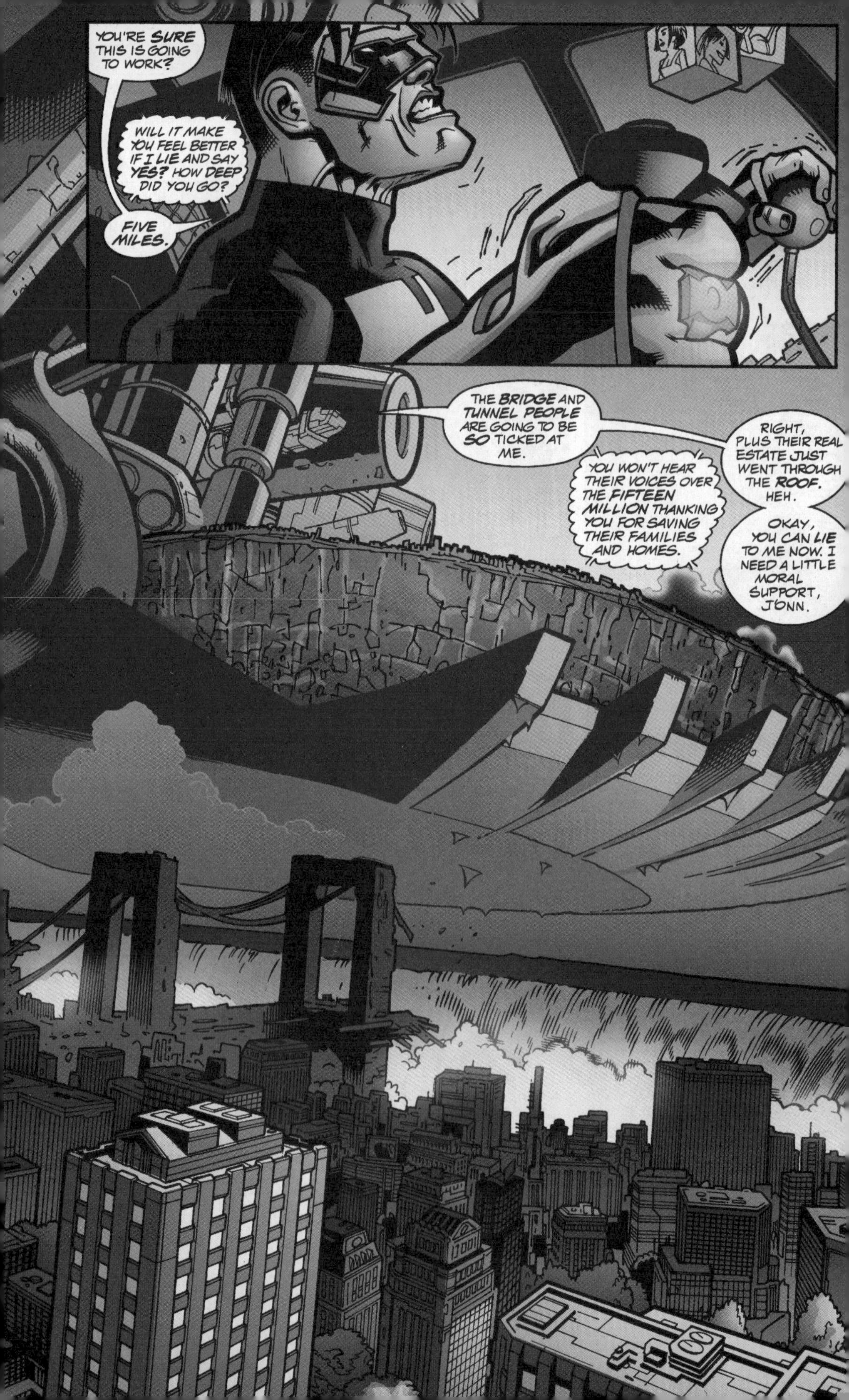
YOU'RE SURE THIS IS GOING TO WORK?
WILL IT MAKE YOU FEEL BETTER IF I LIE AND SAY YES? HOW DEEP DID YOU GO?
FIVE MILES.
THE BRIDGE AND TUNNEL PEOPLE ARE GOING TO BE SO TICKED AT ME.
YOU WON'T HEAR THEIR VOICES OVER THE FIFTEEN MILLION THANKING YOU FOR SAVING THEIR FAMILIES AND HOMES.
RIGHT, PLUS THEIR REAL ESTATE JUST WENT THROUGH THE ROOF. HEH.
OKAY, YOU CAN LIE TO ME NOW. I NEED A LITTLE MORAL SUPPORT, J'ONN.

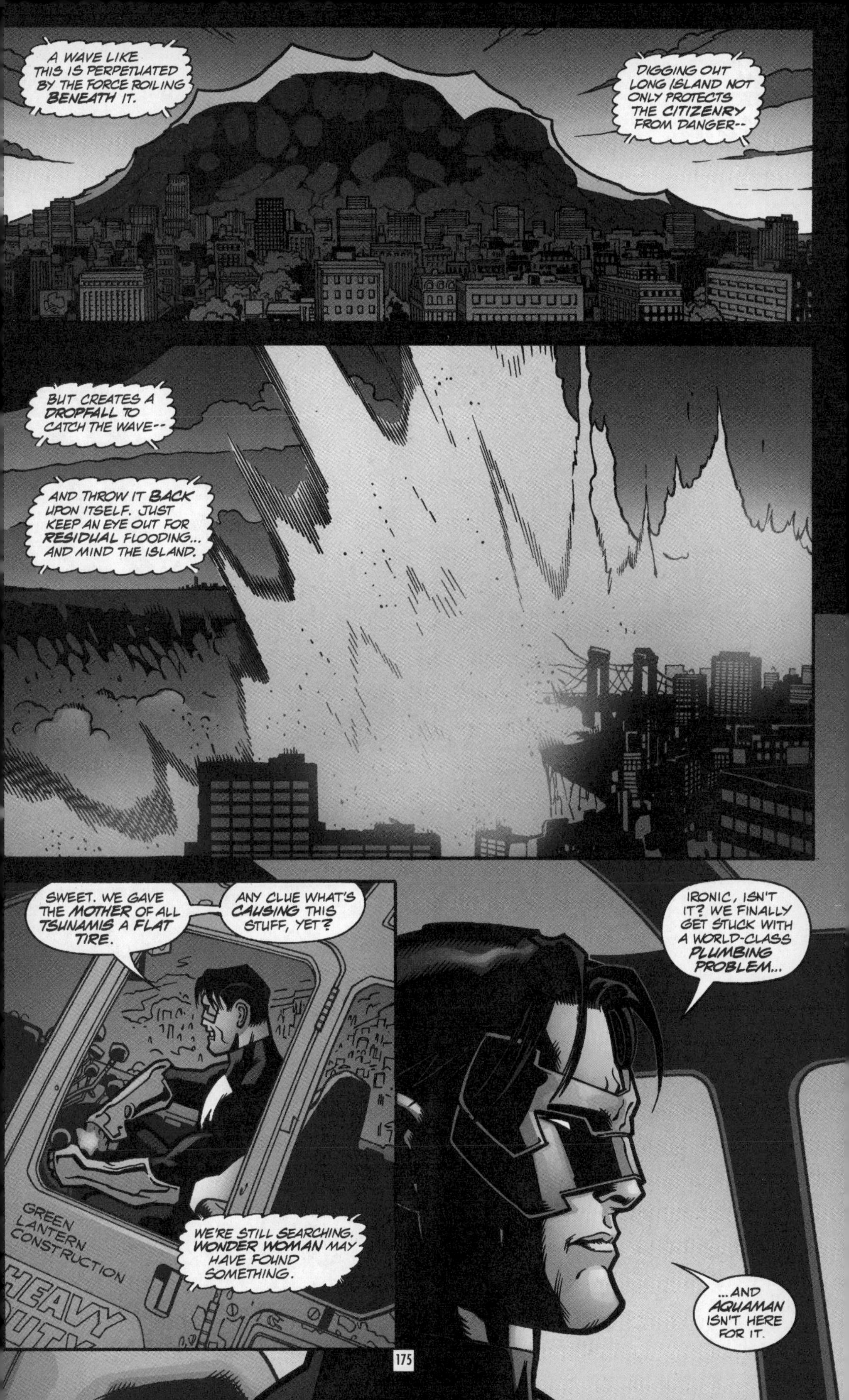
A WAVE LIKE THIS IS PERPETUATED BY THE FORCE ROILING BENEATH IT.
DIGGING OUT LONG ISLAND NOT ONLY PROTECTS THE CITIZENRY FROM DANGER--
BUT CREATES A DROPFALL TO CATCH THE WAVE--
AND THROW IT BACK UPON ITSELF. JUST KEEP AN EYE OUT FOR RESIDUAL FLOODING... AND MIND THE ISLAND.
SWEET. WE GAVE THE MOTHER OF ALL TSUNAMIS A FLAT TIRE.
ANY CLUE WHAT'S CAUSING THIS STUFF, YET?
WE'RE STILL SEARCHING. WONDER WOMAN MAY HAVE FOUND SOMETHING.
GREEN LANTERN CONSTRUCTION
HEAVY DUTY
IRONIC, ISN'T IT? WE FINALLY GET STUCK WITH A WORLD-CLASS PLUMBING PROBLEM...
...AND AQUAMAN ISN'T HERE FOR IT.

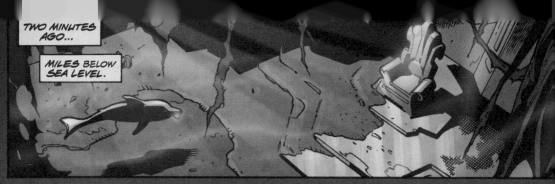

TWO MINUTES AGO...

MILES BELOW SEA LEVEL.

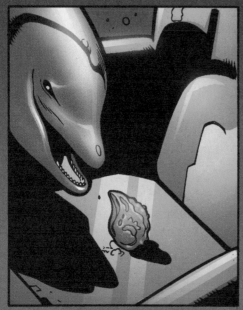

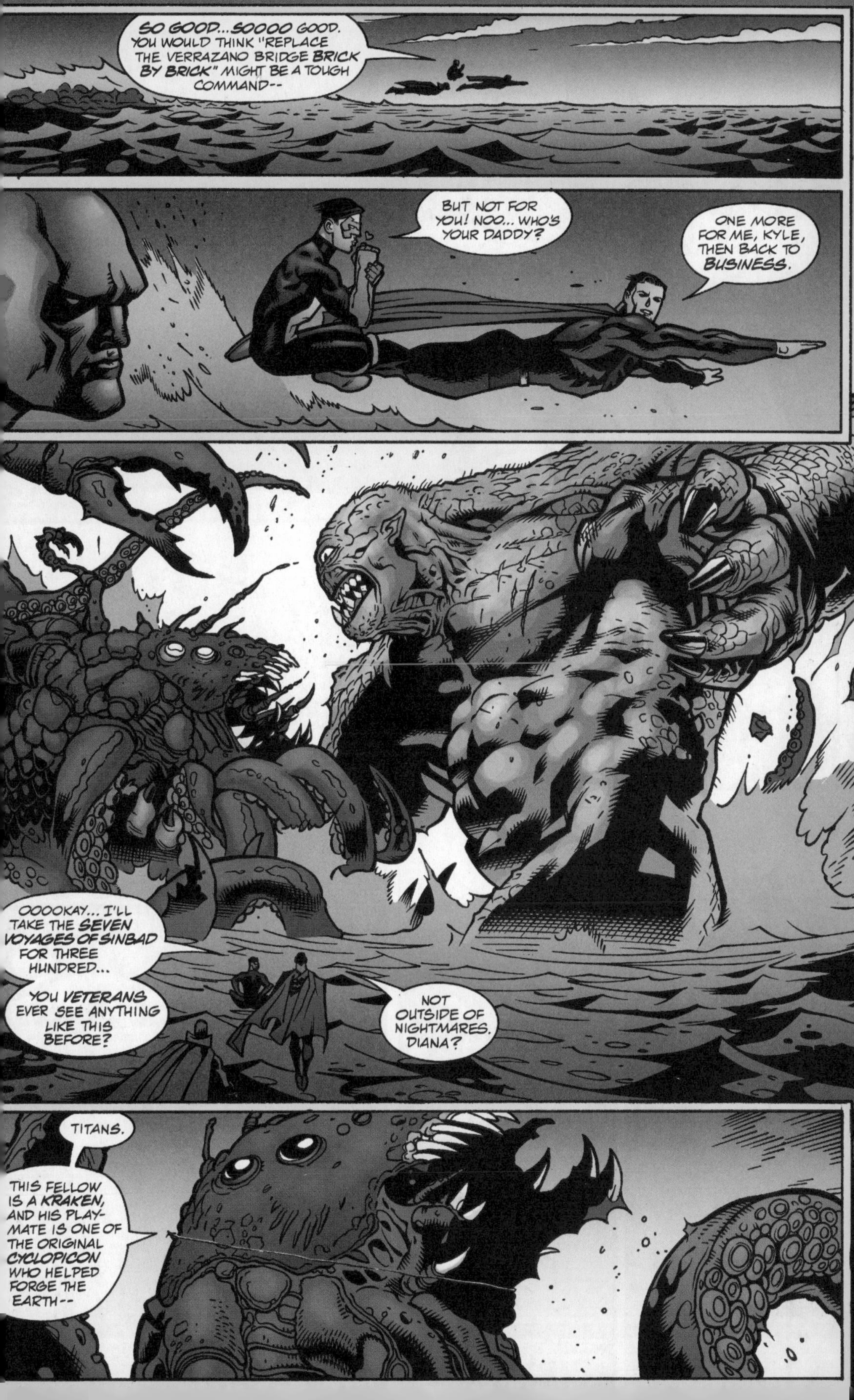
SO GOOD... SOOOO GOOD. YOU WOULD THINK "REPLACE THE VERRAZANO BRIDGE BRICK BY BRICK" MIGHT BE A TOUGH COMMAND--
BUT NOT FOR YOU! NOO... WHO'S YOUR DADDY?
ONE MORE FOR ME, KYLE, THEN BACK TO BUSINESS.
OOOOKAY... I'LL TAKE THE SEVEN VOYAGES OF SINBAD FOR THREE HUNDRED...
YOU VETERANS EVER SEE ANYTHING LIKE THIS BEFORE?
NOT OUTSIDE OF NIGHTMARES. DIANA?
TITANS.
THIS FELLOW IS A KRAKEN, AND HIS PLAY-MATE IS ONE OF THE ORIGINAL CYCLOPICON WHO HELPED FORGE THE EARTH--

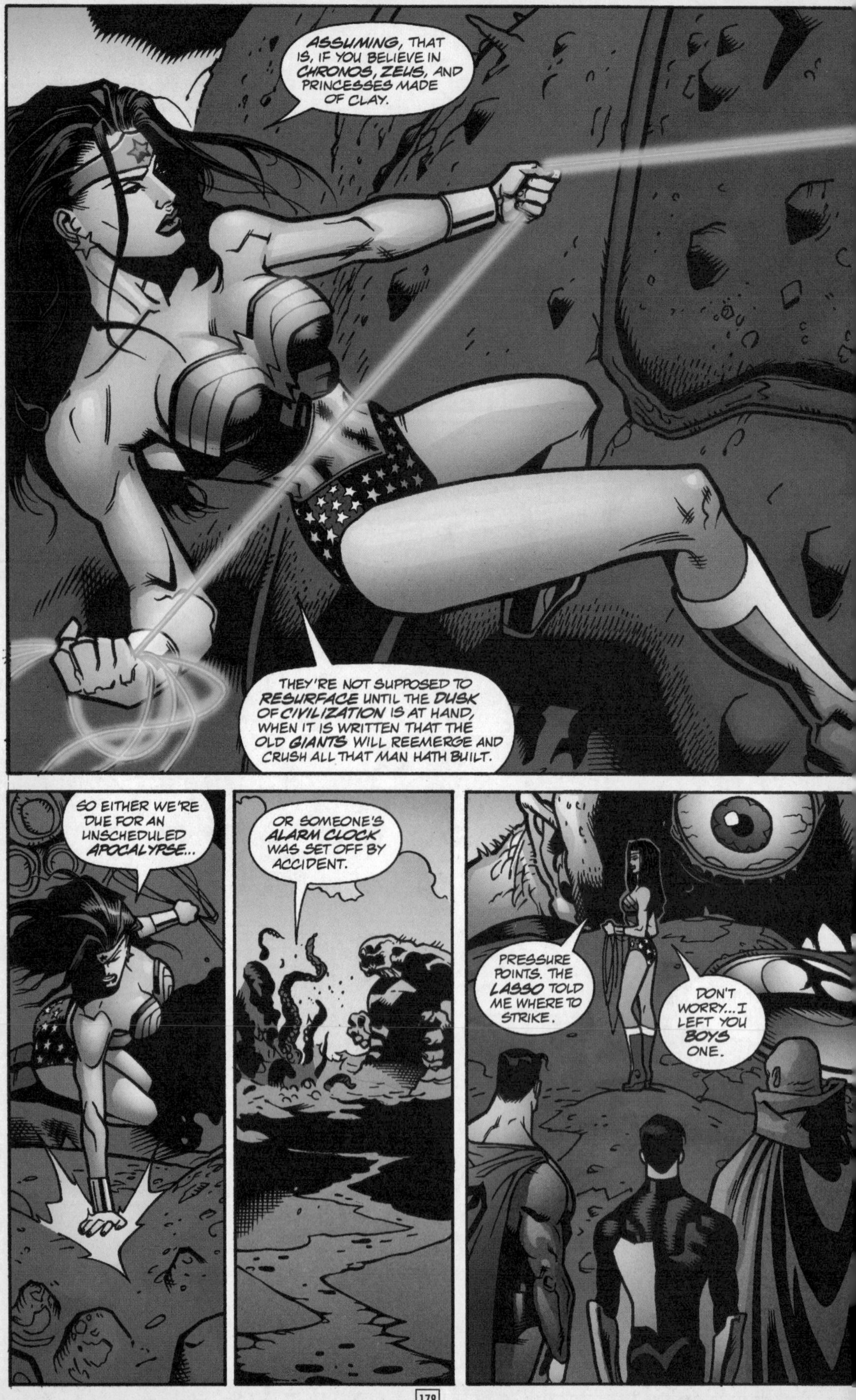
ASSUMING, THAT IS, IF YOU BELIEVE IN CHRONOS, ZEUS, AND PRINCESSES MADE OF CLAY.
THEY'RE NOT SUPPOSED TO RESURFACE UNTIL THE DUSK OF CIVILIZATION IS AT HAND, WHEN IT IS WRITTEN THAT THE OLD GIANTS WILL REEMERGE AND CRUSH ALL THAT MAN HATH BUILT.
SO EITHER WE'RE DUE FOR AN UNSCHEDULED APOCALYPSE...
OR SOMEONE'S ALARM CLOCK WAS SET OFF BY ACCIDENT.
PRESSURE POINTS. THE LASSO TOLD ME WHERE TO STRIKE.
DON'T WORRY...I LEFT YOU BOYS ONE.

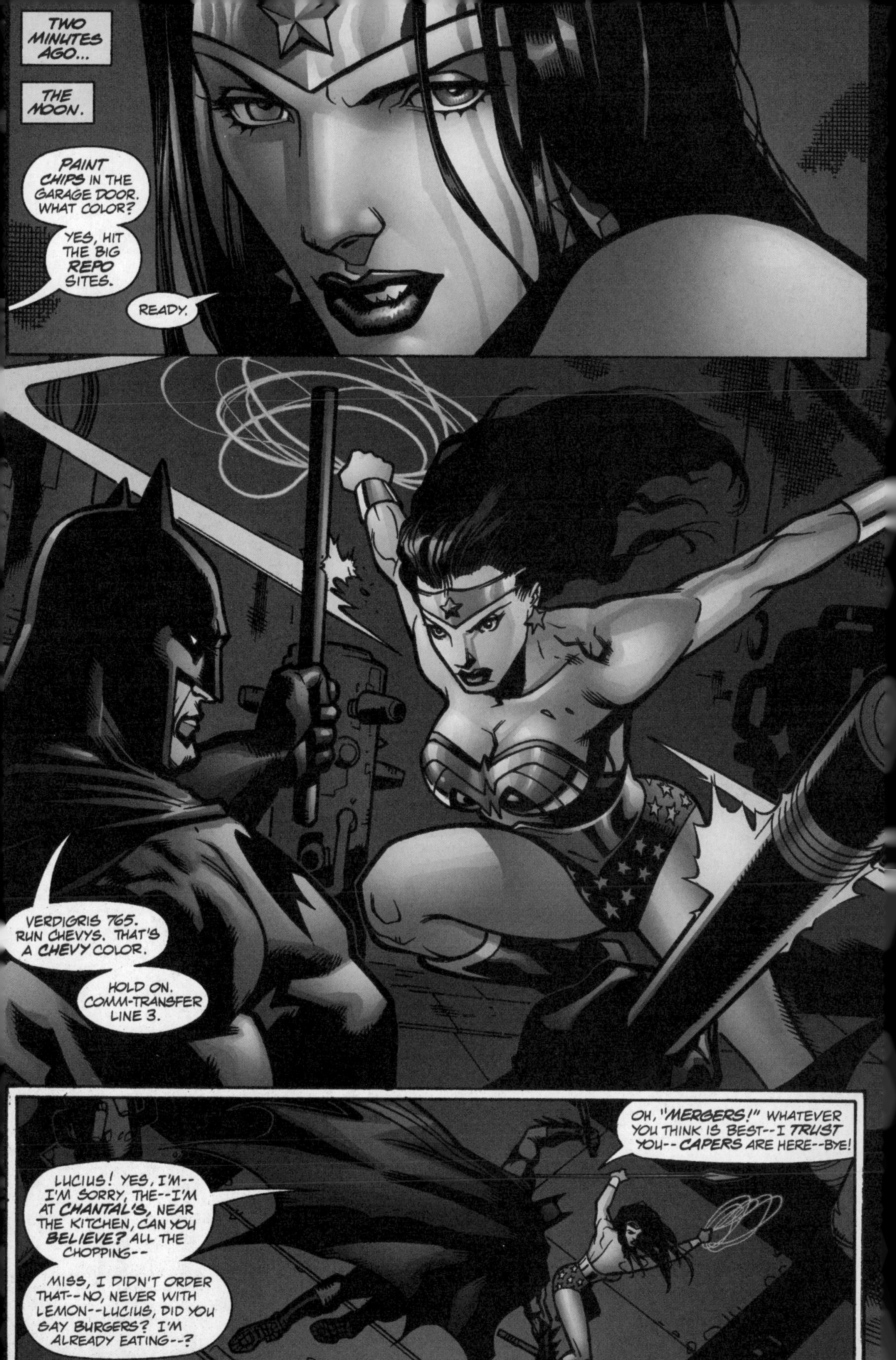
TWO MINUTES AGO...
THE MOON.
PAINT CHIPS IN THE GARAGE DOOR. WHAT COLOR?
YES, HIT THE BIG REPO SITES.
READY.
VERDIGRIS 765. RUN CHEVYS. THAT'S A CHEVY COLOR.
HOLD ON. COMM-TRANSFER LINE 3.
OH, "MERGERS!" WHATEVER YOU THINK IS BEST--I TRUST YOU--CAPERS ARE HERE--BYE!
LUCIUS! YES, I'M--I'M SORRY, THE--I'M AT CHANTAL'S, NEAR THE KITCHEN, CAN YOU BELIEVE? ALL THE CHOPPING--
MISS, I DIDN'T ORDER THAT--NO, NEVER WITH LEMON--LUCIUS, DID YOU SAY BURGERS? I'M ALREADY EATING--?

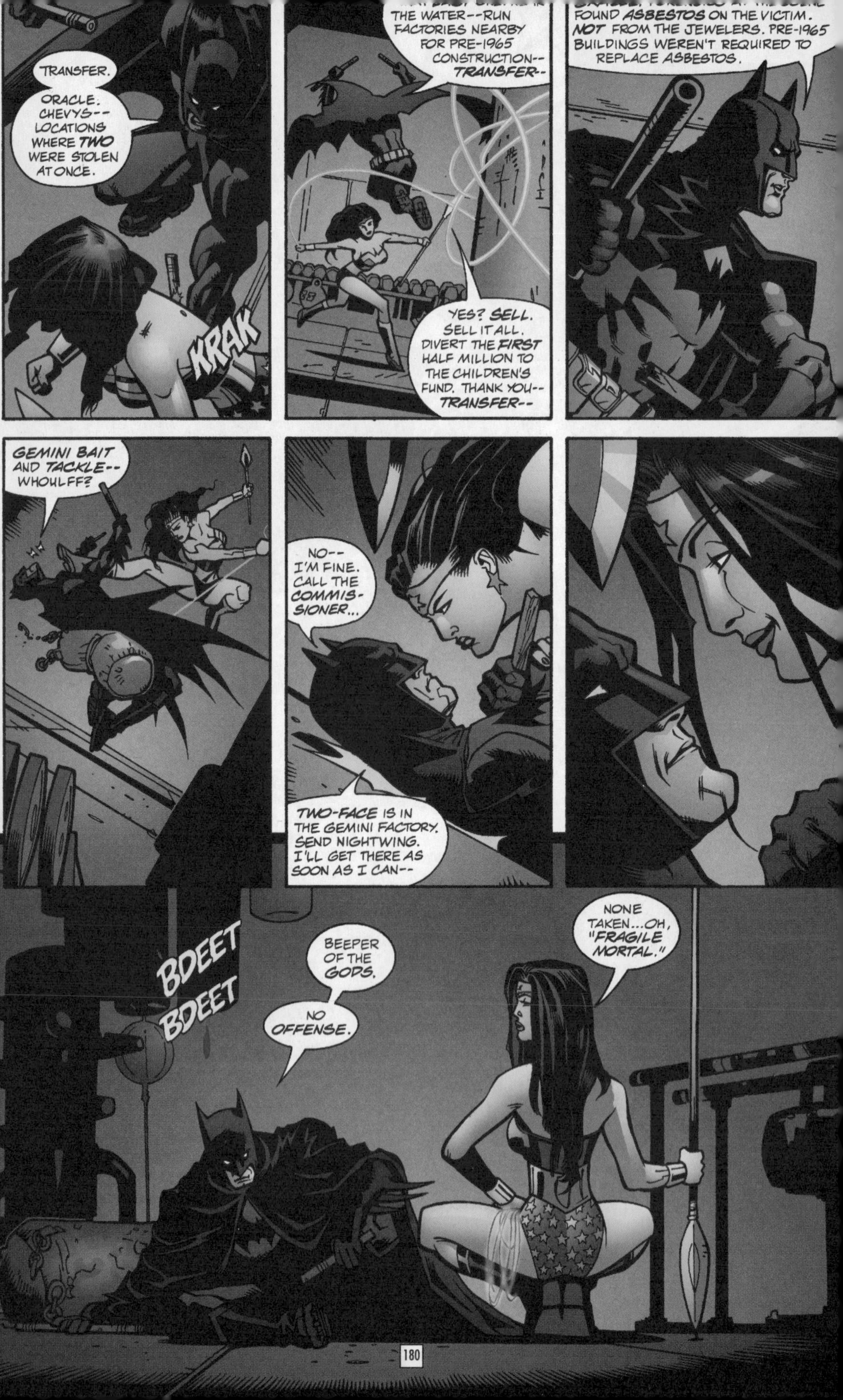
TRANSFER.
ORACLE. CHEVYS-- LOCATIONS WHERE TWO WERE STOLEN AT ONCE.
KRAK
THE WATER--RUN FACTORIES NEARBY FOR PRE-1965 CONSTRUCTION-- TRANSFER--
YES? SELL. SELL IT ALL. DIVERT THE FIRST HALF MILLION TO THE CHILDREN'S FUND. THANK YOU-- TRANSFER--
FOUND ASBESTOS ON THE VICTIM. NOT FROM THE JEWELERS. PRE-1965 BUILDINGS WEREN'T REQUIRED TO REPLACE ASBESTOS.
GEMINI BAIT AND TACKLE-- WHOULFF?
NO-- I'M FINE. CALL THE COMMISSIONER...
TWO-FACE IS IN THE GEMINI FACTORY. SEND NIGHTWING. I'LL GET THERE AS SOON AS I CAN--
BDEET BDEET
BEEPER OF THE GODS.
NO OFFENSE.
NONE TAKEN...OH, "FRAGILE MORTAL."

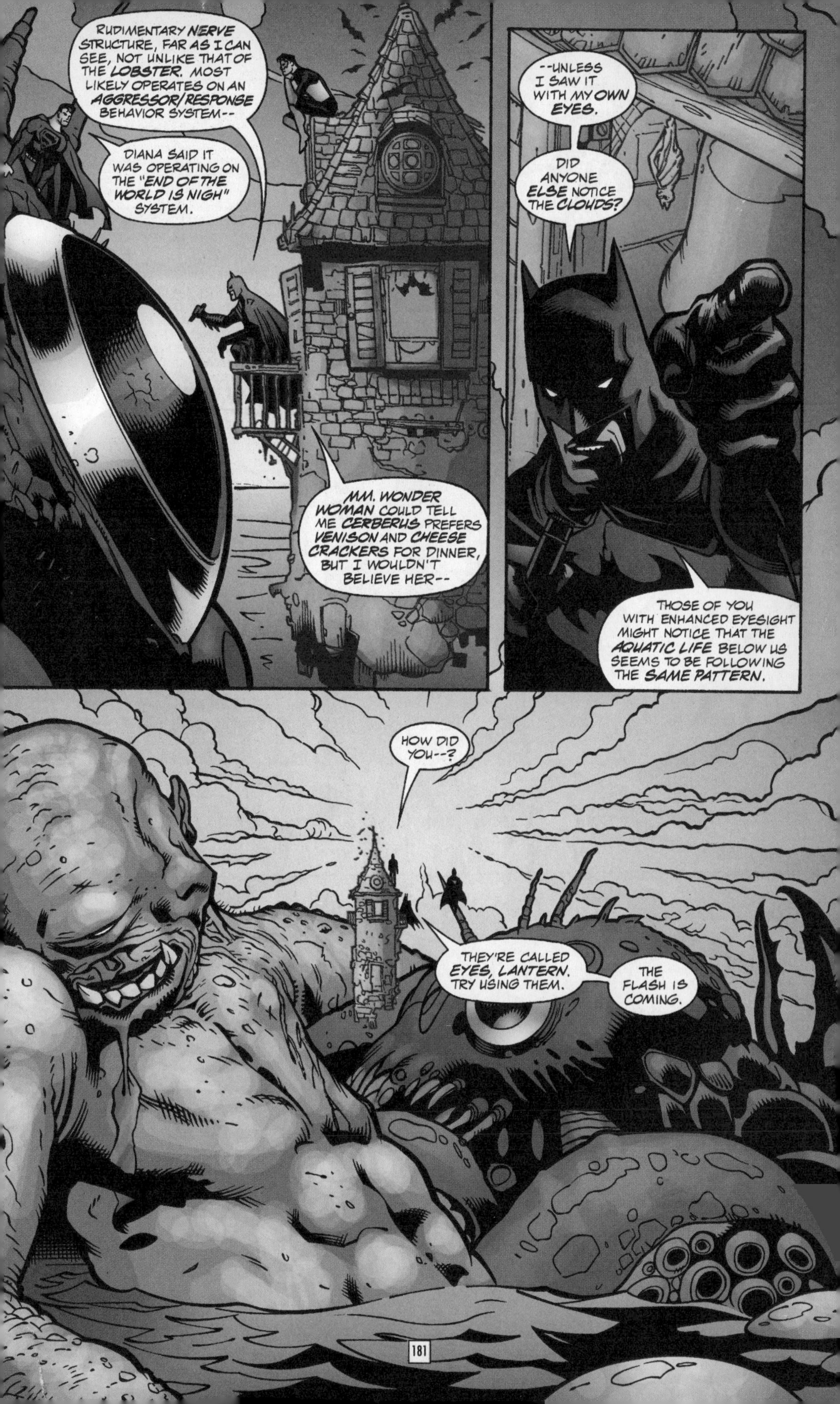
RUDIMENTARY NERVE STRUCTURE, FAR AS I CAN SEE, NOT UNLIKE THAT OF THE LOBSTER. MOST LIKELY OPERATES ON AN AGGRESSOR/RESPONSE BEHAVIOR SYSTEM--
DIANA SAID IT WAS OPERATING ON THE "END OF THE WORLD IS NIGH" SYSTEM.
MM. WONDER WOMAN COULD TELL ME CERBERUS PREFERS VENISON AND CHEESE CRACKERS FOR DINNER, BUT I WOULDN'T BELIEVE HER--
--UNLESS I SAW IT WITH MY OWN EYES.
DID ANYONE ELSE NOTICE THE CLOUDS?
THOSE OF YOU WITH ENHANCED EYESIGHT MIGHT NOTICE THAT THE AQUATIC LIFE BELOW US SEEMS TO BE FOLLOWING THE SAME PATTERN.
HOW DID YOU--?
THEY'RE CALLED EYES, LANTERN. TRY USING THEM.
THE FLASH IS COMING.

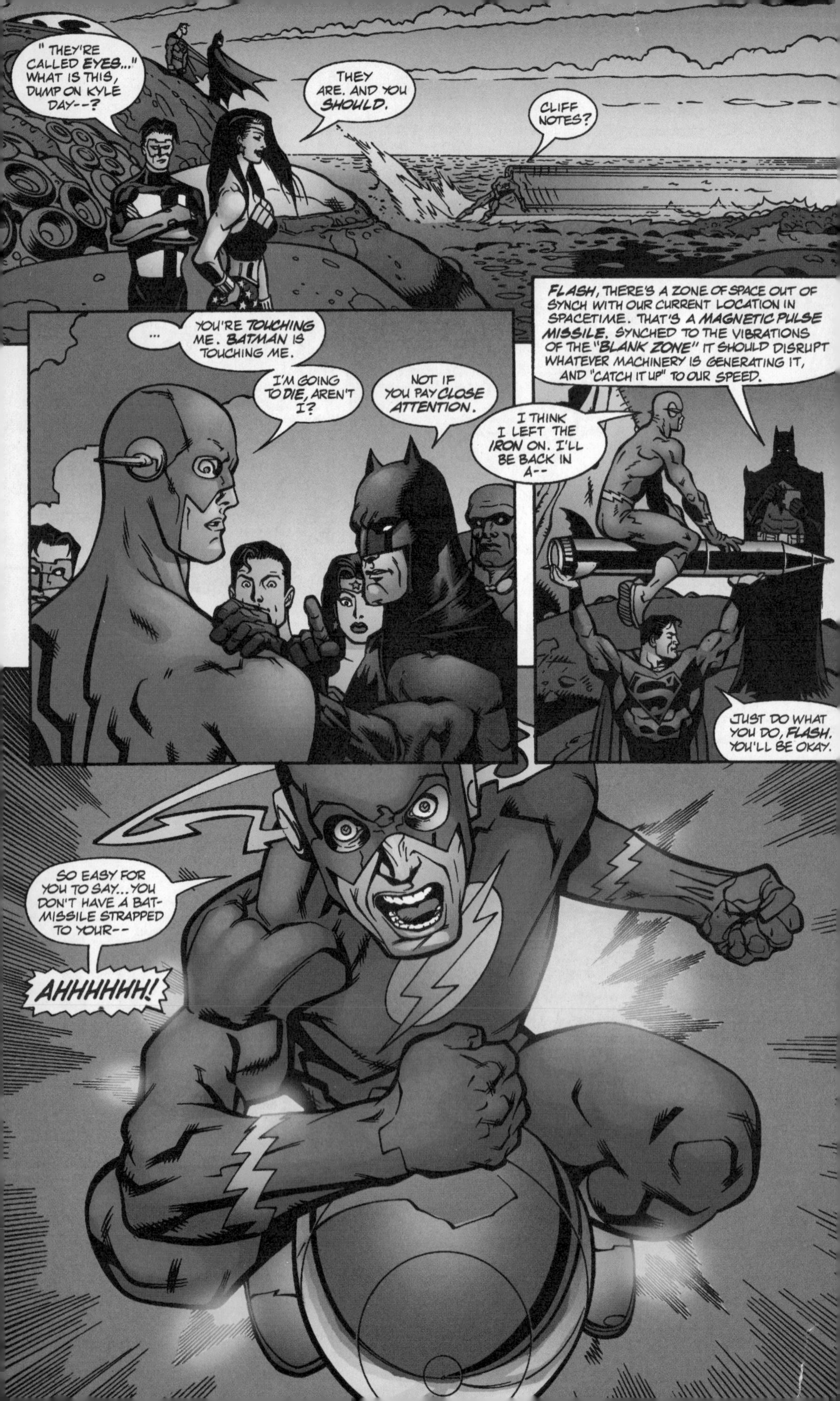

" THEY'RE CALLED EYES..." WHAT IS THIS, DUMP ON KYLE DAY--?
THEY ARE. AND YOU SHOULD.
CLIFF NOTES?
...
YOU'RE TOUCHING ME. BATMAN IS TOUCHING ME.
I'M GOING TO DIE, AREN'T I?
NOT IF YOU PAY CLOSE ATTENTION.
FLASH, THERE'S A ZONE OF SPACE OUT OF SYNCH WITH OUR CURRENT LOCATION IN SPACETIME. THAT'S A MAGNETIC PULSE MISSILE. SYNCHED TO THE VIBRATIONS OF THE "BLANK ZONE" IT SHOULD DISRUPT WHATEVER MACHINERY IS GENERATING IT, AND "CATCH IT UP" TO OUR SPEED.
I THINK I LEFT THE IRON ON. I'LL BE BACK IN A--
JUST DO WHAT YOU DO, FLASH. YOU'LL BE OKAY.
SO EASY FOR YOU TO SAY...YOU DON'T HAVE A BAT-MISSILE STRAPPED TO YOUR--
AHHHHHH!

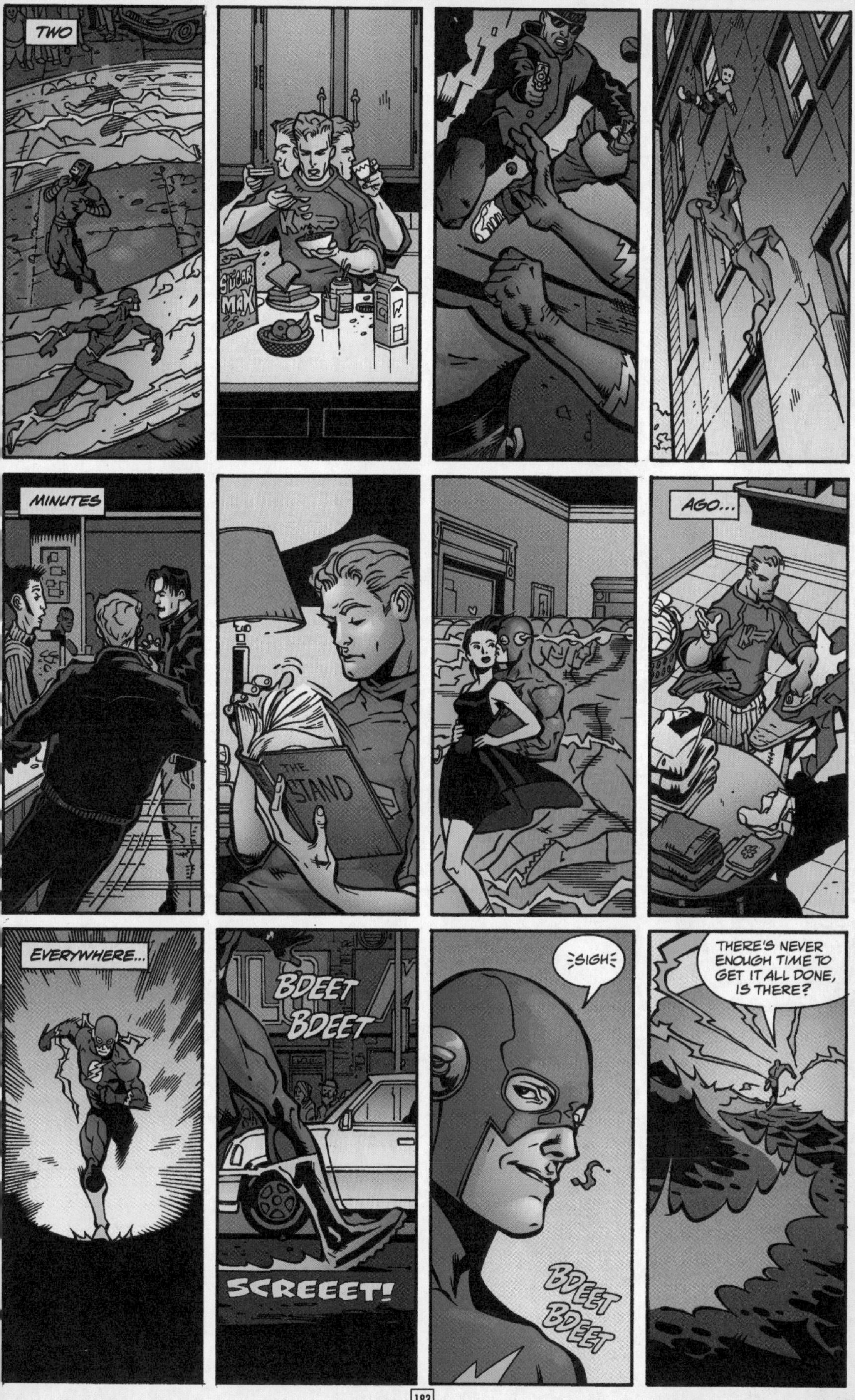
TWO
SUGAR MAX
MINUTES
THE STAND
AGO...
EVERYWHERE...
BDEET
BDEET
SCREEET!
SIGH
BDEET
BDEET
THERE'S NEVER ENOUGH TIME TO GET IT ALL DONE, IS THERE?

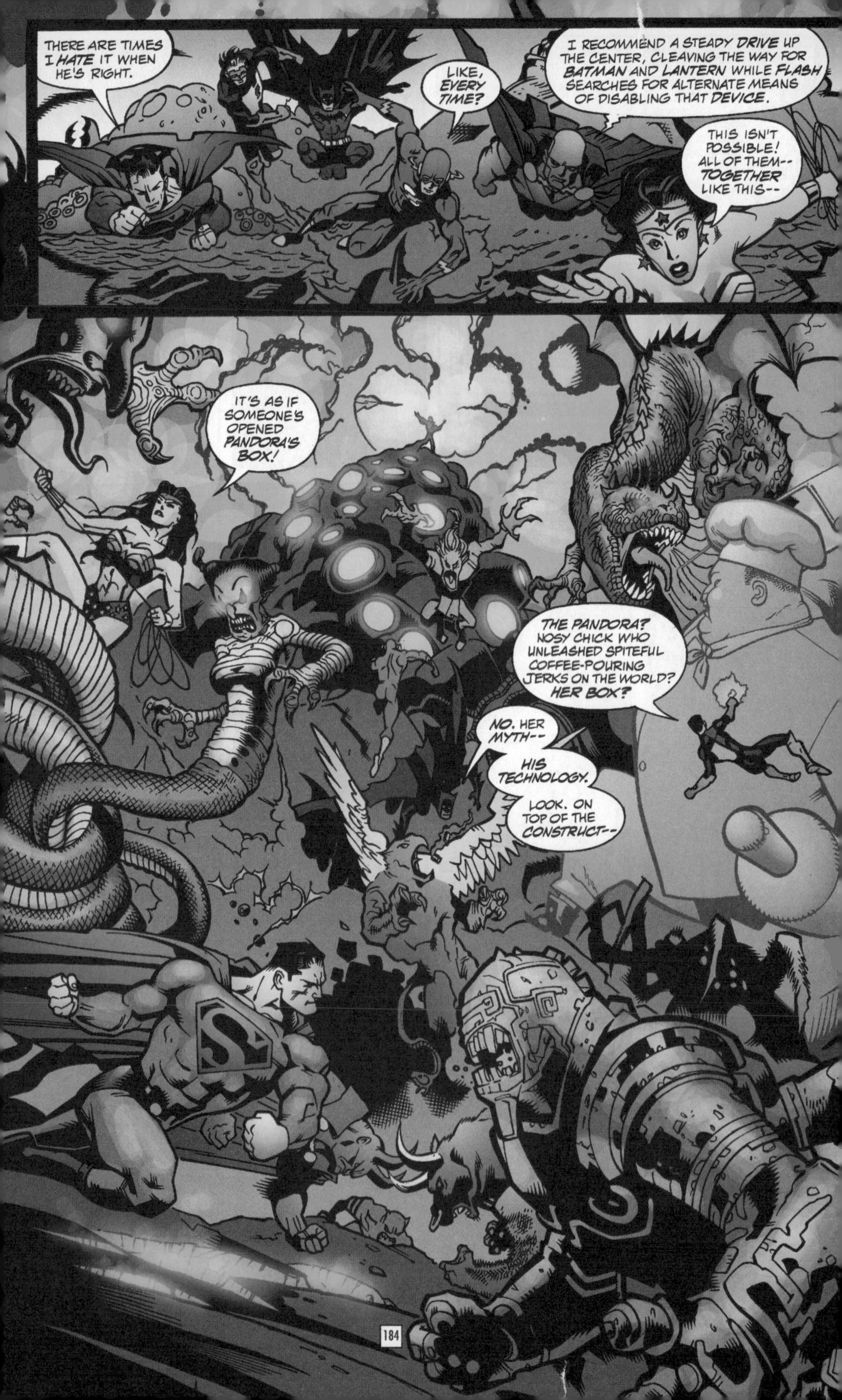
THERE ARE TIMES I HATE IT WHEN HE'S RIGHT.
LIKE, EVERY TIME?
I RECOMMEND A STEADY DRIVE UP THE CENTER, CLEAVING THE WAY FOR BATMAN AND LANTERN WHILE FLASH SEARCHES FOR ALTERNATE MEANS OF DISABLING THAT DEVICE.
THIS ISN'T POSSIBLE! ALL OF THEM-- TOGETHER LIKE THIS--
IT'S AS IF SOMEONE'S OPENED PANDORA'S BOX!
THE PANDORA? NOSY CHICK WHO UNLEASHED SPITEFUL COFFEE-POURING JERKS ON THE WORLD? HER BOX?
NO. HER MYTH--
HIS TECHNOLOGY.
LOOK. ON TOP OF THE CONSTRUCT--

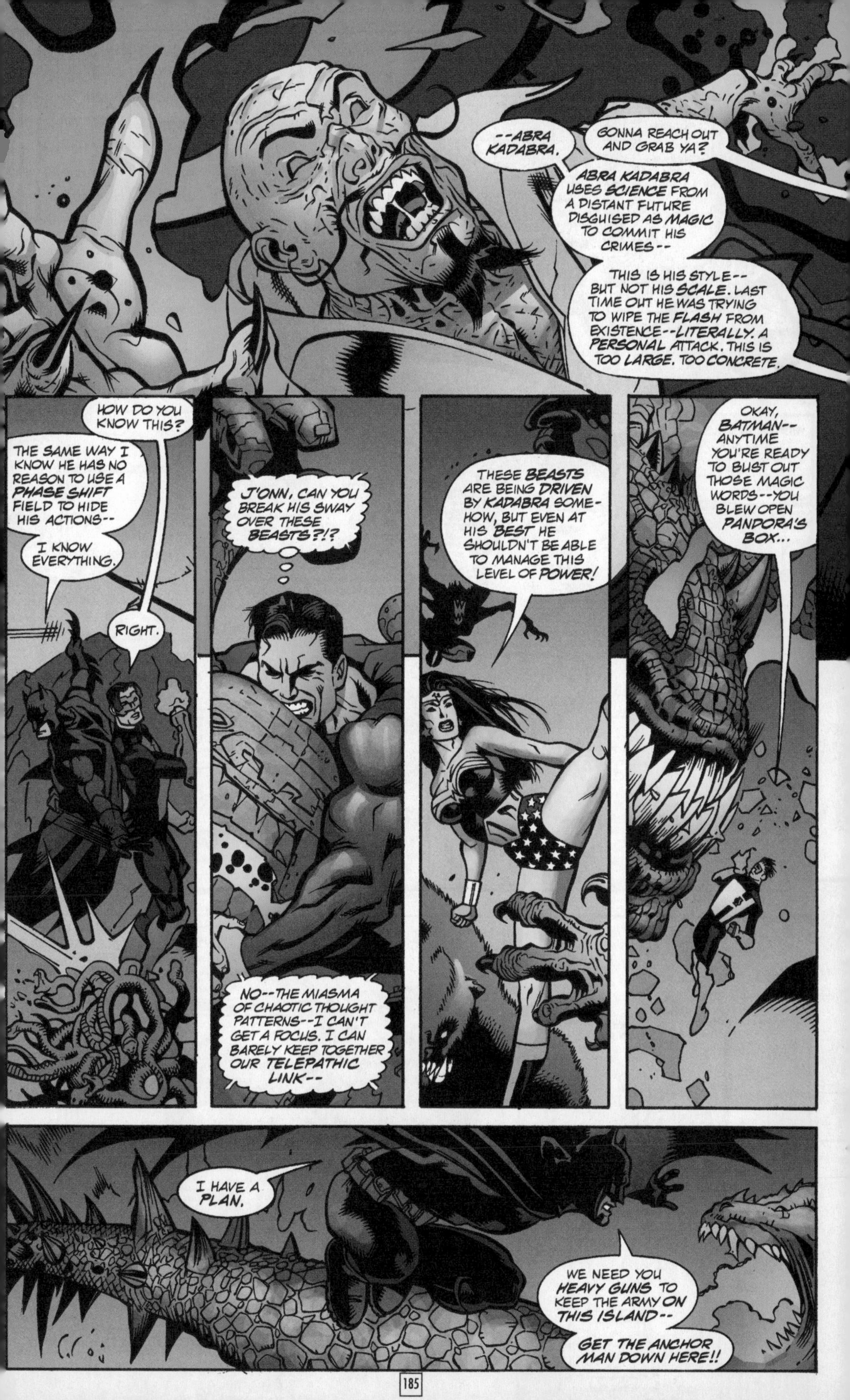
--ABRA KADABRA.
GONNA REACH OUT AND GRAB YA?
ABRA KADABRA USES SCIENCE FROM A DISTANT FUTURE DISGUISED AS MAGIC TO COMMIT HIS CRIMES--
THIS IS HIS STYLE--BUT NOT HIS SCALE. LAST TIME OUT HE WAS TRYING TO WIPE THE FLASH FROM EXISTENCE--LITERALLY. A PERSONAL ATTACK. THIS IS TOO LARGE. TOO CONCRETE.
HOW DO YOU KNOW THIS?
THE SAME WAY I KNOW HE HAS NO REASON TO USE A PHASE SHIFT FIELD TO HIDE HIS ACTIONS--
I KNOW EVERYTHING.
RIGHT.
J'ONN, CAN YOU BREAK HIS SWAY OVER THESE BEASTS?!?
NO--THE MIASMA OF CHAOTIC THOUGHT PATTERNS--I CAN'T GET A FOCUS. I CAN BARELY KEEP TOGETHER OUR TELEPATHIC LINK--
THESE BEASTS ARE BEING DRIVEN BY KADABRA SOMEHOW, BUT EVEN AT HIS BEST HE SHOULDN'T BE ABLE TO MANAGE THIS LEVEL OF POWER!
OKAY, BATMAN--ANYTIME YOU'RE READY TO BUST OUT THOSE MAGIC WORDS--YOU BLEW OPEN PANDORA'S BOX...
I HAVE A PLAN.
WE NEED YOU HEAVY GUNS TO KEEP THE ARMY ON THIS ISLAND--
GET THE ANCHOR MAN DOWN HERE!!

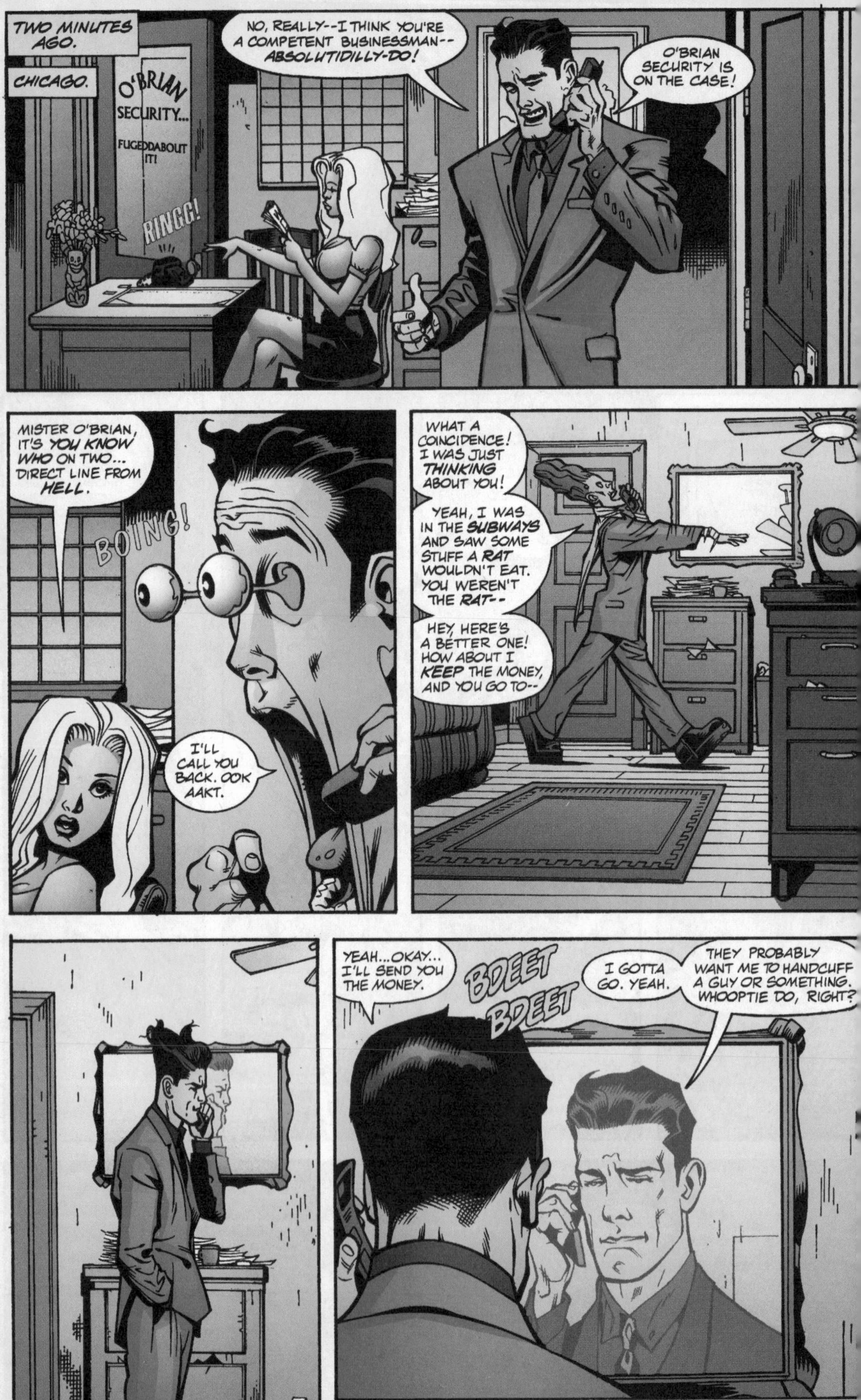

TWO MINUTES AGO.
CHICAGO.
NO, REALLY--I THINK YOU'RE A COMPETENT BUSINESSMAN-- ABSOLUTIDILLY-DO!
O'BRIAN SECURITY IS ON THE CASE!
O'BRIAN SECURITY... FUGEDDABOUT IT!
RINGG!
MISTER O'BRIAN, IT'S YOU KNOW WHO ON TWO... DIRECT LINE FROM HELL.
BOING!
I'LL CALL YOU BACK. OOK AAKT.
WHAT A COINCIDENCE! I WAS JUST THINKING ABOUT YOU!
YEAH, I WAS IN THE SUBWAYS AND SAW SOME STUFF A RAT WOULDN'T EAT. YOU WEREN'T THE RAT--
HEY, HERE'S A BETTER ONE! HOW ABOUT I KEEP THE MONEY, AND YOU GO TO--
YEAH...OKAY... I'LL SEND YOU THE MONEY.
BDEET BDEET
I GOTTA GO. YEAH.
THEY PROBABLY WANT ME TO HANDCUFF A GUY OR SOMETHING. WHOOPTIE DO, RIGHT?

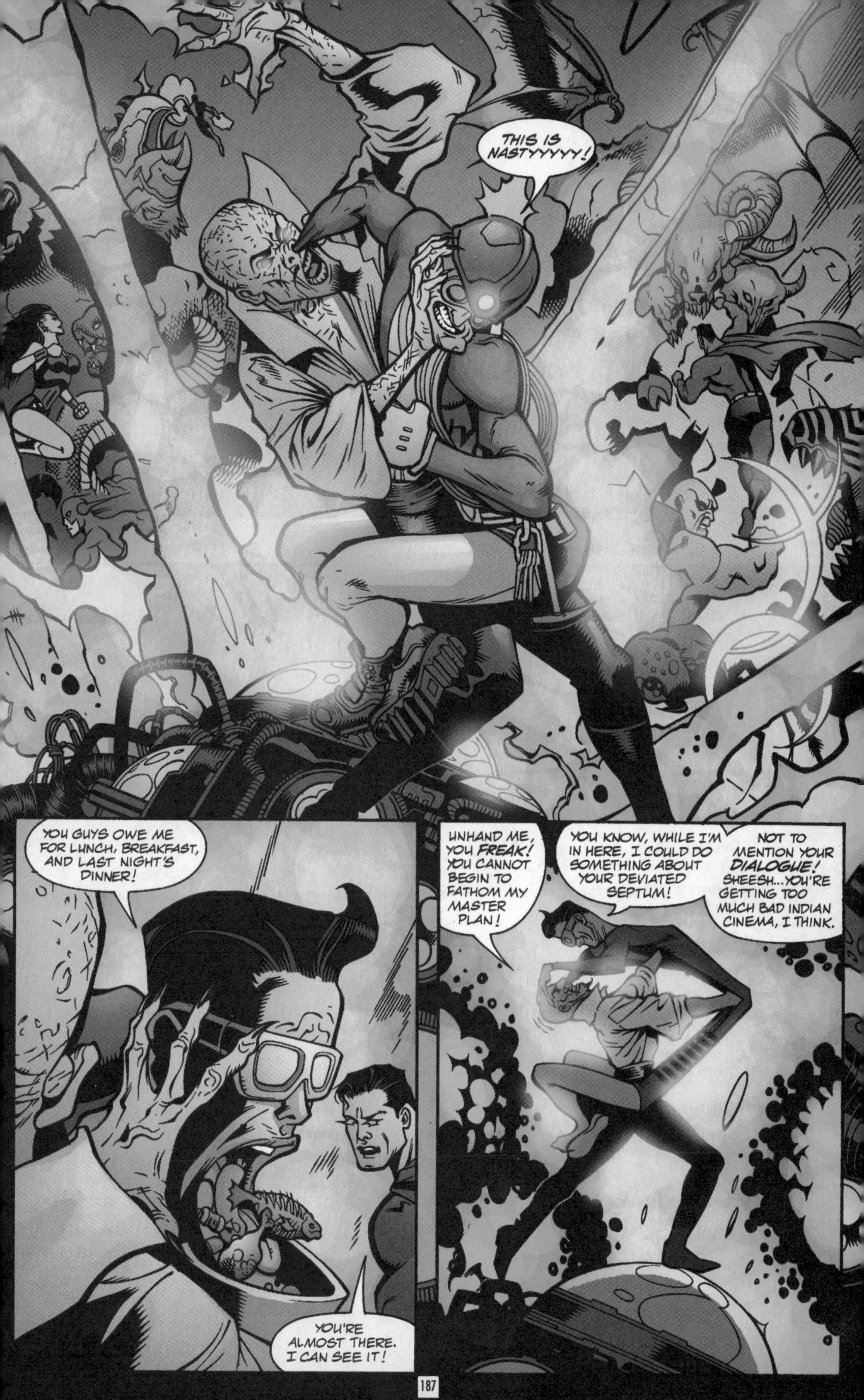
THIS IS NASTYYYYY!
YOU GUYS OWE ME FOR LUNCH, BREAKFAST, AND LAST NIGHT'S DINNER!
YOU'RE ALMOST THERE. I CAN SEE IT!
UNHAND ME, YOU FREAK! YOU CANNOT BEGIN TO FATHOM MY MASTER PLAN!
YOU KNOW, WHILE I'M IN HERE, I COULD DO SOMETHING ABOUT YOUR DEVIATED SEPTUM!
NOT TO MENTION YOUR DIALOGUE! SHEESH...YOU'RE GETTING TOO MUCH BAD INDIAN CINEMA, I THINK.

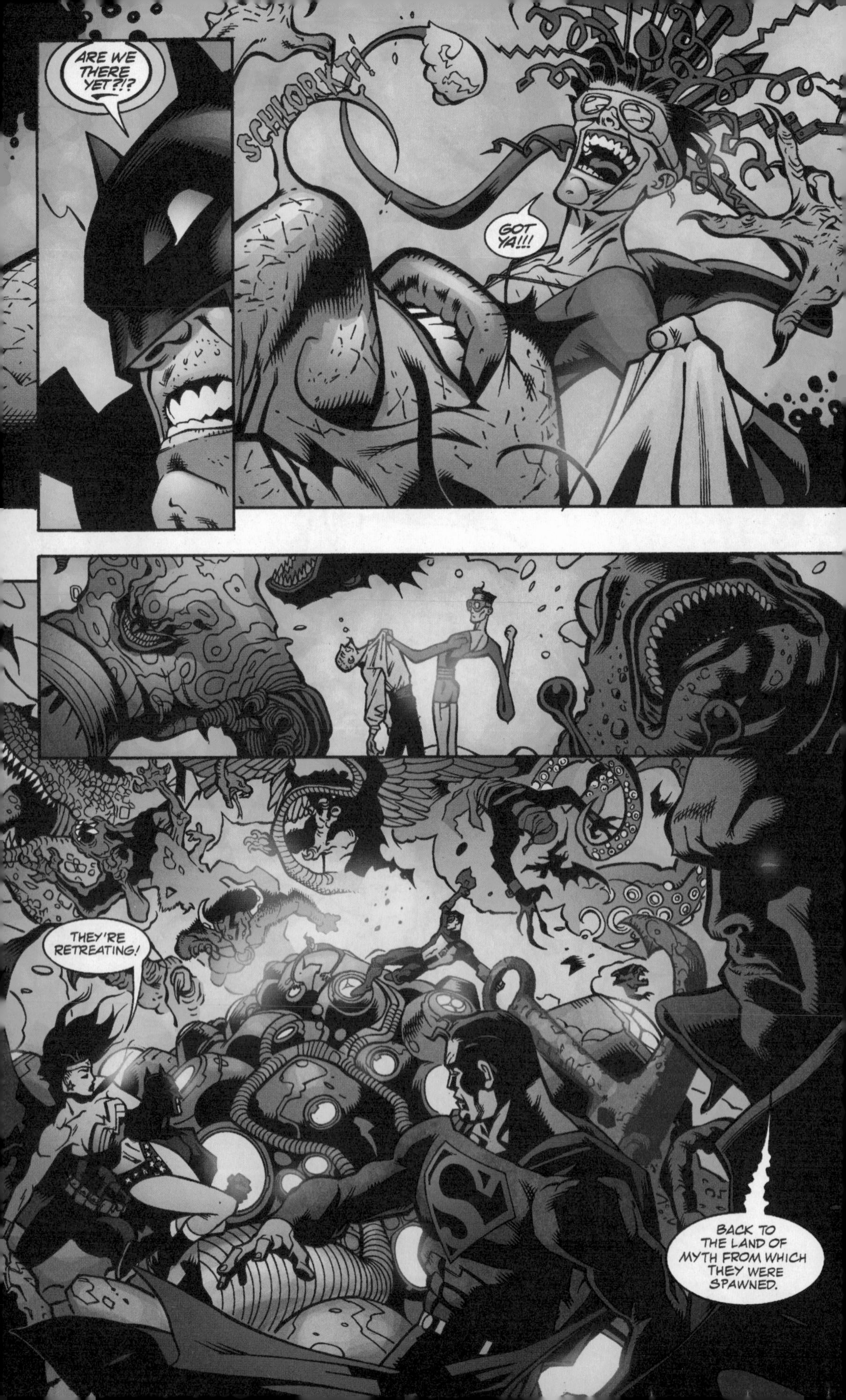
ARE WE THERE YET?!?
SCHLORKT!
GOT YA!!!
THEY'RE RETREATING!
BACK TO THE LAND OF MYTH FROM WHICH THEY WERE SPAWNED.

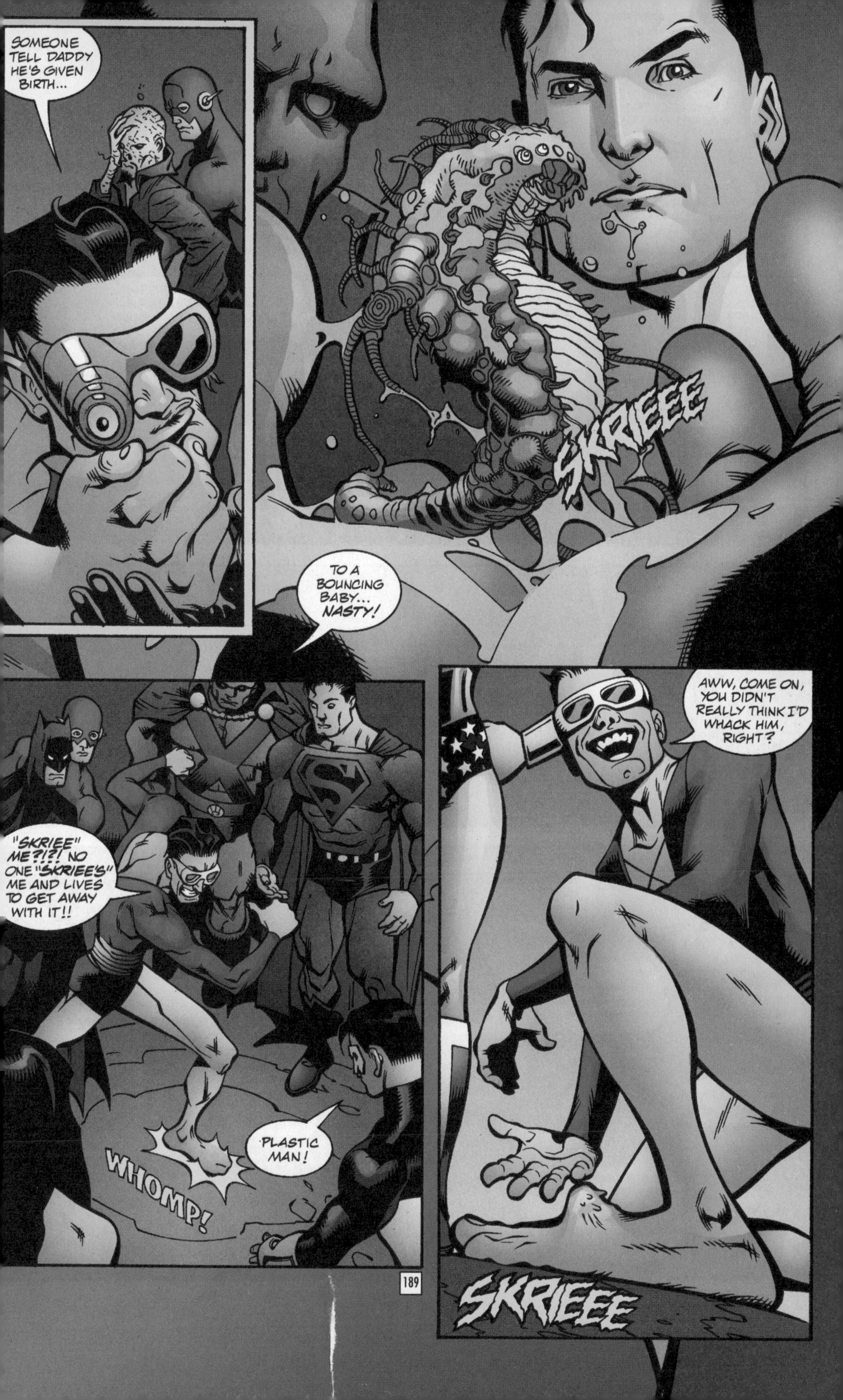

SOMEONE TELL DADDY HE'S GIVEN BIRTH...
TO A BOUNCING BABY... NASTY!
SKRIEEE
"SKRIEE" ME?!?! NO ONE "SKRIEE'S" ME AND LIVES TO GET AWAY WITH IT!!
WHOMP!
PLASTIC MAN!
AWW, COME ON, YOU DIDN'T REALLY THINK I'D WHACK HIM, RIGHT?
SKRIEEE

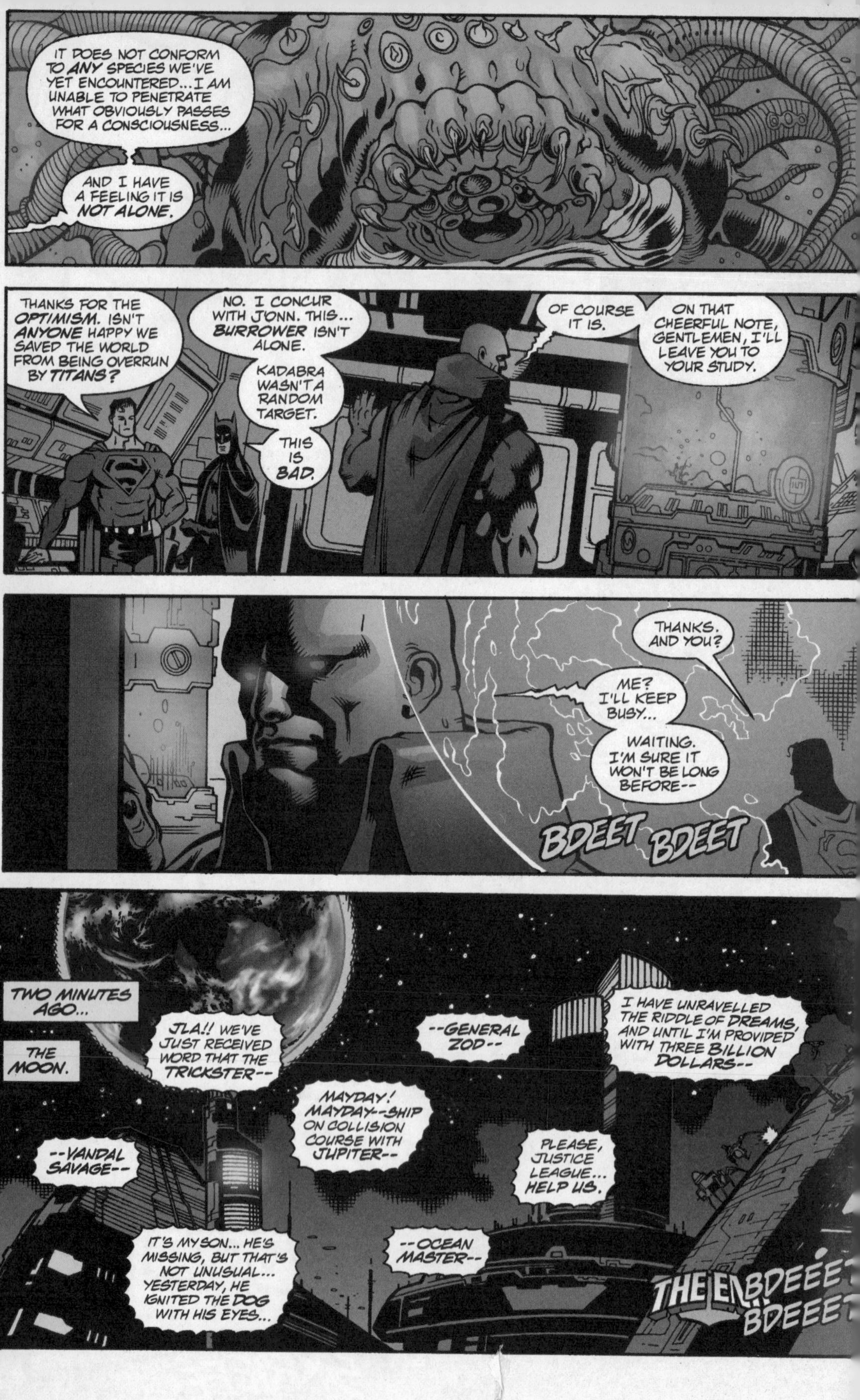
IT DOES NOT CONFORM TO ANY SPECIES WE'VE YET ENCOUNTERED... I AM UNABLE TO PENETRATE WHAT OBVIOUSLY PASSES FOR A CONSCIOUSNESS...
AND I HAVE A FEELING IT IS NOT ALONE.
THANKS FOR THE OPTIMISM. ISN'T ANYONE HAPPY WE SAVED THE WORLD FROM BEING OVERRUN BY TITANS?
NO. I CONCUR WITH J'ONN. THIS... BURROWER ISN'T ALONE.
KADABRA WASN'T A RANDOM TARGET.
THIS IS BAD.
OF COURSE IT IS.
ON THAT CHEERFUL NOTE, GENTLEMEN, I'LL LEAVE YOU TO YOUR STUDY.
THANKS. AND YOU?
ME? I'LL KEEP BUSY...
WAITING. I'M SURE IT WON'T BE LONG BEFORE--
BDEET BDEET
TWO MINUTES AGO...
THE MOON.
JLA!! WE'VE JUST RECEIVED WORD THAT THE TRICKSTER--
--GENERAL ZOD--
I HAVE UNRAVELLED THE RIDDLE OF DREAMS, AND UNTIL I'M PROVIDED WITH THREE BILLION DOLLARS--
MAYDAY! MAYDAY--SHIP ON COLLISION COURSE WITH JUPITER--
--VANDAL SAVAGE--
PLEASE, JUSTICE LEAGUE... HELP US.
IT'S MY SON... HE'S MISSING, BUT THAT'S NOT UNUSUAL... YESTERDAY, HE IGNITED THE DOG WITH HIS EYES...
--OCEAN MASTER--
THE E BDEEE
BDEEE

CONTRIBUTORS

TERRY AUSTIN started out as an assistant to Dick Giordano before teaming up with Marshall Rogers to ink Batman in DETECTIVE COMICS. Since then he has labored on various series including acclaimed runs on *The Uncanny X-Men*, *Star Wars*, CAMELOT 3000, *Dr. Strange*, SUPERMAN, *The New Mutants*, and many others. He also wrote a four-year run of *Cloak and Dagger* and issues of *Power Pack*, *Excalibur*, and *Marvel Fanfare*.

BRETT BREEDING broke in as an inker in the 1980s. His slick style proved popular over a variety of artists at Marvel Comics, before he moved to DC and joined the Superman team, where he worked for many years over the likes of Ron Frenz and Dan Jurgens.

GERRY CONWAY entered the comics industry at the age of 19, first at Marvel, then DC. He had long runs on *Amazing Spider-Man*, BATMAN and JUSTICE LEAGUE OF AMERICA, among others, and co-created a number of DC super-heroes, most notably Power Girl, Vixen, Firestorm, and Jason Todd, the second Robin. Conway eventually turned his attention to television, where he is a supervising producer for NBC's *Law & Order: Criminal Intent*.

JOHN DELL is a prolific inker whose work has been seen on such titles as *Mystic* and *Route 666* for CrossGen, *X-Men* and *Young Avengers* for Marvel, and MAJOR BUMMER, HOURMAN and JLA for DC.

J.M. DeMATTEIS has written for newspapers, magazines, movies, television, and comics, where his work on titles ranging from Marvel's *Spectacular Spider-Man* to Vertigo's MOONSHADOW has received both popular and critical acclaim. His most personal work, BROOKLYN DREAMS, was recently collected in a trade paperback.

DICK DILLIN spent some years in the field of commercial illustration before embarking on a career in comics. Best remembered for his almost 12-year-long run on JUSTICE LEAGUE OF AMERICA, Dillin also had a decades-long association with the character Blackhawk, both at Quality Comics and at DC. It can safely be said that during the 1960s and 1970s there was not a single DC character that the prolific artist didn't draw at one time or another. Dillin passed away in the spring of 1980.

GARDNER FOX began his career as a writer in the late 1930s on Batman stories and went on to create such Golden Age classics as the original Flash, Hawkman, Starman, Doctor Fate, and the Justice Society of America. In the 1950s and 1960s he created and/or wrote such memorable features as the Justice League of America, Adam Strange, The Atom, Hawkman, and, again, Batman. He retired in 1968, and passed away in 1986.

JOE GIELLA first worked for DC Comics in 1951 where, in the 1960s, his style of embellishment became associated with some of the company's greatest heroes, including Batman, The Flash, and The Atom. Giella, who also pencilled and inked a run of the Batman syndicated newspaper strip during the 1960s, retired from comics in the early 1980s.

KEITH GIFFEN is best known for his long run pencilling (and later plotting) LEGION OF SUPER-HEROES, as well as co-creating the mercenary Lobo and the humorous version of the JUSTICE LEAGUE. His latest work includes *Annihilation* for Marvel, *Hero Squared* for Boom! Studios, and co-writing BLUE BEETLE for DC, as well as co-plotting and doing breakdowns for the year-long weekly series 52.

JOE KELLY first gained attention with his quirky run on Marvel's *Deadpool*, and then quickly gained stardom with a one-and-a-half-year run on the highly popular *The X-Men*. He soon came to DC Comics, where he has been the writer on SUPERBOY, ACTION COMICS, STEAMPUNK, LEGACY: THE LAST WILL AND TESTAMENT OF HAL JORDAN, JLA, and JUSTICE LEAGUE ELITE.

KEVIN MAGUIRE got his big break on JUSTICE LEAGUE in the late '80s. From there, he has worked on *The Adventures of Captain America* and *Defenders* for Marvel, as well as JLA: CREATED EQUAL, FORMERLY KNOWN AS THE JUSTICE LEAGUE, and JLA CLASSIFIED for DC.

DOUG MAHNKE illustrated Dark Horse's series *The Mask*, collaborating with writer John Arcudi. He teamed up with Arcudi again on the DC title MAJOR BUMMER before landing a regular gig as the artist on SUPERMAN: THE MAN OF STEEL. From there, he graduated to the monthly JLA series, and has worked on numerous titles since.

FRANK McLAUGHLIN is best known as a longtime inker and associate of Dick Giordano. Joining DC in the 1970s, Frank worked on many super-hero titles including long runs on JUSTICE LEAGUE OF AMERICA and THE FLASH. Since 2001, he has been the artist of the long-running *Gil Thorp* syndicated comic strip.

MARK MILLAR hails from Glasgow, Scotland, and is one of the most prominent writers working in comics today. Millar has worked on SWAMP THING, SUPERMAN ADVENTURES, THE FLASH, THE AUTHORITY, and SUPERMAN: RED SON for DC, and *Ultimate X-Men, The Ultimates, Ultimate Fantastic Four,* and *Spider-Man* for Marvel. He has also launched a multi-publisher line of "Millarworld" books that include *Wanted, Chosen,* and *The Unfunnies.*

GRANT MORRISON found fame with acclaimed runs on ANIMAL MAN and DOOM PATROL, as well as his subversive creator-owned titles such as THE INVISIBLES and *The New Adventures of Hitler.* He has written best-selling runs on JLA and *New X-Men,* and is the creative mind behind the sprawling SEVEN SOLDIERS series of interconnecting miniseries for DC.

TOM NGUYEN has been inking comics for years, mostly over the pencils of Doug Mahnke. He has worked with Doug on various titles for DC, including MAJOR BUMMER, SUPERMAN: MAN OF STEEL, JLA, and JUSTICE LEAGUE ELITE.

DENNIS O'NEIL began his career as a comic-book writer in 1965 at Charlton, before eventually moving over to DC, where he quickly became one of the most respected writers in comics. O'Neil earned a reputation for being able to "revamp" characters such as Superman, Green Lantern, Captain Marvel — and the Batman, whom O'Neil (with the help of Neal

Adams and Dick Giordano) brought back to his roots as a dark, mysterious, gothic avenger.

MARTIN PASKO was one of the regular letters column contributors of the 1960s who then graduated to comic-book script writer in the 1970s. For DC, Pasko is best known for his work on Superman, Blackhawk and Dr. Fate. Elsewhere, he has written such diverse series as *E-Man* and *Star Trek.* His animation credits include the award-winning *Batman: The Animated Series.*

GEORGE PÉREZ's career spans multiple comic companies and thousands of pages of material for titles including NEW TEEN TITANS, CRISIS ON INFINITE EARTHS, *The Avengers,* WONDER WOMAN, *Solus,* and the epic cross-company crossover JLA/AVENGERS. His next project is THE BRAVE AND THE BOLD.

HOWARD PORTER is probably best known as the penciller of the JLA title that relaunched in 1987. He also pencilled the UNDERWORLD UNLEASHED miniseries, and has had runs on THE RAY and FLASH for DC, and *Fantastic Four* for Marvel.

ALEX ROSS studied art at the American Academy of Art in Illinois before turning his attention to comics. Stunning readers with his lushly rendered art for the *Marvels* miniseries, Ross cemented his reputation as the industry's leading painter with the KINGDOM COME miniseries. He is currently one of the most sought-after illustrators both in and out of the comics business.

BERNARD SACHS was one of DC Comics' unsung heroes for nearly twenty years — a solid, dependable inker who tirelessly embellished the pencils of many artists, among them Mike Sekowsky, Gil Kane, and Carmine

Infantino. Sachs worked on both the Justice Society and the Justice League, inking Sekowsky's pencils on the latter feature until his retirement in 1965.

MIKE SEKOWSKY entered the comics field while it was still in its infancy, penciling some of Marvel's top heroes, including Captain America, The Human Torch, and The Sub-Mariner. Sekowsky joined DC in the early 1950s and is best remembered for drawing every issue of JUSTICE LEAGUE OF AMERICA for its first eight years. Sekowsky remained active in comics and television animation until his death in 1989.

SUPERMAN

BATMAN

FLASH

BLACK CANARY

GREEN LANTERN

ATOM

GREEN ARROW